Marakwet

Marakwet

*An Ethnographic Study of Religious and
Cultural Identity in Africa*

Samuel K. Elolia

PICKWICK Publications • Eugene, Oregon

MARAKWET
An Ethnographic Study of Religious and Cultural Identity in Africa

Copyright © 2024 Samuel K. Elolia. All rights reserved. Except for brief quotations in critical publications or reviews, no part of this book may be reproduced in any manner without prior written permission from the publisher. Write: Permissions, Wipf and Stock Publishers, 199 W. 8th Ave., Suite 3, Eugene, OR 97401.

Pickwick Publications
An Imprint of Wipf and Stock Publishers
199 W. 8th Ave., Suite 3
Eugene, OR 97401

www.wipfandstock.com

PAPERBACK ISBN: 978-1-55635-873-9
HARDCOVER ISBN: 978-1-4982-8579-7
EBOOK ISBN: 978-1-4982-4109-0

Cataloguing-in-Publication data:

Names: Elolia, Samuel K., author.

Title: Marakwet : an ethnographic study of religious and cultural identity in Africa / by Samuel K. Elolia.

Description: Eugene, OR : Pickwick Publications, 2024 | Includes bibliographical references and index.

Identifiers: ISBN 978-1-55635-873-9 (paperback) | ISBN 978-1-4982-8579-7 (hardcover) | ISBN 978-1-4982-4109-0 (ebook)

Subjects: LCSH: Marakwet (African people). | Africa, East — Religion.

Classification: BR1440 .E46 2024 (print) | BR1440 .E46 (ebook)

02/12/24

Scripture quotations are from New Revised Standard Version Bible, copyright © 1989 National Council of the Churches of Christ in the United States of America. Used by permission. All rights reserved worldwide.

I dedicate this book to my wife Robin, and our two adult children Kimu and Pippa.

Contents

Acknowledgments | ix
Introduction: The Background and Setting of the Study | xiii

Chapter 1: The Marakwet Social Life | 1
    Physical Environment   1
    Geographical Zones   5
    Kinship and Political Organizations   8
    Economic Structure   16

Chapter 2: The Rites of Passage | 28
    Introduction   28
    Child Naming Rites   32
    The Circumcision Rite   38
    Marriage   56
    Death and Funeral Rites   66

Chapter 3: Religion: Myths, Rituals, and Symbols | 71
    Introduction   71
    The Supreme Creator (*Iriin*)   73
    The Creation   76
    Human and Supra-Human Powers   77

Chapter 4: Marakwet Encounter with the British Colonists and Missionaries | 102
    Marakwet Resistance to the British Soldiers of Ribo Post   102
    Africa Inland Mission   111
    The Roman Catholic Mission   140

Chapter 5: AIM/AIC Christian Communities | 148
    Kapsowar Mission Station   148
    The Mission Outstations   164

Chapter 6: Theological Reflections | 193
    Salvation/Conversion and New Names   193
    Contested Themes   208
    Inculturation/Contextualization   240

Conclusion | 260

Bibliography | 267

Index | 273

Acknowledgments

THE WRITING OF ANY book, especially a book of this kind, is not the work of one person. My thoughts and beliefs are largely informed in communities that shape and give me my particular point of view. It truly takes a village. It is therefore my pleasure to acknowledge them. I wish to express my appreciation to several people and institutions who supported me. Looking further back, I extend my gratitude to Prof. Samuel Ngewa who inspired me at Scott Theological College, and Prof. John Franklin who introduced me to Western philosophy at Tyndale College and Seminary. I am grateful to the university of Toronto Trinity College and Prof. Peter Slater, the dean, for awarding me scholarships and tutorial Assistantships. To my two supervisors, Prof. Martin A. Klein, and Prof. C. Thomas McIntire, who guided my dissertation to completion at the University of Toronto. Their careful supervision, wise criticism and kindly encouragement were invaluable to the initial work that has resulted in this book. Mrs. Pat Sandeman did not only type it but provided needed nourishment for the body through her good cooking. I am forever thankful. I thank my theology professors Prof. Roger Haight at Regis College for teaching me to think theologically and Prof. Lee Cormie at St. Michaels for introducing me to liberation theology. It was in theology seminar classes that stirred my consciousness to a new way of reading the Bible and history where I discovered a liberating God who accompanies the poor in their suffering and their struggle to regain their humanity. The experience of the poor today correlates easily with the people of God in the Bible who often lived under oppressive empires.

I later met some of the great theologians whose writing I had encountered in class who did not only teach me theology but embodied theology's prophetic vision rooted in a faith that is questioning, generous, courageous and compassionate.

I met Prof. James cone for the first time when Black students invited him to Toronto. Although I did not study under him, he influenced me though his books and talks. I was honored when he invited me to Union Theological Seminary reception at AAR/SBL annual meeting and adopted me as his student. I have been 'illegally' attending the Union reception at AAR/SBL since then. I met Gustavo Gutierrez when he gave the Killeen Lectures at St. Nobert in the early 1990s. When I am tempted to give up on the Church, it is the faith and the wisdom of these two giant theologians that gave me hope. They modeled for me that a theologian is not an ivory-tower intellectual, but an organic collaborator and a fellow pilgrim with one foot in the center of reflection and the other in the life of the community. I thank those whom I do not know personally whose publications have shaped me. For those who trusted and gave me vital information for my research, I am grateful. No worthwhile journey is travelled alone so I thank fellow graduate students at the University of Toronto for whom we commiserated and compared notes. They include Akwatu Khenti, Emmanuel Tehindrazanarivelo, David Mensah, and Alix Musoke, among others. We debated and tested our ideas on colonialism, post-colonialism Pan Africanists, and theology. We also, combined our debates with street and sit in activism especially under the biko-rodney-malcolm coalition. Seemingly, we have not solved many of the problems we debated but we continue to be guided by the slogan '*Aluta Continua.*'

Also, I acknowledge colleagues at the African Religions Group in America Academy of Religion and the Society of Biblical Literature annual meetings, whose friendships have encouraged me. They include Tapiwa Mucherera, Gwinyai Muzorewa, Dwight Hopkins, Jacob Olupona, Cynthia Hoehler-Fatton, Musa Dube, Laura Grillo, Teresia Hinga, Kofi Opoku, Afe Odogame, Danoye Oguntola-Laguda, and Fr. Emmanuel Katongole.

I am also grateful to the staff of Kenya National Archives, Nairobi; Billy Graham Archives, Wheaton, Illinois; and Kapsowar Hospital whose courtesies made easily available the documentary material from which some of these pages were written. Above all, I am thankful to hundreds of Marakwet people who answered my questions and trusted me with their stories. Any misrepresentation of their stories in the pages is totally my fault.

In Marakwet, I am indebted to several people beginning with my parents Teriki and Ng'elecha Kisang Elolia, who took interest in my education, speaking of education, I will be remiss if I don't mention my primary school teacher Mr. Enock Suter who introduced me to the basics of education and my high school teacher Mr. Joseph Cheserem "simba" who made history not only interesting but lively and thought provoking. I am grateful to my siblings as listed by their baptismal and given names: Nelly Somokwony, Gladys Jerotich, Ben Kilimo, Eunice Jepkosgei, Metrine Jemutai, Geoffrey Kipkemoi, and Joan Jesinen. They are my cheerleaders. I thank Jane and David Kalessi and fellow Christians in Kerio Valley whose prayers continue to sustain me. Also, I thank Rev. Eustace Meade for welcoming and hiring me as his assistant at the historic First Baptist Church Toronto. He took me as a son and when he travelled to Kenya for the Baptist World Convention meeting in Nairobi, he made an effort to meet with my father and after the meeting and the exchange of gifts, my father was assured of my security in Canada.

My faculty colleagues of Emmanuel Seminary at Milligan University have provided both friendship and stimulating environment. The late Fred Norris who is commonly remembered for his exuberant laughter assured me support when I expressed my reservations in moving to the American South. I thank Phil Kenneson, the head of our academic Area, for giving me professional support behind the scenes within Milligan University. I am grateful for my seminary students whose curiosity and interest in the theologies of the Global South inspired me to complete the book. I thank my professional assistants who read parts of the manuscript. I single out Amber L. Athon whose meticulous ability for detail helped me a great deal in the completion of this book. She went beyond her duties, and I appreciate her. Special thanks to my editorial team at WIPF & STOCK publishers starting with my editor Charlie M. Collier and a few others including George Callihan, EJ Davila, Calvin Jaffarian, and Mike Surber. They were instrumental in shepherding this book through the publishing process.

Finally, and above all, I am indebted to the unflagging love and support of my wife Robin and our children Kimu and Pippa. Their love and support sustained me during the writing of this book. They have no idea how much that meant to me. I particularly thank Kimu who called almost every week to find out if I had submitted the manuscript for this book. I didn't welcome the pressure then but now I am glad he did. This book is dedicated to the next generation of Marakwet who will hopefully carry on these rich cultural traditions and practices. My hope is that by reading it, they will have a better understanding and appreciation of their Marakwet heritage.

January 2024
Samuel K. Elolia

Introduction

The Background and Setting of the Study

MARAKWET IS THE NAME of the people, the land, and the language. They live in the North Rift region of Kenya and are culturally part of the larger Kalenjin ethnic group. The physical topography of Marakwet ranges from the semi-arid climate on the valley floor, the escarpment, and the cooler highlands. The highland glades generate water to irrigate the semi-arid valley floor. The original settlement of the Marakwet was at the escarpment, where the air is cooler at night and free from mosquitoes. Before the arrival of warmer clothing, the highlands were visited only during the dry season for bee keeping and hunting.

Kerio Valley, which takes its name from the Kerio river, is an off shoot of the main rift valley. While it is sealed at the southern end, the main floor stretches northwards to Pokot and Turkana plains to Lake Turkana where the Kerio river empties. The vegetation on the valley floor is semi- arid from being avidly grazed by livestock. Consequently, the soil is bare and deeply scarred. Some of it is sandy loam which is cultivated and irrigated by the Marakwet. The valley floor is flanked by two opposing ridges. The Eastern Wall is reinforced by the rugged Tiati hills which rise nine hundred meters off the valley floor. The western ridge is covered by a lush forest of the Cherangany hills, rising to 3,400 meters at the highest point. Today, the Marakwet reside on the three geographical zones, but the escarpment is still the preferred zone for habitation.

The core of the book concerns itself principally with the formation of the Marakwet person through cultural education. Key rites are critical in establishing a socially mature identity. The most important are the rituals of birth, circumcision, marriage, and death. It is by going through these rites that every Marakwet is believed to become responsible human being in society.

The book is divided into six chapters, and each chapter is made up of several sections. Chapter 1 introduces the Marakwet territory—its topographic beauty and the general activities that promote cultural resilience. The first chapter underlines the physical geography that ranges from the semi-arid climate on the valley floor, the cooler escarpment for habitation, and the colder highlands that form the Marakwet natural forest. It is from here that the highland glades supply water to irrigate the valley floor. Care for the earth is at the center of ethical behavior. The Marakwet understand the earth as a gratuitous gift and all human beings possess an equal claim to it. This also applies to other essentials such as land, air, water, and fire. It is for that reason that land was not private but communal property held by the clan on behalf of the clan. An individual may cultivate a parcel of such land as per their need. This practice is rooted in the understanding that land belongs to God, just like water and air. In that sense, anyone can use the land and leave it in good condition for the next user in the family or the clan for the promotion of life.

Chapter 2 discusses the rites of passage and the role of rituals in managing socio-cultural development. Ritual is the pathway that guides people through what would otherwise be uncharted territory. In fact, the term ritual or rite comes from a context that understands the world as unordered, dangerous, and chaotic. This is equated to a house that requires the order of paths, trees, and a garden for it to become an ordered home. From this perspective rituals are ways of ordering the world and making it manageable. They hold chaos in check, ward off accidents, and regulate life. Every step is approached carefully and with caution because of the vulnerability of life, especially during the rites of passage. Life must be ordered and structured carefully and delicately. Nothing in life should be left to chance. The four Marakwet rituals of birth, circumcision, marriage, and death are marked and ordered by corresponding rites that determine the natural rhythm of life. The last rite of life, which takes place at death, is not the end for rituals continues even after death.

As previously stated, the main purpose for these rites is to create a socially conscious person. It is for this reason that the elders impress these rites upon the young to ensure that they (the young), become responsible members of society. The initiated, in turn, are obligated to observe the rites carefully and pass them on to the next generation in the same manner they had received them. Anyone who rejects the rites suffers social ridicule and alienation.

Chapter 3, which deals with the religious beliefs and practices, is divided into two sections: the first deals with the Marakwet's concept of God (Supreme Power) and God's attributes. The second section deals with the human and supra-human powers that serve as God's emissaries. Like all human cultures, the Marakwet history reveals such dynamic religious elements expressed through symbols, rituals, and stories. This forms their profound beliefs and awareness that their lives are shaped by unseen forces pervading the world with purposes they cannot control but can only understand through religious rituals that give meaning to life. Myth has the primordial power of unlocking human consciousness to another world to show that there is something there in the divine world, or the world of the ancestors, who gives value to human existence. In this sense, religious activities accompany every stage of life from the cradle to the grave and beyond. At the apex of this religious activity is the belief in a supreme deity, *Assis*, symbolized principally by the Sun. While the distinctions are not well-defined, ritual practices seem to signify a supreme deity above the Sun, thus confirming a monotheistic tradition. Prayers are often directed to the creator and seldom to the sun or the other intermediaries.

Chapter 4 concerns the Marakwet's encounter with the British colonial rule beginning with the intruding colonial soldiers from their Ribo post in Kerio Valley. That was followed by the unpopular hut tax. The second and third portion and the most enduring, addresses the arrival of the missionaries and their interaction with the Marakwet people and culture. It was at the school where the African youth came under their tutelage. In that setting the students were taught to despise, denigrate, and undermine their traditional practices in favor of Western culture that was promoted as Christian, civilized, and therefore superior. The third portion underlines the work of the Roman Catholic Missionaries. The motivation of the missionaries, demonstrated through their actions, leads one to think that they did not only preach the Gospel but imposed their own values. In other words, the missionaries confused their understanding of salvation with their own culture. This blurring invariably resulted in the imposition of western cultural values. Incidentally, the Marakwet did not distinguish the missionaries' efforts from those of the colonial government. Moreover, both were united in establishing schools for the natives.

Chapter 5 concerns the making of the protestant Christian communities that began as out stations. The out stations were established and managed by the evangelists, teachers, and nurses who received their Christian orientation at Kapsowar Mission Station. Although their work bore fruit, their early beginnings were not well received by the majority. The early Marakwet Christians were initially understood by the larger community to be marginal figures because they were perceived to have left and abandoned their culture and adopted Western beliefs and practices. It did not help that most of them had left in search of employment in settler farms and overstayed to acquire western education and Christianity. They were further marginalized when they lived around the mission stations and not with their people in the villages. The combination created a separate culture within the larger culture. Their separation was partly orchestrated and accelerated by the missionaries' expectations who were intent to instill Christian values and prevent backsliding. The immediate payoffs of the converts were the benefits of employment and education for their children. They were absorbed in relatively large numbers into the work of the Mission station and outstations, mainly as dressers, teachers, cooks, and casual workers at the hospital and missionary homes. As employees, they were also expected to engage in evangelistic work in villages around the station and beyond. Such evangelistic work often resulted in more converts, most of whom were women and children. Sunday Schools as well as women meetings were started to offer basic literacy instructions. The portion on the Roman Catholic Mission underlines their approach to Marakwet which at first was not different from the protestant missionaries. However, after Vatican II their posture towards African culture was softened. It was probably due to that openness to the culture that gave them an advantage in attracting the adult male population.

In the first section of Chapter 6, I will discuss the subject of conversion. Here, I will analyze more precisely how the Marakwet culture and beliefs interacted with Christianity. I show how both protestant and Catholic missionaries were empowered to give western names to Christian converts, thus estranging them from their cultural roots. In most cases, names were chosen randomly by the missionary with no regard to whether the family of the baptized could pronounce the name.

It is understandable that the gospel message demands conversion and baptism but that does not mean exporting western names that have no relevant meaning in Marakwet. Unlike Adam who encountered a nameless world, the missionaries to Marakwet, did not enter a nameless world. What the missionaries needed to do was not name giving but name knowing and the ability to identify their meaning and correct pronunciations. Unfortunately, that opportunity was missed. What became evident was the missionaries' rejection of Marakwet names sending the chilling message that they did not care about the Marakwet identities and history.

The second section of chapter 6 pays attention to specific themes previously discussed such as rites of passage that have become subjects of controversy in the church. In the early years, the Protestant missionaries attacked key elements of Marakwet culture and beliefs. Initially, the Marakwet met such attacks with indifference. Finally, I will seek to underline how the principle of incarnation or inculturation could be applied as a meaningful alternative in providing meaningful paths to integrate Christianity without destroying the Marakwet culture. Inculturation recognizes that the Gospel is properly communicated not only through the linguistic symbol systems but also through rituals, narratives, parables, metaphors, and rhythm. Without these culturally informed symbolic systems there can be no adequate means of communication.

The conclusion discusses some cultural and theological issues in relationship to the principle of incarnation or inculturation as a methodology of making Christianity relevant to the Marakwet. Listening to the Local Christian communities is paramount, for they surely know where it itches. The African people have often criticized foreign missionaries for scratching where it didn't itch.

The notion of dialogue between Christianity and Marakwet belief is paramount in making inculturation possible. One of the essential methods for inculturation especially in relation to world religions is engagement through dialogue. The term comes from the Greek *dia-logos*, which means mutual communication. The purpose of the communication is to acknowledge the diversity and universality of each culture. No dialogue is possible unless two concerned groups are ready to engage each other on equal terms, but it can be impeded if one side sees the other as a threat; in other words, if any group or party comes with "a priori" assumption that its story is the only true story, the dialogue is doomed to fail even before it begins. To maintain the flow of a dialogue, barriers of prejudice and defensiveness must be overcome. True dialogue, therefore, requires courage to take risks and humility to accept the possibility of change. These ingredients are only gained if there is love and trust. Failure to do so would make room for hypocrisy. Inculturation or contextualization does not change the essence of the Gospel but rather it makes it culturally relevant. That means Christ and his Gospel must become the very heart and soul of the way of life or the very *raison d'etre* of human existence.

— CHAPTER 1 —

The Marakwet Social Life

Physical Environment

THE MARAKWET IS ONE of the seven Kalenjin speaking people in the Rift Valley region of Kenya. Its population is about two hundred thousand and practice agriculture and livestock keeping in an area of 1,595 square kilometers.[1] The others in the Kalenjin linguistic group or cluster are Kipsigis, Nandi, Pokot, Teriki, Tugen, and Sabaot. The term Marakwet was borrowed by the British Colonial administration in 1900 as an administrative designation from one of Marakwet's six ethnic groups. The six territorial groups represented are Endo, Markweta, Almo, Borokot, Kiptani, and Cherangany. Prior to the Colonial period, these six territorial groups existed individually with defined boundaries, distinct cultural habits, style of dress and linguistic variations. For example, the Endo ethnic group, who bordered the Pokot, shared many traditions, and dressed like their Pokot neighbors with head styles of ochre (*siolup*) decorated with ostrich feathers as well as lip plugs on their lower lip. The Mogoro people were reputed to chew dry hide (*mogor*) in time of famine. The said Markweta clan was associated with muddy feet due to irrigation activities to which they were preoccupied.

Over the years, the name Marakwet has gained currency and has come to represent both the district and the people. In the 1920s the colonial government administered the region from Baringo for the main purpose of collecting taxes, and in 1933 the district officer moved to Tambach when Marakwet district was merged with the Keiyo in the South to form the Keiyo/Matakwet District. This merger made the colonial administrative logistics a bit easier and was retained even after Kenya attained its independence in 1963.

---

1. The specific location is within the geographical grid reference 117° N to 45° N Latitude and 35° E and 3542° E Longitude. KNBS, "2019 Kenya Population."

The most notable change was political independence and the shift of political administrators from European to Kenyan nationals as Provincial Commissioners, District Commissioners, and District Officers. In 1994, President Daniel Arap Moi expanded his political power by creating more districts and Marakwet became a distinct district and Kapsowar once again became the district headquarters. In 2010, under President Mwai Kibaki, the government adopted a new constitution and re-drew the country into forty-seven counties to replace the former British seven provinces. With those new administrative arrangements, Marakwet and Keiyo formed the Keiyo/Marakwet County with its administrative headquarters at Iten.

The devolution shifted power to the county governments under elected governors and ward officials. The members of County officials (MCAs) debate at their respective assemblies on development objectives and set the county budget. In the 2010 constitutional demarcation, Marakwet maintained its two constituencies of East and West each represented by a member of parliament and ten wards each represented by a Member of County Assembly (MCA). The Marakwet East constituency wards are as follows: Endo, Embobut/Embolot, Sambirir, and Kapyego. The Marakwet West constituency wards are: Arror, Kapsowar, Moiben/Kureswo, Lelan, and Cherangany/Chebororwa.

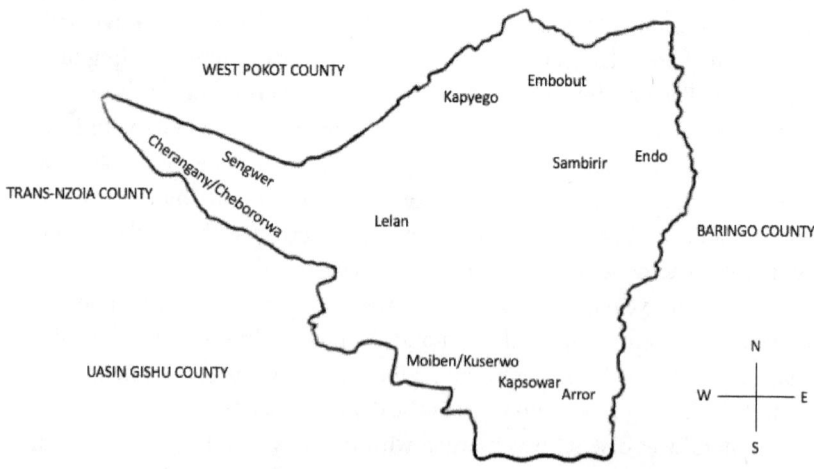

Figure 1: Elgeyo Marakwet County Map

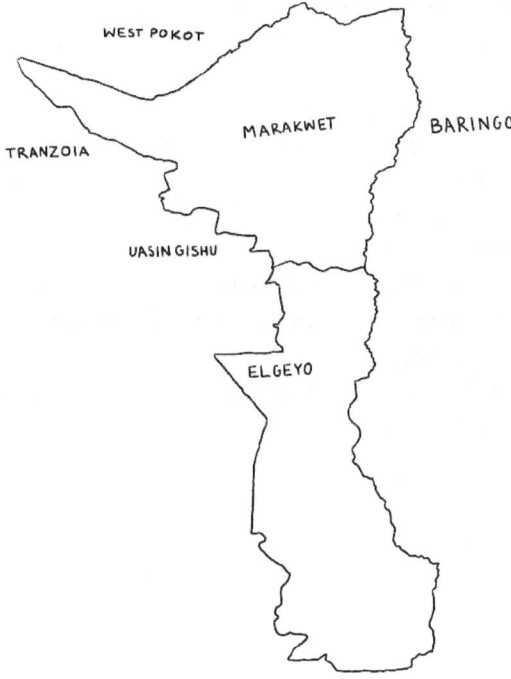

Figure 2: Elgeyo Marakwet County Map

Originally, before the arrival of the British and their colonial rule in Kenya, the Marakwet resided on the escarpment that stretched from Sangurur northwards to Kaben. The higher altitude highlands in the West are covered by forest and therefore too cold for habitation. Similarly, the valley floor on the East along Kerio Valley was too hot and mosquito infested. The escarpment provided the perfect climate as it was free from mosquitoes and Pokot cattle rustlers and relatively warmer than the cold high-altitude highlands on the West. From their central location, they grazed, hunted, and farmed on both Kerio Valley and the cooler regions on the west including Kapsiliot, Chebororwa and the whole Cherang'any forest and its environs that borders Tranzoia. When Kenya became a British colony, better building materials became available, and more people moved into the cooler high-altitude regions. In addition, the colonial government introduced crops that were fit for cooler climates. Today, Marakwet people live in all the zones. The focus of my research is the traditions commonly identified with the original Marakwet residential home in the Kerio Valley escarpment.

Geographically, the Marakwet borders West Pokot to the North, Baringo to the East, Keiyo to the South, and Uasin-Gishu to the South-West. The Marakwet relate to its neighbors, especially the Pokot, Tugen (kamasia), and Keiyo, through trade, inter-marriage, and shared customs. Sometimes, those relationships are hampered by conflicts and disagreements based on anything from encroachment of grazing rights to cattle rusting and theft. The most enduring conflict between the Marakwet and the Pokot has been cattle rustling that resulted in loss of life on both sides. Oral tradition confirms such historic animosity and the most recent began in the 1990s when an incident of cattle raids and retaliations resulted in a prolonged impunity. In each case, the Marakwet territorial groups have united against their aggressor and the same applies to the other side. These raids are not new. The British colonial officers were routinely sent to monitor such activities and keep the peace between the warring groups.[2]

---

2. They initially administered both groups from Baringo. This was much easier for better management tax collection. These arrangements favored the colonial administration more than the Marakwet who would have wished limited colonial presence. In the District Commissioner's report, DC/Elm/3/1, K. Dundas, D. C. Baringo, sent Sergeant Webb with ten rifles to Kolloa to prevent the Marakwet from raiding the Suk (Pokot). Previously one raid had failed owing to a rhino.

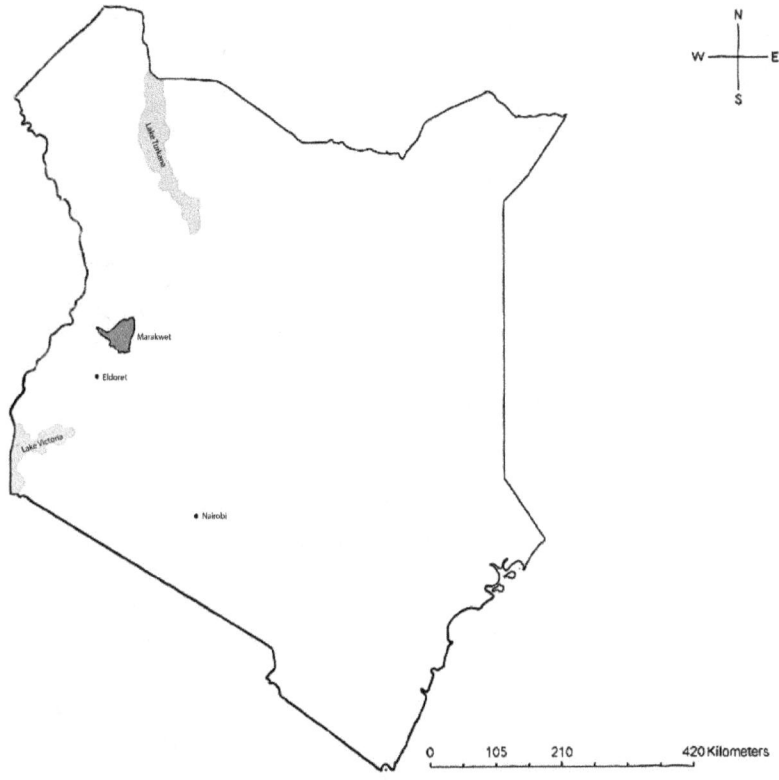

Figure 3: Marakwet Location on Kenya Country Map

Geographical Zones

Marakwet is divided into three specific zones that range from low to higher altitudes. On the East is the valley floor (*kew*), which rises gradually from one thousand meters to 3354 meters. The highland zone has a think forest cover and therefore cooler than the rest of the zones. These zones are distinguished by their geographical vegetation, climate, and function as described below.

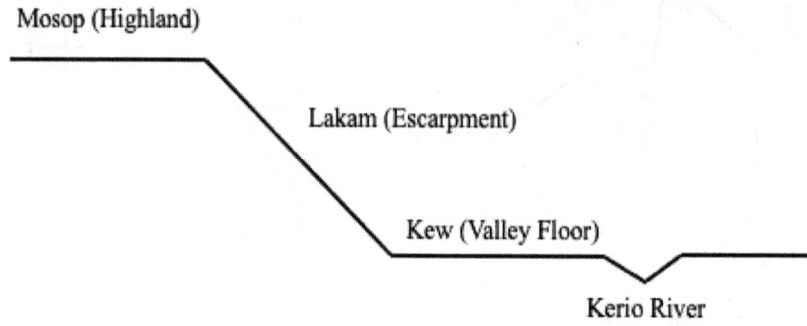

Figure 4: Marakwet Topography

The Valley Floor (*kew*)

The valley floor (*kew*) which extends from the Kerio River westwards to the foot of the escarpment is relatively flat. Its rich soil supports economic activity such as agriculture, grazing, hunting, vegetable gathering, fuel, and beekeeping. Most of the activities in this zone are done during the day for fear of mosquitoes, wild animals, and marauding cattle raiders from the neighboring Baringo district. By sunset (around six o'clock in the evening) most people usually vacate the valley floor except for shepherds and a few men harvesting honey or keeping watch at night.[3] During wartime, this area is completely abandoned as warriors from each side battle for supremacy. On a positive note, the abandonment of the valley at war time allows for the flourishing of the vegetation and wildlife. At the time of peace, the valley experiences unusual activity as more people move freely with their livestock in search of pasture. Moreover, the valley has more land for agriculture, grazing, and wildlife.[4]

---

3. Kipkorir et al., *Kerio Valley*, 2

4. The Valley is irrigated by water furrows from Cherangany hills leading downstream on two principal rivers of Arror and Embobut. The results are good yields of crops of mangoes, bananas, cassava, millet, maize, tomatoes, and watermelons. In the rainy season of March and April, the water surplus go to the main Kerio river where crocodiles flourish. The river travels North and empties at Lake Turkana.

The Escarpment Zone (*lakam*)

Lakam, or the escarpment, extends from the base westward and gradually rises up to three thousand meters. is mostly a residential area because it is safe and comfortably cooler during the night and free from mosquitoes. It also provides a beautiful panoramic view and protection from cattle raiders and wild animals.[5] At night, and during festive days, the escarpment comes to life with recreational and social activities for all ages. They include storytelling, and Marakwet are fond of various types of dances such as *kirong'o* and *Kirap*. Other social activities such as weddings and special religious ceremonies are conducted at the escarpment as well. Also common are the morning and evening gatherings around the fire at several elders' homesteads (*kokwo*). Here the elders informally socialize and discuss important matters of the season and pass on knowledge to the young. The young on the other hand are encouraged to attend such meetings for their own development of local knowledge. The skills acquired here come in handy in daily living or in formal communal deliberations. Certain elders outwit their peers and command the greatest respect and notoriety. The latter are often called upon to settle conflicts and their services are often in demand.

The Highland Zone (*Mosop*)

Above the escarpment is the *mosop* zone, which rises to eleven thousand feet. Apart from being a safety buffer, the Mosop zone is relatively cool and attracts higher rainfall. Most of the area is covered with natural forest of indigenous trees, such as teak, redwood, cypress, bamboo, and cider, and therefore serves as a good source of timber for housing and furrow construction. It also provides game and crops like potatoes, suited to high altitude. Like the valley floor, the highland is also good for hunting, beekeeping, and grazing. Not too many people live in *Mosop*, primarily because of cold temperatures. However, many people commute to their parcels of land at the edge of the forest in the morning and return to their residential area of *lakam* in the evening.

Traditionally, the three zones constitute the integral ecological system of the Marakwet. Most clans, own parcels of land in the three zones stretching from *Keu* to *Mosop*. With such land, they diversify and maintain crop rotation and other responsive farm practices. However, due to population growth and overall shortage of land in the last four decades, fewer families

---

5. Critchley, "Agricultural Developments in Marakwet," 24. Wilhelm Ostberg, "Life Among the Marakwet" Kenya Past and Present, issue 42, (2015) 58.

now occupy land in all three zones, and this has resulted in acute tensions in families, some of which have resulted in fatalities. During the Colonial period, most of the highland zone (*Mosop*) was demarcated as government forest. The clans who claimed ownership of the forest by obtaining a restricted permit from the government could only use it for grazing. After Kenya obtained its independence in 1963, some people moved to the edge of the forest, where they cultivated the newly introduced crops of maize, pyrethrum, and potatoes. By 1970, the crops had grown well, and many people decided to shift their agricultural activities from the valley and the escarpment to the highlands. At this time, maize had become the staple food for many Kenyans. Moreover, the government purchased the maize from the farmers at a good prize through its defunct Kenya Farmers Association (KFA). In a desire to maximize their profit, a few people infringed on the forested area and cleared it for cultivation. The government forest security was unable to curb the invasion. Consequently, the forest shrunk, and reduced the amount of water needed to irrigate the Valley. The illegal deforestation, with its devastating repercussions, necessitated repeated warnings by the government in the '70s and '80s. In 1988, President Daniel Moi issued a presidential decree prohibiting any use of the forest. Those who had enjoyed the use of it for cultivation and grazing were subsequently forced out. Since then, the scarcity of land has created immense tension between families and clans, often resulting in deadly feuds. Also, the growing population reduced the land and as a result, there is little arable land on the escarpment and the valley floor. In the 1990s, Kerio Valley has been affected by cattle rustling that forced many to relocate.

Kinship and Political Organizations

History of Origin

There are several migration stories by almost every clan. The most common and abiding among the Kalenjin is the so called the "Misri legend" that traces the Kalenjin origin to an ancient migration from Egypt. The Kalenjin believe that after the fall of the last Pharaoh, they were driven southwards to the city of Meroe. After some stops, they continued their journey along the Nile southwards all the way to Mount Elgon. The trip was hard, long and might have taken several generations. They must have clashed or negotiated their way with other ethnic groups along the way. Eventually, they settled on the slopes of Mt. Elgon where they found relative peace, sufficient grass for their livestock, and good agricultural land to settle, graze, and cultivate.

With such a promise, they found a home where they practiced their ancient rites of passage, including the circumcision rite. Previously, the rite had been constantly interrupted by enemy attacks on the migration route. However, they kept the traditions in oral history and passed them on to their children and their children's children. Occasionally, they shared their knowledge with other tribes in exchange for food and livestock. Important landmarks such as hills and rivers on the Rift Valley are noted in their songs and folklore. Mt. Kenya (*koilege*—the white colored rock) serves as a distant landmark in their migration.[6] Mt. Elgon is particularly significant in their migration history because it was the point for which significant subdivisions and dispersals occurred. One group headed South-East towards the present day Kericho and later organized into Kipsigis. Another group followed suit and ended up Nandi. The group that formed the Pokot headed northeast and northwest dividing up into smaller families all the way to Baringo. Yet another group that became the Tugen came from another direction and converged in Baringo. The group that became Keiyo settled in lands adjacent to the Nandi, and the group that later formed the Marakwet migrated east towards Kapcherop and settled in fertile lands that stretched all the way past Mt. Kiptaber. The remaining group, Sebei or Kony, continued in their settlement around the slopes of Mt. Elgon and later formed the Sabei/Elgon and remained on the slopes of Mt. Eldon. Landmarks such as the cave of Kitum (*kobeno Kitum*) serve as evidence of that ancient history. It is no wonder all the Kalenjin ethnicities trace its migration stories to Mt. Elgon and the original migration from Misri (Egypt).[7] The Talai, clan to which I belong, traces its origin to *Misri* (Egypt) and this is how they remember it.

> The Talai clan, who are presently scattered throughout the Marakwet region, once lived with other clans on the slopes of Mount Elgon. After some disagreements with their kinsmen over grazing rights, they decided to move eastward to Kiptaber where they resided for a couple of generations. The land was good for livestock grazing and cultivation. On a particular occasion, while dancing at one of their festive occasions, a white-necked crow landed on a nearby tree and warned the people that the rock was going to fall on them should they ignore the warning and run for safety. Some of the people who

---

6. Kipkorir and Welbourn, *Marakwet*, 80–81.

7. African scholars such as Dr. B. E. Kipkorir, G. S. Were, and Dr. Kipkoeech Araap Sambu support the Kalenjin Misri legend in support of the Kalenjin origins. While the *Misri* legend is supported by Kalenjin oral history, it has become a subject of contention (primarily by some Western scholars).

heard the crow's message paid attention and tried to interrupt the dance to warn others, but the rest dismissed the warning and resumed their dance. After the fourth warning, the Pied Crow flew away and the small group, who paid attention to the warning, left for their safety. Before they reached far, the rock fell from the sky and buried left behind with their livestock. Up to this day, this myth is re-told in Marakwet. Interestingly, some herders in Kiptaber have reported having heard voices of people from underneath the Mountain.

The small group which had luckily the incident migrated to different directions in the East in search of food. Some settled at Kapsowar, while others continued towards the warmer Kerio Valley floor and crossed over to Baringo. These travels were not always straight. Along the way, they gathered more livestock and practiced the circumcision rite and traded it for a small fee of grain, livestock, or land rights. Other Talai Clans proceeded northwards and settled in West Pokot, while others branched off in Kerio Valley and travelled Westwards towards the beckoning Cherangany hills. One group settled briefly at Chepkorowo before moving up the escarpment to Boroko where they found the weather attractive for habitation. From there, they hunted and kept bees in the forest above them while some cultivated millet and eleuisine and kept livestock on the escarpment and the valley floor. For irrigation of their crops, they constructed water furrows from Embobut river along with other i clans for which they shared land.[8]

Oral accounts for these travels abound in the Marakwet traditions and are passed on orally from generation to generation. A Talai elder explained to me why some of the Marakwet people differ in size and height. He recounted "the newly arrived people to the Marakwet were relatively tall but they encountered dwarf like people who resided in the forest and lived on honey and game. They tried to interact with them, but they were treacherous and extremely shy. Eventually, they intermarried and assimilated with them. Today, there is no trace of the short people in Marakwet except a few hunters (*okiek*) who still reside in the forest. Some of the colonial administrators and ethnographers recorded these accounts in an attempt to understand the Marakwet social life. The Kiptaber account was mentioned by M. W. H. Beech in his book on the Suk, first published in 1911. Although the falling of the rock and the alleged existence of people underneath Kiptaber may be mythical in nature, the fact of the migration of Marakwet from Mount

---

8. Kisang Kirop, personal interview, December 1988.

Elgon via Kiptaber should be considered in light of their oral tradition and migration patterns. More research is encouraged to unravel and interpret the full implication of such stories in relation to clan origins.

Kinship and Clan Structure

Kinship is an extension of blood lines held together by the ordinary functions of family life. Although there are many variations in African family life, kinship is probably the most common. John Mbiti explains how kinship constitutes the social reality of African people.

> It is kinship which controls social relationships between people in a given community: it governs marital customs and regulations; it determines the behavior of one individual towards another. Indeed, this sense of kinship binds together the entire life of the "tribe" and is even extended to cover animals, plants, and non-living objects through the "totemic" system. Almost all the concepts connected with human relationship can be understood and interpreted through the kinship system.[9]

All those in kinship ritual practice are bound to conduct themselves. Kayongo-Male and Onyango have made the following observation.

> In any rural village, almost everyone was related by blood. That meant all elderly men and women were referred to as father and mother while those closer in age were called brothers and sisters. In polygamous families, children had many mothers, grandparents, aunts, uncles, cousins, and older siblings. Those on the mother's side were uncles and mothers and one was bound or obliged to conduct themselves according to the prescribed ethics. There was no chance of dating anyone from both the mother's and father's side. Older family members exercised authority over the younger members in their nurture and training. When one moves to the urban center for employment opportunities, such a person is bound to contribute to the affairs of the village and visit family in the village whenever they are on holiday. Relatives who travel to the urban centers look for a family member to host them and it is expected for the family member to be hospitable and host their relatives.[10]

---

9. Mbiti, *African Religions*, 135.
10. Kayongo-Male and Onyango, *Sociology*, 6–7.

The Marakwet is organized around family units that form clans in residential villages. These units are geographically and socially divided by physical features such as streams, trees, or rocks. The term *kor* typically denotes both a residential area and a piece of land associated with a particular community. Among the Marakwet, the connection between the social unit and the land *(kor)* it occupies is very strong and carries a sentimental value of belonging. When a baby is born, the umbilical cord is ritually buried near the homestead in the ancestral land, where the spirits of the departed ancestors are believed to reside. Similarly, rituals of initiations are performed on the residential clan land where the ancestors reside. All residential clan groups are divided into lineages called *kabor*, literally meaning 'of', signifying their lineage. *Kabor* members can trace their relationship to a common father or ancestor. Genealogically, the ancestor is traced back to a few generations, as much as can be remembered by the living. Often, they can only be remembered up to four or six generations. This has served to sustain short links with the founding father/ancestor of the clan—*(kabor)* as well as making it easier for the clan to control its social structure and institutions such as infant naming and prevent blood relations in marriage. Each clan is identified by a totem and often the area was named after the totem for identity. Where the clan's name was not used, the relationship between the clan and the geographical location was equally strong.[11]

In villages where there is more than one residential clan group and where intermarriage is possible, members of the clan may choose where to reside.[12] At rare occasions and for the reasons of poverty or insecurity, a man may choose to live near his wife's people *(kapkikoi)* or his mother's people *(kamama)*. In the past fifty years, many of the young men belonging to the *kaplelach* age-set in the Kerio Valley moved their main residence from the escarpment to the valley floor in order to be closer to the modern amenities associated with development and modernity. These centers provided medical facilities, shops, and schools.

Unfortunately, that life was immediately disrupted by constant cattle rustlers. Oral stories of cattle rustling confirm such tensions in the past, but it was revived in the 1970s when deadly confrontation at Kapkamak, Sang'utan and Chesegon resulted in the loss of life and livestock. Organized Pokot warriors had crossed the Kerio river border and attacked the named areas with the intent of taking the Marakwet accumulated cattle. As it happened, the Pokot warriors' spears could not match the Marakwet

---

11. Moore, *Space*, 18.

12. The totemic clans cut across the territorial groups, and many are also represented in other Kalenjin groups. See Kipkorir and Welbourn, *Marakwet*, 6.

poisoned arrows. The clashes resulted in significant death toll. The Pokot did not return until they had acquired sophisticated guns from Ugandan starving soldiers after general Idi Amin was deposed in 1979. With the advantage of AK47, the Pokot prevailed against the Marakwet. Farming in the fertile Kerio Valley was disrupted as Pokot marauded the valley day and night. Also, it disrupted markets and other exchanges leading to famines and untold suffering on both sides. Schools were forced to close for long periods at a time. The government's efforts to mitigate the situation were unsuccessful. In fact, there have been rumors pointing fingers to politicians in government as the castigators especially when the rustlers are constantly in possession of bullets from the government's manufacturing plant.

The Marakwet clans and their corresponding totems are well organized as follows. (see the table below)

Clan	Masculine Singular	Feminine Singular	Totem
1. *Kabon*	Kabonin	Kabon	a. Baboon (majority of the clan)
			b. Frog
			c. Rat
			d. Taiywa (a species of Wildfowl)
2. *Moi*	Kimoin	Kimoi	a. Buffalo or Moiyo
			b. Crested Crane
			c. Osit (a bird)
			d. Kosomyo (ground bees)
3. *Kobil*	Kobilyon	Kobilo	a. Porcupine
			b. Dog
			c. Kipkuto (a burrowing animal)
			d. Black-necked crow
4. *Mokich*	Mokichin	Mokicho	a. Moon
			b. Fire
5. *Saniak*	Saniakin	Saniaka	a. Monkey
			b. Bees (red or brown color)
6. *Sogom*	Sogomin	Sogomo	a. Hawk

Clan	Masculine Singular	Feminine Singular	Totem
7. *Sot*	Sotio	Soti	a. Asiis—Sun b. Mokyo—a worm
8. *Syokwei*	Syokweiyo	Syokwei	a. Black stinging ant
9. *Talai*	Talain	Talaa	a. Ngotuny—Lion b. Kukai—Pied crow
10. *Terik*	Terikin	Teriki	a. Kabongen—large elephant b. Kop Katien—small elephant)
11. *Tingo*	Tingoyo	Tingo	a. Hyena
12. *Toyoi*	Toyoin	Toyoi	a. Ilat—lightning and thunder) b. Ber—Water
13. *Tul*	Tulin	Tula	a. Kipsero—large jackal b. Chepkinjo—small jackal c. Other type(s) of jackal

Table 1.1 Marakwet Clans adopted from Kipkorir and Welbourn, *Marakwet*, 7.

Political and Judicial

The Marakwet had no chiefs before the arrival of Europeans and colonial rule. Judicial and administrative matters were handled through the traditional gatherings of elders (*kokwo*). These were gatherings of men organized for the purpose of discussing village life and activities ranging from irrigation schedules to the settling of community disputes. For the Marakwet, *kokwo* symbolizes the unity of the social group and its judicial strength. Basically, the formal traditional *Kokwo* is used to settle matters that have defeated the family, or the parties concerned. When this happens, the complainant is given a chance to present his or her case at kokwo where the matter will be heard and deliberated openly by a larger group of *Osiis*. The decision by *osiis* is always rendered at the end. The parties will either abide by the said deliberations or make an appeal if dissatisfied. Perisitiany and Huntingford, who had earlier written on this subject, thought of "*kokwet*" as a formalized body with an appointed leader or master of ceremony. What Persitiany and

Huntingford observed might have been the later form of "*Kokwet,*" which was an adjustment to fit the newly established "*African Courts.*" These courts were new and formalized models made up of elders from diverse communities, with the purpose of reinforcing the British colonial indirect rule through the African customary law. This was one of the ideal colonial innovations whose purpose was to serve the colonial system in many ways, including the dissemination of colonial propaganda.

All complaints and misconduct are dealt with at these gatherings, where each case is heard and given fair judgment. Light family disputes are dealt with on a family level where the father, as the head of the household, would resolve the matter, occasionally with the assistance of his clan. Such matters may include allocation of land, water rights, and sharing of food and livestock. In cases of serious concern, the matter is taken to a bigger audience (*Kokwo*). The composition of the gathering depends entirely on the matter to be discussed. If a *Kokwo* is called to settle a marital issue, the adult men and older women from the lineage would be consulted. An issue related to water rights or land dispute is settled by clan or the village men. If the matter is not resolved, the complainant can appeal and ask for another *Kokwo* involving newer voices and probably of seasoned and wiser elders in the wider Community. Matters related to theft are left to the village elders. If the matter concerns murder, then homicide experts are invited; however, in time of grave deliberations involving capital punishment, the final decision is made by the clan (*kabor*) and the maternal uncles (*kamama*). This is often done in the presence of all the residents in the area (*Ossis*). In more weighty matters, such as murder or homicide, only the wise seniors with grey hair (*Karwal)* are allowed to speak. They are trusted for their wisdom that is gained through years of experience and natural wit. Almost every crime, including deliberate and accidental murder, is punished accordingly. Executions are rarely done in Marakwet, but when it happens the maternal uncles of the accused (*Kamama*) have the final word. For instance, if a person were convicted of witchcraft, their arms and legs would be bound by a string tied to two poles in a hot scorching sun. As they lay on the ground, the maternal uncles (*kamama*) watch closely as the examiner/interrogator or an assistant step on the string tightly to inflict more pain until the person confesses.[13] If no confession is obtained, the maternal uncles who had been watching the procedure all along may intercede for mercy or request for another hearing. In all these trials, evidence and witnesses are crucial. In an event where the complainant is not satisfied, the ritual elders administer a blanket curse where the divine and

---

13. Kipkorir and Welbourn, *Marakwet*, 8.

the ancestors may expose the culprit. The results might take generations to take effect and can be visited by the children and the grandchildren. It is not uncommon to witness cases today where the accused had suffered misfortunes due to curses that were done decades ago.

Economic Structure

Land Ownership and Crop Production

The Marakwet engage in mixed farming of livestock and crops. These two preoccupations are the basis of their economy and food security. As in many African societies, land is an important commodity. It does not only serve as a source of food, but also a social asset with religious significance.

> The communal nature of land holding is seen in the context of the bond between the clan and the land. This serves as a basis of their group identity. Thus, the Marakwet community and the land it occupies are quite inseparable.[14]

It is commonly believed that the spirits of the ancestors, who once walked in the land, keep the spiritual bond with the living. This bond is maintained through land rituals, which are often observed in times of misfortunes such as droughts and locust invasions.

The land in Marakwet is divided according to totemic clans, which are, in turn, subdivided by family members. Individuals within a family hold usufruct in a particular strip owned by the clan. They are entitled to use the land during their lifetime and pass this on to the next generation. If, however, a usufruct holder dies without male heirs, the land reverts to his daughters or agnates who would apportion it accordingly. In special cases the land's usufruct is given to a surviving daughter or sister. This piece of land is traditionally referred to as "female's land" (*Para Tipin*).[15]

Technically, a man only gains full ownership of land or livestock when he marries. Until that time, such resources remained under the control of his father. Nevertheless, he is expected to assist his mother, especially when the father is a polygamist. When the son gets married, he is given his share of land by his father or uncles. A woman also acquires rights to land when she is married. This land was given to her by her husband and

---

14. Moore, *Space*, 18.

15. Often these women receive a warm welcome by their male agnatic kin. A visit would demand the killing of at least a goat. Without such hospitality, the women are entitled to ask for payment for the use of their inherited land. On the death of the female inheritor the usufruct of the land reverts to their clan of kin.

will consist of several plots in different parts of the clan area. In principle, the land is under the husband, but the wife is given authority to cultivate it. In a polygamist family, each wife is given her own piece of land, and each is expected to operate independently and provide sufficient food for their children. Although a woman's portion of land is always considered to be hers, she only has usufruct rights over it. Customarily, the land still belongs to the lineage patriarchal clan.

A family usually cultivates several strips of land in the rainy season depending on their numbers. A man without sufficient land to cultivate may lease further strips from other men of the clan or from other clans. Payments for land lease differ, depending on the individual or the economic condition at the time. The most common payments are made with livestock. In Endo location, an axe or a goat would lease a strip of land for a season or two, while a cow would lease for a bit longer. An outright sale may involve the whole clan (*Kabor*). The clan may refuse and stop the transaction if they need the land. The Marakwet not only own the land they occupy, cultivate, and graze their stock, but also lay claim to the entire territory where their forefathers hunted and exerted military control. This claim could go beyond the colonial boundaries. For example, some clans extend their claim across Kerio river to the foothills of Tiaty Baringo, on claims of hunting and bee-keeping rights. Other claims include salt licks, streams, and dams. The woodland and the forest of Cherangany are claimed by Marakwet clans even though this has been a source of tension with the government. Both the Colonial and the Kenyan National government have demarcated the whole area as government forest, thus driving the natives to the edge of the escarpment where agricultural activity does not produce sufficient food. On the other hand, the forest is the source of the water that feeds the numerous irrigation systems that provide water to the land on both the escarpment and the valley floor.

Agriculture

The Marakwet calendar is controlled by the planting, weeding and harvest activities to which other activities revolve. During the dry season, the whole community repairs their water furrows. The work may entail clearing and replacing broken or dislodged rocks. Secondly, the land is prepared for planting before March–April rains. Each clan is assigned to work their own furrows and fields by cutting trees and shrubs for burning. The men would also fence the land while the women turn the soil and seed the land with the traditional crops of millet and eleusine. Sorghum is usually planted in the drier season because of its ability to resist drought. After a month, when the crop is about two or three inches tall, the women begin the weeding season, and this might happen again before harvest. When the big rains stop in the month of May, the irrigation system is employed with fair distribution to each member of the clan. In the final months of August, the crop is ready for harvest. This is also the most critical time to keep off birds and monkeys. It is commonly the responsibility of the youth to rise early and be at their post as early as possible to beat the prey. The post is roughly constructed with three meters acacia posts with platform at the top. From such a vintage point the attendant can see far and throw mud balls by using a long flexible pole to every direction to scare the prey away. They would do so till dark or after sunset when the birds would have gone to their nests for the night.

The task of harvesting is often done by women although a few men also assist to speed up the harvest. Families who need assistance are assisted by communal efforts *(sikoom)* organized to speed up the exercise. There is no payment given to *sikoom* apart from a promise of a good party with food and drink. However, the organizer is given a modest gift for organizing the event. An organizer's acumen and popularity grow over time with experience. The most experienced are sought out for larger events. In the process of harvesting, a better-off family would permit other poorer families or individuals to glean a few paces behind them. As soon as harvesting is completed, livestock would be allowed into the field to forage the grain stalks. The harvest of grain is stored in granaries or the upper chamber of the house (*taboot*). The latter allows the grain to be smoked everyday by the hearth for both durability and longevity.[16]

Traditional agriculture was disrupted when new crops were introduced by the colonial government. Initially, the colonial government took some of the best Marakwet land and gave it to the settlers. Some of that land such as Kapmendi and Kapjongoro/Kapsiliot have been reverted. When the land was initially taken away, the Marakwet became one of the British reserves where labor in European farms was drawn.

In 1923, the colonial secretary in London issued what came to be known as "The White Paper" to address African interests, which until that point had been ignored. Education was provided by the missionaries, and the quality depended on the policy of each missionary agency. For example, the mainline denominational missions and Catholics tended to offer a relatively higher level of education compared to the more conservative mission agencies. The latter were only interested in teaching its members to read the Bible and possibly work as clerks and record keepers in the settler farms. After the second

---

16. Kipkorir and Welbourn, *Marakwet*, 395–96.

World War, Africans who had attended mission schools and fought abroad returned with a renewed zeal to demand for their freedom from colonial domination. In response, the colonial government adopted the Swynnerton plan to strengthen the expansion of African agriculture and provide Africans with more opportunity to cultivate cash crops such as pyrethrum, wool, tea, and potatoes for both local food consumption and export.

The aim of the plan was to create a relatively small family holdings of ten acres each to provide sufficient food and cash for a family. The colonial government envisioned using such incentives to create a middle class.[17] The report recommended for all high-quality native land to be surveyed, consolidated, and parceled into individual holdings. That policy undermined the traditional tribal land system. The individual farmers would be given title deeds and credit which had been previously denied them. In addition, the farmers received technical assistance for their crops and livestock as well as help to access the markets. Previously, these benefits were the reserve of the white settler minority.

In 1951, a few leaders including chiefs from Elgeyo Marakwet were taken on a tour in the Central Province to study land consolidation schemes intended to replace the traditional land system. Unfortunately, the implementation of the plan was interrupted by the MAUMAU protest, and it had to wait until the 1960s. In the end, the consolidation of the traditional land into fewer hands left many people landless and poor. Some of them were forced to work on settler farms, and when there was no work, they became squatters.

During and after the MAUMAU emergency in 1952, the Marakwet Christians were positioned to take advantage of Swynnerton plan and were allotted rich parcels of land by the colonial government adjacent to the forest. Other beneficiaries were the products of government education at government schools such as Tambach and Kabete. One of the beneficiaries was Kibor Talai, who left teaching and became the chief of Lelan. He expanded his own share of land by acquiring more lands and eventually became a renown wool supplier. His reputation increased when he imported Merino sheep from New Zealand and Australia. Talai hailed from Kotut village in the old endo location and was the first Marakwet to go to Alliance High School and Kagumo Teacher's College. In 1947, he was posted to teach at Tambach government school alongside Daniel Arap Moi, the former president of Kenya. Dr. Benjamin Kipkorir recalls his student days

---

17. Roger Swynnerton was an agricultural officer in Tanzania before he was transferred to Kenya in the early 1950s. His agricultural innovations in Tanzania impressed the colonial administration and earned him a promotion in Kenya.

at Tambach and describes Mr. Talai as a stern and methodical mathematics teacher who paid little attention to his body and looks.

> Talai was nicknamed "Chepseng'eny" which though not originally a complimentary name, stuck to him and just about summed him up as someone for whom personal appearance was secondary to what came from his mind. His hair was untidy, and he seemed to apply no oil to his body, which we noticed he scratched often. He had the habit of hoisting his loose-fitting shorts with his elbows—as if to indicate he was aware that his hands were soiled . . . with chalk, dust, or more likely cooking oil, for he was the master in charge of the school kitchen.[18]

After leaving Tambach, Chepseng'eny became an aggressive farmer in the cooler highlands of Lelan where he was appointed chief. He was at the forefront of the government's new agricultural experimentation in Merino sheep and wool as well as potatoes and pyrethrum. At independence, he was already positioned to purchase a huge settler farm in Uasin-Gishu where he kept dairy cows, and large-scale farming of maize, and wheat. It is rumored that he clashed with the second president of the Republic when the latter encroached on his farm during the establishment of Moi University. The animosity might have started much earlier when both were teachers at Tambach government school.

Irrigation

Irrigation has been the most important method used to sustain crop production in the valley floor where rainfall is rather scarce. While that is the case, there are no written records on the early history or the background of the Marakwet irrigation furrows. However, oral traditions abound. One orality suggests that the Marakwet brought the skill with them from the Nile delta in the North from where they migrated. Another tradition implies that the Marakwet people found some of the irrigation furrows when they arrived in the region about eight hundred years ago.[19] This suggests that there were other people in the area before their arrival. Those people may have been absorbed into the Marakwet or driven away. R. O. Hennings, who was once a District Officer in the district recalls one of the oral traditions that on their arrival, the Marakwet found abandoned huts, broken pots, and the

---

18. Kipkorir, *Descent*, 105.
19. Sutton, "Towards a history," 100.

ashes of fire to indicate signs of recent occupation.[20] Whatever the case, the Marakwet inherited and expanded the furrows and added their own innovation to meet the growing population. Evidently, the technology employed to construct these furrows is so complex that Europeans were impressed at such ingenuity. In 1960, Elspeth Huxley noted:

> No rivers would be more difficult to tap for furrows, because they run in deep gorges and are hemmed in by sheer cliffs. A modern engineer would find the task of taking levels difficult. ... That it could all be done so successfully without any equipment was ... in its smaller way, almost as great a feat as the building of the pyramids.[21]

R. O. Hennings was filled with amazement for the extent, ingenuity, and effectiveness of using streams at the top of the escarpment to water the parched fields three thousand feet below. That indeed shows a practical imagination which has sometimes been supposed not to exist in Africa.[22]

There are sections in some of the furrows where spectacular structures were erected to enable water to flow across deep gullies, and jutting rocks. In some places, water furrows are suspended up to four meters above ground. Construction in these areas demanded dedication, endurance, and ingenuity. In some sections, the constructors had to be suspended by a network of ropes, manually held by a team of able men.[23]

Today, there are over forty furrows scattered throughout Marakwet that take their water from the parent rivers of Arror in the South and Embobut in the North that can provide enough water for simultaneous use throughout the year. The furrows are generally excavated out of the main river at an upper intake and then diverted through the escarpment and hills down to the valley floor. The basic alignment and position of take-off from the parent river are dictated by the desired destination of the water and the major physical features to be negotiated.[24] Joseph Thompson saw one of the furrows when he passed through the Marakwet region on a donkey from Kavirondo, early in 1884.

> I here, noticed the employment of canals for irrigation, on a larger scale than in Teita, many of them being conveyed with

---

20. Hennings, *African Morning*, 202.
21. Huxley, *New Earth*, 36.
22. Hennings, *African Morning*, 202.
23. Ssennyonga, "Marakwet Irrigation Systems," 102. Wilhelm Ostberg, "Life Among the Marakwet", Kenya Past, and Present Issue 42 (2015) 59.
24. Soper, "Irrigation Systems," 79.

surprising judgment along the most unexpected places. We contrived to make the descent without accident, and the men camped beside the artificial canals employed to bring the water from the great distance, to irrigate the ground at the base. In camping here, we found we had simply delivered ourselves into the hands of the philistines. The natives at once put the screw on us to extol a large peace offering. Seeing us hesitate, they quietly retired, and the water with them—for they could easily divert it in its upper course. This was sufficient to produce the desired effect. We humbly paid up; and immediately, as if a modern rod of Moses had struck the rock, the water began to flow.[25]

Dr. Kipkorir, who hails from Kapsogom in Arror, thought that the river which Joseph Thompson saw was the Muyeen furrow that is shared by both Kapsogom and Samar.[26] True or not, the technological work seen on the take-off points are of enormous complexity considering the basic tools of wooden sticks, simple axes, and robe that the constructors used. Stones supported by long poles tied together encouraged the growth of grass species with strong root. Similar supporting plants such as *cyperus alternifolia* (*yashan*) grow naturally to sustain the flow. Immediately after the take-off, the flow of the water in most of the furrows is regulated by movable barriers of rocks, logs, and vegetation. This enables the surplus flow to return to the parent river to control the furrow's sustainable volume of water. At this point, water can be cut off to allow repairs whenever necessary. At the close of heavy rains, the furrows will also be closed at this same point to minimize any damages from excess flow or from washouts on the steep slopes.[27]

One of the most spectacular furrows is the Kabarsiran, which waters the fields in the lower part of Sambirir location. The area is otherwise waterless when the small rivulets dry up in the hot season. The Kabarsiran furrow takes its water from the upper part of the Arror river and travels for several miles along the steep side of the escarpment to a gap where it passes over to the slopes above the escarpment. From there it follows a natural water-path to the escarpment edge and flows steeply down a naturally dug out channel to the fields of Kabarsiran on the valley floor. It travels for over ten miles to the valley floor and drops more than 1,200 meters.[28] Intakes are generally located high on the escarpment and are constructed of brushwood, logs, boulders, and grass. Some furrows have partially

25. Thompson, *Through Masai Land*, 310; see also Hennings, *African Morning*, 206.
26. Kipkorir, *Descent*, 428.
27. Soper, "Irrigation Systems," 79.
28. Hennings, *African Morning*, 204.

modernized intakes of wooden aqueduct supported on high trestles. At some points sluices are utilized to control water flow and prevent downstream damage especially during periods of high river flows. At the foot of the escarpment, furrows are directed to the fields.[29]

The former Endo location from Chesongoch to Chesegon has the most extensive system of furrows in the district. The parent river of Embobut begins up on the forested highlands of Cherangany hills and tumbles steeply down through a V-shaped valley cut into the wall of the escarpment. At one point, the river forms a convenient dam with the help of great boulders. Five furrows are created out of the dam, two furrows on the left side and three on the right. These furrows water all the fields in Endo location. The two furrows on the left pass behind Sagat hill, flowing down through natural gulleys and artificial channels to the fields in the valley. The other three large furrows, the most audacious furrow in the region, travel over the saddle at the back of Kapchebai hill, towering to over two thousand meters. These furrows flow precariously along the precipitous slopes, circumventing the boulders on aqueducts made of flat stones, tree trunks, and turf supported on stakes up to ten feet high. At one point, the water of two furrows intersects, one over the other. At another point, one of the furrows passes through a hollow tree.

Once it has passed over the saddle behind Kapchebai hill, two of the furrows flow down gradually for several miles until they reach the fields on the valley floor. The third furrow passes along a rocky hillside until it reaches a stream bed and flows down the rest of the way to the fields. Similarly, the Talai furrow begins above the dam and straddles for miles before it connects to Embo Korengor stream that carries it down to the escarpment before it is redirected at the base of the escarpment. It continues from there all the way to Talai farms of Soyon and Chepkorowo.[30] Similarly, while Kabisioi have their own furrow, Siaban, Kapsiren and Kachepsom have shared water rights for a long time. This shows clearly that Endo location has many furrows leading off from Embobut permanent river.

Water rights are held by the clan and its descendants, and rights to water are equal to rights to land. Similarly, water allocation depends on participation in the maintenance of the furrow. Other groups can only gain access to water by buying rights or through alliance. The general repairs are carried out communally by the males of the clan at least once a year. Every young man from sixteen years old must attend such work and

---

29. Watson et al., "Indigenous Irrigation," 74–75.

30. An interview of Talai elders, namely, Ngelecha, Kariwotum, Karaninyang, Lomukereng, and Lomudang, at Boroko in 2005.

show their clan solidarity. Water is only available to them, although exceptions can be made. For example, once each member has had his share of twenty-four hours, a grace period is given before the next member takes over. That grace period is given to anyone who is in dire need. Non clan members in the village or women may be allocated water during this time, unless they have purchasing rights.

In desperate situations where water demand exceeds the supply, the allocation of water is carefully planned for equitable distribution. For example, in Mogoro location where there are only two small streams for several clans, a system of rotation is employed. Each clan or sub-clan holds the water rights in yearly turns. The system of rotating water rights does not mean that those who were not allocated water are totally deprived of access to irrigation. Water may also be purchased from the holders by the individuals in need. In contrast to Mogoro, the Endo location with its large river, the Embobut, has enough water and therefore agriculture by irrigation is rather extensive. It was the surplus of grain that attracted the German explorer Count Teleki and his porters to Endo fields in 1889. He could have been assisted had he politely asked for food instead of stealing.[31]

The process of irrigation involves men taking water from the furrow and directing it to the concerned fields. This could range in distance from a few feet to four kilometers. The water is then spread out on the dry ground, so that the soil will be moist and soft for the seed which the women plant. During drought, the men again bring in the water and run it among the plant roots. A female may water the fields, as long a male has directed the water from the main furrow. While the men and children may wash in the irrigation channels, sexually mature girls and women are forbidden to do so. This is because it is considered a serious offense for a woman during menstruation to touch or, worse, wash in the furrows and pollute it. It is believed that the furrow will dry up should a woman wash in it.[32] When it does happen, a form of purification rite is necessary. This usually involves the slaughter of a sheep so that its chyme (*errian*) is sprinkled in the stream as a form of purification.[33]

The furrows are maintained communally by the men of the clan. The procedures of maintenance include routine checks of the water level and flow, the cleaning of silt and grass blockages, and other related repairs. Watchmen are appointed to inspect the danger points periodically. These routine checks are done in shifts. Problems are reported to the community

---

31. Hennings, *African Morning*, 205.
32. Moore, *Space*, 181.
33. Personal interview with James Cheserek and others, March 1989.

during the men's evening gatherings. It is at these gatherings that any action regarding repairs is decided. When a furrow breaks, every man whose field is served by that furrow must turn out to help in its restoration. Shirkers are liable to a fine for a goat, beer, or money. The same applies to the work of cleaning and realigning the furrows.[34]

The distribution of land in Marakwet is associated with clan furrows. That means each clan owns parcels of land stretching from the highlands through the escarpment, all the way to the valley floor. Thus, in Endo where the water supply is plentiful, the fields are larger compared to Mogoro location which has only two small streams with which to irrigate. The supply of water also determines the type of crops to be grown. With its water resource, the Endo grow more crops ranging from finger millet, sorghum, maize, and fruits in plenty, while Mogoro prefer to grow drought resistant crops such as finger millet and sorghum.[35]

In the 1950s the colonial government and missionaries, introduced cassava, sweet potatoes, groundnuts, bananas, mangoes, and cotton. In 1979, the Kenyan government established the Kerio Valley Development Authority for the purpose of improving agricultural yield. One of the Authority's priorities was to assist with repairs of the furrows. This involved the supply of modern materials such as cement and steel for reinforcement. Kerio Valley Development Authority introduced additional crops including green gram, cowpeas, kale, oranges, and watermelon. Another staple crop that has grown in importance is an improved variety of sorghum called "serena." It is drought resistant and can be harvested in four months. In the past, finger millet was exchanged for meat or milk from the Pokot, or honey and poison for arrows from the Tugen, Tobacco was also grown and exchanged for goats and salt from the Turkana. Today, the mango fruit has dominated the valley and when the roads are passable, lorries line up to transport it to the urban markets such Eldoret, Kitale, and Lodwar.

Livestock

In addition to crop cultivation, the Marakwet keep livestock. The principal stock are goats and cattle, although sheep are occasionally kept by a few. These animals provide milk and meat for consumption, and the hides and skins are used for leather clothing, shoes, straps, and bedding. The animals are also sold to provide money for buying clothes, food, and school fees. Cattle and goats are also used for gifts and dowry. During the

34. Hennings, *African Morning*, 205.
35. Hennings, *African Morning*, 208.

circumcision period, a boy may acquire his first animals through promises by relatives. In the intervening years, the young man will try through various means, to build up his herd. When he marries, he moves out to a new parcel of land to start his own family. At this time, he is given part of his inheritance mostly in the form of livestock. This will increase his wealth and social standing among his peers.

Keeping livestock, especially cattle, is a man's job, and most of their time is spent looking for sufficient grazing grounds. The women and children are left on the escarpment (*lakam*), where they keep a few goats for milk. During the day, the herding of the livestock is done by young shepherd boys (*mosowo*). Adults are always on call in case of attacks by cattle raiders or wild animals. The ownership of livestock, especially cattle, is a guarantee of status and a voice in society. It also means that one can marry additional wives if they so choose. Men occasionally brag about their animal wealth during drinking parties. At the evening dances of *kirong'o*, men sing praises about a particular cow, mentioning its special qualities. The composition of such songs is done by the individual while looking after animals in the grazing fields. These songs relate the history of the animal, its origins, how it was in its possession, and how it acquired its name. An animal is not only known by name, but also by its family line, particular habits, and virtues, and whether it gives a lot of milk or has difficulty in calving.

In case of a misfortune of one's herd by such as disease, drought, or raids, the Marakwet fall back on an investment security system called *tilya* stock exchange. This is a kind of an insurance system in which a man distributes his livestock widely among friends through lending. For example, one might lend a bull to a neighbor in need in exchange for a heifer. The neighbor takes the bull and promises to give the heifer in the future, or he brings the heifer immediately but after she gives birth, he comes back to return the heifer leaving the calf. A man may borrow a goat from another to feast with his friends with a promise to pay in the future. This kind of relationship goes on indefinitely, hence the name *tilya* which literally means relation. It is common for Marakwet to distribute their surplus livestock to people of the same clan and other clans to ensure wider distribution of livestock. In case of calamity or need, the person can reclaim some *tilya* animals.

Another underlying element in the exchange is the bond or mutual respect, friendship, and solidarity between stock friends. When I was young, a stranger visited our home. My mother asked me to check who he was. I did and reported that he was a man I had not seen before, and his clothing and head gear was unusual. My mother opened the gate carefully to make sure the goats did not escape and let the man in the inner compound and gave him a seat. He was given some water to drink, and he drank all of it and asked for more. He seemed tired and obviously he had traveled from afar. By this time, we had known his identity as a Pokot. He sat there the whole time until food was ready, and he was given his portion. He ate some of the Ugali without touching the vegetables on the side. Just about that time my father arrived and noticed the man. They exchanged cordial greetings like good friends and my father asked if he had been fed. My father's food was served but he didn't eat it. He had a conversation with my mother and before long, he came out with a rope and a knife for a goat slaughter. My siblings and I were excited for the feast in the making. The man must be important to my dad to go to that extent. After a late second meal of roasted goat liver we settled down to sleep, leaving my dad and his friend to talk by the fire outside. After all, he was my father's *tilya*. In the morning we went to school but when we returned in the evening the man had gone. My mother told us that my dad owed the man a cow and that he traveled from Tirioko in Baringo. He was pleased with the way he was received and left without asking for the cow for which he had come. After a hearty meal he was given grain and some of the meat to take with him. We never saw the man again until my dad died in 2015. When we were settling at my father's estate, that man's name had been forgotten. He might have died earlier. On another occasion, my father had planned to take me and my brother to Pokot to collect his *tilya* livestock from people to whom he had given bulls. That trip never materialized due to constant raiding between the Pokot and Marakwet. Besides, it would have taken a long time to trace where those people lived given the constant movements of pastoralists. According to tradition, my brothers and I are expected to inherit our father's stock relations. We have managed to pay in cash nearly all the people to whom our father owed livestock. The last debtor was Ng'imor's family from Cheptulel in west Pokot. Apparently, my father had taken a bull from Ng'imor and entered the *tilya* relationship with him. I agreed to repay him the debt, but he could not accept cash money. I had to purchase a heifer from Lotuma Rengeti, to which he was pleased. In that sense, Ng'imor's son participated in a *tilya* relationship with Rengeti's family. According to the tradition of *tilya*, I am yet to go back to collect a cow from the herd from the same cow. The point of the *tilya* tradition is to help one restock if by misfortune his livestock is decimated by disease or theft.

CHAPTER 2

Rites of Passage

Introduction

RITUALS ARE UNIVERSAL TRAITS that all humans share. That means that in the process of "cultural evolution," humans rely on rituals to manage their lives. It is commonly believed that humans by nature learn from those who precede them and adapt accordingly as they perpetuate the human continuum. The principal technique to sustain this cultural mobility is ritual. In fact, ritual is the pathway that guides people through what would otherwise be uncharted territory. A baby is welcomed into the world and guided safely through life with rituals. Similarly, rituals are performed at the end of life to safeguard life in the next world. As Tom Driver determines,

> A baby emerging from the womb is a potential waiting to be formed into a human being.[1]

Even with human endowments such as a soul and an intellect, these gifts are not yet sufficient to ensure that the baby is truly a functional human being capable of ethical and cultural responsibility. In this sense, the humanity of the infant must be learned and understood through ritual.

According to Theo Sundermeier, the term ritual or rite derives its meaning from the concept of order or regulated behavior. It comes out of a context that understands the world as unordered, dangerous, and chaotic. This is equated to a house that requires the order of paths, trees, and a garden for it to become an ordered home. From this perspective, Sundermeier observes that rituals are ways of ordering the world and making it manageable. They hold chaos in check, ward off accidents and regulate life. They rehearse the values which form the basis of society.[2] Through rituals,

---

1. Driver, *Liberating Rites*, 16.
2. Sundermeier, *Individual and Community*, 54–55.

the community's material life comes into play by non-verbal or symbolic means of communication.

While the Marakwet have learned how to adapt to their natural environment, they are also aware that nothing is safe without the accompaniment of rituals. Human vulnerability is constantly threatened, especially at the crisis points of transition amplified in the rites of passage. At these moments, the community is expected to take adequate measures at every step to address these dangers and provide the needed support. Nothing can be taken for granted. This means the transition from childhood to adulthood is not just left to biological development alone. In every step, the person experiences what might be termed "sacramental death and rebirth." In this case, every ritual deed, from the shaving of hair to replacing old clothing with new, illustrates the process of "losing and gaining." This means one must lose one's childhood in order to gain adulthood. The four Marakwet rituals of birth, circumcision, marriage, and death are marked and ordered by corresponding rites that determine the natural rhythm of life of losing and gaining. The last rite of life, which takes place at death, does not mark the end of life's rituals but a transition point to another set of rituals that continues to be performed even after death.

As previously stated, the main purpose for these rites is to create a socially conscious person. It is for this reason that the elders impress these rites upon the young to ensure that they (the young), become responsible members of society. The young, in turn, are obligated to observe the rites carefully and pass them on to the next generation in the same manner they had received them. Anyone who rejects the rites suffers social ridicule and alienation. Moreover, these rituals are regulated by taboos and breaking any of them would only lead to chaos and eventual breakdown of society. Innovations are permitted, but they must be endorsed by the elders.

These rites are also significant because, in them, religious and metaphysical powers come into play mostly to affirm the African Philosophy as reiterated by John Mbiti, that African culture has no separate compartment for secular and religious life. All of life is sacred with spiritual dimensions.[3]

> The rites of life, with all their religious implications, are the meaningful point by which people feel a sense of connectedness. ... these rites orient the individual to realize his/her place in the society, without which there is no meaningful existence.[4]

---

3. Mbiti, *African Religions*, 107.
4. Mbiti, *African Religions*, 108.

Rituals also play a key role in reinforcing age stratification and power differentials in the family and society. It follows that the elder son occupies an important place of privilege as a result of being closest to his father. In that sense, he is a potential successor to his father and assumes the role of a mediator between his siblings when the father is absent or dead. Moreover, like his father he communicates with the ancestors. Age is believed to come with wisdom; therefore, age seniority determines and commands respect. This applies to women too. In other words, as a person grows older his/her respect increases accordingly.

> The old harvest the fruits of life, for which they previously struggled. Now they can receive from children and grandchildren what they previously owed to parents and grandparents—service, obedience, and respect.[5]

Like other African societies, the Marakwet clans are held together through the observation of rites, particularly the rites of passage. The birth of a child is an occasion for celebration and thanksgiving for a new life. The impending crisis that comes from the impurities associated with birth is mitigated through a host of rites and taboos.

The first rituals at birth alter the social status of the mother and allow the baby to be accepted into society to undergo a lifelong process of orientation. Similarly, the rite of circumcision turns a boy into a man and a girl into a woman. As Sundermeier observes,

> The individual is changed by the ritual. He or she receives a new status and occupies a new rank in other words life takes on a new quality and must be lived in a different way.[6]

The participation of the community encourages the individual to move with ease from one stage of life to the next. Every step is approached carefully and with caution because of the vulnerability of life, especially during the rites of passage. As previously stated, both the individual and the society are vulnerable and in jeopardy at these ritual crisis moments. Nothing should be taken for granted. In order to mitigate any danger, Life has to be ordered and structured carefully and delicately.

While the Western colonial government and missionaries have disrupted some of the African traditions to a degree, nonetheless the majority of those traditions continue to thrive in the rural areas with expected modifications. This is what scholars call social change. For example, the

---

5. Sundermeier, *Individual and Community*, 56.
6. Sundermeier, *Individual and Community*, 57.

qualifications obtained through Western education have given rise to new, competing levels of respect, thus undermining the older system. Such status which used to be the preserve of the elders are nowadays given to a male or female whose education has qualified them to be appointed as a Chief over traditional elders.

This applies to other political offices at the national level. In this case, the older generation, which did not participate in Western education and the status that comes with it feel doubly cheated especially when forced to occupy a subordinate role in their old age, just as they were in their youth. Their opinions are rarely taken seriously in the same manner a youth is not taken seriously. Evidently, this has created a certain crisis and anxiety in many African societies. Some of these are inevitable due to the process of change, but the proper rituals for such transitions were not put in place to ease the pain that comes as a result of change. Thankfully, many African societies, Marakwet included, have learned to adapt, especially when some of the changes resulted in positive outcome. A case in point is the success of women in leadership. In 2010, the Marakwet elected a woman to parliament. In addition, they selected women chiefs in few locations. Evidently, these have expelled some of the old doubts and convinced the elders to trust their daughters.

While that is good and hopeful, there is a dark side to it. One of which is the way money and power has been used and misused to corrupt institutions at all levels. In Marakwet, money has been used to influence voters to ignore the traditional leadership model that is based on the age set system. Today, powerful political self-seeking individuals use money to influence and sponsor loyal youth to do their campaign. This is not unique to other parts of Kenya and the whole continent of Africa. Unfortunately, the change from colonial to national leaders did not bring the expected economic and expected social change. Majority of the new African leaders have become corrupt and irresponsible to their fellow citizens. They have not been different from the previous colonial government for which they fought to replace. It has proven true what an anonymous sage had said, "the forest has changed but the monkeys are still the same."

African societies, including the Marakwet, have the resiliency in their traditions to contribute to its development. The Marakwet people have good land with strong irrigation systems in place to expand their agricultural activities in the valley. What is missing so far is the government leadership to maintain peace and order at the borders. It is not impossible to reverse this trend with good leadership. Above all, the Marakwet should return to its traditional system of electing leaders based on the well tested traditional age set system. In that system, leaders must have attained the right age of thirty and above before they can be entrusted with leadership.

When myths are reenacted, the participants make a connection with the mythical time in the past in which such events took place. In other words, by the repetition of rituals, humans connect to the past and create a continuum. The reenactment gives myth its function and meaning to shape human life in the world. Through rituals, the world can be intelligible and significant. It explains why things exist and to what ends. At the same time through rituals, new ideas are given new interpretations by the designated specialists who assure us that what we do has already been done in the past, thus reducing anxiety to a minimum. In this sense, there is no reason to fear the unknown future because the community knows what needs to be done. For example, in the rites of passage, especially the circumcision rite, the elders (mentors) communicate the cultural myths to the neophytes. They are taught that they are because of a series of events that occurred in a mythical time in the past. While they are not obliged to know that whole history, they are obliged to re-enact some parts of it periodically in order to make the connection to that mythical history; for by knowing the myth, one knows their own origin.

Child Naming Rites

The First Name (Karna Musar)

Names identify an individual as a unique person and as a social being. In a broader sense, names serve as links to ancestors and ethnic history. There are permanent names and nicknames. The latter are mostly acquired at later stages in life and can be dropped at will. In other words, some names lose their usage when other names are added as one goes through the stages of life.

At birth, a baby is given its first name based on the day or the circumstance of birth. The midwife might give the new-born its first name based on the time of day, gender, or the circumstance of birth. Such names include Chemeitoi, Chemisto, Kanda, Kipkiror Krotich Klimo, Kpkore, Kipkech, Chesir, Chemongich, Chepkew, Chesinen, and Kipsigom. Examples of the names given, and their significance are given below.[7]

---

7. Kipkorir and Welbourn, *Marakwet*, 54–55.

Circumstance	Male	Female
Night/Langa	Chelanga	Chelanga/Jelanga
Early morning/Yekat	Kipkech	Chepkech/Jepkech
When cows are let out of the pen	Kipyatich	Yatich
Morning/Grazing	Kilimo	Chelimo/Jelimo
Mid-afternoon	Chebet	Chebet/Jebet
Return of livestock from grazing	Kiprono	Cherono/Jerono
When father or mother are on a visit elsewhere	Ruto	Cheruto/Jeruto
Presence of visitors	Kiptoo	Cheptoo/Jeptoo
Deliverance by the roadside	Kibor	Chebor/Jebor
During rainy season	Kibiwot	Chebiwot/Jebiwot
During wedding ceremony	Kitum	—
Almost died	Chemeitoi	—
In the presence of two mid-wives	—	Arengwony
In the presence of three mid-wives	—	Somokwony
During circumcision period	Kiptorus Kipkore	Cheptorus/Jeptorus Chepkore/Jepkore
In the presence of white people	Kipchumba	Chepchumba
Peacefulness	Kiptalai	—

Table 2.1 Marakwet Names and Their Significance

Motherhood is the ultimate result of marriage. It solidifies a marriage and incorporates the woman fully into her husband's clan. Her personal and clan name, such as *Talaa* (from Talai clan) or *Teriki* (from Teriki clan) are overtaken by her new status as a mother becomes her identity and she becomes known teknonymously as the mother of her first child. For example, if the first child is *Chebor* then she is called teknonymously the mother of Chebor (*Ma-Chebor*), and the husband is teknonymously *Kwombo-Chebor*. She continues to be called so until she has grandchildren, after which she takes the name of her daughter's or son's first child. If *Chebor's* first child is Kiptoo then she is called Ko-Kiptoo (*Kiptoo's* grandmother) and her husband becomes *kuko-kiptoo* (grandfather of *Kiptoo*). However, unlike the women, the men are hesitant to take these names except at special occasions of endearment.[8] These names last as long as the child whose name is taken is still alive. On occasions of death of the child, the bearers shift to the name of the second child. If there are no other children, they revert to their previous names.

Every aspect of a mother's life after giving birth is protected by taboos and rituals. Her giving birth renders her ritually unclean. For this matter, she is kept in seclusion for a month; after which, she undergoes a cleansing ritual.[9] Also, while in seclusion, she is forbidden to cook or eat with her hands. Instead, she devotes this time to the care of her newborn baby. She is not allowed to expose herself to strangers; therefore, she covers her head whenever she goes out of the house.[10]

After a week, she undergoes the first cleansing ritual in which she regains the permission to use her hands, colloquially known as "taking back her hands." She is washed with herbal brew meant for ritual cleansing. The cleansing allows her to touch cooking materials in the house and resume light house duties. A few days later, her hair is cut and kept in a hidden place from strangers, especially those with ill intent. The cutting of hair symbolizes the transition from one stage of life to another (from seclusion to freedom). From then on, she regains the liberty to leave the house and visit her neighborhood. Sometimes she goes to the nearby fields for a few hours, leaving the baby with a babysitter.[11] In most cases, she prefers to stay in the home and nurse the baby until it is over four months old, after which she can leave the baby with a babysitter for a longer time.

---

8. Kipkorir and Welbourn, *Marakwet*, 54–55; see also Moore, *Space*, 69.

9. She is considered polluted until the cleansing ceremony is performed, and she is again entitled to lead a free and normal life. The seclusion also serves to restore her strength. Men frequently have direct parallels between the restrictions placed on women after childbirth and the restrictions imposed on boys at kaptorus when they are considered posited.

10. During this time, the husband requests the assistance of his sister(s) or sister-in-law to help with the housework. Another option is to ask a neighbor, but this might involve some payment or compensation.

11. Babysitters are usually young girls between the ages of six to twelve, mostly drawn from relatives. They are not paid, and they usually stay as long as their parent's permit. With many children going to school nowadays, babysitters are young adult women who are paid monthly salary, and they can perform other household duties such as cooking and cleaning. There has been a debate on social media about the negative influence on children from the hired house help in the urban areas.

Ancestral Name (*Kotkotisio*)

The second naming ceremony, which is done within the month, is called *kotkotisio*. This sacred event invokes the ancestors to give their name to the child. A lot of sacred importance is accorded this ritual name, even more than the first one. The reason lies in the fact that ancestral spirits are invoked to not only give their name but also to protect the named child through the passage of life.[12]

In preparation, the father of the child makes honey beer (*kipketin*) for both libation and celebration. The naming ceremony takes place in the baby's mother's house, already decorated with the ritual creeper plant. Family members, including children and the officiating elder, must be present. The latter conducts the ritual by installing a shaft (*kolomber*) by one of the two front stones of the fireplace. The shaft is used for a boy, and wooden piece from the cooking stick, for a girl.[13] A small gourd (*repes*) containing beer is then placed on the rod to balance while naming an ancestor. Failure to balance the container of liquid on the shaft is interpreted to mean rejection. The attempt can go on until the intended goal is achieved. For the *Talai* clan, the following male ancestors are invoked accordingly until one of them is determined to lend their names, *Ksitien*, is it you? *Loyeleel*, Is it you? *Nebes*, is it you? *Ateratum*, are you the one? All the while, the presider attempts to balance the small guard on the iron rod at each name until one takes on.

When the *repes* balances on top of the shaft without falling, the audience is satisfied. This is translated to mean that the child has received a guardian ancestor. From then on, the infant takes the name of the named ancestor as one of his/her names. The idea behind the whole procedure is to allow the ancestors to assert their influence upon the living. The ancestors chose to reincarnate themselves to show their affinity for the family and maintain a sense of continuity of the family name. Parents with children born outside the residential area make special visits to the village to have such ceremonies performed for their children. If a trip is not feasible, arrangements are made for the elders to travel to where the child lives. When that is not possible, social media has been employed. When my son was born in Wisconsin, I relayed the message home by telephone to my uncle Joseph, who was then working in Nairobi. Joseph in turn found

---

12. Kipkorir and Welbourn, *Marakwet*, 55.

13. The Marakwet believe that iron is used because it symbolizes the boy's permanent link with the family and the clan, while the wooden object, symbolizing impermanence, is used for a girl. A woman moved from her natal home when she marries and joins her husband. In Endo, a woman is referred to as *chebi low kiber*, implying that her home is far from her natal home.

a way to inform the rest of the family in the village. Upon hearing the news, my uncle Lobokong'or is reported to have done the naming ritual (*Kotkotisio*) in our absence and obtained the ancestral name. Similarly, my daughter was given her ancestral name in the same manner. This indeed is a contemporary innovation of an ancient ritual.

There are other signs to watch in identifying an ancestor's intention to simplify the process of ancestral naming. The process is made easier when a child is born with a birth mark or a trait to signify the reincarnation of a particular ancestor, thus making the naming deliberations easier. The name is believed to spiritually link the child to the ancestors, who in turn will be the child's guardian to ensure its social and physical health to a ripe age. Consequently, a wrong name will result in poor health. Often when this is detected, the elders must return to the home and consult the ancestral oracle for another name. It is for this reason that A person who dies while childless does not become an ancestor, and their name is not given to children. This also applies to criminals and lawless characters.

Risk Children

The birth of twins and breech-born deliveries are considered abnormal, and, therefore, are bound to bring misfortunes to the community. For that reason, they need the special ritual of *tiswo* to be successful in life. In case of the birth of twins, the mother is confined in the house for a month where she is attended to by twins or by mothers who have had twins. While in confinement, she communicates in whispers and must leave the house only at night, wearing ritual sandals made for her so she does not contaminate the soil. In order to get out of the confinement, she has to go through the prescribed ritual. This ceremony involves a small amount of honey wine and a sacrificial sheep. The chyme of the sheep is scattered at the door of the hut and the confined twin mother walks over it. Later, the full ceremony of cleansing (*tiswo*) is performed.[14] According to Kipkorir's book, *The Marakwet of Kenya*,

> The serem or tarkanya involved are brought to the hut which is decorated with sinende, palm leaves and branches. . . . The participants are seated round, drinking beer and singing. As they do so, they pat the sheep gently on the back with the palms of their hands, in the rhythm of the songs, and continue to do so till the sheep dies. If it does not die quickly, it is given some beer which is supposed to speed the process. It is then skinned and

14. Kipkorir and Welbourn, *Makarkwet*, 65.

the skin cut into small strips which the participants wear round their necks, fingers, thumbs, legs, etc.[15]

The rite of *tiswo* derives its name from the sound (*tiss*)*usually* made when water drops on fire or anything hot. It means cooling something that is otherwise hot or bringing down the temperature from a tense and heated debate. Heat is often associated with danger that needs to be contained or cooled. The act of *tiswo* therefore is intended to cool down or take away whatever heat of the misfortune in the family that might have come down through birth. The sacrificial sheep and its chyme are believed to possess cooling effects to neutralize hot and harmful powers. In the end, the *tiswo* rite cools and protects the mother, the children, and the whole family from disaster. The slaughtered sacrificial sheep serves as an appeasement to the spirits responsible for the misfortune.[16] Some of the names given to children who have undergone this ritual of *tiso* are as follows:

Boys	Girls
—	Cheserem
—	Chesinen
Kipkech	Cheprech

Owing to the secrecy with which the rite is given, it has not been possible for an outsider to discover the actual *tiswo* procedure. My informant was hesitant to reveal details for fear of repercussions. However, through secondary informers and my own observation at our home, I was able to put together this limited information that might give a glimpse of the ritual. Also, the external apparatus which is visible to anyone reveals a bit of its importance to the participants.

The ceremony begins late in the evening and continues through the night. A procession cycles the hut four times, accompanied by ritual songs. For the rest of the night, the guests celebrate with beer. The mid-wife is given her own guard of beer from which she might share with others.[17] The procession is repeated, and, at this time, the ritual sheep is carried four times around the hut. At a later stage, all the participants go into the hut, where the sheep is brought and placed in the middle so the crowd can see. A smaller group sit in a circle around the sheep singing while patting the sheep gently on the back

15. Kipkorir and Welbourn, *Makarkwet*, 57, 58.
16. Kipkorir and Welbourn, *Marakwet*, 56.
17. Kipkorir and Welbourn, *Marakwet*, 56.

with the palms of their hands. Also, chants or prayers are offered before the sheep is slaughtered and cut open. The diviner gathers certain information by looking at the entrails. Such information might serve as a warning for a looming disaster or war. It may also indicate something positive such as good rains, harvest, and good breeding season for livestock. After that, portions of the entrails are fed to the fire as a form of sacrifice to the ancestors and the creator, who are believed to enjoy the aroma. Finally, the skin is cut into smaller strips and distributed to the participants to wear around their necks, fingers, thumbs, and legs.[18]

Later in the day, the party goes to the nearest stream. There, the main party stops while babysitters (*tibo lakoi*) precede the mother in crossing the stream four times and each time striking the water while chanting their secret chants. This releases the woman from exclusion or the ban, thus permitting her to cross water streams and break the social ban.

The rite is completed with the presentation of ritual ornaments to the mother. Some of those ornaments become part of her regular costume while other ornaments are kept aside for specific ritual events. The ritual qualifies the mother to participate and observe the customary rules for all ritual bearers (*ka-tisen*). On such occasions, she wears ritual-ornaments around her neck ritual-ornaments, which include cowrie shells, medicinal plants of *morgut*, and a small-elongated gourd of oil (*Yombo*). At the end of the necklace hangs another string of dried medicinal herbs of *morgut*. When she meets a stranger with a newborn baby, she bites off a piece of the *morgut* and mouth-sprays them. If she enters the gate of a stranger's homestead or receives food from a stranger, she sprays the objects to make them immune from evil intent. Also, around her neck, she wears a small gourd of oil or an open horn containing fat with which she anoints or rubs her feet each morning before leaving her house.[19] All these concerted efforts are meant to protect from contaminants by either malevolent spirits or unhappy ancestors.[20]

The Circumcision Rite

The Circumcision of Boys

Why do Marakwet practice circumcision? The reasons vary, but I will highlight a few. First, In Marakwet, boys and girls are considered as full members of society through the rite of passage of initiation (*sonok*). The second is its

18. Kipkorir and Welbourn, *Marakwet*, 56.
19. Kipkorir and Welbourn, *Marakwet*, 57.
20. Kipkorir and Welbourn, *Marakwet*, 57.

hygienic and aesthetic value. The foreskin of the penis is considered to be dirty because of the smegma (*meret*) that gathers underneath. Circumcision takes care of that and renders the penis clean. There is a widespread belief that women prefer men who have been circumcised for that reason. On the other hand, the reasons given for the circumcision of women are not convincing. There is a weak argument that the clitoris could grow larger and unruly if it is not cut on time. Another line of reasoning is that it is a verified ancient tradition. While the circumcision for men has not faced many challengers, the women's rite has faced immense resistance. Most men to whom I interviewed did not care whether a woman was circumcised or not. In fact, some did not object to marrying an uncircumcised woman. In my findings, I discovered that the older women in the rural areas are more likely to support women's circumcision than the men. It is for this reason that the circumcision of women famously known as FGM has continued to be practiced in secret despite the government's efforts to stamp it out.

The anthropologist Arnold Van Gennep coined the term "*rite de passage*" and provided helpful insights on initiation rite of circumcision. The three—level processes he presented are: (1) The preliminary rite of separation, (2) Liminal rites of transition, (3) Incorporation. Many anthropologists who have employed Van Gennep's approach as a structuralist methodology meant to reveal the secrets of human existence in the universe.[21]

The goal of the rite of initiation is to instill courage, trust, endurance, character-building and good manners. It is an enduring reminder to the individual about the social bond that is established and continues in the age-set system where initiates remain throughout life. There are FIVE main stages to initiation: (1) the preparation, (2) the cut and surgical event, (3) instructions, (4) the graduation, and finally (5) the induction into an age-set. These five points are what Van Gennep calls "moments of crisis."[22]

Preparation

The circumcision ritual is probably the most significant rite of passage in Marakwet and the Kalenjin society as a whole. It is a rite of passage for both boys and girls at their puberty.[23] Anyone who does not participate in it is treated contemptuously as a child even when they are not. While the cutting of genitalia is significant, the educational process that follows is crucial.

---

21. Gennep, *Rites of Passage*, 26–30.
22. Gennep, *Rites of Passage*, 30.
23. Puberty is marked by physical signs such as pubic hair, change of voice for males, and the physical development of females' breasts.

Evidently, as they approach puberty, Marakwet boys and girls are made increasingly aware of the ordeal. Sometimes they are teased by those who were recently initiated or by intimate friends to test their bravery. Either way, these incidents serve as social pressure and psychological preparation for the rite.

Initially, the boys would present their request for the ritual to their elders, parents or guardians who will in turn bring the matter before the larger community elders for deliberation. Before granting their approval, the elders are to ascertain that all the necessary precautions have been taken to ensure the rite's success. Firstly, the diviners or astrologers study, and interpret positions of the stars or planets such as Mercury, Venus, Mars, Saturn, and Jupiter in relation to the moon. The Marakwet see Jupiter as the husband of Mercury and therefore he rises first. Legend has it that if Mercury rises first, it will urinate on Jupiter and cause all kinds of misfortunes.[24] There must be deeper layers of meanings beneath these metaphors. In any case, no initiation is permitted until these arrangements are propitious. Secondly, spies are sent to the neighboring territories to ensure that no war-like preparations from rivals are under way. It would be a disaster to be attacked when all the potential warriors are engaged in the task of initiation. Thirdly, a goat's entrails are examined in order to determine any other omens in society. If the results prove inauspicious, a second goat is chosen from the man's flock. This could be repeated until good results are obtained. Apparently, the repeated slaughter of goats serves as a ritual prayer to the divine powers to prevent any misfortunes. Finally, there must be a good harvest to ensure sufficient food for the initiates while in the circumcision camp. Earlier on, the duration of the initiation used to run between two to three months. However, due to modernization and the current education system, the duration has been shortened to one month preferably during the Christmas holidays.[25]

When all these requirements are in order, the candidates are then given the approval to proceed. The next step is the construction of the semi-permanent circumcision lodge at the outskirts of the community—physically removed from the mainstream of society.[26] Also, they must ensure that the candidates have procured enough firewood to last the three months duration of the rite. The mentors who belong to the previous age-set have the

---

24. The moon must be in its first quarter on the eve of the circumcision, otherwise the ceremony must be postponed for a month. See Welbourn, "Keyo Initiation," 213.

25. Kipkorir and Welbourn, *Marakwet*, 47. The time spent at the initiation lodge shortened progressively from 1970 onwards.

26. A shrine (*korosion*) is constructed in the vicinity. All the structures are brought down at the end of the seclusion period.

most recent memories to assist in the construction as well as provide general guidance. They must be well versed in traditional matters and respected in the community. The novices are expected to reciprocate by listening and be respectful to their mentors throughout their lives.[27]

On the eve of the circumcision day, the candidates get their heads shaved; in fact, all the body hair is removed. The removal of the hair symbolizes their new status and the beginning of the transition from childhood.[28] The hair is thrown in the direction of the sun (kong'asis) and later collected and placed in a secure place away from suspicious people who could use it for evil intent.[29] At the same time, milk from a gourd is poured four times on the initiates' heads as a form of anointing or blessings (berur). Meanwhile, the body is smeared with white ritual ochre. The religious significance of all these items is beyond the scope of this work. In some parts of Marakwet, red ochre represents normal while white ochre represents liminality.

At this time, the initiates' clothes are taken away and given to the mentors as a reward for their duties. With the new life ahead of them, the boys must not go back to the clothes they wore before the initiation. Instead, they look forward to the new life of being an initiate and come out as a new person with new clothes and responsibilities. Meanwhile, they are given a soft goat skin that will be the primary garment during the seclusion period. Also at this time, girlfriends and relatives can adorn the initiates with beads, bells, and other ornaments. Similarly, Relatives and friends who have travelled from far are welcomed to dress and decorate the candidates. After their final meal, the candidates are escorted to the dancing venue where they meet their sponsors and enter into a whole night of dance of (Kitung'a) or chepyegon. The dances and the songs of Chepyegon are charged with emotions which are meant to encourage the candidates to face the knife bravely and not to disgrace their family and relatives.

---

27. That means helping them with tasks when requested or giving up seats in public places, so mentors do not get tired of standing.

28. Cutting of the hair has taken on a ritual significance, intending to mark the transition from one social state to another and a modification in the status or social condition of the person whose hair is so treated. The similarity between cutting the hair and cutting the sex organ is obvious. See Firth, *Symbols*, 289.

29. The link with kong'asis signifies the act of devotion and prayers to Asis to insure a good circumcision season.

Marakwet	English Translation
Oei! chepyegon kayech oyu . . . kerir oyu	When does it become morning.
kayech mating keochi	the daybreak cannot be reversed
kayechi motingan	It is the morning for cutting
iro tiyatich murono	Fix your eyes on the east facing Tiyati hills
irib korengung kumechur	Do not let your people down
irib katengwong kumechur	Honor your family and do not embarrass[30]

The overriding purpose of the songs is meant to encourage and prepare the initiates for the circumcision act. Some of the songs discourage the faint in heart to quit while there is still time if they think they cannot handle it and save their family from shame. The young unmarried women or potential marriage partners could be heard singing.

> Coward, show your worth.
>
> If you are afraid, let your mother and young sisters take your place. I am not prepared to get married to someone who is a coward and if you know that you will cry, tell me so that I may look for a real man.[31]

At a certain point the women will withdraw to allow the men and the *torus* to proceed to the place of testing. There, they are instructed in the events to take place in the morning, which involve bravery and focus. They are spoken to in symbols and riddles. They are told about such items as fire and water. The fire represents the knife of circumcision, and the water symbolizes the bitter drink and ice-cold water that will be splashed over them in the early hours of the morning.

The candidates are not told exactly how the operation is to be performed. However, they are given the impression that it will be extremely painful and that they must bravely endure the pain. To prove the level of concentration, and readiness, the initiate is sometimes asked to sit while a man pretends to attack his penis with a sharp knife. It might be repeated if any sign of unsteadiness is detected. Songs are sung to constantly cheer them.

---

30. Songs are very important in these events. They are sung before and after circumcision, while the wounds are healing, and after. They are also sung when coming out of *kaptorus*. See Kipkorir and Ssennyonga, *Socio-Cultural Profile*, 115.

31. Kiptoo Kilimo, personal interview, March 1989.

At dawn, the candidates are led to the confession house. This is the solemn moment where candidates gather by the fire before the elders to confess any past wrongdoing such as sharp words to an elder, sexual engagement with an older person, or any taboo broken. Failure to confess may result in slow recovery or worse. The elders remind the initiates that the operation is very painful, and the wounds may bleed profusely and possibly lead to death if they fail to confess any sin. Millet grain is occasionally thrown into the fire and their rattling sound is an indication that someone has yet to confess. Ample time is given so that everyone has a chance to reflect and confess. The most serious sins are full sexual intercourse with older women or having made a woman pregnant. After the confession, the ritual of cleansing (*Lyakat*) takes place. The officiant acts like a priest on behalf of God and the ancestors to absolve the candidates of their previous sins or misbehavior. Libations and prayer of incantations are offered to the ancestors to stay near the initiates in their vulnerable state and protect them from evil.

In the early morning, the candidates are led by their leader (*kiboret*) to the river for cleansing in preparation of the soon to happen event.[32] A few minutes before sunrise, the candidates line up near the main stage where the circumcision master (*kukotum*) is waiting. The lead candidate who had previously been selected takes the honor to sit and face the ordeal in the presence of many witnesses including children, youth, and adults who gathered in anticipation for the big show. The candidates advance one by one and take a seat on the prepared stones where they will each take their turn and show their courage as the circumciser cuts the tip of the foreskin. Currently, the candidates raise their hands and heads and remain stoic as others watch for any signs of flinching, faltering, or running off. Some men stand with spears in hand to threaten any candidate who cries or shows any outward sign of pain. If any of them blinks, he is considered an outcast or coward and scoffed at later in songs of derision for several generations. The same routine applies to the girls during their cut.

When the last initiate has gone through the initial cut, a song signals to the spectators of women and children to disperse leaving men and sponsors to settle down to the longer surgical operation. The men assist in holding the initiates down while the circumcisers perform the operation. At this stage, they are free to cry, moan, or scream while the circumcision songs are sung aloud to drown the screams as each candidate face what is perceived as the "cool knife." One wonders how a knife, fashioned in fire with sharpness

---

32. The leader (*Kiboret*) must be the son of a man from the oldest age-set and must possess good character and leadership qualities. He will be first in all the rituals of the circumcision.

that cuts to let blood, could possess a cooling effect? In this case, the initiation knife is understood to carry ambivalent powers and possibilities. Symbolically, the knife's coolness is realized in the way it evokes enduring meanings of order and balance. In circumcision, the knife cuts off the feminine foreskin of boys turning them into men, and the blood which mirrors menstruation will happen once to show the transition from boys to men.

> It hurts and kills in order to heal and perpetuate; it heats (disturbs) in order to cool (stabilize); It separates in order to link; and it transforms in order to facilitate a never-ending cycle that embodies permanence.[33]

Moreover, the knife defines those aspects in life that constitute the moral education in the areas of personhood, gender relations, sexuality, age, and clan relationships.[34]

> The objective is to prepare the youth for a life beyond adolescence. This is the path to full humanity. Young people become full members of society only at puberty because the passions and fundamental (gender) differences underpinnings are realized only at full sexuality. For such forces to be ordered, education is essential, especially at puberty. This is achieved through combining bodily experience and social interaction.[35]

The Liminal Stage

After the ordeal, the initiates are left to recover at a cool place as they wait to be fed the iron-rich millet porridge. At the end of the day, the initiates are taken to their lodge, where they will have no contact with the public for the duration of the seclusion period. The seclusion at the lodge signifies what Van Gennep calls "*liminal rites of transition.*" It implies the transition from the previous state of childhood to adulthood. Moreover, this period of transition from boyhood to manhood comes with great stress as the initiates' status in society is in limbo—a liminal stage where they are neither boys nor men. At this moment, the initiates are taught the value of cooperation and sharing with fellow initiates. Their care is left to mentors who make every effort to test their wills while teaching them to be responsible men. In order to do that, they have to endure humiliations

---

33. Beidelman, *Cool Knife*, 2.
34. Beidelman, *Cool Knife*, 3.
35. Beidelman, *Cool Knife*, 4.

by the older age-set members. In a way, they are humiliated before they are elevated. When food is brought in by each family, it is shared equally so that those from poorer families should not be made to feel less than the others.[36] The period of liminality serves as a time of socialization and as a preparation for the new status awaiting them.

The duration and isolation make for a conducive environment for the initiates to learn the importance of belonging to the community of kin and clan. It is understood that just as one is nothing without the community, the community is nothing without its members. Stories, songs, proverbs, riddles, and codes are appropriated to instill the wisdom of the elders and the ancestors. The initiates are taught how to adequately use the oral art of proverbs, riddles, songs, and stories. Proverbs are used not only to communicate messages of importance but also to ground relationships. In the west, a well-read person is a cultured person. In Marakwet society by contrast, a cultured person is the one who knows the cultural history of the people and can express himself with wit and humor using proverbs, metaphors and stories. The knowledge and the meanings of innumerable proverbs becomes part of a collective wisdom that is passed down from elders to the young. Once learned, they are incorporated into a discourse, rather than simply retained in the memory. A person uses a proverb to shed some light into something or reveal a hidden truth.

The instructions are primarily concerned with ethical behavior and responsibilities. Images from nature are meant to incentivize the youth to appreciate the intimate relationship between human life and the rest of creation. Some of the proverbs relate to images from the natural world of animals and plants to underscore the significance of interdependence between humans and the natural world. This is based on the principle that nature and persons are woven together by the divine creator into one texture of fabric. This means that by design, humans are to maintain a balance in the universe as an ethical responsibility. Failure to maintain that harmony between people and the natural environment is believed to have provoked the ancestors resulting in catastrophes such as famine, drought, floods, or locust invasions. The actual time frame for such an event is recorded in folklore and the age-set system.

One of the significant factors in the instruction is what Ludwig Wittgenstein called "word games or language game."[37] The elders unpack the deeper meaning of words and reveal their multiple meanings and the way

---

36. Parents with little sometimes fall short in bringing in the regular supply of food to their son. In such cases, the son will be attended to by other families.

37. Wittgenstein, *On Certainty*, 28.

they undergird social relations. The acquisition of fuller skill in speech and thought is one of the important steps towards maturity. This involves the ability to know what to say or not to say at a given time, as well as the eloquence of delivery in public or the ability to conceal information when necessary. The complexity of words and the ambiguity of their meanings constitute a desirable density of imagination. For Wittgenstein, understanding speech depends on pushing concepts and terms to their limits.

Similarly, the Marakwet initiation is about pushing the youth to their limits with the goal of achieving a socially responsible person capable of reason and independence of thought and action. Sometimes, the profundity of the lessons is couched in esoteric ancient language believed to be truer to the tradition. The core of the lessons learned are directed to building and maintaining respectable relationships: first, with the elders and the ancestors; secondly, relationship with ones' family, kin, and neighbors, and thirdly, relationship with the land and its protection. This means pledging to protect the clans' territory from intruders.

The care for the earth is intrinsically woven into the core of Marakwet's ethical behavior. This practice is rooted in the understanding that land belongs to God—a gratuitous gift just like other natural resources like water and air. The ancient African ethic did not sanction private ownership of land. In that sense, anyone can use the land and leave it in good condition for the next user in the family or the clan for the promotion of life. This also applies to other essentials such as water and respect for sacred forests and spaces. These are public properties that have to be cared for and shared according to each community's needs. In this sense, land belongs to the community, and it is managed by the clan members on behalf of the community. An individual may utilize a parcel of such a land for their need for a given season.

Incorporation

At some point towards the end of their seclusion, the initiates are confronted with immense hazing by a symbolic destructive beast of the wild (*kimaket*). The initiates are forewarned of this impending destructive wild beast that could devour them. However, each initiate is encouraged to be strong and fight them off. Help is given to those with good character but withheld from those who seem indifferent to the elder's teachings. Such threats of being mauled and ingested by a wild creature are enough to frighten them into submission to the instructions of the mentors. The initiates are to become aware that their adult identities derive from their ancestors through the agency of the older males who were given the mandate by those before them. In the same way, the new initiates are expected to transmit what they have received to the next generation and maintain the continuum. Paul Tillich made a good point when he stated, "If mystery is expressed in ordinary language, it necessarily is misunderstood, reduced to another dimension, desecrated. This is the reason why betrayal of the content of the mystery cults was a blasphemy which had to be expiated by death."[38]

The last stage of the circumcision rite is the 'coming out' ceremony called "*Kibuno.*" This is the graduation ceremony that marks the end of the separation period and incorporates the initiates back to society. Here, the young men or women have been transformed from childhood into adults. At the end of the circumcision period, the initiates will have learned valuable lessons for life such as (1) the values of belonging to a unit, (2) the intimate connection between human life and the rest of creation, (3) the role of sex, procreation, and sexual taboos, (4) the techniques for survival and the protection of the land, (5) the ethic of self-denial and sacrifice for the good of the community, (6) to keep the prescribed cultural etiquette and other aesthetic requirements, (7) the importance of confidentiality—to never divulge the secrets of the initiation to women and the uninitiated.

Before the 1970s the initiates averaged sixteen to twenty years. The older had reached physical and moral maturity almost ready to get married and start a family. However, with the demands of modern education, and shorter vacation schedules, the candidates, average age is thirteen years and too young to marry. Most of them continue their education and marry later when they are ready. In this case, circumcision rite is no longer a licence for marriage.[39]

The Circumcision of Girls

Before initiation the girls, like the boys, are ignorant of what will take place. However, they will soon experience the previously mentioned five stages of the initiation namely: the preparation, the cut and surgical event, instructions, graduation, and finally the induction into the female age-set.

When girls have reached the age of fifteen or older, either their fathers or mothers request the elders for "the circumcision knife." The elders will, in turn, consult the usual oracle and check the availability of food before

---

38. Tillich, *Systematic Theology*, 109.

39. To honor the confidentiality of the tradition, I have tried my best to summarize some of the lessons taught at the seclusion lodge and hope that I did not betray any confidentiality. I also hope that I have documented the core values that ought to be preserved for posterity.

giving their consent. The matter is then taken up by the girls' families and relatives who are responsible for the necessary preparations of drinks and food. Similar to the boys, they must experience the five stages of the initiation with the help of mentors. In fact, every initiate is handing over all of his/her individual independence and submit to their mentors.

Unlike the boys, girls are not involved in constructing the seclusion lodge. Instead, they are kept in one of the houses in the homestead. This cuts out the time spent in the forest. Also, the girls' rite is more frequently done and therefore their numbers are always smaller than the boys. Apart from that, the pattern is almost similar to that of the boys in the separation, liminality, and incorporation. The mentors (*motiren*) are chosen from among the women and the main circumciser is a woman. However, a few old men are chosen for the purpose of officiating in the ritual cleansing of the female initiates.

In the highland section or the upper Marakwet, a virgin sits on the ceremonial stool, usually studded with beads. At first invitation, she declines to sit on the stool until her father promises her a reward for her honourable behavior. After that, she sits on the stool while relatives and friends shower her with gifts in honour of her virginity. Those who have lost their virginity will be summoned to sit on the floor.

In the early morning the girls are taken to the river where they are stripped naked and lined up behind their leader and dip themselves in the cold water. They are then taken for the main event where they each face the knife. The crowd watch this initial stage as they prove their bravery and courage. This part of the initiation takes only a few seconds, but it is the most important feature of the rite. The candidate must not cry or blink as the knife descends on her clitoris. If she fails at this, she becomes a crier or a coward (*chepite*). The next stage is the actual operation, which takes a bit longer, and the initiates may writhe or cry as much as they want.[40]

The initiates are then taken to the house for their seclusion where they will receive instructions. *Kapkore* provides women with a body of ritual and practical knowledge which is distinct from male knowledge. Women are instructed to take pride in female sexuality, childbirth, and motherhood. They affirm the fact that they can use their sexual powers and charm on men. They do this to affirm and consolidate their position in the tradition. The aspect of motherhood likewise gives women both power and social responsibility. They recognize that although they owe obedience to their husbands, they are generally dependent on them. On the other

---

40. Kipkorir and Welbourn, *Marakwet*, 48.

hand, they are aware that they can influence men easily by refusing to cook or Withrow sexual favors.

These teachings can either be interpreted as constructive in reinforcing female values, or as structural mechanisms through which older women encourage younger ones into accepting their rightful positions with confidence within the Marakwet patriarchal social order. While accepting this position, they also challenge it. Also, women use *kapkore* to further their own solidarity and assert the value of traditional female knowledge which is unknown to men as well as establish ritual links between successive generations of women. The established bond provides the women with their own networks of support and obligations that are separate from those of men.[41]

At the coming out ceremony, the initiates are anointed with castor oil and groomed for the occasion. One of the signifying pieces of jewelry is the oval earings (*siman*) usually made of blue beads replaces the wooden studs they wore as girls. The oval blue earring differentiates women from girls. The young women are often married immediately after initiation, especially if they were over eighteen years old. Those who are still in school may wait a little longer. Pressure to get married is so great that some women marry men for whom they do not love. Some are given as second wives. The practice of polygamy is practiced by traditionalist Marakwet men who see women in terms of procreation.[42]

Most of those who have gone to school or have been under Western influence find husbands at a later time. Those, who do not find husbands, opt for polygamous marriages, while others move to towns in search of employment and a better future for themselves and reduce their economic dependence on men.

Age-Set System

Every Marakwet is initiated into an age-set to which they are attached for the rest of their life. There are a total of eight age-sets for men, and eight for women as illustrated in the table below.[43] However, in a patriarchal society, the men's age-set is given a bigger significance.

A particular age-set takes into its membership any group that is initiated within a span of fifteen years, after which time it closes its doors for another age-set to open. Unlike its distant cousins, the Masai, the Marakwet do not have formal ceremony to mark the closing of an age-set nor opening of a new.

41. Kipkorir and Welbourn, *Marakwet*, 182.
42. Moore, *Space*, 183.
43. Moore, *Space*, 56; see also Kipkorir and Ssennyonga, *Socio-Cultural Profile*, 100.

However, they are cognizant of the moment of transition from one age-set to another.[44] While every generation is initiated into an age-set, there are age-sets that are distinguished by a particular occasion or a particular nickname due to a positive or negative circumstance. A good example of this is the *Kipkoimet* age-set which was nicknamed *Kaberur* because its timing coincided with the arrival of a popular blanket of *kipkaberur*. Another nicknamed age set is the *kakimusik* given to one of the age-sets due to its members' reputation of drinking the dregs of the local *Buzaa* brew.[45]

Each age-set takes over the responsibilities of deliberations and decisions in the community as well as the security of the land during their fifteen years tenure. It is not always easy to tell exactly when that begins, but it gradually takes place when most of its members are at the average age of thirty-five. During this time, they are expected to have attained both physical and mental maturity for leadership. One of their responsibilities is to give guidance to the age-sets under them while seeking the counsel of those above them. They also consult with the elders on whether to go to war in case of an impending threat. However, in cases of extreme difficulties such as a murder case, they must consult with the most senior members in the senior age-set.[46] This method has not only generated a high sense of accountability and respect within the ranks, but also a sense of solidarity within each age-set. For example, if an individual breaks the law and is fined, it is the responsibility of his age group to assist him with the payment of the fine. Because of the age-set bond, the whole group usually feels obliged to help. In most cases, the offender will obviously feel sorry for putting his peers through such an imposition. Sometimes he is ridiculed by his peers for his poor judgement. Should he repeat the offense, the group will reprimand or enforce a harsher punishment such as a stiff fine often involving parting with some livestock.

In principle, the older age-set has the prerogative over certain advantages, one of which is the approval of new candidates for initiation. If for any reason, most of the members of an age-set have not taken wives, the elders may refuse to approve the initiation of the next group of males while at the same time encouraging the initiation of women. The goal is

---

44. Moore, *Space*, 57. In the other Kalenjin groups, such as the Nandi and the Keiyo, there is an official handing-over ceremony to mark the transition from one age-set to another.

45. The name derived from the dregs left over after drinking. This age group is reputed to have drunk everything including the dregs, *musik*, and are, therefore, known as *kakimusik*.

46. In a society without kings or chiefs, the age-set system worked effectively in maintaining peace and order.

to have a sufficient pool of women so that those who wish to marry may do so with little competition. Moreover, some of the older men who are interested in adding another wife might also block the initiation of a new group. While it is obvious that the approval of the initiation of another batch of boys might create more competition, the practice proceeds as per the cultural rhythm.[47] To escape any delay, some of the uninitiated males who are almost ready for marriage often travel to another Marakwet community to be initiated. The only challenge for this is the time it takes to procure provisions for such arrangements. In the past, Marakwet families have contracted for a fee to provide the necessary provisions for any young man who comes to them for initiation. It is economically easier if the host family has a child of their own to be circumcised.[48]

It is traditionally acceptable for older men to marry younger women as long as the young woman is not the daughter of his age-set. The reason behind this is that men who belong to the same age-set see each other as brothers. Their daughters are like his own daughters and to marry one is equivalent to committing incest. Similarly, a man is not permitted to marry the daughter of his age-set to whom he shared a knife at initiation.[49] However, he can marry a younger woman of an age-set below him.[50]

---

47. There was an occasion in the past when an Endo age-set refused initiation to the next group; the reason given was that the Pokot were preparing to attack the land and initiation of the boys should not take place so that the men would be free to defend the land. However, permission was given for the initiation of women. The real reason for holding back the boys soon became apparent.

48. Arrangements to have circumcision elsewhere are not uncommon in Marakwet, and the fee is usually one cow in addition to the goats for the ceremony.

49. The women in the age-set above him are considered as his mother's because they are in the age-set of his mother.

50. Those who were initiated at the same time are believed to have shared a knife. Marrying a daughter of one's age-set is unacceptable and may be treated as an incest which might result in a form of punishment.

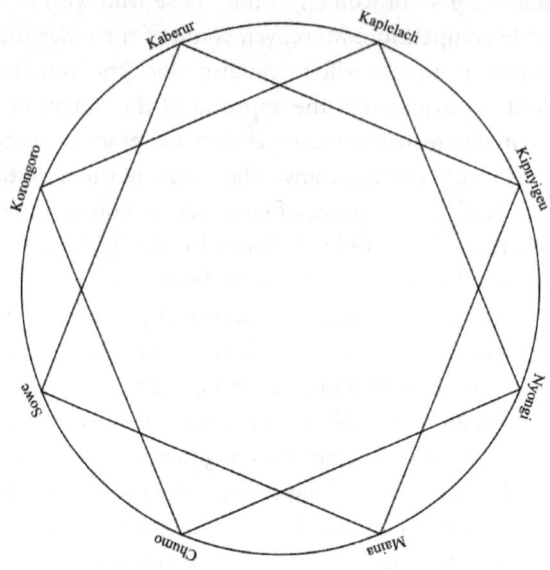

Figure 5: The Age-Set Circle

As shown in the diagram above, the sons of Korongoro age-set are initiated into *Kaplelach*; the sons of *Kaberur* into *Kipnyigeu*; the sons of *Kaplelach* into *Nyongi*; the sons of *Kipnyigeu* into *Maina*; the sons of *Nyongi* into *Chumo*; the sons of *Maina* into *Sowe*; the sons *Chumo* into *Korongoro*. After that, the circle starts all over again and repeats the same endless circle. There are two entry points in the age-set system, namely *Kipkoimet* and *Korongoro*, thus dividing the eight age-set system into two parts.

Men	Women
Kimnyigeu	Cheptentur
Nyongi	Charkina
Maina	Chesyewa
Chumo	Kipturbei
Sowe	Kiptaai
Korongoro	Kasingin (sigingin)
Kipkoimet (kaberur)	Silingwa
Kaplelach	Tabesit

Table 2.2 Men's and Women's Age-Sets

The intricacies surrounding the age-set system do not only control human development but serve as a calendar or event marker. Each age-set is separated by an average of fifteen years which means it takes at least 120 years to complete the eight age-set circle.

Traditionally, one is not expected to live long enough to see the whole circle. At the same time, an age-set cannot be assigned when a person belonging to that age-set is still alive. If that happens to be the case, then the surviving elder has two choices, either to be made an ancestor ritually or face voluntary suicide. The first is done through the ritual of *bore* where the elderly person undergoes a symbolic death and attain an ancestor status while still in the land of the living. Alternatively, one can undergo suicide (*siew*) by falling backwards from a cliff while blind-folded (*tumbo sorun*). A story is told of some elders in a particular village who lived beyond the age of 120 years. When the time came to assign their age-set away, they were faced with the imminent dilemma. They decided to take the second option and commit suicide "en masse." They begged their families to be allowed to die. On the day of the dreadful event, they had their favorite meal, went to the cliff and fell backwards to their death singing a song through their noses hence the designation *tumbo sorun*.[51]

The Concept of Time

The Marakwet concept of time is simply a composition of events which have occurred, those taking place now, and those which will occur almost immediately. The future is virtually absent because events which lie in it have not taken place and cannot, therefore, be a part of time.

J. S. Mbiti has explained the African concept of time thus: time is a two-dimensional phenomenon with a "long past," a "present," and virtually "no future." In this sense, actual time is thought to be the events of the present and the past. Future events constitute only potential time. Events move backwards rather than forwards, and people focus on what has taken place rather than the unrealistic future.[52]

This time orientation within the two dimensions of present and past dominates the Marakwet understanding of themselves. A person experiences time partly as an individual and partly through the social rituals which constitute the dimensions of time. This is realized throughout life's stages: from birth to death and back again, and through the continuity of

---

51. Private interview with David Kalesi, Jane Kalesi, and Samuel Chepkong'a.
52. Mbiti, *African Religions*, 17.

the ancestors. The whole system is viewed in a circle as opposed to the Western linear time with a definite past, imminent present, and infinite future.

	Koyortit	Two days after tomorrow
	Koyorin	The day after tomorrow
	Osun	Tomorrow
Present	Anin	Today
	Omotun	Yesterday
	Orin	The day before yesterday
	Ortit	Two days before yesterday
Past	Kenyinai	Last year
	Kenyisyon	Long time ago

Table 2.3 Definitions of Time

The Marakwet reckon time for specific purposes that are generally connected with events, and not just for the sake of knowledge and counting. These events are accumulated or contained in the phenomenon events, sometimes referred to as phenomenon calendars in which, the events are considered in relation with one another in the sequence of their occurrence.

> An expectant mother counts the lunar months of her pregnancy; a traveler counts the number of days it takes him to walk from one part of the country to another. The day, the month, the year, one's lifetime or human history are all divided up or reckoned according to their specific events, for it is these that make them meaningful.[53]

This notion is further illustrated in the age-set system, in which the eight age-sets move in a circle. It takes at least 120 years to complete the circle, thus creating a cyclical time and there is a period of an average of fifteen years between age-sets. The circle is predicated on the idea that what is "present" will move back and become "past," and what was "past" moves on to become "present." That is inevitable in a cyclical calender.

Like many other African people, the Marakwet have no concrete words to express the concept of distant future. Most of the terms related to time cover the present, the past and the immediate future. Future events

---

53. Mbiti, *African Religions*, 19.

have to fall within the range of these terms; otherwise, such events lie beyond the horizon of what constitutes actual time. The day, the month, or the year is ascertained according to its significance, especially in terms of the economic and religious life of the people. In the naming of children, the time determines the name. The names given below illustrate this point:[54]

Male	Female	Meaning
Kipyatich	Yatich	Born when the cattle go out in the day
Kirotich	Jerotich	Born when the cattle are coming home
Kilimo	Jelimo	Born when the livestock are back in mid-morning from grazing
Kiplagat	Chelagat	Born at night
Kibet	Chebet	Born during the day

Table 2.4 Time Denoting Names

The months are also marked by certain events. There are hot months, cold months, rainy months, and dry months.

Dry Months	December (Kipsiit)
	January (Kiptaam)
	February (Tirtit)
Rainy Months	March (Kiporkoch)
	April (Rekeso)
	May (Poroowo)
Weeding/Irrigation Months	May
	June (Meeltaay)
	July (Meletu)

---

54. Kipkorir and Welbourn, *Marakwet*, 54.

	August (Mukeyoon)
Harvest Months	September (Tapach)
	October (Kokeelyaan)
	October
Dry/Hunting Months	November (Iwoot)
	December (Kipsiit)

Table 2.5 Time Events by Months

Likewise, the year is made up of events and seasonal activities. People generally watch the years come and go in an endless rhythm just like that of days and months. Similarly, the events of the seasons of rains, planting, weeding, harvesting, dry seasons, and again rainy seasons, are in a never-ending circle. Moreover, agricultural activities which predominate Marakwet life are controlled by the rainy and dry seasons. Unusual events, such as eclipses, droughts, famines, or epidemics are generally thought to be intruding bad omens requiring religious attention because they are not anticipated within the normal rhythm of events.[55]

With the expansion of Western education and capitalism the Marakwet have felt the erosion of their values. Some have come to accept these changes as forces which cannot be avoided. Others still cling to some of the traditional rites as resources to anchor themselves. To them, the traditional rites serve as the pillars of their society; without them, the society dies.

The connection with the ancestors and the concept of circular time gives the Marakwet people a sense of responsibility in every facet of activity. Evidently, the Western concept of linear time has undermined the African cyclical time as confirmed by the Kalenjin proverb that "without the calendar and the watches of the white men, we would be immortal."

Marriage

Marriage is another important rite in the Marakwet society. It is in this rite that two people experience the unique joy of procreation that confirms and completes their place in the society. The unity of marriage and procreation embodies social, economic, and religious aspects of the society as a fulfillment

55. Mbiti, *African Religions*, 35.

of life. Biologically, both man and woman are mystically reproduced in their children, thus perpetuating the reality of human continuity. This also embraces the religious aspect through the reincarnation process; in which the ancestors are reborn in their line of descendants. Therefore, a person who has no descendants in effect quenches the fire of life and becomes forever dead.[56] J. M. Mbiti explains the mystery of marriage as follows:

> It is the point where all the members of a given community meet: the departed, the living, and those yet to be born. All the dimensions of time meet here and the whole drama of history is repeated, renewed, and revitalized. Marriage is a drama in which everyone becomes an actor or actress and not just a spectator. Therefore, marriage is a duty, a requirement from the corporate society, and a rhythm of life in which everyone must participate.[57]

Like most people in Africa, it is imperative for all Marakwet to get married and bear children. Marriage gives the individual recognition and a status which he or she cherishes as part of a unit. Marriage is expected to bring harmony and interdependence between a man and a woman to establish an independent productive and reproductive unit. In her study on the Marakwet, Henrietta Moore identifies three things that women bring to a marriage: their agricultural labor, their domestic labor, and their reproductive potential. Both men and women participate in agricultural ventures. The men clear, fence, and irrigate the fields while the women dig, sow, weed, and harvest the crops. Domestic duties are perceived totally as women's responsibilities.[58] A man who regularly carries out domestic tasks will be ridiculed. He will be called derogatory names such as *Sanga-kor* which means "she man" not only because he performs female tasks, but also because his wife obviously refuses to do so. This means that he no longer controls her. A man who is controlled by his wife is no longer deemed a full man.[59]

Women take their responsibilities seriously. They understand that men are dependent on their agricultural and domestic labor, and, if the opportunity arises, they use such powers against men. If they withhold their labors or sexual favors, the men are potentially stressed and lost. The men are equally aware of the women's powers and are careful to avoid conflict which might lead to a withdrawal of labor, services or romance.[60]

---

56. Mbiti, *African Religions*, 133.
57. Mbiti, *African Religions*, 133.
58. Moore, *Space*, 67.
59. Moore, *Space*, 68.
60. Moore, *Space*, 69.

Preparations

Young people get married when they are ready and have gone through the initiation of circumcision. Women usually marry shortly after initiation if they are old enough, unless they are still in school. A man is likely to wait until he has made the necessary preparations to raise a family. After meeting the appropriate partner, the man takes the matter to his parents for approval. The father takes the initiative in checking out some basics to ensure that there is no blood relationship or taboos that might preclude marriage.

As a rule, people of the same clan or totem are not allowed to marry. Where marriage is allowed within the same clan, the couple are scrutinized to ensure that they are not related. Some relationships, especially those by marriage, could be over-ridden if other factors are favorable. Another limitation is set by the age-set system. A man may marry a younger woman, but never a daughter of a member of his own age-set.

> A man may marry a woman of his own age-set and that below, e.g. *Kipkoimet* may marry *Cheptendur* or *Chemeri*. However, he may not marry *Chesyewa*, since this is the set into which his daughters are being initiated and marriage into it would be ritually incestuous.[61]

There are three ways of getting married and all are initiated by the man, and his friends but rarely by the woman. The least and unpopular form is kidnapping or taking the woman by force mostly with the help of friends. The second is elopement. Both are discouraged and therefore unpopular. The acceptable and the most common is a negotiated marriage (*Koyer*). After a mutual attraction and courtship period, both parties may get serious for marriage. The young man plans his first trip to the girl's home often with fear and trepidation. Customarily, the young man goes alone to the woman's home to present himself and declare his intentions. If the woman is agreeable, she comes out to meet him; she exchanges her sile with his spear and places the spear against the granary.[62] The man may be invited to eat, but he must not eat meat if served for meat is considered taboo for such an occasion. Negotiations are annulled should he make a mistake and take meat.

---

61. It is believed that the ancestors are displeased by marriages of close relations and would therefore bring misfortune to their children. *Lakoobo tilya*. Others believe that children of such a marriage might be born or become mentally disabed. Kipkorir and Welbourn, *Marakwet*, 50.

62. *Sile* is a slim walking stick given to young women after their initiation.

After supper, any children and youth are asked to make their way to their sleeping quarters after which the young man is asked the purpose of his visit. By this time, the young woman would have communicated to her mother whether she likes the man or not. In case of likeability, the young man is encouraged to return for further talks that will involve his family and clan elders. If the girl does not care enough for the young man, the parents would know to show him the door. Sometimes, the parents may object the young man based on other insinuating factors such as family background or obvious blood relations.

Following the success of the first visit, it is left to the parents of the young man to make subsequent visits until everything is arranged. The man's father or a senior elder of the clan must take along the ritual spear (*swoger*) to ensure the blessings of the ancestors. They must also take some beer (*komen*) which must be drunk by the elders of both families during marriage negotiations (*Koyer*).[63]

There was no formal bride price in Marakwet until the 1930s. The bond between the two families was sealed by exchange of gifts and a celebration and blessings for good relationships between the two families. After 1920, the majority of the Marakwet were forced to pay a hut tax to the colonial government. Most of the people who could not raise the money had to work in the European plantations in what were then called the "white Highlands" in the current counties of Uasin-Gishu and Tran-Zoia. In the plantations, the Marakwet interacted with the other Kalenjin speaking people, the Elgeyo and the Nandi, and intermarried. This resulted in the Marakwet adopting dowry payments, which were prevalent with those communities. The standard bride price now ranges from ten cows to several goats, as well as blankets, Lezos, and money. In situations where the suitor is poor, the dowry may be four cows, four goats, and a pair of blankets. In some extreme cases, beer only might suffice; In the latter, the man might offer his services to his in-laws.

When the negotiations are completed, an evening is chosen when the groom's close agnates will arrive at the bride's home to escort her to her new home.and they must dress appropriately. The matter is not easy as it sounds. The ordeal could be complicated by the number of people who show up at bride's home to bid her fare-well. First, before the bride leaves her home, her mother pours oil on her head and hands her the equipment

---

63. The use of home-brewed honey beer (*kipketin*) is a significant part of almost every ceremony in *Marakwet*. The drinking of beer makes the elders merry resulting in good deliberations. According to tradition, it is unthinkable to have a marriage negotiation or a wedding without the brew. Drinking is restricted to the elderly. Young people are forbidden to drink with their elders. Unfortunately, today, those traditions have been broken.

She must take with her. This includes an empty bag, a gourd, and a long slim stick (*sile*) or (*sindiit*). By tradition, the children in her neighborhood try and stop her by holding on to her clothes or her stick. The husband's party must be prepared to give "ransom" money to these children until they reach the boundary of the bride's community.[64] The bride too will make stops along the route to get gifts from the groom.

> She will not cross a stream until she has been promised a goat, a sheep, or a grain store. She will not enter her husband's homestead without her husband's promise of another gift.[65]

When she arrives at her mother-in-law's house, she demands a further gift. Before she agrees to eat, a goat must also be promised to her. She stays at her mother-in-law's house for the first few days, during which time she takes food to her husband in his hut. She must not submit to her husband's advances right away, as this would be shameful. She must be persuaded at every stage by the promise of a gift. The most important is the animal she is promised for allowing her husband to undress her.

> Of all the animals a woman is promised she will probably receive at most two or three. These three animals are usually the two she is promised by her mother-in-law for entering the house and agreeing to eat, and the one promised by her husband for agreeing to have sexual intercourse.[66]

Throughout the marriage negotiations, the journey to her husband's home, and for months afterwards, the woman's attitude is often characterized by a semblance of arrogance and contemptuous insolence for her husband. She does not show any signs of affection, The husband, on the other hand, tries to be patient and self-controlled, yet persistent without any show of anger or violence, lest he loses his bride at this early stage. Technically, the marriage can easily be dissolved until the second visit of the marriage is made; this is commonly known as "lighting of the marriage fire" (*kirala ma*).

After staying the first few days at her mother-in-law's house, the bride returns to her parents' home for a brief visit. On this trip she is accompanied by a young girl from her husband's family. After four days, a group of men and women—excluding her husband—follows, bringing home-brewed beer for her parents and relatives Over the beer, the two

---

64. The party must carry a lot of money in small denominations for distribution.
65. Kipkorir and Welbourn, *Marakwet*, 50.
66. Moore, *Space*, 66.

families review all the events leading to the marriage and the bride's first journey and experience in her new home.[67]

> It is important that on this (first journey) no snake or dikdik should cross the path ahead nor baboon be heard to bark. Such an event may indicate an impediment to the marriage which had not been previously considered. Unless it is sufficient slight to be negated . . . the marriage may be annulled.[68]

This is a most anxious time for the groom, wondering at the outcome of the visit. If it is satisfactory, the bride is brought back to her new home and given her allocation of stock and land for cultivation. The size of stock is entirely the husband's prerogative and will include those animals previously promised to her by him and her mother-in-law. If the woman is the first wife, there will be considerable social pressure on the husband to allocate as much as half his herd. Any such allocation would not be an economic loss to her husband, as the animals will continue to be part of his herd and can be used in any way, he deems necessary, with permission of course. A woman also acquires right to land given her by the husband; it usually consists of several plots in various parts of the clan area. She does not actually own the land, although she has use for it. In polygamous situations, each wife is expected to grow enough food to feed her immediate family and the land is eventually inherited by her sons. This also applies to the livestock.[69]

The Wedding Ceremony

Before the marriage is completed, two important ceremonies must be performed. The first one is the ceremony of *barbarisio*. *Kebarbar* means to stir a liquid mixture by twirling a stick between the palms of the hands. The central act of *barbariso* is the stirring of the ritual ochre *ng'eny* with water.[70]

> The purpose is to remove ritual dangers from the woman; it is a form of purification from any sin that might hamper successful deliveries of babies. *Barbariso* is, therefore, performed once the woman is pregnant and ready to have her first child. In preparation for this ceremony, the husband brews the beer at his own

---

67. The woman is asked to report anything she does not like. The dowry is also negotiated at this time and half of the agreed dowry must be paid immediately. The remainder will be paid as soon as the groom's economic circumstances allow.
68. Kipkorir and Welbourn, *Marakwet*, 51.
69. Moore, *Space*, 67.
70. Kipkorir and Welbourn, *Marakwet*, 38.

home with the help of a few friends and relatives. When the beer is ready, preferably honey beer (*kombo moren*), the in-laws and the man's clans-folk, *kabor*, will come; they must bring milk and other foodstuffs. No animal is killed on this occasion as the pouring of blood is unnecessary.[71]

The actual ceremony is conducted during the day so that the sun may witness the event. The groom and bride are seated together with the best man and bridesmaid on either side. The ritual elder takes the mixed ochre and daubs it on the couple. Then he sprinkles some milk on their chests as a symbol of fertility and prosperity. The elder takes a stick to twirl in the direction of the couple and utters words of blessing for the mother and the child she is carrying. Sometimes, while this is taking place, another elder takes some ritual leaves, dips them in the ochre mixture, and applies the mixture generously to everyone. The attending people repeat the elder's incantation:

Chamnyot barbar.	Peace.
Katchenoru tugul barbar.	We have found them all.
Tukubo ng'o barbar.	Whose property.
Tukubo bich barbar.	People's property.
Tukubo anum barbar.	So and So's goods.
A, anyin barbar.	Sweet.
A Sere barbar.	Blessings.[72]

The incantations are combined with confessions of sins by the elders on behalf of the couple. The sins referred to are those committed unknowingly, such as breaking taboos. It may also be a theft or a crime against either of the two families involved in the marriage. Such offenses might incur bad fortune, especially in childbirth.

The second ceremony finalizing the institution of marriage has come to be called the major ceremony (*tum kame*). This is performed any time between the birth of the first-born and his/her initiation.[73] This ceremony elevates the status of the parents and gives the first-born certain privileges. One informant explained it thus:

> When a man is ready for this ceremony, he invites all the members of his age-set, *ibin*, to his house where they will drink the

71. Kipkorir and Welbourn, *Marakwet*, 38.

72. Kipkorir and Welbourn, *Marakwet*, 39.

73. It must be done before the youth is allowed to undergo initiation. Some youths have been barred from this because their parents had not gone through the *tum kame*.

age-set beer (*kombo ibin*). He notifies them of his intention, and, in turn, his peers will pledge their assistance in preparing the ceremony.[74]

A few days before the ceremony, copious quantities of beer are brewed. Relatives from both sides take an active part in these preparations. On the first day of the ceremony, boys and girls from the immediate vicinity and surrounding villages will gather for the grinding of grain (*ng'osho*). The flour will be used to feed the crowd during the three-day wedding celebration. The young boys and girls enjoy offering their services during these festivities, which are regarded as a social recreation, accompanied by songs and jubilation. At the end of the day, the youths are rewarded with food and invited to take part in the dancing. As evening falls, the youths are sent home, leaving the adults to continue with their dancing.[75]

The major dance begins in the evening and continues throughout the night. All the guests are expected to be present except for the in-laws, who do not join until the next day. However, their portion of beer is taken to their home, where they drink with friends. On the second day of the ceremony, the in-laws arrive, led by the wife's father. Her mother, together with the women from her clan, bring food as gifts, and they are all taken to a house reserved for their reception. Before entering the house, the father-in-law takes the ritual plant (*seretyon*) and ties it to the doorpost. When he enters the house, some beer is handed to him. He takes a sip of beer, spits it around the house, and repeats this libation to the ancestors four times with an accompaniment of incantations. After all the in-laws are seated, and are given beer to drink, followed by a greeting ceremony. The people celebrate and socialize throughout the entire day. The women prepare food for the guests, and this is eaten usually around mid-day to late afternoon.

In the afternoon, all the people assemble at the courtyard (*kiror*) for the most important event of the ceremony. The head of the ritual opens the session by pouring beer in four directions in honor of the ancestors. This is followed by prayers, incantations, and further pouring of libations. At that time, the wife and husband are seated on a cowhide in the centre of the *kiror*. After another ritual, the couple are covered by a a ceremonial garment.[76]

74. Personal interview with James Cheserek, February 1989.

75. Wedding dances are started by the uninitiated boys and girls; later, when the youths retire, the adults continue and perform an evening dance called *kiplangatian*. See Kipkorir and Welbourn, *Marakwet*, 51–52.

76. There are many rituals performed at this time, which could not be disclosed to me. Most of these rituals are only known to the ones who themselves have been through these rituals.

The next stage of the ceremony includes the firstborn of the couple, who is the subject of the wedding ceremony. If it is a boy, the father takes him to the house where they make fire together; once this is done, they are asked to run around the fire four times carrying a container of beer. On completion of the fourth round, the ritual expert takes a sip of the beer and spits it on the burning fire wishing them a long life and prosperity. If the first-born is a girl, the mother leads her through the same ritual.

Once this act is concluded, the initiates return to the courtyard where they are anointed with oil and given their status symbols: the woman is given a belt of cowrie shells while the man receives a hat (*kutwo*) made from the skin of a colobus monkey. The first-born is only anointed.

On the third day, the men again gather at the courtyard. At this time, a huge container of beer, *terr*, is put in the centre; the beer is dispensed to groups according to age-set seniority. This being the most important gathering of the men, several of them usually bring their concerns before the elders. These may range from lost property to daughters and sons in the cities who refuse to return home. It is the duty of the most senior elders to bring these matters before *Asis* and the ancestors. In addition, on these occasions, stolen property, an abusive son, or dispute over land is brought before the elders, who may administer a curse to the thief and the wrongdoer. Disobedient children are not cursed, but prayers to straighten their ways are said.[77] It is strongly believed by most Marakwet people that submissions brought to such gatherings will be resolved as the elders are united in heart and mind. The ceremony ends on the fourth day and everybody returns home. The men and women from the man's clan, *kabor*, remain behind to clean up.

Polygamy

Polygamy is an acceptable practice in Marakwet society. In the past, some of Marakwet men aspire to have more than one wife if they can afford it. There are several reasons which contribute to this: the foremost being childlessness, which is considered a misfortune. The most natural reason for marriage almost all African people is procreation and without it the union loses its social credibility.[78]

---

77. The Marakwet draw a line between a curse and a blessing, and, as the two are directly opposed to each other, a man who blesses is not allowed to administer a curse at the same time. The invocations uttered during the two rites do not affect the individuals who administer them.

78. Mbiti, *African Religions*, 141.

> He who has many descendants has the strongest possible manifestation of immortality. He is reborn in the multitude of his descendants.... Children are the glory of marriage.[79]

The absence of children with the first wife of the marriage forces the man to take another wife, to remedy the childlessness and to remove the stigma and anxiety of sterility. This is grounded in the belief that the more productive a person is, the more he contributes to the existence of the society at large.[80]

The second reason is socio-economic. Marakwet people survive on subsistence and often additional hands are necessary to establish and manage new areas of farming and grazing. To make this possible, the husband and first wife try to strike a compromise regarding the second wife, particularly as hiring help is impractical in the traditional economy. In areas where a large labour force is a necessity, an expanding family by polygamy has been the best solution. Each wife is allocated a piece of land which expands as her children increase. This may only apply to the valley where there is still plenty of land. In the highlands things are different; because the land is demarcated into small plots which are usually subdivided further into polygamous families. Due to this dearth of land, polygamy in the highlands is less practiced. Polygamous families have the advantage of ensuring that there is always someone who can help in case of need.

> When one wife gives birth, there are other wives to nurse her and care for her other children during the time she is regaining her vitality. If one wife dies, there are others to take over the care of the children. In case of sickness, other wives will fetch water from the river, cut firewood, cook, and do other jobs for the family.... Where peasant farming is the means of livelihood, the many children in a polygamous family are an economic asset—even if they also must eat plenty of food.[81]

The third reason for polygamy is the quest for status. A man with sufficient wealth in livestock can boast of his position by marrying other wives. This was usually achieved by traditional leaders who, by virtue of their positions, acquired both prestige and property. They included notables such as medicine men and chiefs. After World War II, this list included soldiers, teachers, and businesspeople. After Kenya attained independence in 1963, more businessmen and those who acquired European farms formed most polygamous families, not only in Marakwet, but in all of Kenya.

79. Mbiti, *African Religions*, 142.
80. Mbiti, *African Religions*, 142.
81. Mbiti, *African Religions*, 142–43.

Finally, in a situation when a wife is constantly ill, the husband considers marrying another wife; in this case, the new wife does not only serve the interests of the husband but assists the sickly woman by giving her children motherly support. She will also look after the woman's interests until she recovers.[82]

> Instead of taking drastic and inhumane divorce measures against such a wife, a second marriage is a solution. The man might not enjoy a sexual relationship with his first wife, but he will continue to support her and her children.[83]

Traditionally, the Marakwet did not encourage secret extra-marital relationships. Should such a relationship result in pregnancy, the man was morally responsible to marry the woman for marriage to the mother of the man's child created a better atmosphere for the child. This move maintained the dignity of both the woman and the man. Ideally, a wife should not object to her husband's desire for a second wife, if it does not involve her allocated livestock. Sometimes a wife will even request her husband to take another wife to ease the workload on the family. Some go as far as to find an amicable and suitable candidate.[84]

Death and Funeral Rites

Burials

Traditionally, the Marakwet treat death with apprehension and caution because of its invasiveness and polluting power. Burial preparations vary widely from one part of Marakwet to another. These variations are also based on the age and gender of the deceased as well as exposure to Christianity. Before the Christian influence, a person near dead was taken outside the house if possible. The deceased clothes and ornaments are thus removed, and the naked body is ritually prepared and buried close to the compound. The body of a man is placed on his right side, with his right hand under his right ear. His head must face the East, the direction of the rising sun.[85]

---

82. Usually, the second wife is told the purpose for the marriage beforehand. She has the choice of refusal if she does not want the responsibilities.

83. Mailu, *Polygamy*, 17.

84. Mailu, *Polygamy*, 18.

85. If a man is buried not facing the sun, bad luck will follow his family. The consequences are often observed in sickness in the family or loss of livestock. This has resulted in people digging up old graves to make sure that the bones were positioned properly in the grave.

A woman is buried on the left side of her husband and to the left of her house where the chaff is collected (*kamorir*). The connection with chaff is related to her work of removing chaff when preparing food. Her body is placed on the left side with the left hand under the left ear. Children or uninitiated, who have not yet reached sexual maturity, are buried further away from the house, on either side depending on the sex. As Moore puts it, right and left are not absolutes but relative principles. What is important is that the woman be buried on the left side of the man, regardless of whether this is below her house or beside the chaff.[86]

The death of an unmarried man who has no children is unfavorable and troublesome because there are no offspring to carry on his name. In such cases, the arms and legs of the deceased are bound and pushed over the edge of the grave. Sometimes the family hires a stranger to bury him. The latter may give a better burial, but it is still not a respectable one as far as Marakwet tradition is concerned. To die without an offspring is considered a misfortune. A person who dies without children dies for eternity, and his or her name can never be given to a lineage new-born child. Those who die childless are believed to return as malevolent spirits with the ill intent to take others in their peer group. Similarly, a woman who has not been formerly married in the traditional sense is not buried in her husband's homestead but in her natal home even if she has borne children. Occasionally, a hurried formality is expedited to remedy the situation in order to bury her body at her husband's home.

While the corpse of an honorable person is being carried in a procession to the grave by the old men, another man follows behind throwing stones to drive away bad spirits (*oi*) which are said to be coming to call the living to the land of the dead. Before the grave is covered, some milk is poured on the corpse as a symbol that he may not be hungry on his journey to the land of the ancestors.[87] The grave is then covered with goat's dung and soil. Stone slabs and thorns are placed over the grave to keep children and wild animals away.

After the burial of a man, the widow starts a period of mourning. (The same applies to the man on the occasion of his wife's death.) She turns her clothes inside out and remains in her house for some days until the cleansing period. Other widows in the community will join her and keep her company. Other people stop at the house to comfort and encourage.

---

86. Moore, *Space*, 104.

87. The dead person is said, "to have gone to the spirits." *Asis* has taken him to the ancestral world. In *Endo* it is said, "the baboons have taken him." Similarly, when a child is born it is said, "the child was given by the baboons." All these statements mean that the deceased has gone to a place which the living may not see.

Some offer help in food preparations while others assist where needed. Even though she is assisted by the elders, she is still considered as having performed the burial. For this reason, she is considered unclean and suffers alienation like that experienced after initiation or childbirth. She cannot attend to any important matters nor prepare food for her family; she can only communicate in whispers. To free her, a ritual cleansing called *bito Karin* is performed four days after the burial.

Due to the Western influence through education and Christianity traditional funerals have undergone minor changes. Today, it is common to have a funeral service with speeches, eulogy, and a sermon. Also, the death of a person with social status attracts bigger crowds including politicians who often take advantage of any large gathering. At the end of all speeches and eulogy, the traditional elders take over and complete the interment according to Marakwet tradition. Today, all deceased persons are given descent burials with no discrimination regardless of their age sex or status.

Ritual Cleansing (*Bito Karin*)

A goat or sheep must be killed for the purpose of cleansing the home and the people who participated in the burial. The animal's chyme taken from the entrails is also used to cleanse the ornaments of the deceased. Following the killing of the goat, the ritual master applies the chyme from the entrails on the man's body and along the passage leading outside.[88] Some of it is sprinkled onto the dead man's ornaments. Beer is also used to wash or mouth-spray the ornaments before they are distributed to the heirs or other deserving persons.[89] All the children and agnates of the deceased and his widow must have their heads shaved and anointed. Some of the hair is first shaved from the left side; the man's agnates who have been initiated will shave some of the hair on the forehead and sprinkle it with milk from a black goat. The removal of the hair symbolizes the trauma of a great loss.[90]

The goat's meat is then boiled and eaten by the family and all those who attended the burial. No meat must be left. After the meal, the bones are collected, and the marrow extracted; and mixed with the root of a ritual plant of *morgut*. The mixture is used to mouth-spray the entire compound.

---

88. The ritual master is one who has had experience of losing a family member. He or she keeps company with the bereaved family for a few days.

89. Kipkorir and Welbourn, *Marakwet*, 67. Spittle carries enormous weight for its symbolic association with life.

90. Kipkorir and Welbourn, *Marakwet*, 6 becomes a living dead and 7.

This is followed by invocations. The ancestors are asked not to interfere in the community. In other parts, libations are administered to the ancestors to appease them or reverse any anger towards the people.

After the *bito Karin*, the whole territory observes four days of mourning. During this period people will not work in the fields or engage in any ceremonial activities. Failure to observe this rule is believed to result in a further calamity. After the four days' mourning period, people will resume their normal life in the community. The dead person becomes an ancestor and is welcomed back to give his or her name to the new-born children in the *kotkota* naming ritual. This guarantees personal continuity of the individual through procreation.

Ancestral World

The dead person is believed to continue to live in an alternate world which is almost identical to the current physical world. From there, the living dead will visit the living in various forms. According to Mbiti, the individual remains in the *protracted present (sasa)* period after death until nobody alive remembers him; then he sinks into the *zamani* period.[91] While in the *sasa* period, their appearance is extremely important and is welcomed with libations and their advice and instructions are given serious consideration.

The pouring of libations of beer, milk, or the offering of any other foods are a symbol of remembrance and communion. The ancestors are considered to have mystical ties that bind the living-dead to their surviving relatives. When these acts of libation are performed, the eldest member of the family, with the longest memory of the departed, is given the honour of pouring the libation. The man invokes the ancestors on behalf of the whole family.

This chapter with its sub-sections has shown that when myths are re-enacted, the participants make a connection with the mythical time in the past in which such events took place. In other words, by the repetition of rituals, humans connect to the past and create a continuum. The re-enactment gives myth its function and meaning to shape human life in the world. Through rituals, the world is no longer an opaque mass of objects arbitrarily thrown together but a living cosmos that can be intelligible and significant. It explains why things exist and to what end. At the same time,

---

91. *Sasa* is the period in which people are conscious of their existence. It has a short future, a dynamic present and an experienced past. *Zamani* overlaps with *sasa*; however, it is the period in which every event disappears into the storehouse of everything that ever happened. See Mbiti, *African Religions*, 23.

through rituals, innovative ideas are given new interpretations by the designated specialists who assure us that what we do has already been done in the past thus reducing anxiety to a minimum. In this sense, there is no reason to fear the unknown future because the community knows what needs to be done. For example, in the rites of passage, especially the circumcision, the elders and mentors communicate the cultural myths to the neophytes. They are taught that they are because of a series of events that occurred in mythical time in the past. While they are not obliged to know the whole history, they are obliged to re-enact some parts of it periodically and repeatedly to make the connection to that mythical history.[92] By virtue of repetition, the rite attains an enduring value.

---

92. Beane and Doty, *Myths*, 8.

CHAPTER 3

RELIGION: MYTH, RITES, AND SYMBOLS

Introduction

BELIEFS ABOUT GOD, ANCESTORS, and other supernatural powers are enshrined in myth, and myth supplies models for human behavior that give meaning and value to life. According to Mircea Eliade, an account of sacred history relates to events that took place in primordial time—the fabled time of the beginning/creation. Myth relays how through the deeds of supernatural beings, a reality came into existence, be it the whole of reality or only a fragment of it. Furthermore, myth discloses the creativity of the supernatural beings in the world. It is this dramatic breakthrough of the sacred that really establishes the world resulting in moral, sexed, and cultural beings.[1]

The world owes its existence to a divine act of creation. Its rhythm is the product of events that took place at the beginning of time. The stars in the solar system, vegetation, humans, and animals in the land have their mythical history. In the final analysis, the world reveals itself and speaks through its rhythms. Myth has the primordial power of unlocking human consciousness to another world to show that there is something there in the divine world or the world of the ancestors that gives value to human existence.

Like all human cultures, the Marakwet history reveals such dynamic religious elements expressed through symbols, rituals, and stories. This forms their profound beliefs and awareness that their lives are shaped by unseen forces pervading the world with purposes they cannot control but can only understand through religious rituals that give meaning to life. In this sense, religious activities accompany every stage of life from the cradle to the grave and beyond.

---

1. Beane and Doty, *Myths*, 5.

At the apex of this religious activity is the belief in a supreme deity symbolized by the sun and other supernatural principles. Linguistically, it is hard to draw the distinction between the sun and the supreme creator since both are referred to interchangeably. However, ritual practices and sacred incantations seem to indicate a higher power behind the Sun. The sun's brightness symbolizes God's watchful eye, and its warmth represents God's generosity. Like God, the sun too is identified by many names, such as *Chebeto Chematau, Cherelmo, Chibo Yiim*, which implies the one generous one that rules by the day. The sun is a daily reminder of God's presence and generosity. The sun makes things grow, while the thunder provides rain to nurture the earth so humans, plants, and animals can enjoy its abundance and thrive. The other powerful entities include the big stars and the moon, which represent God's activities in the night and serve as calendars and signals to remind people when to plant crops and conduct rituals, ceremonies, and festivals. For example, astrologers interpret the positioning of the stars in relationship to the moon to determine the rains or when best to conduct life-cycle rituals. God needs all these representations, without which God would remain unknown to humanity. Unlike the Europeans deists of the nineteenth century, who believed in God's distance and complete removal from the earth, the Marakwet believe that God is both transcendent and partially eminent and is actively involved with the world either directly or indirectly through intermediaries. Moreover, humans sense God's mystery in extreme limits, namely in the fullness of life and in the emptiness of life (life and death).

However, God is beyond human grasp, yet at the same time God is believed to encompass everything in nature. Unlike nature, God is intangible but real. While God is not directly seen, God discloses God's sacred presence in the most diverse ways in nature and human creativity. Unlike Christian anthropomorphic perspective, the Marakwet traditional concept of God is understood in cosmic terms and views creation as interdependent on both God and on itself. They see God as the principal cosmic force animating every aspect of the universe, while at the same time maintaining a level of independence from the universe. Simultaneously, there is a sense of co-dependency of creation that makes room for a greater role for stewardship and preservation, as opposed to the exploitation of nature. This reciprocity is an intact component in Marakwet practices of hunting, grazing, and working the land, where the restoration and preservation of the natural environment takes place.

The Supreme Creator (*Iriin*)

Like the rest of the Kalenjin groups, the Marakwet recognize a principal deity who created and brought everything into existence; therefore, God is principally referred to as the creator (*Iriin*). This deity is understood to be beyond human scope and can only be related through intermediaries. In his study of God in Africa, Mbiti rightly uses a wide range of terminologies, most of which understand God as the creator, preserver of life, and arbiter of justice. God is the giver of light, darkness, and rain and the granter of the fertility of humankind, animals, plants, and the soil. God is also the dispenser of both good and evil and chooses to use both at will to fulfil God's intentions. Disobedience to God or to God's agencies results in misery. The Supreme Creator is represented principally by the sun, and, most often, the creator and the sun are used interchangeably. It is believed that the sun in itself has no power of its own. Rather, its energy and illumination reflect the purity and kindness of the Creator.[2]

God is wise and knows everything, even the unknown secrets to the elders.[3] The sun, moon, and the stars are God's great eyes, and they always keep a perpetual watch everywhere in both the physical and spiritual world. This metaphor of divine seeing (omniscience) explains how God relates to the creation. For example, some days a man may be too busy or too lazy to look after his flock, therefore he lets them graze unattended saying:

> "*Bo chebet anin rokony*—God will look after the flock to-day."[4]

Similarly, God stretches beyond human imagination or thought, so that as far as humans can see, God is also present there. Metaphorically, the Marakwet believe that God is always present but invisible, like air, light, and wind. In this regard, J. Mbiti's description is appropriate:

> African people acknowledge the omnipresence of God. He may be in the thunder but not thunder; He may shoot forth like a waterfall, but God is not the waterfall; He may be associated with the sky, but he is not identical with it.[5]

This might have led to the Western caricature of Africans as animists. It is perhaps more appropriate to say that Africans are Panentheistic, believing

---

2. The sun attained its purity status by burning all impure materials, thus radiating the characteristics of God.

3. The Elders are believed to have extra insight because of their acquired wisdom through years of experience in public life.

4. Kipkorir and Welbourn, *Marakwet*, 14.

5. Mbiti, *Concepts*, 8.

that God is in everything. In other words, there is a divine element in everything.

Furthermore, the Marakwet believe that God is eternal and infinite; in other words, there is no time when God was not. From time immemorial (*kenyision*) the Supreme Deity was in existence and will exist beyond today, tomorrow, and the distant future. All creation, including trees, land, and ancestors going back to the first ancestors, were made by God. The notion of the past and future are understood differently for all African societies, as articulated by the late John Mbiti who advances the theory of the African concept of time. In order to underline an African view of time and of reality in relation to God, Mbiti recognizes three epochs of time, namely the past (*Zamani*), present (*Sasa*), and future.[6] From this perspective, the Supreme Being is seen in and beyond the past, present, and the future.

> God is the origin and sustenance of all things. He is older than the Zamani period; He is outside and beyond His creation. On the other hand, He is personally involved in His creation, so that it is not outside of Him or His reach.[7]

In terms of space, the Supreme Being is thought to be far beyond human search and reach, but, paradoxically, God is near and observes everything one does. This is often done through God's intermediaries or emissaries.

The transcendence of God means limitlessness, for God is Spirit and fills every space everywhere. Mbiti further affirms this argument that:

> As Spirit God has no limit and transcends all boundaries. There cannot be and there is no "beyond" God for his is omnipresent and there is no vacuum of existence which he does not fill up. He is or has the most abundant reality of being, lacking no completeness and possessing all fullness of being. He is the ultimate, the final and the absolute Supreme Being beyond the aspiration and imagination of man.[8]

On a clear night, the sky invites one to gaze as far as the eye will reach. This exercise suggests great distance, thus aiding one in trying to comprehend and describe the transcendence of the Supreme Being.

---

6. *Zamani*: is a Kiswahili word for "past." Mbiti uses it to designate the time that passes on from the "present." It is the period beyond which nothing can go. *Zamani* is the graveyard of time, the period of termination and the dimension in which everything finds its halting point. It is the first storehouse for all phenomena and events, the ocean of time in which everything becomes absorbed into a reality that is neither after nor before. See Mbiti, *African Religions*, 23.

7. Mbiti, *African Religions*, 29.

8. Mbiti, *Concepts*, 14–15.

RELIGION: MYTH, RITES, AND SYMBOLS

Because of the transcendence of God, the use of intermediaries suggests a link of communion between God and human beings. This supports the paradoxical notion that God is both far and near. In his omnipotence, God oversees all things, in both the material world and the Spirit world. Things are only possible when God allows them to happen, for nothing happens without God's permission.

The Marakwet turn to God in times of crisis such as epidemics, droughts, locust invasions, disease, and wars. They pray to God with the aid of sacrifices to appeal to God and God's power and greatness, which is above and over any human and ultra-human force. Most of the time, the appeal is done through the recognized intermediaries who represent the ultimate knowledge of the Supreme Deity. This is based on the overall presumption that

> the Supreme Being is more powerful than the living dead, the spirits, and the medicine-men which are generally considered to be more powerful than men. In this context, power is viewed hierarchically, so that God is at the top as the omnipotent; beneath him are the spirits with lesser power; and lower still are men with comparatively little power.[9]

Although the Supreme Creator occupies a particularly important place in the Marakwet world view, formal worship is not routinely observed. In other words, there are no sacred places of reverence or priests. Everybody knows and shares the common body of beliefs. In this case, worship is observed indirectly. B. E. Kipkorir's observation is worth noting:

> There is not a compartment earmarked for expression of one's beliefs and religion. There are times when one is conscious of religious obligations and there are also times when one is not particularly so. When one is going through personal or family stresses, one takes remedial steps, like offering sacrifices and prayers. At those times the person focuses attention on the operation of other worldly phenomena. Equally, there are times when an individual is in a philosophical mood. He is pensive and contemplative.[10]

In his book *The Prayer in the Religious Traditions of Africa*, Aylward Shorter gives six models of prayer. The one he calls *"The Asymmetrical Mediation"* is similar with the Marakwet worship tradition for it addresses

---

9. Mbiti, *Concepts*, 12.
10. Kipkorir and Ssenyonga, *Socio-Cultural Profile*, 13.

the indirect relationship with the Supreme Deity. This is where the mediators act principally as channels of formal prayer.[11]

The Creation

The Marakwet commonly believe that the sun, moon, stars, and earth and all the things in them came into being a long time ago (*Kenyision*), though no one knows exactly when and how. Some people have told stories related to the origin of things. The only Marakwet creation story I have heard is recorded by B. E. Kipkorir.

> Once upon a time, sun, moon, elephant, man and other animals were resting together on their sides. They continued thus for a long time. But one day, sun noticed man turn his head. Sun became suspicious but took no action. Some time afterwards, however, man was found by the others to have turned completely over onto his other side. Sun could no longer contain his suspicions and said to elephant: "Do you see this being called man? He is dangerous." Elephant looked at man and laughed, saying "He is too tiny for me to worry about." But moon shared sun's suspicions; and they went away together, up to the sky where they would be safe from man's designs. A short time afterwards man got up and walked away. Later, the other animals got up and walked away. They saw man sharpen a stone with which he killed one of the smaller animals. The grim truth dawned on elephant and the others that sun and moon had been right in their suspicions. It was too late to flee to the sky. So, they fled to the forest away from man.[12]

It is a common belief that the creation of the universe, including the sun, is the work of God. Unlike the Judeo-Christian tradition that try to explain evil away from God, the Marakwet hold that the Supreme Creator, made both good and evil. Their ultimate purpose is to be at the service of the Supreme Creator. The conflict between these two forces is constantly at play in the human arena. The manifestations of the evil forces are observed in misfortunes such as illness, droughts, and famine. The good is manifested through good health, wealth, procreation, and other positive aspects of life. Evil things come through any disruption of health and social harmony. Quite often, the Marakwet attempt to keep the two opposing forces side by side while at the same time trying to observe the proper conduct in society. This

---

11. Shorter, *Prayer*, 4.
12. Kipkorir and Welbourn, *Marakwet*, 13.

conduct includes keeping all religious rites, ceremonies, proper burials, and respect for the elders and the ancestors. Such observations will not only keep people in line with God but will free them from the machinations of the evil spirits. In case of any misfortune, one must try to obtain God's benevolence or manipulate other power sources by the help of the religious experts. This manipulation might include offering gifts and libation to the ancestors, making peace with wronged relatives, or paying one's debts.

The Marakwet seem to acknowledge God's transcendence above God's immanence. The indirect involvement of the Supreme Deity is daily manifested through a variety of executioners. As a result, there is very limited direct relationship or means of reciprocal communication between God and people. This might be the reason why there is ambiguity on direct knowledge of God. However, none of this has diminished the people's allegiance to God, even when details of God are limited. The emissaries are organized in a format that is complex but easy to understand. At the apex of the hierarchy is the Supreme Creator and under that are the human and supra-human powers as explained below.

Human and Supra-Human Powers

In between the Supreme Creator *(iriin)* and humanity, there is a body of other forces that are human and supra-human by nature. They act as intermediaries or remedial agencies when things go wrong. Their duties towards humanity may either result in good or bad, depending on the dispensation of their agencies. Some of these supra-human forces are the Sun, Thunder/Water Spirit *(Ilat)*, Ancestors, Witchcraft, Divination, Oath, Incantation, and Healers. These are chosen because they form the cosmology of the Marakwet beliefs.

The Sun *(Asis)*

As previously mentioned, the Sun *Asis* is God's visible representative. It existed all along with God; though in essence, it was created at some point before the creation of humans. The sun acts on God's behalf daily by watching and supervising matters at closer range. It faithfully does this by rising dutifully every morning and making its way across the sky. As God's visible symbol, the sun shines on people, animals, plants, and even those creatures in the deep sea that do not get sunlight are sustained by God. As the sun illuminates, it exposes human actions and draws attention to what is right, just, and good. From time to time, the sun or other supra terrestrial entities are to intercede for the people and the planet. This happens not only in the time of crisis, but also in daily, mundane matters where balance is required.

In human relationships, the oath, *muma*, is the most powerful and fearful rite that the Marakwet know. An oath is a self-endorsing act of coercion used to determine truth in a conflict. The swearing, which enforces the oath, functions to guarantee the credibility of the person's words. Failure to say the truth may result in something terribly deadly happening to whoever conceals the truth. The common consequences may come in the form of sickness, death, or loss of property. Such misfortunes may follow the family up to the fourth generation. Nothing can be hidden from the principal watchful eye of God, which is the sun.

God alone is understood to control the effects of oaths and God has endowed the sun with the attribute of judging everyone's behavior on God's behalf.[13] For instance, if a theft of stock is committed and the culprit remains unidentified, a community may administer a curse (*muma*) on the suspect and call on the sun to inflict the appropriate punishment. The offended party may claim innocence and would likewise appeal to the sun to intervene and show justice by reversing the curse towards his accusers, thereby proving his innocence. In another sense, the sun acts as the last or final recourse in a civil dispute. If two parties disagree over the boundary marks of their fallow land, and the elders are unable to settle the matter, the sun is invoked to reveal the truth. Further, the sun is invoked in any matter where a curse is involved. For example, an elder may curse any youth who behaves in a manner contrary to custom. For this reason, youth often take careful precautions in their conduct lest they incur the curse of the elders. In the case of minor offenses, such as negligence of duty, an elder is believed to nullify the curse by spitting on his chest. If a crime is committed by an unknown offender, or property stolen, the victim may be cursed incognito. The curse takes the following form:

Marakwet	English Translation
Borokok!	Attention!
Rotwana Asis	Behold my case, sun
Borokok!	Attention!
Barin Asis	May the sun kill you

13. What the Marakwet attribute to the sun are indirect acts of the Supreme Being.

Marakwet	English Translation
I'orisitu	May you turn pale
Kuyamin morok	May your throat go dry
Tiarin ilat	May thunder strike you

The Marakwet believe that *Asis* has some instruments, which it employs to manage its will and judgement. A recognizable instrument is *Ilat* (thunder and lightning). *Ilat* is also one of the divinities subject to the omnipotence of the Supreme Deity. Presumably, acting as the Creator's agent, *Ilat* will strike the property of any offender. In these cases, time will eventually determine the culprit.

Thunder/Lightning/Water Spirit (*Ilat* [sing], *Ilot* [pl])

The Marakwet spirit world is made up of spirits which are divisible into two categories. One group comprises the clan spirits, which are believed to live invisibly in the clan territory, preferably in the nearby forests and hills. The second group, which we will now discuss, is made up of the spirits of the unknown beings (*Ilot*) believed to roam at night when people are asleep. The *Ilot* are also believed to dwell in streams, waterfalls, pools, and isolated spaces. Generally, they are considered hostile to humanity, especially when offended. For that reason, people fear to come into contact with them. Children and women avoid travelling alone at night in fear of encountering them.

By nature, (*Ilot*) are spirits, but they are tricky in that they impersonate people to conceal their identity. Sometimes their appearances are unique and mysterious. Some are believed to come in the form of one-legged or dual bodied creatures. The latter is one half human and the other half metallic. They are also known to transform themselves whenever they wish. *Ilat* (sing) The Toyoi clan consider Ilat to be their totem and in a broader sense, Ilat's principal duty is to execute justice on behalf of the Supreme Deity. For this reason, every effort is made to obey the Marakwet moral and social conduct which include respect for the elders, refraining from theft etc. The opposite may result in a drought or personal disaster. Sometimes, Ilat's activities are akin to that of a thief. It may strike someone or burn down a house. When that happens, the community concerned may seek the services of a diviner or a rain maker who has the ritual apparatus to intervene. People and cattle that have been swept away by floods or drowning are attributed to the work of *Ilat*. The most common fingerprints of *Ilat* can be seen when lightning strikes a tree or a piece of ground. In such cases it is offered sacrifices composed of lamb and honey-beer, (*kombo-moren*). The lamb's meat is cut and ritually distributed throughout the area affected, and the beer poured onto the ground for *Ilot* consumption. This act is believed to appease them so they will not strike again. It is a kind of peace offering.[14]

A while back in Kaben location, a man whose house was destroyed by lightning and lost everything sought answers from a diviner. The man was asked to give an account of how he had acquired the lost property and the materials used to build the house. The Marakwet do not believe that things happen by chance. Everything has a cause and effect and, in this case, it was believed that either the man or his kin were responsible for provoking the divinities; otherwise, none of these misfortunes would have happened. The only solution was to offer a sacrificial animal to appease the avenged ghosts, otherwise something serious would follow. The man sacrificed a sheep as advised, and the meat was cut into small pieces and distributed around the homestead.[15] With the help of his tools, the diviner discerned that the man had stolen in the acquisition of his livestock. The diviner also prescribed a solution in the form of a black sheep and monetary compensation for the stolen property to the one he had stolen from.

The Ancestors

Although the Marakwet do not, in their tradition, concern themselves directly with the act of creation, they are concerned with the reality of being in the present and hereafter. For them, it is not a matter of concern to speculate on when life first started. That moment is wrapped up in the realm of the unknown past, and it is of no use to speculate on the matter. The present human life is the continuation of a life that began in the past and continues to be lived today, and in the future. The incident of this first life is carried on through procreation, and that is why childlessness in a marriage is taken as a curse that has undercut the process. It implies an end to human existence. For an illustration, I was once hosted by a long-time friend in Nairobi. His relative was also visiting, and at one point after dinner my friend's daughter asked the man "*unaitwa baba nani,*" which translates "to whose father are you?" When the visitor replied that he had no child, the girl nicknamed him "*Baba zero,*" which implied that he was not a father. The Marakwet consider children to be a sign of blessing and continuity.

14. Kipkorir et al., *Kerio Valley*, 14.
15. Personal conversation with the Assistant Chief responsible over Sokotow village.

A man must therefore ensure that as he (of the present) in the continuation of his father is (of the past) so his "flame of life" should continue flickering long after he is dead through the birth of a son (of the future). And given the ageless process of procreation and recreation: the future, like the past, has no definable limits. Bodies of events of the future can be anticipated based on the precedents of the past.[16]

One who dies after obtaining a certain level of respectability (marriage and children) in the society assumes the status of an ancestor.[17] According to Mbiti, they are referred to as the living dead because they are still active within the present period, *sasa*,[18] and their process of dying is not yet complete.[19]

When a Marakwet speaks of ancestors, they think of the departed spirits of their progenitors with whom the living maintains filial relationship. Nonetheless, not every departed person receives consideration or recognition as an ancestor. To qualify for consideration, one must have lived a life of honesty and attained an enviable old age. Also, before dying, he or she must have left behind good children and good memories. Children and youths who die prematurely, barren women and infertile men, and those who have lived reckless lives or committed suicide are excluded from consideration.

A man's father, after death, becomes for him the most important figure in the spirit world. The father is seen as the one who links the individual to the ancestor's lineage. Although the Marakwet is a patrilineal society, the ancestors are inclusive of male and female members.

As the guardians of the community's laws, family affairs, traditions, ethics, and general daily activities, the ancestors exercise protective and disciplinary influence on their children. Offenses in these matters are, ultimately, offenses against the ancestors and are punishable unless something is done to correct the wrong. The idea behind this is that of reciprocity which means the respectful treatment of the ancestors is expected from the descendants. This involves careful observation of the community's

---

16. Kipkorir, "Sun in Marakwet Religious Thought," 176.

17. An ancestor is one from whom a person descends. It refers to lineal descent through fore-parents or progenitors. Merriam-Webster, s.v. "ancestor," https://www.merriam-webster.com/dictionary/ancestor

18. J. S. Mbiti's analysis of the concept of time by using two Kiswahili words, *sasa* and *zamani*. *Sasa* covers the "now period"—where people are. Events in the *sasa* dimension cover the experienced past, the dynamic present, and the short future. *Sasa* is tangible and practical. Events move from now *sasa* to the past *zamani*. See Mbiti, *African Religions*, 16–23.

19. Mbiti, *African Religions*, 83.

code of ethics and keeping the prescribed taboos. Such actions will, in turn, result in good and harmonious living.

The Marakwet, like other African people, do not worship the ancestors. It is, therefore, wrong for Western scholars to conclude that Africans are ancestor worshippers. Bolaji Idowu feels that ancestor worship is a wrong nomenclature for what, in fact, is not worship but a manifestation of an unbroken relationship between the parent, who has departed from this world, and the offspring, who are still here.[20]

By virtue of their position in the societies of both the living and the dead, the ancestors play the role of immediate intermediaries between the living and the spirit world. They are indeed believed to be nearer to the divine emissaries and can plead to them effectively.

> The living dead are bilingual: they speak the language of men with whom they lived until recently, and they speak the language of the spirits and of God to whom they are drawing nearer ontologically.... It is through the living dead that the spirit world becomes personal to men.[21]

Ezekiah Kaino narrated to me a story about a dispute that had developed in the 1930s between the clans of *Shaban* and *Kabisioi* over the boundary of their land. The dispute continued for a period of ten years with no solution. Finally, the tension erupted into violence, leading to physical casualties. The community of *Kokwo* was called in to settle the matter, but still no solution was achieved. The meeting was adjourned until the following day. Before the adjournment, the community elders (*Ossis*) took the matter in prayer to God by the Sun and the ancestors.

In the dawn hours of the following morning, someone in the village spotted an elephant in the residential area on the escarpment. Usually, elephants are on the valley floor and rarely on the escarpment where people reside. The man gave the alarm cry to warn people of potential danger. Within an abbreviated time, the village men had assembled at the village. The elephant charged down the escarpment, and the men followed in pursuit. Strangely, the elephant followed a straight line through the contested land, from the top down to the valley floor. When the meeting resumed later, a decision on the boundary was easily determined. The disputing

---

20. The ancestors are benevolent to their earthly kin, but they can also be ambivalent. When they are neglected or forgotten by their living relatives, they are said to be angry with them and are capable of sending misfortunes as punishment. Their anger is usually appeased through prayers of incantations and pouring of libations. See Nyamiti, *Christ as Our Ancestor*, 16.

21. Mbiti, *African Religions*, 83.

clans were satisfied by the extraordinary intervention. Finally, prominent elders were asked to seal the meeting with libation and incantations of blessing so the disputing clans may live in peace.[22]

As pointed out already, the supernatural status of the ancestors is due to the good life the clans led. They are believed to be the source of harmony and stability. They are expected to provide care and protection from sickness, strife, death, or other calamities. Furthermore, living expects from them various benefits such as longevity, many children, and wealth. When recourse to ancestors fails to procure favorable results, the living usually turn to the Supreme Deity as their last resort.

Witchcraft

The Marakwet perspective of witchcraft must be understood in relation to the larger African context. One of the leading authorities on the subject of witchcraft in the west, John Evans Pritchard described witchcraft as a psychic act free from the use of rites, spell, or medicines. In his observation on the Azande of Sudan, he draws a sharp distinction between witchcraft and sorcery; he attributes the use of magic and medicine to the practice of sorcery.[23] Other writers, among them John Middleton, who edited a book on *Witchcraft and Sorcery in East Africa*, make similar distinctions.[24] The Marakwet, however, do not make such distinctions. They use the broader term *kiban*, meaning witchcraft, to describe both terms. For our purpose, we shall use the term witchcraft to refer broadly to all harmful employment of mystical powers.

The training of witchcraft is acquired in diverse ways. Some people are believed to have been born witches, others inherit it from their relatives, and others procure it through material means. The apprenticeship of the art takes a long time to master—sometimes a lifetime. Older witches are, therefore, considered dangerous and are extremely feared.

The practitioners of witchcraft keep their practice in extreme secrecy. They are sometimes referred to as night people. To cast a spell on a victim, the witch is believed to secretly collect all manner of items which had once been in contact with the person. These items may be portions of food, pieces of hair, clothes, feces, finger and toenail clippings, or any other personal effects. These items are used with other articles belonging

---

22. Personal interview with Kisang Kariwotum and my own father, Kisang Kirop Elolia, January 1989.

23. Awolalu, *Yorùbá Beliefs*, 80.

24. Middleton, *Witchcraft and Sorcery*, 27.

to the witch, such as human bones, snakes, tobacco, etc. The success of the practice results either in sickness, bad luck, or death. For that reason, people are afraid to leave any of their personal possessions lying around carelessly, including spit.

Consultation of a witch is not the acceptable norm in Marakwet society. Problems are often solved communally at *Kokwo* and, when that fails, the institution of communal curse is invoked. Individuals who feel betrayed by either of these tools may consult a witch in secrecy. Also, individuals whose intent is to hurt others, for whatever ulterior reason, will resort to a witch practitioner in secret and pay them handsomely, depending on the challenge at hand. Sometimes, witchcraft accusations may be a result of jealousy, suspicion, or pure hatred. If the children of one of the wives in a polygamous marriage prosper while those of the other do not, the latter group would attribute their misfortune to acts of witchcraft by a jealous stepmother.

I was informed about a woman from the village of Kowow who had appeared before the village elders; she had an accusation against her co-wife for causing the death of her first child. It was later discovered that the accused was driven by jealousy to kill. It started when the husband spent more time with the other wife thus neglecting her. Besides, she had a few miscarriages, which she blamed on the other woman.

A *kokwo* was convened at the request of the husband and his family, and the case was brought forth. The accused woman denied any wrongdoing and was brought to an open field in the middle of a hot day. She was fastened to two poles with strings on both of her hands and feet. The strings were stroked repeatedly to induce pain while being interrogated. The procedure continued for three hours while she denied the accusations. Finally, she was asked to take an oath saying:

> May this oath kill me if I witched the son of my co-wife. . . . May this oath return to my accuser if I am innocent.[25]

She was freed after that. I learned that she died a few years later. It is a widespread practice for a person convicted of witchcraft to be killed. However, in cases where there is no strong evidence, the victims are left with an oath. The oath is believed to be a form of a link between the ancestors and the creator, who are believed to know human secrets. This process is believed to take longer, but its effects can impact many generations until it is reversed by restitution through a larger gathering of arbitrators.[26]

---

25. Personal conversation with two Kowow women concerning witchcraft, January 1989.

26. Personal interview with Kochemeitoi Kasenyang, January 1989.

One of the most celebrated stories of witchcraft took place in 1955 in a village in Endo location. In this case, a man (name withheld) was accused of being responsible for the death of his six stepbrothers. Some of the members of the family grew concerned and consulted with two independent diviners. Each time, the diviner pointed a finger at the oldest brother, who lived close to the clan's irrigation furrow. A series of meetings were called to discuss the matter, but the older brother denied the accusations. Witnesses were brought to testify against him. At the final meeting, which was attended by elders from the corners of Endo, Mogoro, and Sambirir, deliberations were drawn, and the accused was found guilty. There was no other solution but to kill him. The surviving brothers were the first to hit the accused, followed by the maternal relatives, *kamana*, as expected. He was hit with sticks and stones until he died. Afterwards they pushed him with sticks into an open ditch, and he was left there to be eaten by hyenas during the night. According to the Marakwet custom, people who die in that manner are neither touched nor given a proper burial. The occasion was celebrated as victory over evil.

When the British Colonial Administration heard of this, they sent some soldiers to the village. The two brothers who participated in the execution were taken to the District Headquarters at Tambach. They were judged by the colonial law and were each given several years in jail with hard labour.[27]

During the colonial era, witchcraft was widely condemned. Similarly, witch-killing in the village was prohibited by the colonial law. Anybody involved in doing so was to be punished. The chiefs and their assistants were instructed to report any accused witches, especially when houses belonging to suspects were set on fire. Instead, the government intervened by sending the suspected witches to jail and relocating them to another area after their release to avoid village rage and attacks.

Today, witchcraft is still practiced despite its negative implications and severe punishment. The exercise is basically a way of projecting a philosophy of life. It is also an attempt to explain the problem of failure, sorrow, misfortune, or death. Awolalu correctly asserts that

> when anxieties and stresses arise in social and domestic life, when things do not go according to plan, when there is barrenness or sterility, depression or misery, ghastly accident or premature death, failure in business, in academic or other pursuits, the Africans pick on witchcraft as the cause. In this

---

27. Personal interview with Ng'elecha Kisang Elolia, March 1989.

way, things that otherwise would have been difficult to explain, easily find explanation.[28]

Most Western scholars influenced by the enlightenment tend to ridicule the African practice of witchcraft, claiming that the cult is an illusion or superstition. Most of those holding this view, especially the missionaries, have argued that Africans will be relieved of the fear of witchcraft when they convert to Christianity. Others thought that beliefs in witchcraft would disappear with Western education and improved medical facilities. Surprisingly enough, that has not been the case, even with all the influence of Western education, Christianity, and technology.

On the other hand, it is rare to find an African who thinks witchcraft is an illusion. One still finds accusations of witchcraft between fellow workers competing for positions, political opponents, and even among contending brothers. Through various personal experiences, most Marakwet are convinced of the reality of witchcraft as an evil and destructive force in society. The practitioners are not easily identified, but they are embedded in society. Their services are constantly sought by those who wish to cause harm to someone who might have wronged them. In my experience in the village, I have never met anyone who identifies himself/herself as a witch, but I have known people who have been accused of the practice. This goes to show that the practice is conducted in secrecy. The majority of witches in Marakwet are women and a few men. In Marakwet

Divination

Divination is the act of obtaining information about unknown happenings and future events from supernatural sources by means of signs and occult techniques. Besides penetrating the unknown and the future, which has been a challenge to humanity from the beginning of time, diviners also detect witches and act as intermediaries between the living and the dead.[29]

The Marakwet diviners are usually men that belong to the category of mystics, since that is their primary objective. However, unlike other healers such as herbalists, diviners can deal with the living dead and general spirits.[30] In some cases, some diviners are possessed by spirits, especially when they infiltrate the spirit world on behalf of clients. During such a time, the diviner loses his own being or sense and becomes an instrument of the spirit

---

28. Awolalu, *Yorùbá Beliefs*, 87.
29. Mbiti, *African Religions*, 171–72.
30. Mbiti, *African Religions*, 172.

in him. He can then be led to act or speak according to the wishes of the spirit. The experience generates ultra-human power, giving the medium the ability to perform both physical and mental activities that would otherwise be extremely difficult. During the possession, useful information is obtained from the spirit world concerning a given matter.[31]

Like most Africans, the Marakwet generally believe that the world is influenced by certain forces such as witchcraft and evil spirits. Thus, to survive, it is expedient to have better control over such powers. The best way to do that is through the diviners, who have been endowed with the powers to detect events. They are to ascertain the proper link to the unseen world of divinity. By virtue of the nature of their office, they are able to know what the ancestors and the Supreme Deity's desire from the people.

Diviners are often consulted in catastrophic situations such as illness, death, failure of crops, and any other misfortune, usually believed to be caused by witchcraft. Normally, diviners do not prescribe cures, but they may divine the mystical cause which itself determines the further steps to be taken. B. E. Kipkorir has classifies some of the methods used by different diviners as follows:

> The client takes milk, preferably obtained from a neighbor. The (diviner) pours a little into the lid of a gourd, examines it and, perhaps after questioning his client, states what he believes to be the cause of the trouble. A second type, known specifically as kibarbaris, (not related to barbarisio) keeps a number of hard objects such as stones in a gourd. On being consulted, he rattles the gourd, pours its contents on the ground and divines from the arrangement. A third type has a bag containing such things as feathers, pieces of cloth and animal skin, which he empties into a bowl of water in order to study their arrangement.[32]

If a diviner, upon consultation, accuses a person of the misfortune of another, the client will take the case to *kokwo*. At *kokwo*, the community elders will have a chance to hear the case and give a fair judgement. If convicted, the accused will be punished accordingly.

The wife of a certain man in Kabarsumba location had several miscarriages and later could not have children. She and her husband consulted a diviner, who confirmed their suspicions of a neighbor's wife who had bewitched them, by closing the wife's womb. Based on this accusation, a *kokwa* was held. The neighbor persisted that she was innocent, which to many seemed to be true. Finally, it was decided not to proceed any further.

31. Mbiti, *Concepts*, 22.
32. Mbiti, *Concepts*, 23.

The elders performed the ritual of incantation, kiseeno, to exhort all members of the two families to live in harmony.

> O let it be sweet (anyin)
> O let it never happen
> Be always spiritual
> Be always at peace.
> Let it be so.[33]

The most common means of divination in Marakwet is through dreams. Here, the diviner is able to foresee the future and prescribe the remedy as it is revealed to them. In most cases, the prescription of a sacrifice is required in order to correct the matter. The offer of sacrifice is to ensure that predictions of good fortune happened and those of ill-fortune are averted.

In 1969, a diviner from Kasagat village dreamt that an enemy was to attack Kaben location from the northeast. The diviner advised the people to sacrifice a black bull within a period of four days. The head of the bull was to be buried on the Pokot border and the chyme to be sprinkled along the borders. This advice fell on unreceptive ears, as there was no one willing to offer a bull for the prescribed sacrifice. Less than two months later, the Pokot raiders, (Ng'oroko), raided by simultaneously crossing from both borders of Chesegon and Kerio rivers.[34] A sizable number of cattle were taken from the Marakwet side, and a few lives were lost in the conflict.

In April 1989, I interviewed one of the famous Endo diviners known as Chemosop. We met at a shopping center in Kabeldemet near his home. In the interview, he remembered that his call to be a diviner started at the age of twenty. By then, he was working at a colonial settler farm in what was commonly known as "The White Highlands," near Eldoret. One night, he had a dream that somebody was going to die. A few days later, someone with whom he worked was injured and died. Soon after that, he had another dream in which he saw himself leading a group of men. A month later, he was promoted to the position of a fore man, responsible over a number of workers.

When he returned to his village, the diviner kept dreaming of things, and they would happen. He admitted that in the early years of his career

---

33. Personal interview with Ngelecha Kisang Elolia, March 1989.

34. "Ngoroko" are identified by the Marakwet as the cattle rustlers from Pokot and Turkana territories. They repeatedly raided the Marakwet area from 1969–80. It was stopped by government intervention through the paramilitary police. The term was later used in Kenyan politics to refer to any subversive group or attitude.

people did not take him seriously. They only believed after the incident had happened.

In another dream or vision, Chemosop was to go and warn the people of Kitony in Embobut location about an impending disaster. To prevent the disaster, he was told to tell the people to prepare honey beer. The honey was to be obtained from the home of one Lotekemetwa, and a cow was to be sacrificed from the home of another man, named Lopusinyony. Some parts of the cow and the beer were to be offered to the local ancestors, who had been displeased.

Chemosop sent the message to the elders of Kitony, asking them to do exactly what was revealed. Some of the Kitony elders dismissed the idea mockingly, asking for the diviner to deliver his own message in person. When Chemosop arrived, a big crowd had gathered to hear him speak. Unfortunately, he was dismissed and driven away. A year later, the diviner reported that a boy had disappeared from Kitony and had not been found. The diviner was convinced that the river spirits (*ilot*) had taken him as a punishment for the people's disobedience to take his (diviner's) instructions.[35]

Often trusted diviners are taken seriously, but there are cases when self-styled diviners have gone around deceiving people for gain. A good example is Tuliangole of Katilit, who later converted to Christianity in 1985 and was an active Christian elder in Cherutich Church. In conversation with me, he admitted that he had gone as far as Kericho territory collecting unlawful fees on the pretence of being a diviner. His motivation was purely material gain. Thankfully, he acknowledged and amended his ways and regained his respectful place as a respected elder in his community.

Most of the diviners in Marakwet are paid an average of Sh.200 ($2) for private consultations. However, in more complicated cases, the fee is a bit higher. It also depends on the economic worth of the client. The payment can be made in grain or livestock. In situations where diviners are shown visions to warn the whole community, monetary payments are not demanded. As members of the community, it is the diviner's rightful duty to render their services for the good of the land.

Oaths (*muuma*)

Muuma is a powerful instrument of justice and is used only in the most extreme cases. It is a last resort when there has been a failure to find an acceptable solution to a dispute. Traditionally, the Marakwet had no chiefs or

---

35. Personal interview with Mr. Chemosop, a diviner from Koibirir location, March 1989.

kings. However, law and order were maintained through the elder's council. In severe cases where the accused denies responsibility, the most extreme measures of the oath are administered as a last resort.

The administration of *muma* depends on the seriousness of the case and the characters of the people involved. This also determines the material symbols to be used in the ritual. The respected seniors of good reputation usually administered the rite. In administering ordinary oaths, a gate is made and personal effects of those involved are placed on top of the gate. Sometimes, spears are planted on both sides of the gate. The accused or defendant must pass through the gate saying, "If I lie, I shall never see the new green grass spring up." The same process is repeated with the other party.[36]

The more serious oath precludes young men and women who have not passed the stage of menopause. In this case, the elders (with grey hair) mark out a path in their midst of approximately twenty meters in length. Both the accused and the accuser must pass along the path carrying a white stone (*Sengwet*) saying, "Should I be lying, I shall obtain no property and if I have a wife, she will be childless, and I shall die or live a solitary life all my days."[37]

In a dispute over livestock, such as claims of a cow or a sheep in another's possession, the one in possession will slit the ears of the disputed animal so that it runs madly, sprinkling blood on the ground. The claimant will then be welcomed to take the oath animal if he is innocent. Should this claim be false, he will die within a year. After this time, the animal will be returned to its original owner. Should he by any means fall sick or experience any other misfortune in his family, he will automatically link it to the oath. He will then return the animal, confess to the elders, and ask them to perform another ritual to neutralize and reverse the powers of the oath. In this case, a sheep must be sacrificed, and its blood used to cleanse the convicted victim.

Another kind is the oath of peace (*miis*), taken as a commitment to peace by two warring tribes. The ritual requires a sacrificial animal whose blood is applied on specific items common to both parties. When my father was growing up, this ritual was rarely used but it has happened in my time more frequently to bring peace between the Marakwet and the Pokot. The elders of both tribes would meet at their common land boundary. After negotiating and agreeing to the grounds for peace, a sheep is killed to seal the agreement. A long sinew is extracted from the animal's foreleg, and the representatives of each tribe are invited to hold on to either end of it. The sinew is then cut in half, and each side will depart with half. It is believed that the tribe who breaks the peace treaty (*mis*) will suffer not only defeat in war, but also social misfortunes. The latter requires a blessing which is commonly known as *kise'eno*, which is the next topic.

36. Personal interview with Ng'elecha Kisang Elolia, March 1989.
37. Personal interview with Ng'elecha Kisang Elolia, March 1989.

Incantation (*kise'eno* or *ayebisio*)

Incantation is a rite involving prayer offering in chants purported to have special appeal before the divine powers. Sometimes, the words are coupled with charms to enhance and increase their vitality for better results. Normally, the rite is done by those with good moral standing. Incantations are used on different occasions for separate purposes to preserve harmony or promote restoration of relationships. Practical examples range from a woman having a protracted child-birth labour to a settling of family disputes.

Before a man sets out on a journey, it was customary for him to gather his neighbors and request their prayers for safety and success. The leader stands up holding a piece of ritual plant and begins to open with general words to address God and the needs of the person requesting God's blessings. After that, he leads the audience in an incantation.

Marakwet	English Translation
Aa le nyone, le nyone	It is so
Aa anyin. Anyin	It is sweet
Aa Baibai. Baibai	Happy
Aa Le chi anum	May this person . . . (qualification)
Aa Anyin, aa rutor	Have a successful trip
Aa Inyoru, aa kelyen	We wish you luck
Aa lmila! Aa Irotu	Return
Aa Katongung	To your home
Aa Torokun aa lakokuk	Come back to your children
Aa Isutu aa berur	Bring back blessings
Aa sere. Aa sere! Sere!	Blessings. Blessings!
Anyin, baibai, sere	Sweetness, happiness, blessings[38]

All the people present spit on a bowl that contains ritual leaves/grass. The collected mixture of saliva in the ritual leaves/grass is sprinkled or splashed generously over the disputants while the elder utters incantations of reconciliation and harmony thus:

> May there be harmony
> May the bad go away
> May it never happen again

38. Personal interview with Lobokong'ar Kwananyang', March 1989.

Let there be peace
Let it be so.[39]

Incantations may be used on any occasion without necessarily any overt need, but simply to offer blessings (*sere*) and happiness (*baibai*). A man who suspects that he is unpopular may brew beer and invite his adult neighbors over. Over the beer, he will explain his worries. The elders will give him words of encouragement, followed by incantations to wish him well. The incantation constitutes a binding oath that the participants will let him live at peace with neighbors. Any animosity that might have existed will no longer be there. Further, the incantations are supposed to give him good luck with people to increase his popularity.[40]

Before I left Kenya for Canada my father invited a few people from the community to come and give me their blessings. After enjoying a good meal, the occasion was concluded with incantations directed by one of the elders, Mr. Ng'imor from Cheptulel. He made a big ring out of a creeping plant (*seretyon*) and put it around my neck. He then took another green plant and recited incantations accompanied by spittle to bless me for a safe and fruitful journey. I was blessed.

Healers

The Marakwet generally perceive illness and misfortune from a religious point of view. In fact, they consider bodily disease to be caused by either supernatural or natural phenomena. Mbiti calls it physical and psychological or physical and spiritual.[41]

The natural illnesses are those stemming from biological pathology such as malaria, while the supernatural/spiritual are those caused by someone directly or indirectly using mystical powers such as sorcery, curse, or witchcraft. The supernatural also includes those sicknesses that come because of disobedience to the ancestors or the Supreme Deity. Sometimes it is difficult to tell whether a sickness is naturally or supernaturally transmitted. For example, malaria might be attributed to a mosquito bite, but the patient might still want to know why it bit him and not another person. This gives room for speculating on the possibility that someone sent the mosquito to sting that individual by means of supernatural manipulations.

---

39. Personal interview with Ng'elecha Kisang Elolia, March 1989.
40. Kipkorir and Welbourn, *Marakwet*, 15.
41. Mbiti, *African Religions*, 169.

In seeking treatment for the sick, the Marakwet healer will, therefore, try to determine the cause through various means.[42] The healers, who might be either male or female, are also aware of the religious dimensions of illness; therefore, they make necessary attempts to meet the need from a religious approach. Some of the activities involved in dealing with such illnesses in Marakwet are spiritually and psychologically vital and obviously play a significant role in healing the sick. In this case, the means are less important than the end.

Most of the illnesses on the supernatural or impersonal level are thought to be caused by *ngoki* (sin). This is indirect or direct disobedience to God, often through the infringement of moral rules. On this level, causation is thought to involve the agency of spirits, the ancestors, or directly from the Supreme Deity.

Therefore, in explaining the cause of illnesses, the Marakwet usually begin with a primary definition of the illnesses, which is natural. If that is not sufficient, they will then move onto the supernatural level. In this sense, the developmental process of the illness begins at the "how" and proceeds on to the "why" levels. Sometimes both biological and supernatural causation are combined in one individual's ailments. In such cases, the treatment is given with consideration to the two levels of causation.

Supernatural or spiritual related illnesses are rather complicated and cannot be dealt with by empirical treatment. A common illness in this group is that caused by "people with evil eyes." Usually, in this case some men and women discover to their horror that they have "evil eyes." Merely looking at an object or a person, without any overt intention on the part of the looker, may cause harm. Stories have been reported of how certain people have walked into a house and, upon looking at a gourd, the gourd bursted. Small children have also fallen sick because of someone casting an evil eye on them. The most common sign of an evil eye is the development of rashes (*kiberber*) on the exposed part of the body, especially the head. Traditionally, babies are covered to prevent stranger's evil eye. If by chance the baby is not covered, the person with an evil eye will spit on it and say *imilda* (defeat me; do not let me harm you). If people know that they have evil eyes, they announce the fact on arrival at a homestead, and the inhabitants hold before them a skin or pot of water on which they can gaze.[43] In doing so, the evil is temporarily transferred to the said items.

---

42. "Healer" is used here generally to refer to those specialists interested in human health and welfare such as herbalists and diviners.

43. Sometimes worms are left in the water to show the powerfulness of the evil in the person's eyes. See also Kipkorir and Welbourn, *Marakwet*, 18.

Another example of supernatural related illness is the person with a mental problem (*chewosot/chebiywo*). This term covers a wide range of conditions, from mild psychological disturbance to complete madness. One type of *chewosot* is said to develop from any disease which enters the head and spoils it. Such mental illness is treated with material medicines only. However, most mental illnesses may be perceived to result from supernatural causations such as witchcraft, sorcery, or a curse. It may also result directly from displeased spirits. In such cases, a healer takes preventive measures by supplying the clients with countermeasures. These would include performing rituals, supplying charms, or administering medicines that are swallowed or rubbed into the body.[44] In the case of sin (*ng'oki*), the patient must confess and receive the appropriate cleansing ritual.

It is the duty of the medicine experts to rid community of witches, detect sorcery, remove curses, and control the spirits and the ancestors. They are believed to have access to the forces of nature and other forms of knowledge unknown to the public. The public, therefore, entrusts them with the duty of protecting the community from any impending danger.[45] The duties of the medicine experts are varied and sometimes overlap. In the Northern part of Marakwet, the medicine-man also doubles as a diviner or "reed blower" (*kipses*). These people seek to discover the cause of an illness, diagnose its nature, and apply the right treatment to treat the illness or prevent its recurrence.

Most of the experts in Marakwet can be categorized as herbalists (*chepsagitin/chepkirichin*). Their objectives include curing, restoring, and preserving health. They employ different substances from material medicine (*materia medica*) to treat or prevent disease. These include plants, leaves, roots, barks, animal parts, and minerals.

In all the cases, herbalists have some magical words to accompany the preparation and the administration of their herbs. When collecting their medicine in the forest, herbalists normally invoke the spirits of the ancestors. At other times, they recite incantations, while on other occasions they do not speak until they have returned home with their medicine. In this way, medicine is believed to carry some potency to cure the sick. The patient who is prescribed to wear a ring or an amulet or to apply a special powder into the incised portion of his body, believes definitively that the medicine is charged with mysterious powers. Because of these beliefs, the treatment is shrouded in mystery.

While the practice of healing is done by both men and women, the women seem to be the majority. Traditionally, all medicine experts acquire

---

44. Mbiti, *African Religions*, 170.
45. Mbiti, *African Religions*, 170.

their knowledge from their family line, and the skill is passed on from parent to child, potentially extending many generations. There are a few occasions where an herbalist claims to have been called into their profession by the spirit of a certain ancestor.

The apprenticeship usually begins at an early age, with a parent taking the child to the forest to observe the nature of the herbs. At a later age, they are allowed to practice under close supervision of an expert until they are confident enough to practice on their own.

The success of a *chepsagitian* (sing) depends on the ability in both diagnosis and treatment. Her knowledge of plants is vast. Should she discover that symptoms are best treated with certain herbs, she tries to keep this knowledge to herself. For this reason, she collects her herbs in secret. When my maternal grandmother went out to look for herbs, she made sure that no one knew what she was doing. She often pretended that she was collecting wild vegetable or firewood but in reality, she was looking for medicinal plants. Also, as she sets forth to the forest to look for the herbs, she listens to nature, attuned to make sure that good omens are on her side. For instance, striking a stone with her right toe is a sign that she will find whatever herbs she is searching. On the other hand, if her left toe strikes a stone, her quest that day will be fruitless. Often when that happens, the trip is cancelled. Similarly, the landing location of a woodpecker symbolizes the same misfortunes.

Medicine experts are believed to treat almost all kinds of ailments using herbs and other methods, such as massage, or scarification. If a person does not receive a cure from one herbalist, the family may consult another herbalist or a diviner.[46] Many abdominal ailments are managed by using herbs to soothe or induce the patient to vomit. It is believed that the forces which cause illness are brought down when one vomits. An excess of acid or stomach worms are expelled with purgative medicine.

The Marakwet also use the method of scarification (*wetisio*). This is done only by experts who know how to apply the right concoctions of medicine on the cut. The medicine is usually in powder form, often the ash of particular shrubs mushrooms or animal parts. Vertical incisions are made on specific regions of the body. The powder is then rubbed into the body. This method is used for illnesses which are not located in the alimentary canal or on the surface of the body.

Bonesetters are another commonly used technique of treatment. When a bone is dislocated, it is set back. They use bark splints, skin casts, and wet leather string to keep fractured bones in place. The powdered bark

---

46. Modern medicine is just an alternative when traditional methods fail.

of cedar is used for cushioning.[47] For swellings, a wide thick leaf is warmed on the fire and then applied gently onto the affected surface.

A form of massage is used for treating abdominal uneasiness and fatigue or "stiff muscles," as the Marakwet call it. In most cases, bare hands are used for gently rubbing the stomach repeatedly with the help of a slippery liquid from the bark of a particular tree. This is repeated four times to complete a dose. Most birth attendants use this method to manipulate the abdomen of a pregnant woman in order to set the baby in the right direction.

In cases that require a surgical operation to remove a tumor or set broken bones, the Marakwet have surgeons. There are few of them because the apprenticeship takes several years to master. The establishment of modern health facilities has also contributed to the decline of traditional surgeons. Nonetheless, the few that are available are mostly found in Marakwet East where there are no good hospitals. Most of the traditional surgeons in that region are known for their expertise as head surgeons. They still use crude instruments and herbal concoctions in their surgical intervention (*trepanning*). Some surgeons can graft bones from bigger animals to set a fractured human skull.

In the process of *trepanning*, broken bones are removed. The Marakwet surgeons use antiseptics made from leaves which are crushed or chewed into a paste. This stops infection. There is also a particular sap used to prevent flies from landing on the wound. *Trepanning* is also performed to release evil, which is believed to cause sickness.[48] When someone experiences severe and continuous headaches, a cut is made with a razor on the forehead so that the blood pressure is reduced, thus relieving the patient of pain.[49] Usually, when any of the treatments are carried out, prayers are offered simultaneously to the creator who is believed to help the patient recover quickly. The patient is given the best food available to speed up recovery and is never left alone. Members of the family, friends, and relatives take turns to care for and give their moral support.

---

47. While bone-setting is the work of the adult men, women often assist in the care of the patient.

48. The Marakwet surgeons use plant and animal fibers to stitch cuts and hence speed up recovery.

49. The impure blood comes out, thus leaving the patient clean. This process is used to replenish the blood.

General Sacrifices

Sacrifice is the act through which a relationship is established and maintained between the human and the divine through the efficacy of material objects. Turner describes sacrifice as a symbolic action intended to restore the relationship between two parties. Sacrifice must, therefore, be the product of faith in the supernatural and its power. Its sacredness and action bring about a change which benefits the sacrificer.[50]

The objects used for sacrifices are usually familiar. The most common are animals—their blood becomes the gate-way through which the relationship flows in both directions. The blood from the animal is visible proof that the sacrifice has been offered. Of all the physical elements in an animal, blood has been deemed the actual life and must be rendered back to God. Its special quality gives it the efficacy to reconcile two parties. Sacrifices are handled ritually because they are religious acts. This is the reason why menstruation and childbirth—both involving blood—are considered religiously unclean.[51] The act of sacrifice is, therefore, a religious expression of great significance between both the supernatural and humanity. It keeps the people's faith alive and active.

The offering of sacrifices is widespread practice in Marakwet. There are sacrifices that are offered exclusively by men, women, or children. These sacrifices are made on special occasions at locations. Some are offered during the rite of passage, planting season, and specific ritual moments. The sacrifices can be divided into two distinct categories, namely the sacrifices of good husbandry and the sacrifices of crisis. I shall now examine each of the categories separately.

Sacrifices of Good Husbandry

The sacrifices of good husbandry are marked by celebratory spirit. They occur when a person, or a group of people, experiences a good yield in their crops. A lamb is provided to celebrate the harvest, usually the first harvest of the season. The lamb must be of one color and in perfect condition. A man whose firstborn is a girl is invited to perform the ceremonial ritual of killing the animal and then offers the prayer of thanksgiving. This is based on the belief that the man associated with a daughter symbolizes humility

---

50. Turner, "Sacrifice," 190.
51. Ashby, *Sacrifice*, 24.

and peaceful acts as opposed to war acts often associated with males. As a result, their hands are considered clean.[52]

These celebrations of feasting with a lamb as a sacrificial act of thanksgiving are repeated every year after a good harvest. After four years a bigger feast, called *mooy*, is celebrated at designated sacred locations in the community. The young uninitiated girls dance the whole day while the parents and men watch. The girls are usually decorated with white ochre, applied on their bodies in magnificent designs.[53] *Mooy* used to be widely celebrated in Marakwet has declined since the arrival of the Protestant missionaries. Now, it is only practised in a few places by those who have not converted to Protestantism.

When livestock is prospering, a special sacrifice is made to the divinities. This also is celebrated with great joy by everyone. One of the important practices under this category is the killing of the firstborn of a goat or sheep at four months old. The ritual is expressed thus: *kakileb wawa mwatian*,[54] This celebration is confined within the family. To ensure continued health and the fertility of the stock, another ceremony is performed. The roots of the morgut plant are crushed, mixed with water and special soil applied over the animals each morning for a period of four days. A young girl of about thirteen years old is asked to perform this rite. No visitor is allowed within the homestead during those four days of ritual.

The Sacrifices of Crisis

Sacrifices arose out of the need to deal with estrangement from the divine powers resulting from sin. In this case, therefore, the sacrifice acts to put things right and avert the expected danger. Failure to do so might result in trouble in the land; often the consequences manifest themselves in the form of sickness, floods, droughts, or locust invasions.

To determine a plan of action, a diviner is approached and asked to consult the oracles and prescribe the appropriate sacrifices.[55] The oracle

---

52. I could not find any reason for this requirement, apart from the supposition that such men are more peaceable. This concurs with the symbol often attributed to women—as harmless and less aggressive. Some of the men in this category qualify as rainmakers and general ritual leaders.

53. The notion of associating sacrifices with girls symbolizes peace, humility, and absence of aggressiveness.

54. Kipkorir and Welbourn, *Marakwet*, 33.

55. The consulting of oracles plays a vital part in *Marakwet's* religious life. Through oracles precautionary measures are taken to prevent imminent danger and disaster. Before a person undertakes a journey or executes a planned important action, he or

may reveal what offenses have been perpetrated by an individual or community. Sometimes, calamities are not due to wrong-doing or negligence, but because evil spirits have used their powers to harm others. In such cases, sacrifices are usually prescribed to propitiate evil spirits.

The sacrificial animals vary in accordance with their function.[56] However, they must always be of uniform color, without bruises or cuts and must be blameless *(lubwob)*. This idea corresponds with the Jewish Levitical sacrifices:

> If anyone of the ordinary people among you sins unintentionally in doing any one of the things that by the Lord's commandments ought not to be done and incurs guilt, when the sin that you have committed is made known to you, you shall bring a female goat without blemish as your offering, for the sin that you have committed. You shall lay your hand on the head of the purification offering; the purification offering shall be slaughtered at the place of the burnt offering. The priest shall take some of its blood with his finger and put it on the horns of the altar of burnt offering, and he shall pour out the rest of its blood at the base of the altar. He shall remove all its fat, as the fat is removed from the sacrifice of well-being, and the priest shall turn it into smoke on the altar for a pleasing odor to the Lord. Thus, the priest shall make atonement on your behalf, and you shall be forgiven. (Lev 4:27–31)

The preparation of the sacrifice must be done according to ritual prescriptions in which the officiating person must satisfy a certain criterion, such as being the father of a first-born girl, as mentioned previously. Moreover, they are worthy and acceptable before the Supreme Deity who is holy, peace-loving, and just. It is expected of them to observe certain taboos and code of conduct such as avoidance of certain foods, conflicts, and fights. The man must be ritually clean, faithful, and sincere, and bear no malice against anybody.

The sacrifices are often offered in isolated and consecrated areas such as forests, rocks, or hills. The expert, accompanied by the people concerned, leads the sacrificial animal at a given time to the place of sacrifice. Upon arrival, the ritual leader kills the animal as instructed and offers the blood

---

she must consult the oracle regarding the future and what dangers may lie ahead, and for guidance to obviate and change them. Neglect to do so may result in unpleasant consequences.

56. The victim acts as a symbol corresponding to the intent of the sacrifice: some require a goat, others a sheep or even a cow.

as libation to the deities. This is often followed by invocations, so the divine personalities may hear and accept the sacrifice.

The sacrificial animal is then dispersed in different directions. The blood, which is regarded as an indispensable constituent of the whole event, is scattered around the area. The nucleus of life of an animal is believed to be its blood, and when this life is offered, another life is expected in exchange: they want the deity to accept the offered blood or life of the animal so that the supplicant may live long and enjoy prosperity. This is in agreement with the Yoruba beliefs as described by J. O. Awolalu that;

> The divinities and the spirits therefore drink blood, and this is their main share of the sacrificial victims. And when they take blood, they are believed to have taken the whole victim because when blood is drained from a living creature it dies. Blood, it is believed, invokes the pleasure and the blessing of the divinities and the spirits and blots out sins and averts illness and death.[57]

The chyme is ceremonially scattered over the area, similarly to the blood. Some of the chyme is put on the bodies of the people on whose behest the sacrifice was offered. Finally, the rest of the meat is roasted and shared amongst everyone. Some parts are dispersed in various directions in the hope that the ancestors will be able to eat them.

After the prolonged drought of 1985, which devastated the Marakwet crops, the elders of Kowow in Endo location decided to perform a sacrifice for rain. The place chosen was above the escarpment under a tree near the Embobut River. The ritual leaders were chosen from the two clans who shared the same furrow *arakapterik*. They had officiated at such rituals before and knew exactly how to conduct this one so that no detail of the sacred act would be missed.

Everyone assembled at around midday. The ritual elders girded their clothes around their waists and began the ritual by killing the goat. The stomach was cut open and the bowels emptied. Each elder took part of the stomach content (chyme) and threw it towards the sky. They asked *ASIS* to provide rain, fertility, and good health. The rest of the meat was roasted. Tiny pieces were cut from the internal organs (liver, kidneys, and heart) and scattered around for the ancestors who were believed to attend as unseen guests. Some pieces were thrown towards the main river for the spirits of the river *ilot*. At the same time, one of the elders stood and led an invocation requesting rain.

---

57. Awolalu, *Yorùbá Beliefs*, 92.

Marakwet	English Translation
Soruech na we chibo kaptoyi	Rescue us, man of the river
kole nee si kuyam kore	Why do you let the land get dry?
acha we, nukech!	Moisten us
anyinita kore!	Make the land sweet
konech berur!	Bless us

When the prayer had been completed, the people sat in a semi-circle. The rest of the meat was then distributed and eaten. The sacrificial act was believed to have forged a strong relationship between the Supreme Being, ASIS, and the people. ASIS will remember his/her people and see to it that they are helped in their need.

There are no specific days scheduled for worship in African Traditional religion as other religions like Christianity and Islam, but religion permeates all of life. This affirms Mbiti's statement that Africans are notoriously religious.[58] This religiosity is not practiced in isolation but rather within the concrete relationship with which the individual finds himself or herself within the culture.

In the practice of religion, the Marakwat utilize all the supernatural and metaphorical power at their disposal. They can communicate with the unseen world by interpreting the seen. Somehow in the process, the unseen world of spirits intermingles with the world of living constantly. For traditionalists, the living dead are a constant form of reference for all important activities. Their favor is being always sought. Similarly, the Supreme Being, who is the ultimate resort, is frequently sought to assist in daily life. The Western missionaries have interrupted some aspects of the traditional life, but they have not uprooted it.

---

58. Mbiti, *African Religions*, 1.

CHAPTER 4

Marakwet Encounter with the British Colonials and Missionaries

Marakwet Resistance to the British of Ribo Post

THE BRITISH COLONIAL RULE in Kenya was established in several stages from 1895 to 1963. As the conquest advanced, it increasingly became violent reaching its climax when Africans resisted. There were episodes of African resistance through the colonial century. The process of control was uneven. Sometimes it would begin with compliance in one instance and coercive in the next. Either way, the British soon discovered, that their level of success depended upon African allies and confederates enhanced by their communication and organizational strategies. The railway line from Mombasa to Uganda opened the colony up for easy management, and the British government money was loaned to construct and protect it. However, further away from the railway line, the native populations lived their lives with little interruption except for tax collection, ivory trade, Christianization, and the recruitment of workers for settler farms.[1]

In those years, the territory under Uganda protectorate which included Nakuru in the Rift Valley was the home of the Kalenjin people and was colonized from a colonial post at Eldama Ravine. A Maltese ex-soldier James Martin who had previously worked for Joseph Thompson in charge of human resource and material supplies was appointed the District Commissioner in Eldama Ravine. Although he was reputed to be the only District Commissioner who could neither read nor write, he utilized his organizational skills to recruit Nubians from Sudan as soldiers (Askari) for the colony.[2]

1. Lonsdale, "Conquest State of Kenya."
2. Hennings, *African Morning*, 29.

The Kalenjin did not take kindly to the provocative intrusions of the British rule and were constantly on the look-out. After all, before the arrival of the British, they had been independent groups, controlling their own economy and a large territory of flat fertile land which they generously appropriated to graze and grow crops. Also, prior to the arrival of the Europeans the Kalenjin had interacted with Arab trade caravans for a half a century.

The Arab traders had traversed the territory from the coast to the Rift Valley and Northwards along Kerio Valley all the way to lake Turkana in search of ivory. They knew when and where to purchase food supplies for themselves and their porters along the way. However, to maximize profits, the traders organized a band of porters to carry trading goods into the interior and return with ivory, leopard, and crocodile skins leaving no space for food.

> Food had to be obtained from the local natives to feed the porters; for it was the regular practice of the traders to load them up with trade goods on the outward journey, and with ivory on the return journey, to rely on what they could get up-country to bring them back alive to the coast.[3]

In addition to the ivory cargo, the traders captured (kidnapped) young women and children and brought them to the coast where they were sold or traded. British colonial administrator R. O. Hennings states:

> Sometimes, too, the hunters carried with them young girls and boys of the of the up-country tribes, destined for domestic slavery in the rich Arab mansions and plantations at the coast, where the sultan of Zanzibar held sway.[4]

In the mid-1970s, an old man by the name of Lokitel returned to his village of Kitony village, Kaben location and retold the ordeal of his capture by the Arabs in Kerio Valley and slave labor in different Arab homes. One of the noted among the Arab traders was Sadi Ben Abedi whom at one point controlled the Kerio Valley ivory trade. The Swahili traders would sell the ivory to the British at a profit or to other buyers in Asia. Soon the British got interested in the ivory trade and tried to push out the Arab traders. The competition drove the traders deeper in Kerio Valley along the elephant path (*ara beel*) in search of a bigger and better supply of quality ivory tusks. Profits were maximized in pioneering fresh fields where there was little competition. The success of finding good ivory came through local intelligence and a network of collaborators in the local communities.

3. Hennings, *African Morning*, 17.
4. Hennings, *African Morning*, 18.

In the protection of their commercial interests, traders guarded their knowledge of the most profitable remote regions by diverting traders or exaggerating the dangers of local atrocities to discourage outsiders. For instance, Sadi Bin Abedi misled Englishmen with false information about the Pokot atrocities in Baringo. The goal was to keep Europeans out of the ivory hunting grounds.[5] Also, the Arab traders replenished their food supply by buying grain from Marakwet farmers and at the same time discouraged them from selling the same to the British.

At that time Kerio Valley was part of Uganda territory under the protection of the imperial British armed forces.[6] In 1899, Sir Harry Johnson, the special commissioner for the Uganda British Protectorate, adopted an environmental policy to protect the endangered wildlife in Kerio Valley, especially the elephants. As noted earlier, the ivory trade was rampant, and traders were not paying taxes at government post at Eldama Ravine as expected. Johnson became aware of that and planned to stop the illegal trade. Sir Harry Johnson planned to create a game reserve scheme along the Kerio river from Lakes Baringo and Turkana to preserve the already depleted herds of game from marauding hunters. Big settlers such as Lord Delamere, who were notorious hunters of the big game, were not happy with Johnson's conservation plans and worked hard to undermine them. Johnson was adamant and to advance his plan he established a government post in Kerio Valley at Ribo near Koloa that would be run by a Sudanese Sergeant Major and a garrison of African police. The objective was to impose heavy taxes on ivory to discourage elephant hunting. However, the approval of Johnson's plan from the foreign office in London was delayed till April 1900.

For the plan to succeed, the British needed an assurance of a steady source of food supply. Earlier on, they had established a post among the Il Chamus at Lake Baringo where grain was in good supply due to advanced irrigation systems. The British had knowledge of another group within Kerio valley that had an impressive irrigation system and a good supply of grain.

> Trading Caravans made use of allies at whose stations they stopped to refuel (grain, donkeys, etc) in the northern hinterland, the most important of those allies were the Il Chamus,

---

5. The corridor along Kerio River, otherwise known as Kerio Valley stretches from the South all the way to lake Turkana covering the land occupied by the Keiyo, Tugen, Marakwet, Pokot, and Turkana. The ivory in this area attracted Arab Caravans from as far as the Coast and Abysinia (Ethiopia).

6. In the early 1970s, he tried to make verbal claims of that territory, but President Kenyatta told him that he was well prepared to defend Kenyan territory. Idi Amin discontinued his threats.

better known as Njemps of lake Baringo. A little farther north from the Il Chamus were the Marakwet who sophisticated irrigation system and probably more surplus grain for purchase by the itinerant travelers.[7]

On his way back from Lake Victoria in 1884, Joseph Thomson stopped at Lake Baringo and crossed over to Marakwet territory. He was the first European to record the Marakwet irrigation furrows. He recounts his experience of camping there for a few days and the natives extorted a bribe from him and when he did not comply, the natives attempted to divert the water from the source. They paid up and the water was released.

> In camping here, we found we had delivered ourselves into the hands of the philistines. The natives at once put the screw upon us to extort a large bribe (*hongo*). Seeing us hesitate, they quietly retired, and the water with them-for they could easily divert it in its upper curse. This was quite sufficient to produce the desired effect.[8]

Similarly, the Austrian Karl Peters who had explored lake Rudolph (today's lake Turkana) traveled back along Kerio river. When their food ran out, they sneaked into Marakwet fields and harvested their ready grain. When the Marakwet found them in their fields, they attacked and injured several of Peters men. Judging from the two accounts it is possible that the British feared the Marakwet. On the other hand, unlike other Kalenjin groups the Pokot had been friendly to the British. They voluntarily paid their taxes on a relatively timely basis. They might have had other reasons for doing so but the colonial government saw that compliance positively. Finally, there is a possibility that the British did not distinguish the Pokot from the Marakwet and their territories, which at that time was difficult for a foreigner to distinguish. Whatever, the reasons, the British did not station their post on the Marakwet side of River Kerio. Instead, they chose to put it on the Pastoralist Pokot side with a plan to obtain the needed grain from Marakwet.

When the approval for the new post was granted, Johnson assigned a European officer Harold Hyde-Baker to proceed, with immediate effect, to Kerio Valley and establish a government post at Ribo as the first of a chain along Kerio Valley to lake Turkana/Rudolf. Hyde-Baker was dispatched from Eldama Ravine with less than eighty men, most of whom equipped with Snider and Remington rifles. The journey was described as difficult due to the scarcity of food and water. It had proved impossible to procure

7. Kipkorir, *Descent*, 389.
8. Kipkorir, *Descent*, 390.

grain along the way so the Caravan relied on the little game they could hunt along the way.[9] On arrival at Ribo, the local Pokot had little food, forcing Hyde Baker to look for food purchase in Marakwet. That was not to happen either because the British had gathered that the Arab traders had poisoned the Marakwet minds with their propaganda against the British.[10] For some reasons, the Marakwet listened to the Arab caravan traders and refused to trade with the British. The Swahili traders disliked the presence of the British in their trading zones and were successful in fermenting the same among the natives with whom they traveled and traded.[11]

Within a few days of their arrival at Ribo, two of Hyde-Baker's porters were speared to death by the Pokot. Fearing a full-scale attack, Hyde-Baker requested assistance from Ravine and from the Il Chamus in Baringo, with whom he had earlier established a good rapport. In April 1900, the new commander at Ravine, Archibald Bagnall, who was described as belligerent and headstrong, received the devastating report and was furious. He advocated a violent revenge against Africans who did not cooperate with the British goals. He notified Johnson in Kampala of his plan and took his force of forty-five *Askaris* and forty-two Il Chamus warriors from Lake Baringo. Bagnall took the native's reluctance to trade with the British as a direct challenge. His response was swift and brutal. Two attacks were directed against villages that had refused to sell food to Hyde-Baker. Almost two thousand sheep and goats were confiscated in the first attack and eight hundred sheep and a large quantity of grains in the second.[12] The Marakwet villagers were driven out of their homes into the safety of the hills above them.

It was Bagnall's second attack that signaled a victory for the British. Bagnall's ruthless attack seemed to have succeeded when a group of elders came to settle with Hyde-Baker. The Marakwet elders agreed to trade

---

9. Lonsdale, "Conquest State of Kenya."

10. Bagnall confirmed Hyde-Baker's mistrust of Swahili traders when he noticed that the Swahili traders nearby were freely trading for a large quantity of locally grown grains while Hyde-Baker was not getting any.

11. While the Swahili traders might partly be blamed, Hyde-Baker had a very limited range of trading goods which was mainly inferior beads. It may also be possible that the local communities did not have surplus grains to furnish both Europeans and the Swahili Caravans.

12. The British colonial writers had difficulties distinguishing the Endo Marakwet from the Pokot of Cheptuleel because both shared common features and cultural practices. However, the distinctions were known between the two groups. Moreover, they have been historical rivals over livestock and grazing grounds. Contrary to the British report, it was the Endo of Marakwet and not Cheptuleel Pokot who overpowered and slaughtered a company of nearly fifty Nubian police and subsequently stormed a government outpost at Kollowa by Kerio river.

with the British and not with the Arab/Swahili Caravans. Although the Swahili traders were responsible for Hyde-Baker's predicament, they were not punished other than a fine of three cows. Bagnall returned to Ravine, taking with him his forty-five soldiers and the grain and livestock that was confiscated from the Marakwet.

After that show of force, the relationship between Hyde-Baker and the Marakwet deteriorated further. At the same time, the shortage of food continued to persist, and when it became difficult for Hyde-Baker to acquire sufficient food for his eighty men, they resorted to stealing. With the encouragement of his boss at Ravine, Hyde-Baker decided to send out forty-two of his Nubian *Askaris* to cross over the Kerio river into the Marakwet farms to steal the grain in the early hours of the day. They had taken some beads to pay in case they were caught. Upon noticing the soldiers on their farms, the Marakwet sounded the war alarm. Within a short moment, the Marakwet warriors from every village had assembled, and surrounded the colonial government soldiers (*Askaris*) and wiped them out. None was spared and their bodies and weapons were never to be found by the British.

As if that was not enough punishment, the Marakwet warriors, numbering several hundred strong, proceeded to attack Ribo Post and flushed out the remaining ten *Askaris* and eight porters of Hyde-Baker. Hyde Baker took cover in the bush. Some of Hyde-Baker's remaining men travelled all night to seek help from the Il Chamus Maasai warriors from Lake Baringo. The Il Chamus responded and sent a force of over sixty warriors. They reached Ribo post on July 4th, 1900, and succeeded in repulsing the Marakwet siege. Eldama Ravine did not respond to Hyde-Baker's cry until six months later because all the available military forces had been deployed to deal with the Nandi Resistance. Others guarded the stock captured from the Nandi, while others protected the station from possible Tugen attacks.[13]

In January 1901, the British launched a punitive attack on the Marakwet. The British force led by Captain E. H. Gorges consisted of five European officers, two companies of the Uganda Rifles, and nearly six hundred recruits drawn from Uasin-Gishu and Il Chamus Maasai. The latter were brought from Lake Baringo. The British attack was well-coordinated. Beginning at dawn they attacked one village after another village in the two locations of Mogoro and Endo. The "very drastic punishment" meted out by this patrol was among the most brutal of any punitive expedition in the colonial history of East Africa, with approximately three hundred

---

13. Anderson, "Massacre," 49.

Africans being slaughtered and over five hundred cattle and ten thousand sheep and goats being seized.[14]

One of the colonial government's successful methods was the burning of houses. The residents thought that they would stop the burning of houses by dousing the fires in the houses, but that did not help because the attackers had matches. The Marakwet weapons of arrows and spears were not a match to the British guns. In February 1901, Gorges stopped his punitive attacks, and shortly thereafter Ribo was abandoned.

In March 1901, Sir Johnson wrote to Hyde-Baker and asked him to close down Ribo Post and relocate to Lake Baringo post.

> I am becoming much disturbed in mind about the advisability of you remaining on at Ribo. The plain facts are that the Post is 140 miles from any base of troops, the natives all round about it seems to be thoroughly hostile, food supply is very bad and there is little or nothing in the country worth its present development.

This marked the end of Sir Johnson's ambitious scheme in Kerio Valley. Evidently, the rudiments of colonial control could not be established in Kerio Valley. The Marakwet resistance was a sign that the British policy was unwelcomed. That prevailing attitude remained for half a century. In addition to the defeat at Ribo, there was the humiliation suffered at the third campaign against the Nandi in July 1900. In the end the British forces suffered their heaviest casualties yet in East Africa. 127 men were killed, including a European doctor and additional 117 men were wounded. In October 1900, Johnson had reported that the Nandi problem would be settled only by conquest.

The British ambitious plan to have a chain of posts along Kerio Valley from Lake Baringo to Lake Turkana failed because it had misjudged their ability and underestimated the strength of the native population who controlled the resources on the ground. Moreover, they did not consider the presence of the Arab caravans that had dominated the ivory trade for a half century. Neither did they understand the intricacies of the lucrative batter trade, or they were just driven by their own blind ethnocentrism. Marakwet resisted the British because they considered them rude and took by force what did not belong to them. On the other hand, the Arabs who were also visitors and had preceded the British in the region appeared to be friendly and traded peacefully. On their part, the British learned from their mistakes and introduced indirect rule by appointing chiefs in locations.

---

14. Anderson, "Massacre," 50.

Since the partition of Africa in Berlin in 1884/5, the representatives of British and German governments contested for land rights in East Africa. Needless to say, Kerio Valley became one of the early attraction by both parties partly because Arab traders had made them believe that Lake Baringo could be the source of river Nile "Some map-makers in the 1860s and 1870s seized upon it as yet another source of the still mysterious River Nile, and showed a river flowing from lake Baringo westwards into lake Victoria."[15] It took Joseph Thomson's expedition in 1883 to verify and show that Lake Baringo was an enclosed lake with no outlet. In 1888, the Hungarian explorer Count Teleki accompanied by an expedition of two hundred men traveled through Kerio Valley on his way to Lake Turkana. He claimed to be the first white man to discover the lake which he named after his Royal Imperial Highness Prince Rudolf of Austria. As the expedition returned, they passed through Endo villages in Marakwet. When their food supply was running low some of Teleki's men sneaked into the Marakwet farms to steal grain. While foraging in the millet fields, they got engaged in a skirmish with the people of Endo.

> The thefts committed by our men in the Endo plantations, were detected, and led to a struggle with the natives in which showers of arrows were discharged, one man only being seriously wounded in the abdomen, and he recovered completely.[16]

In 1890, the German explorer Dr. Karl Peters arrived in Baringo. He had previously been in Tanzania signing contracts with local chiefs with plans to advance the German sphere of influence in East Africa. In a short period, Peters had obtained 124 treaties giving him exclusive sovereignty over about 2,500 square miles of what became eastern Tanganyika resent day Tanzania and obtained an imperial charter in 1885.

Two days after his arrival in Baringo he negotiated a treaty with the Njemps people whom he referred to as Wakwafi. He told them stories of the greatness of his country and how he defeated the Maasai and therefore he could offer them protection from both the Maasai and the Pokot. The only condition was for the Njemps to submit to him and ask him to make an application to the German chancellor for the incorporation of the Baringo country into the German protected territory in East Africa. After obtaining their consent, Dr. Peters hoisted the black, white, and red flag of imperial Germany over Baringo and Kerio Valley. The motive underlying Peters'

---

15. Hennings, *African Morning*, 19.
16. Hennings, *African Morning*, 21.

treaty with the Njemps is the ivory trade in Kerio Valley. This is revealed in his letter to the German committee which had sent him to Africa.

> A Baringo nation would be of the very greatest importance for the opening of Central Africa and for the great plateau over which our way led. Here, in what resembles a peaceful oasis, the expeditions can rest and gain strength for the further difficulties that lie before them. It is also known that Njemps and the Baringo form one of the great centers of the ivory trade.[17]

He was aware that Germany would be concerned with expenses for such an undertaking, so Peters presented a less costly option of a small personnel of five Europeans and twenty-five African soldiers (*Askaris*). He also suggested that such an establishment in the rich Kerio Valley would eventually pay for itself as a commercial post. With all those efforts, Dr. Peters plans to secure the ivory rich Kerio Valley did not materialize. He left a frustrated man and travelled through the Marakwet escarpment using his rifle freely. His treaties with native elders were rendered void by the Anglo-German agreement of July 1890 and Kerio Valley fell under the British.[18] For the next few decades Kerio Valley became the attraction of expeditions and trade caravans. When Prime minister William E. Gladstone brought Uganda under England, in 1894, Kerio Valley was incorporated as part of the new protectorate, a status it retained till 1892.

In 1901, At about the same time the railway line from Mombasa to Lake Victoria had passed away off Kerio Valley receded into the background. It was believed by the Native population, that the railway line was a fulfillment of an early prophecy by a Nandi seer named Koitalel Arap Samoei that a snake like creature would crawl along the ground through their land, belching fire and smoke.[19] The caravan trade of the nineteenth century opened the interior, bringing many African peoples into the world economy as suppliers of ivory or slaves or producers of food or local products that provisioned caravans. The pioneers of all the major routes were African traders caravan porters and porters. an. Nyamwezi caravans from central Tanzania, reaching the coast about 1800, developed the most important route from their homeland to Bagamoyo on the mainland directly opposite Zanzibar. Kamba ivory traders from central Kenya opened a route

---

17. Hennings, *African Morning*, 22.

18. Peters served as director of German East Africa, during which time he developed a reputation for brutality in his dealings with Africans. In 1891, he became imperial high commissioner for Kilimanjaro, but was deprived of his commission in 1897 for misuse of official power in his treatment of the Africans.

19. Personal interview with David Kalessi, Eldoret, Kenya, June 14, 2000.

that ended at Mombasa. Eventually, this route crossed Kamba and Maasai country, branching east towards Uganda and north to Lake Turkana.

Africa Inland Mission

Historical Context

The modern missionary societies coincided with the formation of European colonial empires and thrived in the colonized parts of the world. In that sense, the missionary found himself side by side with the merchant and the soldier. In the fifteenth century, Portugal, and Spain with the blessings of the Pope dominated the world outside Europe where they planted their colonies and their church. In the nineteenth century, the Protestant nations and their missionaries entered the scene but turned a blind eye to the dehumanizing slave trade that had been earlier practiced in Africa by the Portuguese. In fact. European nations were more interested in signing treaties that favored slave trade than in organizing scientific expeditions into the African continent. The demand for slaves on the plantations of the Americas occasioned the rapid growth of slave trade. The triangular trade route, as it was called, meant that ships left Europe with tradeable items such as cloth, alcohol, guns and exchanged them with slaves in Africa that would be sold in the Americas for sugar and tobacco which were in turn sold in Europe. The staggering profits were used to boost the European economy and build cities such as Liverpool, Nantes and Bordeaux.

In the nineteenth century, mounting opposition from Christian anti-slavery and abolitionists in England and America eventually, brought slavery down. When slavery was no longer a viable business it was replaced by tropical raw materials such sugar, coffee, tobacco, tea and spices. These products came to depend on the exploitation of the conquered African land and labor.

The curiosity of Africa led to the exploration ventures of the eighteenth century followed by the partition of Africa and modern missionary endeavors. In 1894/5, European leaders met in Berlin to divide Africa amongst themselves. Britain took the lions share followed by France. The partition was followed by the soldiers who wielded the gun and not far behind was the missionary. The missionaries followed their national flag and operated in those colonies. For example, France displaced the American presbyterian missionaries in Gabon similarly, the Portuguese erected surmountable obstacles to the Protestant missions in their colonies. After WWI, French and English missionaries replaced German missionaries in Togo, Cameroon,

Ruanda, Burundi, and Tanzania. This meant that a change of sovereignty in Africa was a change of missionaries.[20] At home the French Republic was anticlerical but when it came to their colonies, France stood behind their missionaries and was unsurpassed in its number of catholic missionaries in the colonies. In fact, secularist France helped build churches and financed education in their colonies something they could not do in France. In Algeria, the French government provided a great deal of financial assistance to Christian religious institutions and seminaries. In 1843, the Holy Ghost Fathers signed an accord with the French colonial administration that the missionaries would endeavor to bring the moral influence of evangelized black people under the control of the French colonial administration and the government for its part would provide the missionaries with the necessary grants for its mission. Similarly, the British provided similar financial support and protection to the missionaries in its colonies.

To bolster interest in the recruitment of missionaries at home, the missionary press and mission agencies raised awareness and funds for their respective mission. In the literature, images of distant lands with a missionary appeared as a hero venturing to bring light to the dark continent. For the readers of exotic literature, Africa was a pitiable continent of darkness, diseases, slavery, and ignorance. This is what contributed to the "dark continent" myth that aroused Christendom Europe to an active generosity and enthusiasm. This Eurocentric view of Africans is captured in the words of the nineteenth century explorer Samuel Baker "An African savages is quite on the level with that of the brute and not to be compared with the noble character of the dog. There is neither gratitude, pity or self-denial; no idea of duty, no religion, nothing but covetousness ingratitude, selfishness and cruelty."[21]

Not all Europeans were insensitive or ruthless. A few were sympathetic to the Africans and often did not fully support their government's colonial policies. On occasion, the mission opposed colonial conquest, and aimed to limit its effects through education, medical work and a message that promised a better life beyond. Philanthropists (travelers and writers) who were interested in Africa formed a society of the friends of the Blacks in 1788 and abolished slavery in their convention in 1794.[22] The daughters of Mary founded by Pere Levasseur rescued enslaved women in East Africa. The nineteenth-century Protestant missionary movement was mostly antislavery. William Wilberforce was active in abolition movement

---

20. Ela, *African Cry*, 16.

21. Davidson, *Africa in History*, xxiii. Basil Davidson, Africa Episode 1 Different but equal youtube. https://www.google.com/search?different+but+equal+youtube=

22. Ela, *African Cry*, 21.

in England and the Quakers led the abolitionist movement in America and Canada. Unfortunately, those efforts did not challenge colonial practices in Africa. In the long run, the mission churches in the colonies became appendices of the mother churches in the West.

The formal colonial period in Kenya started in 1895 when Britain declared its Protectorate over the territory it had previously granted to the Imperial East African Company. The initial attempts to administer the Protectorate through the Imperial East African Company up until 1895 was deemed to be unsuccessful due to poor management. When A. H. Hardinge, the first Consul General, took over in 1895 and declared it the British East Africa Protectorate, he was faced with the challenge of establishing an economically successful British administrative system. However, his efforts to move into the interior were constantly resisted by the African people who were opposed to foreign rule. Such resistance inevitably led to a military retaliation from the British. Similar military tactics were used to subdue any tribal resistance throughout the colony as discussed in the previous chapter. For example, the Nandi people were attacked in 1901, 1905, and 1906. Force was constantly used by the British not only to take land, but also in the collection of taxes and directing casual workers to settler farms.[23]

One of the bold colonial government's efforts was the construction of the Kenya-Uganda railway. The African labor force as well as importation of Indian laborers embarked on the construction of the rail reaching Kisumu on the Lake Victoria in 1901. Now with easy transportation into the country, more foreigners started coming in as traders, settlers, and missionaries. They arrived from Britain, South Africa, Australia, New Zealand, and Canada. On the whole, most of them brought more capital than their predecessors.[24] The highlands of Kenya in Uasin Gishu and Tran-Zoia which is the most fertile was allocated to the new settlers, while the rightful owners were displaced. They chose Eldoret as their commercial center.

> This town (Eldoret), beautifully situated on the Uasin-Gishu plateau, 2096 meters above sea level boasts of fine hotels, banks, up to date stores of all sorts, several churches, European and Native hospital and a white population of about 2000. This plateau itself is the loftiest and probably the healthiest district in Kenya colony. . . . The plateau is bounded on the North by deep valleys which separate it on the Northwest from Mount Elgon, and on the Northeast from the Cherang'any range.[25]

23. Rosberg and Nottingham, *Myth*, 21.
24. Ogot, "Kenya under the British," 260.
25. Ogot "Kenya under the British," 260. See also Miller, "Annual Report," 20.

Due to these favorable conditions, many British farmers acquired large tracts of land on the "White Highlands" and by 1904, the population increased by the influx of a large party of Afrikaner farmers from South Africa. They all acquired large tracks of land and benefited from the Kalenjin labour force organized through the governments' hut tax laws. Some of the farmers assisted in the missionary work and a few enrolled to be missionaries.

Before proceeding to the history of the Mission in Eldoret area and in Marakwet in particular, it is necessary to give a brief history of the founding of the Africa Inland Mission in order to understand the missionaries' backgrounds and recruitment strategies.

The Mission Background

The Africa Inland Mission was founded in 1895 by its first missionary to Kenya, Peter Cameron Scott. Scott was born in Glasgow, Scotland, on March 7, 1867. At the age of twelve his parents immigrated to Philadelphia. While still a teenager, he discovered his singing ability brought him offers to perform professionally at the opera, but his Christian parents discouraged him. An accident while he was still a youth affected his health and was sent to Scotland for a year. At this time, he had decided to dedicate his life completely to God.[26]

Upon his return from Scotland, he entered the New York Missionary Training College in preparation for missionary work. However, before completing the three-year programme, he was accepted by the International Missionary Alliance and, in 1891, sailed for Congo. After a short period, he was joined by his brother John, but within a few months John died of fever. Two years after this, Peter Scott's own health forced him to return to the United States. Later, he travelled to Scotland and slowly recuperated.

Peter Scott spent the next two years reading and lecturing in America and Great Britain on the challenges of missions in Africa. At this time his attention was drawn to British East Africa where the physical conditions seemed favorable to Europeans. On a visit to Westminster Abbey, he knelt by the grave of David Livingston and was gripped by the inscription "other sheep I have which are not of this fold, them also I must bring" (John 10:16). At that moment, his plans for East Africa were confirmed. He envisaged a chain of mission stations stretching westward from Mombasa in the East to Lake Chad in the very heart of Africa.

Scott was not the first missionary to propose such a chain across Africa. J. L. Krapf, a German who came to East Africa under the Church Missionary

---

26. Miller, *Peter Cameron Scott*, 16–19.

Society in 1844 referred to such a plan. Another Church Missionary Society missionary to East Africa, Alexander Mackay, envisioned a similar chain of stations that would serve as educational centers for native agents who would spread Christianity throughout the continent.[27]

In 1895, Scott had recovered from his illness and returned to Philadelphia. Within a short time, he had organized a supporting team out of the recently formed Philadelphia Missionary Council—a non-denominational group organized to assist in world evangelization. Scott described his plans to return to Africa to establish a chain of mission stations from East to West. He pointed out the benefits of such a venture in thousands of African converts. Thus, the Africa Inland Mission was conceived, for African mission and the Philadelphia Missionary Council agreed to raise funds for him and others who would be willing to join him. The Council promised not to exercise any control over the activities and decisions of the missionaries except in their support of the work, which could be withdrawn at any time. Their responsibility was to spread the knowledge of the Mission's work and to function as a clearing agent for finances and new recruits. This conformed to the Africa Inland Mission's financial policy of faith-reliance as it appears on its literature "as to needs full information, as to funds no solicitation."[28] Thus, all funds were to be of a voluntary nature.[29]

For the recruitment of missionaries, the Mission recognized that it would be difficult to find people with full theological education. Furthermore, the few ordained clergy went with the denominational mission organizations. These two factors informed the decisions of the evangelicals of the time that Africa did not require any scholastic ability when it comes to missionaries. Instead, great emphasis was put on recruiting dedicated laymen full of zeal and devotion. Education was of a secondary concern. However, the need for trained workers soon became apparent when the complexities of translation of the Bible into African languages demanded it. The various African tongues had no written language and translation of the Bible and other Christian literature into these languages required well-trained minds. This is confirmed by Willis Hotchkiss' letter, after being in the field for three years:

27. Harrison and Mackay, *Pioneer Missionary*, 462.

28. *Hearing and Doing* 1.1 (1896) 5. The journal *Hearing and Doing* was to print letters and articles of information of the labors in Africa, as well as serve as the official organ of the Philadelphia Missionary Council. It came out monthly and was edited by Charles E. Hurlburt, president of the Council, and James H. McConkey, the treasurer.

29. *Hearing and Doing* 1.1 (1896) 5.

Africa needs hundreds of the very finest scholars to grapple with her hundreds of still unwritten dialects.[30]

Almost concurrent with the launching of the Africa Inland Mission was the founding of the Philadelphia Bible Institute, a school that was to play an important role in the life of the new Mission.[31] Its purpose was to equip young people with the knowledge of the Bible and prepare them for the Mission overseas. The accounts of both the Philadelphia Bible Institute and the Philadelphia Missionary Council appeared in the official magazine *Hearing and Doing* which they shared. The same officers served in both the Philadelphia Bible Institute and Philadelphia Missionary Council. One of these was the Rev. C. E. Hurlburt who became the Mission's first general director and served for twenty-five years.[32]

In August 1895 Peter Cameron Scott sailed with a party of six to be joined in Scotland by Walter McLellan Wilson. The US team members were Lester Severn, Margaret Scott (Peter's sister), Minnie Lindberg, Bertha Reckling, Willis Hotchkiss and F. W. Krieger.[33] They arrived in Mombasa at the end of October and were received warmly by the Church Missionary Society members who had already started work on the East African coast. The Church Missionary Society provided a house where they could live until they were ready and able to find a suitable caravan to the inland. The sheer volume of supplies required for each missionary was was staggering. As it were, assembling caravans involved complex and skilled routines for recruitment, pay, inventory packing and organization. In most of the time the recruitment for porters was often difficult due to changing demands for local labour during the agricultural circle, epidemics, conflicts between different ethnic groups of porters, availability of desirable trade goods used for payments and competition from other travelers. Failure to have the right porters could lead to defection, theft, or insubordination.

On November 12, 1895, the five men in the party left the three women in Mombasa and travelled inland. Their luggage was transported by the Smith Mackenzie company, a firm that had a lot of porters and camels at their disposal.[34] They stopped at Nzawi, on December 12th, where they established their first station. Peter Scott left the others to construct a temporary house and returned to Mombasa to escort his sister and the other two women back to Nzawi. With his staff of seven missionaries, Peter Scott opened other

30. *Hearing and Doing* 3.11 (1899) 7.
31. *Hearing and Doing* 1.1 (1896) 7.
32. Gration, "Africa Inland Mission," 22–23.
33. *Hearing and Doing* 1.3 (1896) 4.
34. Stauffacher, *Faster Beats the Drum*, 18.

stations: Sakai was opened in March 1896 with Willis Hotchkiss in charge. A month later another site was chosen in Kilungu under F. W. Krieger. At Nzawi, Margaret Scott established the first school, and dispensaries were opened at all three stations followed by out-schools.

In July, Peter Scott set off to Mombasa to meet a new party of eight missionaries from America. Among them were his parents and sister Inez.[35] Once back at Nzawi, some of the new arrivals were sent to Sakai and Kilunga; another station was opened in the densely populated area of Kangundo. Peter's parents were assigned to this new station. A military house, which was no longer needed by the British, was offered to them at a modest rent.[36] In his report of that year, Peter Scott said:

> In humble dependence upon God, we have moved steadily forward, no doubt in our blindness making many mistakes for we are only human. Four stations have been established and manned in less than ten months. We have had time of trial, also time of blessing, times of sorrow and times of joy. Men, beasts, fever, the very prince of darkness himself, all sought to keep us out of Nzawi valley, God raised up helpers to furnish the means; . . . God raised up kind friends to welcome and care for us at Mombasa; . . . God saved us from ravenous beasts; God raised us up from fevers; God gave us favour with the African people and with Government officials.[37]

Though Peter Scott's leadership of the young Mission showed a lot of promise, it was brief. In December 1896 he died at Nzawi station after a brief illness and was buried by his parents in front of his grass-thatched house.[38] Now left without a leader; the Mission was terribly affected. Those remaining began leaving work one by one; some because of ill-health, others sought employment outside the Mission. Peter Scott's parents and their daughter Inez resigned to work with the British government. Peter Scott's sister Margaret married Walter M. C. Wilson, one of the original parties. They resigned in November 1897 and settled in Machakos. That left only four workers with the mission.

Another problem arose when it was found that a debt of $1,800 was left unpaid by Peter Scott. The Philadelphia Missionary Council had made a definite agreement with the Mission that no debts should be incurred, and that the Council would not be responsible for any financial obligations.

---

35. *Hearing and Doing* 1.10 (1896) 10–12.
36. Richardson, *Garden of Miracles*, 30.
37. Stauffacher, *Faster Beats the Drum*, 20.
38. The remains were later removed from Nzawi to Nairobi by his parents.

Their sole role was the distribution of funds collected from donors. The Philadelphia Missionary Council investigated the matter and discovered that there had been a mix-up between family and mission expenditures. The Council issued a statement to this effect and immediate payment was made. At this time, F. W. Krieger, one of the original members, sent in his resignation stating his unwillingness to continue work with the Mission under the doctrinal basis adopted by the Philadelphia Missionary Council.[39] He established a different mission in Kikuyuland.

By July 1897, only Hotchkiss remained in the Mission. Two of his comrades had died of fever, and the two remaining women were forced, by health reasons, to return to the United States. The original three stations had to be closed. Kangundo was kept open by Hotchkiss who was tethering to leave the mission altogether.

Meanwhile, at home, the Philadelphia Missionary Council debated the fate of the Mission. In October 1898, the Council sent the new director of the Africa Inland Mission, Charles Hurlburt, to visit the field. He was accompanied by a recruit, William C. Bangert. After six months, Charles Hurlburt returned to the United States via Britain. He travelled widely expounding the needs of the Mission. The recruitment of missionaries became his immediate objective.[40]

While the Rev. Hurlburt was recruiting candidates, another crisis had arisen in the Mission field. Hotchkiss resigned to start a mission with the Friends Church of which he was a member.[41] Bangert, who had just joined him, was left to continue the work alone. With the severe famine raging in the whole of Kambaland and little knowledge of the people's language, Bangert came to a point of desperation. In a letter to Hurlburt he wrote:

> Go in any direction and you are bound to stumble onto dead bodies. The drawn agonized look on every face plainly speaks of the horrors of death by starvation. . . . This has been part of my revolting work for the past few weeks. Less than one fourth of the Kamba tribe remains to tell the story of their awful sufferings and before crops a still smaller percentage will remain.[42]

---

39. The Africa Inland Mission had no official doctrinal statement when it started. The first party had gone out as a group selected by Peter Scott. Later on, the Philadelphia Missionary Council took the initiative to formulate a doctrinal statement and circulated it for adoption. Obviously, some of the members did not agree with it.

40. Famine had tightened its grip on the area at that time killing thousands. This was a possible reason which caused the closing of the mission stations.

41. *Hearing and Doing* 3.5 (1899) 6.

42. Stauffacher, *Faster Beats the Drum*, 23.

In October he was encouraged by the arrival of two men, C. F. Johnston and Elmer Bartholomew. Within a few months William Bangert's health broke down and he had to return to America and could no longer return to Africa due to poor health.[43] About this time, Lester Severn, who had been a member of the first party in 1895, returned to Kenya to direct the mission work at Kangundo. Shortly after, the British Colonial government sent twenty-seven orphaned children to the Mission whose parents had died during the famine. A house was built for them, and Johnston took over their education. Most of the orphans remained at the station for a long time while others proceeded to Kijabe for further training and became successful teachers and evangelists in the Mission's outstations.[44]

Hurlburt, who was named to succeed Peter Scott, took up residence in the Mission in 1901. He had been the superintendent of the Philadelphia Bible Institute and had involved the Institute with the work of the Mission from the start. He resigned his position at the Institute in order to give leadership direction to the Mission which was almost collapsing. By October 1, 1901, he had assembled a group of seven people including Dr. J. Henderson, the first Mission doctor, and Lee H. Downing, who was to become a prominent leader in Kijabe. The rest of the team was Hurlburt's five children. They all settled in Kangundo where the other three missionaries were stationed.

The influence of Hurlburt was soon felt. Within a year of his arrival, three new stations had been established, two among the Kikuyu, and one among the Kamba. At this time, the colonial government designed a plan to designate different missions to areas in order to avoid competition. An agreement was made among the Church Missionary Society, the Church of Scotland Mission and the Africa Inland Mission on the spheres of work responsibility. The Africa Inland Mission was given the area between Nairobi and the Maragua river near Fort Hall.

By 1901, the railway line had reached Kisumu on Lake Victoria. Now the question arose as to the best location for the Mission's headquarters. It was deemed necessary that the location be near the railway line where telegraph and mail services were available. The railway ran about forty miles from Kangundo.

In 1903, Hurlburt discovered the ideal place in Kijabe with healthy climatic conditions and only two miles from the railway line. The location was 7,500 feet above sea level and surrounded by a forest of cedar and wild

---

43. *Hearing and Doing* 3.11 (1899) 7.
44. *Hearing and Doing* 3.11 (1899) 8.

olive trees. Due to its high altitude, and cool climate it was free of mosquitoes. Without hesitation Hurlburt established his headquarters at Kijabe.[45]

Another young missionary, who later accompanied the director on many pioneering trips, arrived at Kijabe in 1903. He was John Stauffacher, a Wisconsin dairy farmer who had attended North Central College in Illinois. He started the Mission's work with the Masai who settled near Kijabe. Within a year he was given permission by the colonial government to settle amongst them. By this time, the colonial government had taken the Masai's grazing land for European settlers after ordering the Masai to move north to the Laikipia plains. Many refused to leave, and soldiers were sent to burn down their *manyattas* (kraals).[46]

As opportunities for outreach increased year by year, constant pleas for new missionaries were made to the Philadelphia Missionary Council. The Council, in turn, issued challenges within the Philadelphia Bible Institute and the America churches. It soon became necessary to appoint deputation secretaries whose duties were to visit churches and present the needs of the Mission. This method proved to be quite successful, and people enquired about the Mission from as far west as Chicago.

In 1905, the Philadelphia Missionary Council assumed additional responsibility in the control and screening of Mission candidates. When Hurlburt returned to the States on a recruiting drive that year, the Philadelphia Missionary Council agreed to the establishment of the office of a home secretary to serve full time as executive director of the Council. In January 1906, J. Davis Adams was elected to that post. One of his main duties was the recruitment of missionaries.

By this time, most volunteers had some training beyond high school; they were generally laymen. Many were enlisted by the Student Volunteer Board and were taking instructions through the Young Men's Christian Association; these YMCA centres were often visited by the Council's executive director. It was through these centres and through the various church groups that many felt called to the service of God in Africa.[47]

In 1907, following Hurlburt's visit, the greatest influx of missionaries arrived in Kenya. Among them was Albert Barnett, an Australian, who had gone to America to study flour milling. There he attended one of the revival meetings and responded to a full-time service to God as a missionary. After training at Moody Bible Institute, he joined the Mission and sailed

---

45. Kijabe became one of the largest mission stations in the world with over one hundred missionaries in residence. It has a school for missionary children.

46. Stauffacher, *Faster Beats the Drum*, 27.

47. *Hearing and Doing* 11.2 (1906) 16.

to Kenya with the largest party of twenty-three. They reached Mombasa in December of that year and with the new railway line, they were able to reach Kijabe in a shorter time. After spending a few weeks at Kijabe, Albert Barnett joined Charles Hurlburt on a field survey for new stations. He was left to work among a branch of the Masai people at Kilombe on Lake Baringo. A little later he moved to Rumuruti to relieve the Stauffachers. Barnett married Elma E. Nicher, a Swedish massage therapist who had Bible training in America. She was no stranger to the station at Rumuruti as she had lived there previously.[48] In 1913, the Barnett's returned to the Kamasia (Tugen) and established another station at Eldama Ravine where they worked until Mr. Barnett's death in 1965. His sons Eric and Paul and daughter Ruth joined the Mission. Ruth Barnett was married to Tom Collins who started the Liter mission station among the Marakwet. When Tom Collins died in 1964, Paul Barnett joined his sister Ruth and continued with the mission work at Liter. Like many others in the Mission, the Barnetts of the third generation are now numbered among the AIM (African Inland Mission) missionaries.

By 1914, after being in existence for about fifteen years, the Mission was firmly established in Kenya. Its sixty missionaries were active together with their African agents in fifteen stations and the Mission was ready to expand not only towards German East Africa (Tanzania) and the Congo (Zaire), but also into small communities in the interior parts of Kenya. By this time, the Mission had begun to expand their recruiting base and accepted missionaries from other mission boards to serve in Africa under its direction. Several of the new recruits came from Baptist, Mennonite, Anglican, and the Gospel Missionary Churches.

The British AIM Missionaries in the North Rift

After the First World War, most of the British missionaries expressed their dissatisfaction in working with and under American missionaries. In the 1920s, when the Mission was experiencing expansion, the British missionaries voiced their desire for a British-only area, or a separate Mission. They wanted to be free from the American control, both in the field and New York (the Mission headquarters had now moved to New York from Philadelphia). However, they still wanted to remain within the Mission. The autonomy would give the British a better control and advantage, after all Kenya was a British colony. We shall revisit this subject in greater detail later.

Earlier on, in 1912, a branch of the Africa Inland Mission was opened in Nandi by Mr. and Mrs. Lawson S. Probst. They leased a site from the Church

---

48. Richardson, *Garden of Miracles*, 66.

Missionary Society at a place that came to be known as "Chebisas."[49] In 1914, the Probsts were joined by two Swedish women, Marie Hansen and Signe C. Kristensen. Encouraged by the colonial government, the missionaries started a school. The government was interested to educate the sons of the chiefs who would later assist in the British colonial administration.

When the first world war broke out in 1914, most of the male missionaries went into the army, and for some reasons known to them, the women could not be permitted to remain at Chebisas on their own. They moved to temporary buildings at a station near the government offices at Kapsabet where another missionary George McCreary and his wife resided. For the next five years while at Kapsabet there was little expansion. Apart from a few porters and police from Nyanza (Kavirondo) they had no Nandi converts.

In 1922, they and the McCrearys returned to Chebisas and reopened their school. Some of their former students returned. Those who had converted to Christianity were taught to reject the Nandi traditions especially the girls' circumcision rite which seemed to be the most repugnant to the missionaries. While the missionaries discouraged the circumcision rite for the girls the Christian boys were to be circumcised in the hospital. The Nandi took this as an attack on their tradition and responded swiftly. Some of the girls who resisted the customary initiation were forcefully seized by their parents and forced to submit to the rite. Those who managed to escape were given sanctuary at the station or taken to another station. This raised tension between the local people and the Mission.

In 1924, the McCrearys returned to the United States leaving the two women missionaries on their own again. The Nandi planned to take advantage of this situation, by attacking the station to rescue their girls. "Let us go and bring our children to have them circumcised; the men have gone, the ladies have no strength."[50] After being secretly notified of the plan, the missionaries decided to evacuate the girls during the night to a nearby railway station to travel to the mission station at Litein in Kericho. When the Nandi men learned of this plan from the schoolboys, they sent a messenger to the District Commissioner at Kapsabet. Instead of helping the Nandi men, the commissioner offered the girls protection and the needed assistance to Litein where they stayed until things had cooled down in Nandi.

49. The term *Chebisas* has two meanings. The first meaning is the hissing sound that comes out of a pressure lamp commonly used by the missionaries. The second meaning is Saas which means hate referring to "those who hate" in reference to the Africa Inland Mission followers who had developed disdain of anything traditional such as drinking beer, dancing, smoking, and initiation rites.

50. Langley, *Nandi Rituals*, 50.

In 1925, the two women missionaries and their protégés returned to Chabisas. Three new missionaries had arrived, Elizabeth and Mr. and Mrs. William A. Mundy who had worked for a time with the Luo in Western Kenya. A decision was made to move the station to Kapsabet where there would be some government protection, especially in the matter of circumcision pressure regarding their young converts. While the girls' circumcision rite became a national matter when missionaries' lives were threatened.

Although the colonial government did not subscribe to the Mission's view on circumcision, it offered them protection whenever necessary. This was evident when one of the chiefs sued the Mission for custody of his daughter who was ready for marriage and needed the rite.

> The test case brought by Nandi against the Africa Inland Mission for custody of his daughter was compounded by the defendants who paid dowry for the girl in stock. I question whether these people are making much headway.... Generally, speaking, the Nandi are opposed to all Mission enterprise principally on account of propaganda by native teachers to the effect that not only female, but male circumcision is sinful.[51]

The chief wished to benefit from the cattle which were the bride-price. Finally, payment of the bride-price was guaranteed by the Mission in the event of marriage. From then on, the Nandi attitude to the Mission began to change slightly. More of their children were enrolled in the school. Moreover, candidates were baptized, and the church increased its membership. Among the newly baptized was Samuel Gimnyigei, who was later responsible for translating the Nandi Bible and the first Nandi to be ordained by the Africa Inland Mission. Another convert was Reuben Seroney, who later left the Africa Inland Mission and became an Anglican evangelist and the first Anglican vicar of Nandi.

The first church marriages followed in July 1925. Leah Cheptorus, the chief's daughter, was married to Reuben Seroney and another convert, Martha, was married to Mica Bomet. The bride-prices for the two women were paid by the Nandi Christians. The Kapsabet station became an active centre for the Mission's activities, such as translation work, boarding school, Sunday School, and weekly church services. The Nandi evangelists and teachers went out from the station every weekend to the villages as itinerant preachers. These efforts yielded many Africa Inland Mission churches in the district. However, more progress was achieved when one of the elders, Elijah Chepkwony, was chosen by the colonial government

---

51. Langley, *Nandi Rituals*, 52.

to be a chief over a large area. Through his influence, Africa Inland Mission churches were established in his territory.

In 1927, after furlough in Australia, the Rev. and Mrs. Stuart M. Bryson were sent to work among the Nandi people in Kapsabet. Earlier he had worked for two and a half years at Kijabe where he had learned both Kiswahili and Kikuyu and before taking his first furlough, he had relieved the Inness at Nyakach during their absence and while there, learned Jaluo. Past experiences in different stations had given the Brysons a good ear for languages, making it easy to learn an additional language at a new station.

The Brysons were convinced that if Christianity was to be established in Nandi, they must have a Bible in their own language. With the help of Nandi converts, the Brysons began to learn the language. They wrote Nandi words on slips of paper and collected them in a biscuit tin.[52] When they had mastered the language, they started the translation work. Samuel Gimnyigei (mentioned above) helped them tremendously. The translation of the whole Bible was completed and published by the British Bible Society in 1938. It was the first vernacular Bible in Kenya.

Due to this early missionary involvement by the British, whether from Australia or South Africa, coupled with the coming of the settlers, the British Mission office felt obligated to take total control of spiritual matters within the territory. They were also somewhat contemptuous of the American leadership.

In July 1929, the Rev. Roland A. Smith, the president of the British Council of the Africa Inland Mission, wrote to the American Africa Inland Mission head office in New York explaining their desire for an autonomous sphere of operation:

> Without a vestige of control on the field, without possessing a brick or rod of territory in its own name, the British Council has, for nearly two decades, furnished men and means, besides those spiritual forces, which if less material are possibly for that very reason, more potent. . . . Such a condition is one which we have come deliberately to feel is inimical to the best interests of the work and does in fact militate against and even retard the influence and interest of the Africa Inland Mission in Britain and in our colonies. Indeed, the parents of missionaries and friends in our constituency hold that such a one-sided method of administration is inadequate and inequitable, and evidence is not lacking the with-holding of considerable financial support, until this state of affairs has been regularized. . . . The proposal which we are now led to make after a most exhaustive enquiry

---

52. Richardson, *Garden of Miracles*, 79.

and prayerful concern, in consultation with our missionaries on furlough ... is that the Eldoret Area be handed over to the British council, with the work in the Nandi tribe together with the stations of Kapsabet and Kabartonjo, with a view of reaching the untouched tribes of Northern Kenya.[53]

On October 15, 1929, the British Council sent another letter to New York and offered to purchase the two mission stations in the Eldoret area. The stations had been established earlier by American missionaries using American funds.

With regard to the two stations, Kapsabet and Kabartonjo as base for work among the Nandi tribe, we should, of course, reimburse the American section of the Mission for the capital value of buildings ... on these stations in exchange for the title deeds giving the British section control of the property. This matter of alteration of title could presumably be dealt with on the field through the British Colonial Administration at Nairobi.[54]

When the New York office received the letters, they were obviously displeased. However, they responded positively lest the Mission divide. They stressed unity and amicability in dealing with the issue at hand. With the assurance of the British influence and control in its own sphere of influence, the American office was convinced that the British office would deepen and foster a spiritual concern within its churches. That would lead to a definite commitment to Missions in Great Britain, Ireland, and the colonies. The only issue they objected to was the notion of the sale of the two mission stations.

The Committee agreed to all that you have written before....
Until it came to the request for purchase of Mission stations and surrender of title deeds held by the Africa Inland Mission to the British Council.

Our committee holds that all real estate belongs to the [Mission] and that no property rights are vested in any Home Council or individual missionary. The Home Council here cannot sell buildings or land as requested, and must decline to sell the stations, since the American Home Council does not hold sole rights to land and buildings. The Council does not believe that the section requested would make for the unity of the work

---

53. Roland A. Smith, letter to Mr. Campbell, General Secretary for the North American Africa Inland Mission in New York, July 1929.

54. Roland A. Smith, letter to Mr. Campbell the General Secretary for the North American Africa Inland Mission in New York, October 15, 1929.

of the [Mission] but on the contrary would separate it into two quite independent bodies.[55]

After several months of negotiations and adjustments, the North American office officially authorized the British Council to take over the Eldoret area in 1931. This sphere included Kapsabet and Kabartonjo with the objective to open other mission stations in other nearby communities. To maintain unity in the Mission, the British Council was asked not to recall its missionaries from other fields, nor dislodge American missionaries already working in the Eldoret area.

The Rev. Albert Barnett, who opened the mission station in Eldama Ravine in 1909, was the one most affected by these changes. Being an American, he strongly opposed the idea of handing over his station to the British. He challenged the American office for making decisions without consulting those in the field. The matter was discussed once again at the annual meeting of the North American Council of the Africa Inland Mission held in Montrose in July 1932. After careful consideration of both the earlier agreement and the current opposition from Barnett, the following steps were taken:

> (a) We are willing that the British take full responsibility for Eldoret and for the Nandi tribe including Kapsabet station and for the Northern half of the Kamasia tribe including the Kabartonjo station, the Elgeyo, the Marakwet, the East Suk and the Turkana tribes and all other available tribes in the Kenya colony field of the Africa Inland Mission north of Kapsabet. The Eldama Ravine station, including the Tugen people of Kamasia and the Njemps tribe in Lake Baringo were to remain under the direction of the North American Council.[56]

The British Council appointed the Rev. Reginald V. Reynolds to head the new work in the Eldoret area. Reg Reynolds was born in Australia in 1901. When still an infant, his parents moved to South Africa and settled in Johannesburg. After completing his education, he accompanied his father on a business venture in East Africa. In Tanganyika (Tanzania), his father bought hundreds of cattle and left them in the care of his son. While herding the cattle across Tanganyika, Reginald Reynolds met many missionaries; he was quite fascinated to hear their stories and their commitment to the spreading of Christianity. After selling the cattle, Reg travelled to Nairobi to

---

55. Mr. Campbell, letter to Roland A. Smith, December 18, 1929.
56. Mr. Campbell, letter to Mr. H. F. Garwood, British Home Secretary, August 2, 1932.

join his father who had started a motorcycle business. In 1920, he became a Christian, influenced by the AIM missionaries he had met in Nairobi. Shortly after his conversion, he was encouraged to attend Moody Bible Institute in Chicago in the United States of America. There, he met Zan Hamilton, a Canadian, whom he married after graduation.

In 1925, the couple returned to Kenya to resume work with the Africa Inland Mission. Following a short assignment at Githumu, the Africa Inland Mission British Office asked them to survey the proposed British sphere of influence in Eldoret area. Later he was made district superintendent of the region that had been given for the British Mission.

Africa Inland Mission in Marakwet

In 1931, Rev. Reginald Reynolds, accompanied by Stuart Bryson, Harry Lunn and A. M. Anderson, travelled to Tambach and to Marakwet district with the intention of opening new stations for the Mission to be managed by British missionaries. Marakwet was then categorized as a "restricted reserve," and foreigners needed a special permit from the District Commissioner to operate in the area.

Later, when Rev.Reginald Reynolds visited the District Commissioner at Kapsowar to make a formal request to open mission work in the region, the District Commissioner also invited the Roman Catholic missionary Father Hartman who was based in Eldoret to the meeting. He advised both missionaries that it would be desirable that they agree on the allocation to each Mission of a reserve to avoid any inter-mission conflicts. Father Hartman agreed to concentrate on Keiyo, while the Rev. Reynolds was to work in Marakwet. This policy was later broken when both missions competed for stations in each other's assigned territory.

A year before Rev. Reynolds went to Kapsowar, a church that had been established at Laboret by Mr. Lunn, a settler, and an active supporter of AIM agreed to send a couple to prepare the way. Most of the converts at Laboret Church were workers in settle farms. Among them was the evangelist Joel K. Chemibei and his wife Jeni.[57] Joel Arap Chemibei had been an active member at Laboret Church as well as at other settler farms; however, Laboret became their home church, and it was from there that they were sent to pioneer the Mission's work at Kapsowar.[58]

Joel Kipchumba arap Chemibei was born in South-Eastern Nandi on the edge of Kano plains. His parents had been displaced from their land and

57. Miller, *Central Africa*, 49.
58. Personal interview with Bishop Ezekiel Birch, February 1989.

were forced to become squatters on a European settler farm. In 1927, his father moved to Kabiyet in Northern Nandi and Kipchumba, being the eldest boy, had to move with him, leaving the rest of the family behind. After they had settled their livestock, the father returned to Songhor to collect the family. It was at Kabiyet that Kipchumba had the chance to visit Kapsabet and became aware of the Mission. Before long, he was enrolled in the Mission school at Kapsabet where he learned to read and write. He was also converted and baptized and given the name of Joel. He became an active Christian and brought many children from his village to Sunday school. Through his efforts, the Mission opened an out-station at Surungai where a small church was started under Joel's leadership. He married a Nandi Christian girl, Jeni, who had been converted while at the girl's home at Kapsabet. With his wife's support, Joel proved a capable evangelist and was sent, with others, to establish small churches throughout the district. He travelled to European settler-farms and converted some of the workers.

In 1933, Joel and Jeni Chemibei were joined by two young Marakwet men, Daudi Kisang and Elijah Kilimo. These two were to become the prominent lay agents of the Mission in Marakwet. They were responsible for opening many of the stations as well as dispensaries under Kapsowar Mission Station. Joel Chemibei, his wife Jeni, and the two Marakwet evangelists Daudi Kisang and Elijah Kilimo resided in the houses vacated by the government administrative officers.

> No rent or other charge has been made hitherto in respect of the land occupied by these catechists. Negotiations commenced tentatively with the Africa Inland Mission towards the establishment at Marakwet of a hospital with properly qualified staff. A site was selected by Rev. Reynolds and Dr. Allen and was approved by the Talai elders. The Hon. C.N.C. (Native Affairs) approved the scheme and it now remains to receive the formal application from the missionary society.[59]

By 1933, Reynolds had completed negotiations with the District Commissioner regarding the purchase of the land. In fact, the administration had been pleased with the Mission's plan for the requested hospital. The colonial's records of 1933 had the following agreement:

> The Africa Inland Mission has completed the purchase of the old Government *boma* at Marakwet and 30 acres have been surveyed and granted to them for mission purposes under certain conditions, the chief being that a resident trained medical

---

59. Sylvester, *Annual Report*, 1.

practitioner or nursing sister be in continuous residence on the plot and that adequate medical and hospital equipment be provided.[60]

At the conclusion of the purchase, the mission wisely sought the signatures of the original owners of the land. It is hard to know how the colonial government obtained the land in the first place. It was likely by force given their history. But with the promise of a hospital this time around, they all agreed to sign.

> We the undersigned elders of Talai, Marakwet so agree to hand over to AIM the portion of land as pointed out to us by the district officer for the purpose of building a hospital mission and housing for staff provided only such land is confined to the top of the edge. Kiptum Arap Cheptiot, Kipsewa Arap Keture, Chepto Arap Kaino, Moyot Arap Kiptoi, Chepkiyeng Arap Chemurmet, Chepkochoi Arap Kimetet, Murongwet Arap Kiror.[61]

On October 19, 1933, the Reynolds's moved from Kapsabet to Kapsowar to supervise and manage the construction of the station and remained at Kapsowar for a year before returning to Kapsabet where he would manage all the mission stations in Edoret Area. Within six weeks at Kapsowar, the Reynolds' were joined by Bessie Mildenhall, a nurse from England who had arrived at Kapsowar to work at the hospital. Nurse Mildenhall won the confidence of the people, and many patients were treated on the grass outside her home. Meanwhile, plans were under way to erect a building for medical work as required by the government's medical department. On March 11, 1934, the first peg was struck on the ground, and when the main road was diverted a few months later, the chosen site had a most commanding position. It was also conveniently near a group of brick huts/rondevels, which had once been police lines, but were now available to the Mission in connection with the medical work. Some of the brick round huts are still standing.

The plans were accepted by the medical department and the building began in July 1934. Most of the bricks needed were obtained on the station by demolishing some of the huts left by the District Commissioner. Timber was obtained from the nearby forest and cement, iron sheets and other materials had to be brought from Eldoret town.

When construction of the hospital building was completed in October of 1934, European guests were invited from Kapsabet, Kipkaren and

---

60. Sylvester, *Annual Report*, 1.
61. Kibora, "Growth and Development," 108.

Eldoret. The District Commissioner from Tambach also came to the opening ceremony. A large number of Marakwet men and women gathered to witness the occasion. The Rev. Reynolds, the Mission superintendent of the Eldoret field, led the prayers and Mr. H. A. Lunn, a settler farmer at Laboret and a member of the British Home and Field Councils, was asked to replace Mr. Laurie Walker who had fallen ill and died. Mr. Laurie Walker, had been invited to come and lay the foundation stone of the hospital, but he passed away suddenly while traveling. He was buried in Mombasa. In his speech Mr. Lunn reiterated how[62]

> Mr. Laurie Walker's work, prayer and gifts were largely responsible for the funding of the work in this new sphere, "we praise God for all that was accomplished through the devoted ministry of our late beloved Chairman and for the inspiration to wholehearted discipleship which remains to all who hold dear his memory. It is most appropriate, therefore, that the new hospital—the first building to be erected in Marakwet to the Glory of God should be dedicated to the memory of Mr. Laurie Walker".[63]

Mr. Lunn continued to speak of how God had planned and brought about this work; he stressed that the building had been erected to the Glory of God for the healing of the bodies and souls of the people. He referred to the life and work of the late chairman, and he dedicated the hospital and the work which would be done therein to the memory of Mr. Laurie Walker.[64] By opening day, the conditions laid out by the government had been met; the resident nurse Bessie Mildenhall, and a medical doctor, Dr. Leigh Ashton, were in residence. Dr. Leigh P. Ashton, who arrived on October 16, 1934, was borrowed from the South African General Mission, which was also interested in working in Kenya. Within a year he was joined by Dr. Marion L. Tyren, and the two doctors eventually married and continued serving at the Kapsowar hospital until 1939, when Ashton was drafted into the British Army.

In 1937, Dr. Ashton negotiated a merger between the South African General Mission for which he represented and Africa Inland Mission. The union was officially acknowledged in the Inland Africa Mission Annual Report:

> We wish to record with deep thankfulness to our heavenly Father, the fellowship which we enjoy in the Eldoret area with Dr.

---

62. Sylvester, *Annual Report*, 22.
63. Collier, "Kapsowar Report," 21.
64. Reynolds, "Annual Report," 36.

Leigh Ashton and Marion Ashton who are the representatives of the South African General Mission. The record of progressive development at Kapsowar is a cause for encouragement and an indication that God has set His seal to the coming together of these societies.[65]

Dr. Ashton, the first resident doctor, began his outreach work with immediate effect. He visited the villages to preach and persuade the people to come to the hospital for medical treatment. Sometimes he went with either of the two early converts, Elijah Kilimo or Daudi Kisang as interpreters. The Marakwet listened to him politely but were not always willing to accept his message and change their ways. Judging from his experience and with little understanding of Marakwet ways, he concluded that the Marakwet were a most backward people. In his disparaging report he described them in the following words:

> This is the country where these tribes eke out their isolated existence deceived by their father, the devil that this is the best that can be experienced in this life or the next.... As they plodded along the mountain paths which passed through the Mission ground, fear and sin were clearly seen in their features, for their atrocious tribal customs and religious rites reveal they are the slaves of the devil, who exacts unmitigated service from them in this life, and pays his full wages at the end—even eternal death.[66]

This response convinced the missionaries that success of their work in Marakwet depended on the "native agents." Besides, the physical ruggedness of the territory would be managed best by the Marakwet people themselves who were used to the terrain of their land.

> The physical feature presents many real problems for evangelistic work. There is growing conviction among our brethren on the field that this task can be best undertaken by the natives themselves ... let us give praise for the continued blessing among the Marakwet and for their growing interest among these somewhat difficult people.[67]

It became imperative, therefore, for the Mission to establish schools and medical facilities as a means of out-reach. Between the two institutions, the school became the major force behind the establishment of out-stations, and the schoolteachers were also evangelists. In fact, both school

65. Ashton, "Annual Report (1937)," 39.
66. Ashton, "Annual Report (1935)," 19.
67. Ashton, "Annual Report (1936)," 1.

and church were closely aligned, if not synonymous. Sometimes the same building was used for both school and worship. This point is confirmed by J. S. Mbiti who makes similar observation from a comparable situation among his Kamba people:

> Schools became the nurseries of Christian congregations.... The same buildings were used as schools from Monday to Friday, and as churches on Saturday (for catechumen classes) and on Sunday (for worship services).[68]

The method of education adopted by the mission was directed towards evangelism. Any attempt to carry education beyond the proficiency needed for evangelism was considered improper use of the missionaries' time and resources.

> School work provided one of the most fruitful fields for soul winning; every effort should be put forth to conserve this avenue of approach.... Although the Mission is not constituted to give advanced education in any general sense, nevertheless it should be remembered.
>
> Because of the need for Christian leaders for church, school, medical and other places of responsibility in African life, suitable education should be considered for key people such as are in the extension of Christ's Kingdom as pastors, evangelists, schoolteachers, outschool-teachers, dispensers, and nurses.[69]

Kapsowar Boy's School was started in the second year of the Mission's existence in 1934. By 1936, Ashton reported timely progress.

> The number of the schoolboys has been increased in the last term and there are now quite a few little fellows staying here attending school every day. They are so much easier to reach while they are young and will make the future evangelists.[70]

The training given in the schools was often on rote learning aimed at Bible knowledge. The day usually began with assembly, where prayers were offered, before the pupils went to their respective classes. Before lunch break, all the pupils attended Bible classes taught by one of the teacher evangelists. At mission stations (where missionaries resided), like Kapsowar and Liter, missionaries engaged in teaching. At Liter, for example, Mrs. Paul Barnett, the Sunday school instructor, also taught the Bible classes at

---

68. Mbiti, *Concepts*, 303.
69. Smith, "British Council Business Report," 9.
70. Ashton, "Field Report," 16.

the Primaryschool. Her classes were well attended, as many were attracted out of curiosity of seeing a white person. My childhood friend Stephen a student in one of those classes attests:

> I attended the Sunday school and Bible classes at school more out of curiosity than religious interest. The missionary who taught the classes spoke our language in a funny way (accent). She was also, quite huge. Her lower arms were dangling when she conducted the singing. Everything about her was quite amusing.[71]

The hospital and the dispensaries served as the second means of outreach. Every morning at Kapsowar hospital the patients assembled for a prayer period. The message was given by either one of the Marakwet nurses or a missionary, and then an appeal for salvation or conversion to Christianity was made. After that, the patients were treated. An example of a day's activities at the hospital was reported by Dr. W. B. Young as follows:

> At 8.30 a.m. the dispensary service is held, by which time all the patients must arrive. The service is held in a nice little sort of a chapel. After this, the patients file into my room one by one and present their cards which they have obtained before the service by either showing their numbers, or if they are new, by getting a new number and a card. . . . I keep each patient's card and put it in its right file on my table. If any patient requires any thorough examination, there was little room for this purpose. The patients then go outside again and if there are cases for dressing or injections, after awhile their names are called by the boy in the surgery . . . and carries out the treatment. Patients for medicine hear their names called by the boy on duty. . . . Having got through the patients by about 10.30 a.m. Patients arrive who are connected with the school. Also, workmen and other station employees. When they are finished, then we do any odd minor operations or special treatment.[72]

Through the week, the nurses and other medical staff visit each patient for Bible reading and systematic instructions on how to live a Christian life. Those who were not Christians were also visited, admonished, and encouraged to consider conversion. In most cases, the patients acknowledged and accepted the Christian message with gratitude, especially after recovering from their illness.

---

71. Personal interview with Stephen Rutto, January 1989.
72. Young, "Field Report," 39.

The dispensaries in the out-stations were also active centres of evangelism. Elijah Kilimo, who spearheaded the early hospital extension work in Endo conducted services for at least an hour before treating patients. Those who heard the message and believed were encouraged to attend the catechism classes in preparation for baptism. At Boroko, a few people managed to go through the catechism classes; however, most of the people who heard the message did not follow through. The adults listened politely but remained unsure about converting to a foreign religion.

In 1942, Dr. and Mrs. W. B. Young arrived at Kapsowar. Dr. Young was born in Northern England in 1916. He entered Cambridge in 1935 to study medicine. While at Cambridge he became a Christian through the influence of an evangelical Christian movement. He also became a close friend of Philip Morris, another medical student whose parents were missionaries in the Congo. It was through Philip Morris that he became interested in missionary work in Africa.

He graduated from Cambridge in 1941 and married Nancy Brown, whose three brothers were missionaries elsewhere in Africa. She too was interested in missionary work in Africa. At the end of 1941, they went to the Africa Inland Mission office in London to inquire about the possibility of going to Kenya. As it happened, the Mission was looking for someone to go to Kapsowar hospital, which had been left without a doctor due to the War.

At the beginning of 1942, the Youngs started their journey to Africa. However, due to the War, they had to take a very roundabout route, first to America, then took a boat to South America and across the Atlantic to South Africa. From there, they flew to Kolandoto in Tanzania where they were given orientation on tropical medicine by Dr. Nina Maynard, who had worked in Africa for many years. After the orientation, they boarded a steamship to cross Lake Victoria to Kisumu, and then by car to Kapsabet. In October 1942, they arrived at Kapsowar.

A short time later they were followed by Ms. J. W. M. Banks, also from England, who had come out to replace Nurse Bessie Mildenhall who was due for furlough. Dr. Young was a Cambridge Rugby Blue who had participated in Scottish International games. With such an athletic background, he walked up and down the *Marakwet* hills and valleys. He learned the language in record time and quickly gained the confidence of the people. His years in Marakwet helped in the Mission's progress. Apart from his zeal for the faith, Dr. Young had a positive attitude towards the people. In one of his yearly reports, he wrote:

> Mrs. Young and I both have felt for a long time that the Marakwet don't deserve the title "degraded." They are a fine athletic

type, brave enough to tackle leopards single-handed, armed only with a spear and dagger. They have a very definite moral code. . . . They have a system of mutual help in danger, all the warriors respond instantly to a danger cry. They are cheerful, friendly and show care for their children. Their huts are well built, and their system of agriculture is a good one. . . . Their irrigation trenches, sometimes carried on aqueducts thousands of feet up the precipitous escarpment, are real feats of engineering skill. None of those things justify the epithet "degraded" and we would be glad if that could be erased from the annals of the Kapsowar work.[73]

Dr. Young's observation is quite opposite of the uninformed view of the earlier explorers like Samuel Baker who were blatant racists. Although his responsibility lay in hospital work, he did not confine himself to the station. He made several trips on foot down to the valley, promoting both the Word of God and the medical work. Initially, the Marakwet were not keen on Western medicine. They regarded it as a last resort when their native remedies failed. However, taking the medicine to the villages encouraged more people to use Western medicine. In turn, this established a better relationship with the Mission.

Dr. Young's efforts brought a lot of changes. Many boys converted to Christianity, mainly from the Mission's out-schools. Some of them volunteered to spread evangelism during their weekends. On completing school, some were posted as assistants to the out-schools, others as evangelists.[74]

> Doors are opening on all sides for us to go out preaching in small villages. There is a sense of urgency amongst the Christians to reach their brothers and sisters before it is too late, and they have been going out in ones and twos telling the Good News.[75]

Also, at this time, the evangelists got wind of the East African Revival movement, which was sweeping through East Africa[76] Besides, Dr. Young himself had been affected by the Cambridge Evangelical Students Movement. They stressed the new birth and the cultivation of Christian piety

---

73. Young, *Inland Africa* (1944) 32.

74. In the same year, Chebara out-school was opened. The buildings of the school were put up by the Kapsowar Christians without pay. They camped on the site in wet weather for a fortnight.

75. Young, *Inland Africa* (1945) 32.

76. The East African Revival Movement was a renewal movement that started in an Anglican Church in Ruanda in 1948 and spread across denominational lines in Uganda, Kenya, and Tanzania.

through daily prayers and Bible readings. Once the complete Nandi Bible arrived in 1939, the new believers found Bible studies much easier, especially those who had become the nuclei in the mission station at Kapsowar.[77]

In 1953, Dr. Stanley Lindsay came to Kapsowar and remained in Marakwet until 1978. He married Pauline Driskell, one of the nurses, and together they gave inspiration and leadership to the medical work in Marakwet. They were able to raise money for new wards, medical equipment, and expanded the hospital. A generator to supply electricity was also acquired. Like his predecessors, Dr. Lindsay travelled all over Marakwet. In 1959, the new road from Kapsowar to Kerio valley was completed by the government thus making travel to the valley much easier by car.

> Quite recently a new road has been cut through between Kapsowar and Liter. It is very important to us in the preaching and spread of the Gospel, because it goes straight down the escarpment in a most spectacular way to where there is an enormous population.[78]

Dr. Lindsay made use of the new road to the valley weekly. During those trips he opened additional dispensaries. Previously, without transportation, many sick people could not reach the hospital; some died on the way. Now they could wait at the dispensaries for the doctor's monthly visits, and the most critically ill were taken to the hospital in the doctor's Landover.

The greatest challenge then was finding enough African staff for the ever-expanding mission work. The hospital reported some sixty inpatients and several thousand outpatients every year. The school at Kapsowar had become an intermediate school and had 120 boys. Both institutions required trained African staff.

> Dr. Lindsay has been trying unsuccessfully to get more trained African staff to help in the work, but it seems difficult to find those with the necessary qualifications who really love and serve the Lord.[79]

To meet the hospital needs, nursing training was started at the hospital and the candidates were recruited from the out-schools. Those who showed

---

77. The Nandi Bible, which was translated by Bryson and Kimnyigei, was printed in England in 1939. It was also to be used by all the other Kalenjin-speaking people: Kipsigis, Keiyo, Marakwet, Tugen, and Pokot.

78. Driskel, "Kapsowar Report," 15. Pauline Drisdell joined Kapsowar mission hospital as a nurse where she met and wedded Dr. Stanley Lindsay. They got married and raised their family at Kapsowar.

79. McMinn, "Progress in Marakwet," 12.

consistency in their Christian life and had abandoned the old traditional ways were accepted into the programme. Their spiritual qualifications were more important for the job than their academic abilities. A few, who showed competence in both, were sent to Kijabe for further training. Unfortunately, the first Kijabe trainee had to be dismissed later for drunkenness.

The church was also experiencing steady growth, especially at Kapsowar due to the expanding school and hospital. The Christian teachers and hospital nurses conducted Sunday schools in the communities nearby.

> We now have about twenty-three places where meetings are held under the shade of a tree, some in a school building and six in a church (building). The small meetings have five or six folk attending, others fifteen or twenty and the larger ones over a hundred. All these meetings are led by men who have had no special training as pastors or evangelists for we have no such one in the tribe. Sometimes a woman may lead (the service) when a man is lacking.[80]

The twenty-five years of Dr. Lindsay's stay at Kapsowar witnessed a great expansion in the Mission's health work. Dispensaries and clinics were opened in remote places throughout Marakwet. With his proficiency in the Marakwet language, he was welcomed in several communities for which he visited regularly. As a good doctor, he respected the traditional medicines of the Marakwet. There were rumors that he sought treatment from Chebo-Kamichan, a famous Endo herbalist with whom he was in regular professional consultation.

Dr. Lindsay was also a preacher. He helped in the Kapsowar church. While encouraging the training of medical staff, he was equally supportive in the training of church workers. In 1962, two young people were sent by the church to the Bible school at Kapsabet. One of them dropped out after the first year; the other, a woman, completed her studies and married a Pokot man in Kapenguria. It was not until 1965 that another group was sent to the Bible school. By 1970, there were five trained African pastors in the Marakwet district. The first to be ordained was the Rev. Samuel Yego from Kabetwa. He became a pastor at Tot in Endo location for ten years. He would later resign due to rumors of infidelity.

In 1978, Dr. Lindsay left Kapsowar and was replaced by Dr. Brian Carson, a native of Northern Ireland. Dr. Carson had migrated to South Africa to work in a black university. While there, he met people who had worked with the Africa Inland Mission in Kenya. Mr. Jack Pinner, who was responsible for the construction of Kapsowar hospital, and Dr. Ethel Schaeffer,

---

80. McMinn, "Report from Kapsowar (1952)," 2.

who had worked as a nurse in Kapsowar hospital both influenced him in his move to Kenya. Like his predecessor, he expanded the hospital and, in addition to new dispensaries and clinics, he organized community health services and mobile eye clinics. Also, like those before him, he encouraged the training of African church and hospital workers. He employed qualified clinical officers trained at the University of Nairobi. During his tenure, many short-term doctors, and medical students, mainly from Great Britain and Canada, worked at the hospital. Some of them extended their stay to a year or more, while others came during their summer holidays. In his annual report of 1988, Dr. Carson acknowledged them and their sponsors:

> The year has brought many new faces to work for both short and long periods at Kapsowar. We are grateful to the Canadian Evangelical Medical Missionary Aid Society for again assisting us with short term doctor help on three occasions during the year. . . . Again, we have had much help and encouragement from a number of medical students from both Europe and North America. . . . We are especially grateful to "Samaritans Purse" in America for their generous help with the water project and two new staff houses and Christoffel Blinden Mission in Germany for its continued financial assistance each month and the contributions towards a new landrover for the eye work in the Kerio valley . . . we also thank CIDA in Canada for helping us with our Community Health Work.[81]

In the early years of the AIM work in Kenya, the form of the church structure and government depended on the missionary who worked in the specific area, thus creating different church structures in various areas of the country. From 1918, the missionaries began to discuss the possibility of uniformity within churches. By 1943, an organizational structure that resembled both Presbyterian and Congregational forms of church government structure was formed. This structure provided for the creation of local church councils, each made up of individual Christians. (A group of Christians who met to worship on Sundays formed local churches.) Several local church councils formed a district church council which in turn joined up with other district church councils in a wider area to form the regional church council. Each regional church council accordingly formed the national governing council called the Central Church Council (Baraza Kuu). At this time also the African based church officially became known as the Africa Inland Church. In 1947, it was officially registered with the government as an entity able to hold property but as a joint trustee with

---

81. Carson, "Hospital Annual Report," 2.

the Mission. The Mission on the other hand, refused to be absorbed into the Church under the African leadership and chose instead to co-exist independently, parallel to the Church. While this did not sit well with the African Christians, it continued to exercise a strong paternalistic control, extending discipline to the Church members and officers.

The tension between the African Inland Church and the Africa Inland Mission over partnership in the field provoked heated debates that continued throughout the decade of the 1960s and the 70s. While the Africa Inland Mission remained adamant on maintaining its autonomy, the general thinking of other mainline Protestant missions was towards the integration of indigenous church and mission. Also, the African Christians had found it difficult to understand the Mission's insistence on maintaining a separate organization from the same entity to which it owed its existence. An African leader's affirmation of this polarization is as follows:

> We have had several meetings, and every time we talk about the getting together of AIM and AIC. I am surprised that the AIC had to put pressure on its parent AIM to get something. It amazes the government people in Kenya . . . when Uhuru (independence) came, many denominations tried to bring forward the Africans in the church, even the Roman Catholics. But it appears that AIM is not going forward, but backward. . . . If we speak of bringing the Africans forward, then we are talking of something that AIM is not interested in.[82]

In 1970, the Rev. Wellington Mulwa replaced the Rev. Andrew Gichuhi as the leader of the Africa Inland Church and took the title of bishop. At the time, the Mission and the Church were still running parallel to each other and constantly in conflict. However, to reduce the tension, they compromised to bring all the departments, such as education and medical, under the roof of AIC. The Mission insisted to exist as a separate entity, and missionaries who worked in these departments were not considered an integral part of AIC but worked on secondment.

Bishop Mulwa noticed the racist elements in the mission and led the church into becoming autonomous from AIM. In October 1971, he presided over a large gathering of twenty thousand African Christians together with Mission delegates at Machakos where the autonomy of the church was officially declared. The Africa Inland Mission field secretary turned over most of the Mission properties to Africa Inland Church. The Mission interpreted this move by Bishop Mulwa as rejection of the mission. Some of the missionaries left the Kenyan field for other parts of Africa. As a result, the church faced

---

82. Cited in Gratian, "Africa Inland Mission," 320.

personnel and financial shortages which affected the running of the schools and hospitals. This was interpreted by bishop Mulwa and other African Church leaders as a financial sabotage on the part of AIM.

In 1978, Bishop Mulwa died from a road accident, and his assistant, Rev. Ezekiel Birech, succeeded him. Birech did not have the nationalistic leadership qualities of Mulwa, but he was a spiritual man of prayer. He had another leverage in Kenya's president Daniel Toroitich Arap Moi, also a member of AIC for whom he had known since he was a student at Africa Inland Mission school at Kapsabet. In fact, Bishop Birech had been the president's teacher at Kapsabet. Throughout the 1980s, the church continued to suffer from lack of funds to maintain its schools and hospitals. It has been forced to rely on the parent Africa Inland Mission and other development organizations such as the British Consul, Tear Fund, Canadian International Development Aid and World Vision International. Above all, President Moi donated and raised funds for the Church on several occasions at Bishop Birech's request.

The Roman Catholic Mission

The Mill Hill Fathers

In 1930, the Roman Catholic Mission, under the Mill Hill Fathers had also started work in Eldoret and were interested in expanding its work to the Elgeyo and Marakwet district. They sent Fathers Hermann Hartman and Hans Burgman to visit the government school at Tambach, hoping to place an African catechist who would teach religious studies. In the following year such a placement was realized, and an African catechist moved to Tambach. Most of his work was with the students.

The Mill Hill Fathers who extended their mission from Uganda came to Kenya in 1903 when the railway line had reached Kisumu. Their first mission in Kenya was at Ojalla among the Luo, followed by Mumias among the Abaluhya, and Nyabururu among the Kisii, all three under Kisumu. After the first World War, the Mill Hill priests followed the railway line to the Rift Valley to provide pastoral work to the Goan Catholics who had been brought from India to work on the railway line. They established a Chapel and purchased a house in Naivasha that served as a place of rest. Naivasha was, at that time, the British headquarters for the Rift Valley. In 1925, Eldoret was linked with Nakuru by a railway extension thus opening the way for the Roman Catholic Missionaries to the Kalenjin territory. By 1929, Eldoret had a church and a resident priest. Also, Chapels were opened in

Turbo, Soy, Moisbridge, and Kitale. From Eldoret, the missionaries spread to other communities in the Rift Valley.

In 1932, Fr. Nicolas Stam and his young assistant Fr. Joseph Kuhn left Mumias to work among the Kalenjin people. Before coming to Marakwet, Fr. Kuhn had established a Catholic mission at Chepterit in 1934. In 1948, he was sent to Tartar in West Pokot, and from there he traveled to Marakwet and prepared to start a Catholic mission at Sinon. That was not permitted by the Colonial District Commissioner due to its proximity to the Africa Inland Mission at Kapsowar. However, he was advised to look for another location within Marakwet. Fr. Kuhn moved twelve kilometers to Nerkwo where he cleared the local Nerkwo trees and established the Catholic mission in 1948. He was assisted by Fr. Koos van der Weijden. The Catholic mission in Marakwet was slow but in time, it expanded to the nearby homes around Nerkwo, Cheptongei, Kaplenge and Chebiemit.

After World War I, The Catholic evangelizing strategy concentrated on three key methods. The first was education. At the time, the colonial authorities had exerted a far greater influence on the missions through government grants in aid of schools. The colonial government realized then that an African self-government was inevitable in the colonies. Several studies were done, including Phelps Stokes Commission, which recommended an alliance of all Christian missions to achieve the required educational standards. Phelps Stokes policy aimed at education to improve social and community development, but not so much on the notions of citizenship and political rights. The British Colonial government as well as the missionaries embraced these general aims in order to resolve the mounting tensions over the colonialism of Africans. Based on this factor, the Mill Hill missionaries among others began to look seriously towards the provision of tertiary and secondary educational facilities.[83]

The second notable approach was the recognition that the evangelization of Africa depended on Africans bearing witness for the gospel to their own people. That meant the recruitment and training of African catechists/evangelists under European supervision. The third distinctive feature was a more sympathetic approach to African cultures as compared to the previous centuries where African cultures were demonized. This

---

83. During the 1920s and 1930s American strategies for racial justice had a major impact on colonial education policy in Africa. The ideas of the American educator Thomas Jesse Jones held a broad audience among Christian missions and colonial governments and the recommendations he made in the two Phelps Stokes Education Commission reports he authored became the basis for educational reforms primarily in British held African colonies but and other colonial regions. Jones, *Education*, 3–15.

distinguished the Catholics from the Protestants who waged war on African culture, especially the African Traditional Religion.

Following that strategy, the Mill Hill missionaries made contacts with the schools that were being started by the colonial government. The priest visited such schools and made contacts with the students. The next step was to place a catechist where a greater number of students showed interest. In fact, the priests recruited and trained their first catechists from the schools they visited, such as Tambach government school and Chesoi Intermediate. The Mill Hill Fathers and later the Kiltegan missionaries that replaced them took advantage of the government incentives and established schools up to intermediate level thus paralleling the AIM schools at Kapsowar.[84]

When the Mill Hill Fathers were phasing out their work in Eldoret region, the priests of St. Patrick's Society (SPS), founded in Kiltegan, Ireland, were invited to take over. In December 1951, a group of five Kiltegan Fathers set sail for Kenya aboard the SS Durban Castle and arrived in the port of Mombasa twenty-three days later. They were placed in five stations alongside the Mill Hill Fathers, whom they would soon replace. On June 29, 1953, the new missionary district was recognized as the Apostolic Prefecture of Eldoret and officially entrusted to the Kiltegan Fathers. By 1955, twenty-two Kiltegan missionaries had been sent out to the Rift Valley to serve in the districts of Uasin Gishu, Baringo, Nandi, Kericho and Elgeyo Marakwet.

Before going further, let us look at the first missionary to Marakwet. Fr. Michael Brennan (1924–2010) was the first missionary to be sent to Nerkwo mission. He was among the group of five who set sail for Kenya aboard the SS Durban Castle on December 6th, 1951, and arrived in the port of Mombasa twenty-three days later. Fr. Brennan went directly to Nerkwo to join Mill Hill missionary Fr. Lester Weech, who was to hand over the mission. Fr. Brennan was a man who did not spare himself in the work of spreading the gospel. In the early days, he would trek for up to two weeks, visiting outstations, sleeping in the houses of teachers. He was sustained by potatoes, the only food he carried with him, and whatever else the local people offered him. He was also a man of prayer who had a great love of the Virgin Mary and worked throughout his life to spread devotion to her. He regarded the Legion of Mary as an indispensable agent of evangelization. He promoted it everywhere he went and was, for a period, a full-time chaplain to the Legion in Eldoret Diocese. Fr. Brennan was also known for his evangelistic style that included the selling of religious items such as bibles, rosaries, medals, and other devotional objects. He believed strongly in the power of images and symbols in nourishing faith. After a

---

84. Baur, *Christianity in Africa*, 258–59.

year in Marakwet, he was sent to open Kituro mission. Some years later, he was one of the first priests to live and work in the Turkana, a closed area in which outsiders, including missionaries, were not allowed unless on famine relief work. That is how he founded the missions of Lorugum and Kakuma along with Fr. O'Brien. He died peacefully at Kiltegan at the age of eighty-six, being the last to die of the original five.

As previously stated, the school served as the main recruiting ground for converts.

During the holiday when schools were closed for a month, the priests brought catechumens to Chesoi for a crash course of catechetical program. Those who did well and were deemed ready were baptized. Some of the catechists include Josephat Chepkurui of Cheptongei and Raphael and Dominico of Kaplenge. The latter was knighted by the pope. The baptism of 1961 included Zelaya of Kakisegei and Kapkechir of Katemko, among others. In 1966, there was a large Catechetical class at Nerkwo sponsored by Fr. McNicholas. When the candidates were asked for their birthdate, most candidates had no way of knowing since such records are non-existent in the village. To solve that problem, the baptized candidates were given a uniform birthdate of 1955.[85]

Kerio Valley

The Mill Hill priests from Nerkwo sponsored a school at Chechan to parallel the AIM outstation school at Ngecher also known as Cheptororio. Gabriel Koyelel was the first teacher and several of his students included Justice Charles Chemuttut, John Suter Longura, Dominic Cheptoo, John Kilimo, Emmanuel Yano, and Michael Chereko. That school was later moved to Chesongoch in 1959. In 1968, the AIM mission dispensary at Chesongoch could no longer meet the health demands of the population. Chief Kisang Chemuttut and his development committee asked Dr. Lindsay to expand the facility to a health center. When Dr. Lindsay declined, the chief raised money through the community efforts to start the health center and asked the Catholic mission at Nerkwo to take over from where they left. Fr. Morgan O'Brien (1929–75) came and lived on one side of the health center while the construction was underway on the other side. He facilitated the Catholic work at Chesongoch until he was transferred to the newly established prefecture of Lodwar in Turkana. He died tragically in a car accident in Turkana on January 1, 1975, and was buried at Turbo.[86] Fr. McNicholas

85. Phone interview with James Kimisoi, October 8, 2021.

86. He gave me a ride in his VW beetle to Eldoret, that being my first time to a big town.

continued to manage the work from Nerkwo with the help of the faithful Catholic Christians who had been baptized either at Nerkwo mission or Chesoi outstation. Among them were the early converts like Zilaya of Kakisegei, Kapkechir of Katomko, Raphael Cherop (catechist) of Kwenoi, and Peter Cheboi (catechist) of Kakisegei, who later joined politics as councilor. The second batch to be baptized include Antonio Murkomen Chelimo, Dr. Joseph Kibiwot Litamoi, and James Kimisoi. Others who came later were Ernest Chepkonga of Kakisgei, James Cheboi of Kobil, Wilfred Kiptoo of Kacheturgut, and Edward Chelimo of Kakisegei.[87]

Among the women who were baptized include Mary Jeruto Biwott, Anyesi Chesir, Susana Cherop, Colleta Cheboi, Magdalena Kirop, Florence Cheptoo, Mary Chepkonga Anthony, Florence Kitum, Florence Peter, Veronica Cherop, Catherina Kipchumba, Sabina Biwott, Anna Yano, Margarina Biwott, and Annah Chelimo. These and many others shaped the local Roman Catholic Church at Chesongoch. It was also a common practice to baptize the whole family in those early days.[88]

The Benedictine Monks

In 1971, the Benedictine missionaries of St. Ottilien, Germany were invited by Bishop Emilio Njiru of Eldoret Diocese to conduct missionary work in Kerio valley. They arrived at Eldoret and were soon sent on their new mission in Kerio Valley. They settled at Chesongoch in 1972. The Benedictines did not have any mission in Kenya; therefore, they had to be under their East African base in Peramiho Abbey in Tanzania.[89]

The aim of the Benedictine Missionaries is to combine the Benedictine contemplative and active way of life in the mission field among the semi-nomadic people of Pokot and Marakwet in Kerio valley. The early missionary monks were Fr. Paul Steinman, Fr. Peter Meiberg, Fr. Winfred (kipchurmet), and Fr. Benedikt Ruegg. From Chesongoch, they dispersed

---

87. WhatsApp interview with James Misoi, July 20, 2021.
88. WhatsApp interview with Cheptoo Lotirghor, October 23, 2021.
89. The Benedictine Missionaries of St. Ottilien is a congregation of religious houses within the Benedictine confederation, founded by Fr. Andrew Amrhein, a monk of Beuron Abbey in the year 1884. The aim of the Benedictine Missionaries of St. Ottilien is to combine the Benedictine way of life in the mission field. Benedictines are contemplative and active. The work of the Benedictines of St. Ottilien Spread to Africa and Asia in 1887, when pope Leo XII entrusted the Benedictines with the Apostolic prefecture of South Zanzibar, in what was then German East Africa, presently Tanzania. Since there was no Benedictine work in Kenya so they had to follow their society's protocol and operated under the Peramiho Abbey in Tanzania.

and started parishes in other parts of Kerio Valley. In 1973, Fr. Lucas and Fr. Reinhard went up hill to Chesoi and established a Parish. In the same year two sisters, among many to follow from the community of missionary Benedictine at Peramiho, were sent to Kerio Valley to spearhead the medical work. The team, including Sister Eva Maria and Sr. Wilcart (koko), was instrumental in instructing catechetical classes to the Kipnyigeu age group including Pius Cheserek, Raymond Agui, Dr. Kiplegunya, and the late Kampala and others. Sr. Eva Maria later joined Fr. Benedict and Fr. Winfred (Kipchurmet) at Aror, which was established in 1975. The first converts to be baptized were John Cherwon, Jennifer Komen, Philip Kipkwomei and Sogomo Loyei.

In 1978, Fr. Reinhard Bottner (1940–2020) left Chesoi and pioneered a new work in Embobut. Previously, he had been a missionary among the Zulu people in South Africa in 1970s but left South Africa only because of his clash with South African apartheid laws. It all started when he was accused of breaking the apartheid law by giving a lift to a Zulu man to whom he knew. As a result, he faced subsequent harassments and threats from the secret police, forcing him to leave South Africa in January 1972. He was reassigned to Kerio Valley.

While in Embobut, he worked hard in building roads, schools, churches, and health facilities. He undertook countless trips on foot in the mountainous area, gave baptismal instructions, and celebrated many Masses under trees. He also trained catechists and set up parish councils. Today, there are churches at Lemeiywo, Korou, Kapchebau, and Wewo, as well as St. Michael's secondary school and health center. His success is partly attributed to his openness to the Marakwet traditions and the resources he brought to develop the area. However, he tried with little success to discourage the old Marakwet rite of passage commonly known as Female Genital Mutilation. It proved more difficult than he anticipated. On the other hand, he supported the men's rite and contributed resources to the initiation lodge (Kaptorus).

His gift for creating networks and supporting personal initiatives was helpful in his versatile activities, especially in gaining a wide circle of helpers. Another concern he had that was not fulfilled in his lifetime was peace between the warring tribes of the Pokot and Marakwet. In 1998, his house was broken into and robbed. That was a big blow considering his contributions to the community. As a result, he left Embobut for another mission at Kamwosor in the neighboring Keiyo district. Fr. Reinhard died in Nairobi in 2020 after five decades of successful missionary work in Africa.

Fr. Winfred made trips Northwards and established a mission outreach station at Sikip in Kowow in 1977. The catholic priest's relationship with the

AIM missionaries at Liter wasn't easy at first, but I think it improved later. In 1984, the mission outreach moved to its current location of Sebero on a land that was donated by Kapterik, Kasukut and Shaban clans.

Father Benedikt Rüegg was a Benedictine missionary of St. Otmarsberg. He was born in 1927 in Switzerland. After elementary school, he went to the St. Josef Institute at Gouglera for one year and transferred to the gymnasium in Disentis and Schwyz. On October 2, 1948, he entered the Benedictinum in Fribourg and pursued studies as a Missionary Benedictine preparation at the University of Fribourg. He was ordained to the priesthood in Saint Michel on the feast of St. Benedict, March 21, 1953. In November 1954, Father Benedikt was assigned to the mission of Peramiho in Tanganyika, before it was Tanzania. Until 1971, he had various parish postings in the southwest of the country. Father Benedikt offered himself along with other confreres for new mission in Kenya. For more than twenty-five years he served as a missionary with other Benedictines in the Kerio Valley region in Marakwet.

In 1999, Father Benedict returned to St. Otmarsberg Switzerland and worked for ten years as priest at Maria Bildstein. In 2011, he moved back to St. Otmarsberg due to poor health and enjoyed his last years in a retirement Abbey. He died at the age of ninety-four, on November 25, 2021. A month before his death he was visited by Teresa Cheserem Makail, a Marakwet woman who lives in Zurich.

While a missionary in Marakwet, Fr. Benedikt was easy-going and open. He embraced the culture with little inhibitions. For example, like most of the local adults, he was known to enjoy snuff tobacco. Occasionally he carried a tobacco snuff container and shared its contents with the adults he met on his village visits. As a result, he gained popularity among the locals instantly. Unlike the Protestant missionaries in the nearby station of Liter, Fr. Benedikt attended traditional ceremonies whenever he was invited and enjoyed the local brew of mead (*kipketin*). While he abhorred the traditional initiation of girls, he supported the initiation of boys. Occasionally, he contributed food stuff whenever possible. In fact, he earned the nickname '*Kaberur*' during the initiation of Kipnyigeu that took place on December 24, 1980. He found out that he was of the same Kaberur age as the initiates fathers. He paid his dues to the elders and was formally accepted into the Kaberur age set. Moreover, he frequently contributed food items, especially cases of soda, to a few circumcision lodges, thus increasing his popularity in the villages. Among the first converts to be baptized at Kowow location were Chilanyang and family, Arukwomoi and family, Kiberenge and family, Anyaman and family, Loikwotome and family, Rionoki and family, among many others. Samuel Berekimoi was their first catechist.[90] The author's grandmother, Maria Kochemeitoi Kasenyang, was among this group. She often boasted of purchasing her baptism and her name, Maria, with a huge bag of finger millet. She was baptized by Fr. Kaberur, as she preferred to call him.[91] Through the initiative of Fr. Benedikt Ruegg, St. Abraham Church was constructed, as well as the clinic. The sisters of St. Joseph were invited to care for the sick at the newly opened clinic and, out of that, grew the health center. In 1988, Endo Mission became a Parish.

Both Protestant and Catholic missionaries were white Westerners who shared the same views about Africans and their cultures. They were Eurocentric and operated as such within the colonial system. Like the colonialists, most of them treated the African people as inferior with the assumption that Christianity and western education would make them civilized and human. That is the base line in my view. While the two mission agencies in Marakwet were united in their Eurocentric outlook, they differed in their delivery methods. Evidently, Protestant approach was quite invasive while the Catholics were sympathetic to the culture. But to what extent? I pose this question to further discussions that will result in a robust Marakwet theology.

---

90. WhatsApp interview with Elijah Kamla, September 30, 2021.

91. Due to cattle rustling in Kerio Valley, she relocated to Kamendi in Cherangany to live with one of her sons. I paid her a visit one Sunday in 2004. I always enjoyed her wit and this day, and I wasn't disappointed. I asked her if she went to church, and she replied that she attended the nearby church but did not stay long because she did not understand the Turkana language. I found out later that it was a Protestant church in Kiswahili. She said she came back home and had her own church where she sang her familiar songs and prayed.

CHAPTER 5

AIM/AIC Christian Communities

Kapsowar Mission Station

THE CHRISTIAN COMMUNITY AT Kapsowar was not only the largest in the Marakwet but had also developed Kapsowar into a relatively active commercial town. Some of the Marakwet Christians started small businesses while active in the life of the church. The missionaries continued to offer leadership but only in the administration and training, otherwise the work of the school and evangelism was left in the hands of the Marakwet teachers and evangelists some of whom were new entrepreneurs. Today, Kapsowar has grown to a sizeable town of ten thousand people with schools and government offices, and the mission hospital is going strong as the only hospital in Marakwet. The mission hospital mission has remained the same for almost one hundred years. It has had resident doctors continuously and a successful school of nursing that has gained national recognition. Next to the hospital is the Kapsowar School of Theology. In 2023, a large Church structure with a capacity of seating over two thousand people was opened under the leadership of Rev. Robert Chesorom. The impressive structure was designed by Architect Eunice Kibor the daughter of Drs. Esther and Jacob Kibor and grand daughter of Mr. and Mrs. Zablon Kaino a pioneer Christian of Kapsowar Church.

When Rev. and Mrs. Reynolds established the mission station in 1933, they were received by Joel Arap Chemibei and his wife Jeni who had been sent earlier by the Nandi Church to evangelize the Marakwet and prepare the way for Marakwet AIM mission. Mr. and Mrs. Chemibei started a school in one of the government buildings. After a few months, they were joined by Elijah Kilimo and Daudi Kisang Koikoi, two Marakwet Christians, who had been converted in Uasin-Gishu and had been students at Kapsabet. They were recruited by the Rev. Reginald Reynolds to help with the work of the Marakwet mission. In time, they become the backbone of the Marakwet

Mission. Also, Reuben Seroney from Kapsabet joined them and taught for a while but left shortly after a disagreement with the missionaries. Seroney later left AIM and joined the Anglican Church. His son Jean Marie Seroney became a distinguished politician in Nandi and the deputy speaker in parliament during the rule of President Jomo Kenyatta.

It did not take long for the Reynolds and the other Christian workers already at Kapsowar station, to start their first outreach to the villages surrounding the station such as Cheles, Kapchsewes, Rorok and Sinon. To their surprise, they were met with a strong opposition by Mr. George, the former D.C. clerk, Mr. Kitum, the chief and three Somali Muslim traders, whose shops stood adjacent to the site allocated to the Mission. The mission asked the Muslim families to move elsewhere in the town, but they refused. One of them by the name of Ibrahim is rumored to have vowed that the missionaries would settle near his premises only over his dead body. Incidentally, this same person died suddenly, and presumably, his vow came to pass. There is no record available as to how he died, but the story made a great impression in the community. Eventually, the remaining two Muslims relinquished their resistance to the work of the Mission. In fact, one of them by the name of Abdi Garbush married a Marakwet woman, and for a while professed to be a Christian, although he returned to Islam.[1] Rev. Reginald Reynolds moved the school to the shop previously owned by the Somali Muslim Ibrahim who had just died. Ironically, the house served as a school and church until a new church was built in 1952.

The early missionaries at Kapsowar mission station were preoccupied in a wide range of tasks from evangelism, teaching, road building, medical work and running of the station. As converts and staff increased, Africans were employed not only as servants and manual workers but as evangelists, teachers, dispensers, nurses, and junior administrators. With such help, the missionaries had more time for administration. T. O. Beidelman observation applies to almost all the Protestant mission stations in Africa.

> A mission station has a developmental pattern; an initial stage of success with its routine and understanding in relation to the rapidly growing number of converts and a final stage when increase in converts and scope of enterprise leads to further routinization and lower standards in staff... the station forms a cultural security nest... isolated from the indigenous culture.[2]

This resulted in three subcultures. The station culture of missionaries, Marakwet Christian culture, and the larger non-Christian culture. The

---

1. Personal interview with Elijah Kilimo, February 1989, and Luka Suter, June 2016.
2. Beidelman, *Colonial Evangelism*, 23.

missionaries had an advantage at the station because of its enticing material culture of cash employment represented by the mission station. In fact, the rectangular modern buildings modelled what was expected of the converts. The rectangular houses were associated with Christianity and modernity while the African circular huts were associated with backwardness and heathenism. In this case, the type of house one lived defined a modern or Christian life over primitivity of non-Christians. Many have wondered if the missionaries were ever cognizant of the contradictions they portrayed when on the one hand, they promoted materialism while on the other hand discouraging their followers from material pursuits. On a similar note, the natives were discouraged from wearing the traditional dress which Karl Barnett used to call primitive or *"nguo za kishenzi."* He must have heard that reference from his parents or other missionaries. The contradiction lies in the fact that the natives were criticized for materialism when they purchased Western fashions of clothes, shoes, and ornaments and equally criticized when they wore their traditional attire.

Right from the beginning the missionaries had discovered that the success of their mission depended on their African agents who doubled as evangelists and teachers. The two prominent pioneers in Marakwet Christianity Daudi Kisang Koikoi and Elijah Kilimo served that purpose. It was in fact through their contact with the missionaries at Kapsabet that the missionaries came to Kapsowar in the first place. It is therefore appropriate to highlight these two pioneers.

Daudi Kisang Koikoi was converted to Christianity in a settler farm in Uasin Gishu after which he left the farm and went to Kapsabet to attend the mission school. There, he received not only an education, but further instruction in Christianity. He was soon joined by Elijah Kilimo Kleu, a fellow Marakwet from Endo location. The two became good friends and later worked together for the mission for many years. When the new mission to Marakwet was being planned, they were both involved. While at Kapsabet, Daudi Kisang's mother died, and he had to leave school to be with his father at Kamogo. After two months, Elijah Kilimo felt lonely and went out looking for his friend and managed to bring him back to Kapsabet. This is what Elijah Kilimo told me.

> When Daudi Kisang did not return after two months, I got quite lonely and decided to go and look for him. I walked for several days before I reached home. After resting for two days, I walked from my village of Sibow to Kamogo village, where I met Daudi in the field, harvesting millet with his father. I stayed overnight at his home, persuading him to return to school. I told him I was

not returning to Kapsabet without him.... On the following day, we set out together for Kapsabet, a journey of four days by foot and were welcomed by the missionaries and the other students.[3]

After their training at Kapsabet the two returned to Marakwet and were involved in the work of the mission. Daudi Kisang "Koikoi" became an excellent teacher at the mission station and a key leader at Kapsowar Church. Elijah Kilimo Kleu worked as a dresser and championed the establishment of out-stations or bush schools further out in the remote villages.

Daudi Kisang Koikoi and Elijah Kilimo Kleu were baptized at Kapsowar in 1934 by Rev. Reynolds. After that they immersed themselves in the work of the mission and were the first to evangelize their own people. At this time, they were in their mid-twenties, and the missionaries were concerned that they might end up marrying non-Christian women. This imminent concern inspired the missionaries to design a plan to find marriageable Christian women elsewhere. They had been made aware of the girl's school at Kabartonjo mission station over the ridge in Baringo. After making the contacts with the resident missionary at Kabartonjo mission station, they informed the two young men who were already curious and thrilled by the proposition. In 1935, Rev. Reynolds took the two young men by foot across river Kerio over to Kabartonjo to find wives among the Christian girls at the girl's home. The ordeal was difficult, but they pulled it off eventually. My visit and conversation with Mr. and Mrs. Elija Kilimo Kleu at his home at Suwerwo in 1990 confirmed what I had heard. He narrated the events of that unforgettable day. The preparation for the trip was nerve-wracking as he recalled. It involved getting ready, traveling the whole day by car, and most of all meeting strange people for which one had to select a lifelong partner. Upon arrival they were kept waiting in a different area as the missionaries conversed among themselves. When the time came, they were led to a line of girls for whom they had to inspect carefully before making their individual selection.[4] After inspecting the women students, Daudi Kisang Koikoi selected Ruth Kiplabat of Sacho, while Elijah Kilimo settled for Maria Komen Chelalam of Talai clan of Kapcheserem. Although the two young women were still at school, they were of marriageable age of 18 years. After a month of preparation and payment of dowry, they returned to Kabartonjo for the wedding. The combined wedding was conducted by the Rev. B. Dalziel, the missionary in charge of Kabartonjo on July 22, 1935, after the wedding, the

---

3. Personal interview with Eljah Kilimo, December 1988.
4. Personal interview with Elijah Kilimo, February 1989.

two couples returned to Kapsowar where they settled and started their families while continuing with mission work.[5]

Joel Arap Chemibei took Daudi Kisang Koikoi as his assistant at the school, while Elijah Kilimo Kleu assisted the missionaries at the station. Apart from a few trips to start new out-stations, Daudi Kisang Koikoi devoted most of his time at the school at Kapsowar as well as being an advisor to the out-stations "bush" schools. He eventually replaced Joel Arap Chemibei as head teacher and continued in that capacity until the government brought in better qualified teachers in the early 1960s. The educational schedule in those early years was very simple but strict. The class sessions for standards one and two were half an hour each and forty-five minutes for standards three and four. Much time was spent on manual work such as cleaning rooms, working the school garden, cutting wood, and fetching water for the school and the teachers. The allocated time for instructions was divided between subjects. For standards one and two, 40 percent of the time was given to secular classes, 20 percent Bible, 10 percent breaks, and 30 percent work and games.[6]

In addition to his teaching at Kapsowar, Daudi Kisang Koikoi was also instrumental in establishing a few out-stations, including Ngecher near his home where he constructed the first building that was used as dispensary, the school and church. Daudi Kisang Koikoi returned to Kapsowar, leaving Abraham Ngelech, one of his former students at Kapsowar, to run Ngecher station. Some of the fruits of Ngecher school include Jonathan Barsiron who became a teacher at several outstation schools in Marakwet. Two years later, after Ngecher, Daudi Kisang Koikoi was involved in the opening of Kapcherop out-station. When Ngecher experienced difficulties in the late 1950s, Daudi moved the school to his clan land at Kamogo.[7] In 1965, Daudi retired from active mission work due to poor health. He settled in Kapsowar where he opened a business. In 1970, he joined other fellow Marakwet Christians and bought a settler farm (scheme) in Suwerwa, Trans-Nzoia. He died in 1986, leaving his wife and several children and grandchildren. The funeral was attended by hundreds of church leaders and other dignitaries, including the then President of Kenya, His Excellency Daniel arap Moi. It turned out that Daudi Kisang's wife, whom he selected from among the Christian girls at Kabartonjo, was related to President Daniel T. Moi who ruled Kenya for twenty-four years and died in February 2020 at the age of 95.

In addition to Daudi Kisang and Elijah Kilimo, other Christian leaders emerged majority of whom came as students and stayed on as evangelists. They include Isaiah Chemwal, Zacharia Kipkech, Joseph Arap Kore, Ezekiel Chebet, Barnaba Kalacha, Marko Kotut, Josiah Marir, Cheserek Kipkech,

---

5. Kilimo, *Cultural Transformation*, 16–18.
6. Personal interview with David Chelimo, Kapsowar, 2016.
7. Personal interview with Joseph Kipkore of Kapsowar, January 1989.

Simon Chesang, Amos Cheserek, Isaia Chemwal, Solomon Chemwal, Noah Chesos, Marko Kimengich, Josiah Kasororot, Musa Kipkeres, Jeremiah Cheratum, Mariko Kimengich, Barnaba Kalacha, Amos Cheserek, Zakariah Kiptabara. The women include Ruth Daudi Kisang, Mariah Kilimo, Rebecca Zechariah, Leah Isaih, Ziporah Job, Flora Joseph, Grace Paulo, Peris Muna, Silvah Kileu, Milcah Daniel, Lillian Kirop, Helen Stephen, Salome Cheratum, Grace Katisei, Zaniaka Zakayo, Diborah Gidion, Hana Ezekiel, Prisca Herman, Tabrandich Parapiy, Cictoria Cheboi, Deborah Clement, Susana Tiren, Clara Keres, Lois Solomon, Milkah Boit, Jane Philip. Several of them attained the basic education of standard four, after which they were either employed at the Mission as dispensers, evangelists, or teachers. Most of them were already adults and ready to advance the work of the mission but they needed to learn how to read. In that case, they attended the afternoon adult education. On the weekends some of them were dispatched in small teams to the neighboring villages for evangelism. The prescribed method for evangelism was simple. First, the team would meet at Kapsowar, before they were dispersed. The missionary in charge would pay each of them five shillings at the beginning and another five shillings when they returned. They traveled in small teams, and when they reached the destined location, they divided further into smaller teams of two or four. Upon arriving at a homestead, one of them made the introduction and another gave the reason for their visit and introduce the gospel message, after which an invitation for response is offered. If someone believed, they prayed with them and took their names for future follow up. They would then proceed to the next home, and this would continue till evening. At night, the team would stay at a Christian or at a relative's home. When neither were available, they would ask to stay at any home willing to accommodate them. One informer related to me of an evangelistic team in which he participated. He recalled their total number as four and each received five shillings from the new medical doctor at Kapsowar, Dr. W. P. Young to travel to Sambirir—a distance of about two hours by foot. They arrived in the afternoon, and they visited a newly converted woman who led them to her village. In the evening they stayed at the woman's house only to be disrupted by her drunken husband who came at night. They didn't know where else to go in the middle of the night, so they stayed and persevered against the man's insults. Apparently, the man was furious because his wife no longer brewed alcohol after she converted. That meant a loss of income and status for him. The woman continued with her faith regardless and received support from other women who had converted to the Christian faith. Later, she started a Sunday school at her village and the Sunday school grew into a church. She was instrumental in joining other women in the newly founded women's group called *Kelyekab Chepyosok* (women's feet). *Kelyekab Chepyosok* focused on evangelism in the early days and later supported missionaries who dared to go far. Some of the missionaries who received support were sent among the Luo, Turkana and Rendile communities respectively. Village visitation was a prominent method of evangelism from the beginning. Pastor Paulo Chepkiyeng who participated in such evangelistic outreach in 1950s along with Barnaba Kalacha of Kapkamak described an evening in which a woman by the name of Linah Chemurey of Kapkomoro with whom they had shared the gospel one afternoon invited them to stay overnight at her home. There was a drinking party, but their host put them on the upper deck of the house (*tapoot*) where she felt was safe for them, but they were disturbed all night long.[8]

The response to those evangelistic visits was slow in the early years. The Talai clan, who lived adjacent to the mission station, resented the white people primarily for taking their land. Consequently, their relationship to the mission remained cold until the second generation. In fact, some of the clan members attempted to frustrate the work of the mission, quite often through theft and other tricks. One of the main culprits was Jeremiah Kisang. He stole building material, kept some at his home and sold the rest to neighbors. He also stole sheep and goats from the African staff that worked at the station. He abhorred outsiders. Noticeably, the thefts stopped when the mission employed him as a watchman over the station. Later, Jermiah Kisang became a forceful evangelist.[9]

In 1936, the Mission established a girl's home at Kapsowar, like those at Kapsabet and Kabartonjo. The primary purpose was to protect Christian girls running away from the traditional rite of circumcision. In preparation, three rondavels were to be constructed for them between the hospital and the missionary houses. Tom Collins, who was temporarily at Kapsowar awaiting assignment to the Pokot territory, assisted in the construction.

> After much prayer, we all feel the Lord would have a definite girl's work begins at Kapsowar. We are therefore building three or four round burnt-brick huts for them fairly near the missionary's residence, the first of which should soon be ready.[10]

8. Personal interview with Rev. Paulo Chepkiyeng, June 2018.

9. In 1947, Dr. Young took Jeremiah Kisang on one of his trips to Boroko, where Elijah Kilimo had moved to open a dispensary and a school. Jeremiah Kisang carried the dispensary supplies on the two-day journey on foot as there was no road then. While at Boroko, Elijah Kilimo held an evening service at his house where he read the Kalenjin Bible and explained it in Marakwet. At the end of the service, Jeremiah Kisang repented of his sins and confessed all his thefts at the mission station that included Elijah's sheep. On his return to Kapsowar, Jeremiah returned the stolen some of the property to the mission. He also enrolled at the school and later became an evangelist, notably at Kapsowar market. Personal interview with Jeremiah Kisang, February 1989.

10. Collins, "Kapsowar News," 79.

By this time, the Marakwet mission was fully established, and the Reynolds had moved back to Kapsabet for other administrative duties. The boy's school was making good progress under the leadership of Daudi Kisang and the girl's home under Eileen Mahood. The hospital was also gaining a good reputation, as were its medical staff. Patients returning to their respective homes after being cured of their ailments spread the news, and before long the hospital was very busy as people came not only from Marakwet, but also from the surrounding districts of Baringo, Keiyo, and Nandi. The patients who traveled from far, were often accompanied by family members who needed places to lodge while their sick relatives received treatment. Since there were no hostels or guest houses, and Kapsowar being too high in altitude for unsheltered living, it was necessary for the Christians to open their homes to these strangers. Such hospitality was common among the Christians. When Elijah Kilimo and his wife Maria were at Kapsowar, their home was often crowded with visitors mostly from all over Marakwet and Tugen in Baringo.[11]

Medical work was seen as Christian sacrifice and an opportunity to evangelize. In caring for patients and alleviating human physical suffering was thought to persuade many to accept the gospel. In this sense medical work was subsidiary to the real work of evangelism. In both Kapsowar Mission hospital and its outstations, the doctor and other health providers combined medical work with prayers, preaching and religious instructions followed by an invitation to confess sin and accept salvation in Jesus Christ. African patients would easily connect sin with their illness. Similar routines were repeated by the nurses at the outstations where the doctor visited periodically to see patients. Difficult cases would be referred to Kapsowar hospital.

Unlike the African Christians, the missionaries' houses were in a gated section of the station far removed from the African quarters. The only contact with Africans was at the hospital and at church services. That may be attributed to the general Western racial overtones in which white people, including missionaries, were warned to minimize their social engagement with Africans. Missionary children were not to be trained by native teachers. They were carefully isolated and could rarely mix with the native children.[12] The duty of entertaining "strangers" was left solely to the African Christians living around the station. Several of them had been employed in the hospital as casual workers or dressers. Amongst those who were permanently employed in 1935 was Isaiah Chemwal, who gave a lifetime service to the

---

11. Personal interview with Mrs. Maria Kilimo, December 1988.
12. Personal interview with Mrs. Maria Kilimo, December 1988.

hospital. Abraham Ng'elech, was assigned to Ngecher outstation as well as Kapsowar until he moved to Kapcherop for good. Others at Kapsowar included Amos Cheserek. This latter group was absorbed into the Mission as teachers and evangelists. Pilipu Chepkong'a from Mogoro became a prominent teacher at Ng'echer and Kamogo. Others who had joined and were active in the Christian community at Kapsowar were Joshua Chebobei, Samson Chelang'a, Pilipu Chepkong'a, J. Chemaringo, Daniel Morugeu, and Job Kibor Kabiron. Although most of them had been converted elsewhere, they chose to settle at Kapsowar to receive further Christian instructions, education, and employment at the mission station.[13]

Samson Chelang'a and Job Kibor Kabiron discovered the business opportunities in the growing town and took advantage of it. Samson Chelang'a started a variety shop, while Job Kibor Kabiron opened a small tea-room. At first, the missionaries encouraged them, but later objected to their new ventures. They attempted to accuse the two entrepreneurs of pursuing material gain instead of striving for the spiritual matters of the heavenly Kingdom. As a result, Samson distanced himself from the missionaries and concentrated on his business.[14] Job Kibor Kabiron, however, kept his business at a minimum and gave more time to the church and maintained a close relationship with both the missionaries and African Christians and eventually, became one of its main pillars. He earned the respect of many. Later, he was selected by the government to serve on the African Native Court at Kapsowar.[15]

Job Kibor Kabiron was born in Kaptol in Mogoro location. He traveled to the settler farms at the age of twenty in search of cash employment. He found a job as a herder to a colonial officer. Once, while herding goats, he became involved in a fight and hurt his opponent severely. Fearing punishment, he ran back to his village. He was pursued and captured by the colonial soldiers and taken to Eldoret where he was tried and sentenced to three months in jail for assault.[16] While in prison, he was visited by Elsie Clarke, a settler and an AIM contact, whose ministry included visits to prisoners in the Eldoret area. Through Elsie Clarke, Job became a Christian. Upon his release from prison, Elsie Clarke directed him to Kapsowar station where he enrolled in catechism classes for baptism. Finding many Christian friends at Kapsowar, Job decided to settle down there. He opened a small kiosk by the hospital where he sold tea. Later, he applied for a plot at the shopping centre and opened a small restaurant.

13. Personal interview with Joseph Kore of Kapsowar, February 1989.
14. Personal interview with Gideon Chelanga of Kapsowar, February 1989.
15. Personal correspondence with Dr. Stanley Lindsay, October 1991.
16. Personal correspondence with Dr. Stanley Lindsay, October 1991.

In the meantime, he had married Zipporah, one of the Christian women from the girl's home at Kapsowar. Unfortunately, Job and Zipporah never had children. During the early years of their marriage, Job was pressured by his clan to consult a diviner regarding their infertility, but Job rejected this advice citing his Christian convictions. Some of his people asked him to divorce his wife and acquire another woman who could give him children to carry on his name.[17] Job did not yield, and he and his wife remained together throughout their lives, and their love and commitment to each other served as a good example for many young Christians. Job often compared his faith to that of his namesake in the Bible. Evidently, he found courage from that biblical story.

Although Job and Zipporah did not have children of their own, they opened their home to all the Christian youth who ran away from their homes to get an education at Kapsowar and grow their faith. The pupils who completed their lower primary education in the mission out-schools were admitted at Kapsowar intermediate boarding school. Those who could not afford the boarding fee stayed in Christian homes and that is how many found themselves in Job's home. From the early 1960s, Job and Zipporah Kibor's home was buzzing with activities. Many of them eventually became teachers, pastors, and government workers. Others, including Erik Cheserek and Robert Kipkorir, who resided at Job's home while going to school and later succeeded in politics as members of parliament of Marakwet East. Job's home was also open to people who brought their sick relatives to the hospital. Some patients stayed for weeks as they receive treatment. Those who could not pay the hospital fees, either borrowed from Job Kibor or have him bail them out of the hospital to go home and look for the money.[18] Patients who had no means of paying their hospital fee were given manual work at the hospital after their recovery. Some sought permanent employment and stayed on, adding to the growing population. After a decade, the number of the Christians at Kapsowar had outgrown the land acquired from the government which was sufficient only for the purposes of facilities of a mission station, hospital, school, and a church. The growing number of converts in the settlement was not part of the consideration. It became

---

17. Traditionally, the Marakwet people become hysterical when a marriage does not produce children. This is the reason that, sometimes, a divorce is granted.

18. Cash was always hard to come by in Marakwet. To obtain money, people often had to sell livestock and such transactions took time. Those who did not own livestock were given manual work at the hospital once they had recovered. Some, who had converted, were given long-term employment, and they helped to swell the Kapsowar Christian community and delighted the missionaries whose intent was to grow a large mission station.

apparent that the growing population, otherwise known as "*Nganaset*," required more land for cultivation and livestock. The indigenous landowners were livid and resented the encroachments on their land by the migrants. In those days, an individual or a family who converted to Christianity would also desire the accompanying benefits of Western education and commerce entrepreneurship which could be obtained by living in the township.[19]

Dr. W. B. Young came to take charge of the station in 1944 and recognized the growing Christian community and its potential to spread the Christian message to the whole of Marakwet. He saw an opportunity for an outreach strategy that moved from the center to the periphery.

> We have a small group of Christians living near the station, an average of 80 at the Sunday services, a station school of 50 and two out-stations. . . . From this people have come the few whose hearts God has touched, and we are seeing the fellowship of the spirit deepening amongst them. They are coming in increasing numbers to the Bible readings and more and more of them are getting up early in the morning to seek God before the days' work began.[20]

With enough help at the station, Dr. Young combined his hospital duties with village visits. He started with the villages closer to the hospital. Occasionally, he visited distant locations, not only for medical purposes, but also to do evangelism. However, most of the village visitation were conducted on a regular basis by the evangelists and the station staff. After 1945, regular preaching journeys to the villages were organized. In most cases, audiences were not receptive, despite continuous attempts at several places, and efforts centred on schools and dispensaries.

> Several young men have come to school. They are our hope for future evangelism as outschool teachers and evangelists.[21]

In 1946, Sunday school classes were started in the villages around Kapsowar under the direction of Mrs. W. B. Young and Miss J. W. M. Banks. Teachers were recruited from the hospital staff, the girl's home, and the boy's school. Every Sunday morning, these teachers went out to the villages to hold classes, usually under a tree. Eventually, these classes turned into Churches when a few adults, mostly women, showed interest and attended. The Rev. Philip McMinn, who was briefly at Kapsowar and witnessed some of these developments affirmed it in his report:

19. Kipkorir, *Descent*, 61.
20. Young, "Marakwet Report," 32.
21. Young, "Marakwet Report," 33.

The shade of a large tree would be a meeting place of many who wanted to hear the word of God and have fellowship with fellow Christians. Very few of these folk could read, but many could sing hymns by heart, and some had learnt portions of Scripture. The number of these meeting places gradually increased.... At several places, simple buildings were put up.[22]

Some of the churches which started as Sunday schools around Kapsowar include Kapchelos, Kapchesewes, Sinon, and Cheles among others. Initially, they were under Kapsowar mother church through lay volunteers some of whom had other responsibilities at the station. Some of the early supply preachers could hardly read, but they would preach from some of the Scripture verses they had memorized. However, short Bible conferences were held periodically to equip volunteers who could not read but were willing to preach. While most of these small churches were led by male evangelists and volunteers, and most of those attending were women and children. There were some exceptions, like Suwerwa, where a woman named Kopilo was the leader; she became a Christian while at Kapsowar hospital and was later baptized by Dr. Young at Suwerwa.[23]

As Kapsowar community expanded with the help of the hospital, it attracted many Christian youth from the outstations. Some of them found employment at the hospital and the missionary homes, others joined the boy's boarding school. This influx created a major housing problem for the mission staff. The Talai people were not willing to give any more land. Eventually, the Mission managed to acquire a piece of land below the shopping centre which was too steep for farming. Several members of the staff, particularly the casual workers, were given a small piece of land on which to construct a dwelling and grow some maize and vegetables. As the population grew, the village of Kapanda became crowded and the solution to move some families out of Kapsowar became a reality. The first significant move was to Chebara in 1946 where many Christians relocated and established a school and a church. Because they were already entrepreneurs, they were interested in new farming, dairy skills, and trade.

In addition to the hospital, the school expanded from a handful of students to hundreds. They were drawn from the communities around Kapsowar at first and later, from the outstations. The boarding school for the boys was called Logo and the girl's residence was Kaptipin. The recruiting of students was difficult. The parents did not trust the white people and thought that their children were being enticed to work in settler farms

---

22. McMinn, "Report from Kapsowar (1946)," 3.
23. Personal correspondence with Dr. W. B. Young, January 1992.

through the pretense of school. The recruitment of girls was nearly impossible. Some of the early female students escaped the circumcision rite and early forced marriage arrangements. They were welcomed and protected by the mission at Kapsowar. Their families made attempts to return them with little success. While Daudi Kisang, was a pioneer, other teachers were to follow some of whom had been Daudi Kisang students and had gone on to receive the required training. They include Philip Chepkong'a, William Muna and David Chelimo.

David Chelimo enjoyed a long career as a respectful and disciplinary headmaster. He attended Kapsowar in 1950 along with Philip Chepkonga After Kapsowar, hewent to Kapkenda from 1955-58 and sat for the primary education exam (KAPE). Unlike his classmate Jonathan Long'aile, his grades were not high enough for a government school, therefore he joined the mission teachers training College at Kapsabet under Julian Jackson. Among his classmates was Elias Chesir of Kapcherop. In 1960, Julian Jackson moved the College to Mosoriot. In 1961, David Chelimo completed his training and was posted to Kapsowar mission station with a letter of authority to teach from standards five through eight. At this time, both the girls and the boys, streams joined to become Kapsowar intermediate school under his leadership as Headmaster (1965-86). The students he taught went on and attained successive careers. They include the following: Johnstone Chepkwony (senior prison officer), Rebecca Hezekia Kilimo (nurse), Rev. Edward Cheboi (pastor), Edward Talam (banker), Joseph Biwot Kirop (Navy), Jacob Kirop Lokiles (teacher), James Cheserek (Sr. Chief), Robert Kipkorir (MP), Boaz Kilimo (MP), John Marimoi (MP), David Suter Sudi (MP), Truphena Yego (councilor), Lord Ben (teacher), Helen Yego Cheburwa (homemaker), Johnsotone Chepkosir (teacher), Jacob Kibor (theologian), Edwin Suter (pastor/Bible translator) and many more.

As Kapsowar became an active Christian center (*Nganaset*) or kachebisas, it acquired its own notoriety of rejecting the traditional customs. Sunday services were fully attended, and weekdays were equally filled with Christian programmes, both at the church and in Christian homes. The Mission was convinced that, the reading of God's word would largely change the Marakwet from their old traditions and eventually the whole area would be Christian. That grand optimism proved to be difficult to achieve as time went on. While the missionaries encouraged regular weekly Bible study meetings, they did not attend them. Instead, they had their own separate meetings in their quarters. Those contradictions were not lost to any observer.

On Mondays, Bible studies were conducted in people's houses on a rota. A list was posted at the church and the hospital advising the location and name of the leader. In most cases, the classes were in the homes of Christians who worked at the hospital. The meetings often lasted an average of three hours, starting at 7:00 PM. Singing and spontaneous sharing of testimonies took up the first portion followed by the actual Bible study. Bible study materials were available in Kalenjin from Kapsabet printing press. One of the early ones was *Sobondab Betut age Tugul* (daily life). It was replaced in the 1970s by *Naam Ak Iam* which translates "Take and eat." These devotional materials were intended to deepen Bible knowledge as well as promote literacy. Many were motivated to read so that they would be able to read the Kalenjin Bible and the hymn book. These two books often comprised the whole library supplemented by a Bible study material. *Sobondab Betut Age Tugul* became so popular that it was often used in Evangelism.

On Wednesdays, prayer meetings were held at the church, and the believers were expected to attend. These meetings were, initially, conducted by missionaries, but gradually Marakwet evangelists and elders took over. Job Kibor Kabiron and Joseph Kore were the two elders that provided leadership on a more regular basis. Isaiah Chemwal assisted occasionally when he was not on duty in the hospital. Later when he retired Isaiah moved back to Chebara where he joined his brother Solomon and other Christian elders at Chebara Church.

One of the most important aspects of the church not only in Kapsowar but throughout Marakwet was the involvement of women. Women's participation in the early life of the church was significant and was initially spearheaded by Ms. Mahood, who organized women's meetings at Kapsowar on Fridays. Women in the small communities surrounding Kapsowar and beyond were also encouraged to meet at least once a week. Margaret Halliday, who worked with Ms. Mahood, reported on the women's progress:

> The women's meetings on Fridays have been going on nicely. One woman in the hospital who was recently converted asked for a book in which to learn how to read. She has taught herself and is now the very proud possessor of a Bible and a Hymn book. How she loves her Bible, and whenever you go into the ward, the first thing she wants to do is to read the Bible. . . . Pray for her as she will soon be going home. She will be the only Christian in her district.[24]

The women's work became one of the pillars in the life of the church not only at Kapsowar but also throughout the Marakwet region. Once every year, a week-long women's conference was held at Kapsowar. Many women from outstations attended and were given Christian lessons on

---

24. Halliday, "Annual Report," 39.

various aspects of life. The speakers at the conferences were the female missionaries or an invited quest. The women's organization known as *Kelyekab Chepyosok* sprang out of this group and still active today in advancing the gospel and the mission of the church. Today, the organization raises money to support missionary work in unevangelized parts of Kenya and South Sudan.Most recently, it has raised money to support a Marakwet missionary couple Reverend and Mrs. Zechariah Cheboi in their mission work among the Turkana in Northern Kenya,

Saturday afternoons were allotted to catechumen classes to prepare new believers for baptism. These classes usually ran between one to two years prior to baptism. During this period, candidates are taught facts of the Bible and theology, but above all their conduct is monitored.[25] Failure to meet the moral requirements would lead to delay or denial of baptism. These obligations include abstaining from alcohol, smoking, and sex outside of marriage—and the rejection of traditional practices of dancing and the circumcision rituals.

From 1950 on, the Africa Inland Mission applied to the government for new centres to erect churches, clinics, and schools. The Mission's objective at that time was to take over the whole of Marakwet before any other mission staked a claim. The Roman Catholic Mission[26] was already at Nerkwo, some twelve miles from Kapsowar and imminent threat to the AIM work. Lately, their work in Marakwet had intensified, especially in the field of education, and the Protestants did all in their power to thwart their efforts.

In 1958, the two missions fought over a piece of land in Suwerwa, near Kapsowar. The dispute went as far as the government's board of education, who mediated in the matter. In the end, the Africa Inland Mission was given permission by the government to develop the site and a year later a church building was erected.

> We thank the Lord that a church site has been granted in this location right on the edge of Kapsowar. . . . We do praise the Lord that it is no longer a site but now a church building with one baptized member and others attending the catechumen classes.[27]

---

25. Personal interview with Elijah Kilimo, February 1989.

26. Fr. J. Kuhn, a German belonging to the Mill Hill Mission, first became responsible for Nandi, Elgeyo, Marakwet, and Tugen when he first arrived in 1927. In 1935 he moved to Nandi and continued to visit the other districts from there. In 1948 he opened the Marakwet station at Nerkwo.

27. Jackson, "Battle for a School," 9.

Two years later the two missions fought over another site at Maina, a mile away from the previously disputed location. The Catholic Church claimed to have been given the site to build a school by the District Education Board. The Rev. P. W. McMinn, the Africa Inland mission station manager at Kapsowar, who had laid claim to the site, dispatched a letter of complaint to the District Education Board.

> I wish to place a very strong and serious objection to the above school.... The school was granted to the A.I.M. late in 1959 and a visit paid to the area by the manager, Assistant Supervisor, local headmen and a few of the people. A suitable site was chosen, and arrangements made to have the levelling started and materials bought. The work had hardly begun when Fr. McDonald from Nerkwo visited the site and without consultation either with the District Commissioner or Education Officer stopped the work as he made a prior claim to the site. The government education office stepped in and after brief investigation, A.I.M. was given an alternate school at Tuturung.[28]

The Roman Catholics constructed better schools than the Protestants, which gave them an edge and Villages invited them to start schools in their communities. This competition became a threat to the Protestants missionaries who had enjoyed an early monopoly of sphere.

The Rev. A. R. Checkley of the Africa Inland Mission wrote to the field director in Nairobi alerting him to this imminent threat in Marakwet.

> The very great problem facing the Marakwet church council is that the Roman Catholics have said they are prepared to build for the people and naturally if we fail, the people will turn to the R.C.'s.[29]

From this competition, Chebara Secondary School was established by the Mission to provide higher education for the young people who had completed the intermediate level. With the financial contribution by English school children, through the Council for Education in World Citizenship, the construction of classrooms was done, and the school commenced in 1965. In thanking the organization's director for their donation, the Mission's head-teacher wrote in 1961:

---

28. Philip W. McMinn, letter to Mr. R. F. Roberts, Education Officer Elgeyo/Marakwet, July 8, 1960.

29. A. R. Checkley, letter written to the Africa Inland Mission Field Director, October 8, 1963.

With your generous gifts we have bought some fine books for the school library, items of furniture, farm equipment and have put up a nice single classroom of much improved design to the usual mud walled type. Part of the money donated has been used to complete a fine new brick building comprising two classrooms with a store and office.[30]

The Mission Outstations

Some of the Christians reached out from Kapsowar to farther villages and established a dispensary and an out-school where they would evangelize on the weekends. This approach was in tandem with the missionaries' agenda to use native evangelists to reach their villages with the Christian message. Elijah Kilimo Kleu and Daudi Kisang Koikoi, for example, were the early pioneers of this simple approach that yielded several outstations and eventually Christian communities. Several medical trips were also made by the missionaries in the company with Marakwet interpreters. The combination of these activities resulted in the formation of several Christian communities chronologically as per their years of establishment. On a cautionary note, the number of the mission evangelists who doubled as teachers or dispensers were few, therefore it was necessary to rotate them as per the needs of the mission. In that case the same person might appear more than once in the records of different out-stations.

Kibuswa

In 1936, Elijah Kilimo Kleu and his wife Maria were sent by the mission to open a dispensary at Kibuswa location. It was the first out-station of the Mission. After choosing an appropriate site at Katkok, Elijah started building a simple shelter.[31] He was assisted in the construction by Tom Collins, a missionary from England, who was at Kapsowar preparing to begin his mission work among the Pokot of Baringo. On his visit to Katkok, Tom Collins observed:

Yesterday, I came back from choosing a site and starting work on our first Marakwet out-school—a full day's journey from Kapsowar. The Lord has given us a magnificent centre for it,

---

30. Philip McMinn, letter to Mr. Terence Lawton of Council for Education, November 21, 1961.

31. Personal interview with Elijah Kilimo, December 1988.

and I feel that the position will play its part in keeping up the morale of the teacher who is to be there. He is not a particularly bright fellow, but he has a good wife who was trained in the girl's home at Kabartonjo. When this first out-school is built I imagine we shall be ready to choose the exact position for the second; after we have built that, we shall have used up all the available teacher/evangelists.... At the out-school which we are now building, the chief said that he himself would see to the getting of poles and thatching for the teacher's house which I thought was a very nice gesture.[32]

Elijah settled down quickly and introduced the work of the mission to the people. Curious minds came to the station, and the chief encouraged them to utilize the facilities offered by the mission. Soon, Elijah's dispensary received some visitors. He treated the sick in the morning and turned the dispensary into a school in the afternoon. The first few approaches to the dispensary comprised simple ailments such as cuts, ulcers, and malaria. In most cases, people came to try Western medicines and compare them with their traditional village doctors. Unlike the dispensary, the school had a slow start, as parents were reluctant to send their children. The boys and girls were expected to assist their parents from a very early age.

> From an early age, children are taught to help their parents. Boys are sent out to herd cows, sheep, and goats. Girls help their mothers fetch firewood, water, and help with the weeding of the garden. They must invent their own toys and games. Boys soon learn to play with bows and arrows and later when grown up, will have to use these as well as spears to protect themselves and their livestock from animals such as leopards and hyenas. Girls learn to sew skins together and ornaments of beads.... In many parts of Marakwet, parents are opposed to their daughters going to school as they cannot see any advantage in it.[33]

On several occasions, Elijah went to the parents to beg them to send their children to school. The parents on the other hand preferred that they look after their livestock instead of wasting time in classrooms. A few of the boys, however, were able to attend the classes forming Elijah's first school. After a year, he had five regular pupils, including his young brother Wilson Kilimo, whom he had brought from Endo for the purpose of receiving an education. Wilson Kilimo later found employment with

---

32. Collins, "Kapsowar News," 79.

33. Philip McMinn, letter to Mr. Terrence Lawton of the Council for World Citizenship in London, November 1961.

the government and rose to become a senior officer in the motor vehicle department. There was also a girl by the name of Elizabeth among the five pupils. She later went to Kapsowar girls' home and was married by George Kendagor who taught at mission schools at Kapsowar, and Kapcherop before becoming an independent missionary in West Pokot. The son of Abraham Ng'elech, Dr. Benjamin Kipkorir attributed his academic success to the discipline of George Kendagor.[34] Later, pioneer missionary in Kapenguria West Pokot. George Kendagor died in July 2018, but his legacy lives on in the churches and the schools he founded and above all, the people he influenced and trained.

Within the year, Elijah also introduced Sunday services, but these were poorly attended. The only regulars were his pupils and their friends. The adults were not interested in going to church, including those who attended the dispensary for medical attention. They were content with their own system of beliefs.[35] Having so little success, Elijah Kilimo became discouraged. Also, with work in the dispensary in the morning and school in the afternoon, he did not have any time for evangelism within the community. Meanwhile, at the mission station at Kapsowar, a young man identified as Samuel, came to the hospital for treatment, converted and was baptized. He showed a keen interest in mission work and expressed a desire to become an evangelist. Being aware of Elijah Kilimo's full program, the Mission intended to send Samuel to help him, but discovered that Samuel's reading ability was inadequate:

> We found that Samuel's knowledge of elementary education was very small, so he went for three months to Kapsabet to get special training in the school there under Miss. Collier's supervision. He has worked very hard, and she says he has made good progress and is now fit to teach the elements of reading and writing, which he will have to do at the out-school as well as medical work. We are hoping that he and his wife will be out at Kibuswa in the course of the next two months.[36]

When the Second World War broke out in 1939, Elijah Kilimo was recalled by the Mission to return to Kapsowar. Apparently, all the British male missionaries in Kenya were drafted into the army. Dr. Leigh Ashton had to

---

34. George Kendagor started several churches in West Pokot and later settled in Kaperguria where he established a training centre for evangelists. His son, Timothy Kendagor, was the principal of Kapsabet Bible Institute for a long time. Nathaniel Kendagor runs a successful Christian school in Kapenguria as well.

35. Personal interview with Elijah Kilimo, December 1988.

36. Reynolds, "Kapsowar News," 6–7.

pass his medical responsibilities at Kapsowar to his wife Marion, also a doctor, and Bessie Mildenhall, a nurse. Elijah Kilimo was brought back to assist and conduct the worship services in the mornings before treatments.

The recall of Elijah Kilimo resulted in the collapse of Kibuswa. A replacement was sent, but he did not have Elijah's flair and drive and the community rejected him. Moreover, the Kaptol clan did not want their land used for a hospital with a potential burial ground as they had seen at Kapsowar. Eventually, the station was closed, and the remaining pupils transferred to Kapsowar.

In the early 1960s, some students from the area who were studying at Kapsowar, started a small church at Kaptabuk, near the place Elijah Kilimo had founded a school in 1936. Through that school, other small ones have. One of the students, Paulo Chepkiyeng, later went to Bible college and returned to be the pastor of Kaptabuk is a product of Kaptabuk school. Paulo Chepkiyeng attended Sangurur primary school in 1936 where he heard the gospel. However, he converted in 1960 through the influence of his cousin Ezekiel Chebet who later became a prominent teacher and leader at Chebara. Before joining Kapsabet (Kalenjin) Bible School, Paulo Chepkiyeng was an evangelist for two years. As an evangelist he joined the ranks of the second-generation evangelists including Amos Kipkech of Samar, Marko Kandie of Komolwo/Suwerwo, Sylvano Kipkatam of Kapkamak /Koitilial. In 1965, Paulo attended Kapsabet (Kalenjin) Bible School and graduated after three years. The curriculum then was in Kalenjin language and his teachers included Philip McMinn, Samuel Kipnyigeu, and Jane Baxter. After serving as a pastor for many years, Paulo Chepkiyeng returned to school for additional studies for a year in preparation for ordination.[37]

Ng'echer

By the end of 1936, the second out-station in Marakwet was opened at Ngecher. It came as a result of Daudi Kisang's request for a station in his home area. Obviously, Daudi volunteered to spearhead the work and did so single-handedly. First, he constructed a two-room house to serve as both a school and dispensary. After that, he constructed a house for his own family. His wife, Ruth Tabarno, had converted and trained at the girl's home at Kabartonjo mission, and assisted Daudi during village visitations. As Daudi knew the area and people very well, it was easier for patients to use the dispensary and for parents to send their children to school. Within

37. Personal interview with Paulo Chepkiyeng, January 1989.

the first year, Daudi's work showed a better success rate particularly regarding dispensary enquiries.[38]

After a year at Ng'echer, Daudi Kisang Koikoi and was recalled to Kapsowar where Daudi took over the school from Joel arap Chemibei who had to return to Nandi. Daudi's successors at Ngechar were the first products of the school at Kapsowar namely Isaiah arap Chemwal from Moiben location and Abraham Ngelech from Arror location. Later they were joined by Pilipu Chepkonga from Kakisagur in Mokoro location. Pilipu took charge of the school, while his companions worked in the dispensary as evangelists.[39]

In 1938, Abraham Ng'elech was transferred to the new station at Kapcherop. That left Isaia Chemwal to manage the dispensary until he was recalled to Kapsowar. When the Second World War broke out in 1939, AIM work scaled down. The War years did not only affect Ng'echar but all the AIM stations that depended on male missionaries. The departure of Dr. Leigh Ashton from Kapsowar affected both the hospital and the out-stations. Throughout the war years 1939–45, the dispensary did not run at full capacity due to a shortage of workers. The school, however, continued to function under the able leadership of Pilipu Chepkonga.

Towards the end of the War, Dr. Young came to resume the medical work. He made several visits to out-stations assisted by Daudi Kisang Koikoi. He re-activated the dispensary at Ng'echar and Paulo Katisei, who was helping Abraham Ng'elech at Kapcherop dispensary, was relocated to Ngechar. The school, still under the leadership of Pilipu Chepkonga, had moved from Ngechar due to the declining number of pupils to the more populated area of Kamogo. Daudi Kisang had offered their clan's land to accommodate the school in the new location.

Paulo Katisei was born in the village of Kapsogom in Endo location about 1915. At the age of seventeen, he went to Kapsowar to visit his older brother Johana Kaino who was working at the District Commissioner's offices. While at Kapsowar, Johana heard the Christian message through Joel arap Chemibei. In 1932, he returned home and was initiated into the Korongoro age set. After the initiation ceremonies, he joined some young men from Endo, and they travelled to Ziwa in Tranzoia to work on a settler's farm. While at Ziwa, he visited Kitale and was introduced to Salvation Army preachers who converted him. In 1940, he returned to Kapsowar and was employed at the hospital as a casual labourer at a monthly wage of twelve shillings. In 1943, he married Grace Cherop Cheboi, a young woman from

38. Personal interview with Elijah Kilimo, December 1988.
39. Personal interview with Elijah Kilimo, December 1988.

Kasang who was at the girl's home at Kapsowar. Grace had fled to the girl's home to avoid circumcision on the grounds of her new faith. She was ridiculed from her village but that did not sway her.[40]

Paulo learned to read and write and was promoted to dresser. In 1947, he was transferred to Kapcherop dispensary to assist Abraham Ngelech. Two years later he was moved back to Ngechar to reopen the dispensary. In 1953, he was posted again, this time to Chesoi in Sambirir location where a government dispensary had been turned over to the Mission. He remained at Chesoi until January 1956 when he was relieved of his duties following a disagreement with the Mission. He moved his family to Kamogo where Daudi had given him a piece of land.

He left his family at Kamogo while he proceeded to Tot to start a business. While at Tot, he married a second wife; however, she left him as his first wife refused to allow him to conduct a traditional wedding ceremony.[41] Early in 1989, after thirty-three years, Paulo returned to the church and asked to be re-instated. He has six children with his first wife Grace and two from the second wife. The first-born, Obadiah Kiptoo, who married from a Muslim family at Kapcherop worked as an eye clinical officer at the government provisional hospital Nakuru and later at a district level in Marakwet. The second born Sarah was the first female schoolteacher at Liter Primary school. While at Liter she was married to Benjamin Logere a high-ranking officer of Kenyan prisons. They later relocated to Moiben where they had purchased a farm.

When Paulo left Ng'echer in 1953, he was replaced by Ezekiah Kaino of Sibow location. By 1960, most of the people at Ngechar had relocated to their fields on the valley floor near Kabetwa. This resulted in a decline in attendance at the dispensary and its subsequent closure. Ezekiah was transferred to Chesongoch to run the new dispensary started by Dr. Stanley Lindsay. In 1968, a clinic was opened at Kamogo under Benjamin Kilimo, an elder and evangelist of Kamogo Church. He was not a trained nurse but knew enough to manage the basic needs of the clinic and prepare the ground for the monthly doctors' visit from Kapsowar hospital. Grace Katisei the wife of Paulo Katisei became a prominent pillar at Kamogo Church. She organized a strong women's group and founded two other churches at Kapchebau and Chawis. Initially, the two churches began as Sunday school outreach of Kamogo Church. In 1982, Job Kisang, one of the youth members who attended Sunday school at Chawis, completed

40. Songs were composed on how Cherop ran from the knife of womanhood. Those songs are still sung during beer parties and other festivities.

41. Even though tradition allows one to marry more than one wife, it must always be done with the consent of the first wife.

studies at Kapsabet Bible College and became the pastor in charge of the three churches. Pastor Job Kisang has since relocated to Cherangany along with others who purchased a settler farm at Kamendi in Tranzoia. Since many were already Christians, they reconstituted a new church and called it AIC Baraka. The prominent church edifice was constructed under the leadership of Dr. David Kimaiyo, a high-ranking police officer who later rose to e the rank of Inspector General of police in Kenya. The church was officially opened by the then President Daniel Arap Moi.[42]

Kapcherop

In 1938, the Mission sent Daudi Kisang to open a new dispensary at Kapcherop. Samson Chelang'a and Joshua Chebobei had gone there the previous year to construct a square structure of eight-by-eight meter that was to be utilized as the dispensary. After opening the dispensary, Daudi Kisang 'Koikoi' left it under Abraham Ng'elech who doubled as a schoolteacher especially when there was a shortage of teachers. Unlike other stations in Marakwet, Kapcherop School flourished from the beginning because of interest from the local community. Moreover, Kapcherop was closer to settler farms which were keen on hiring literate workers as clerks. The dispensary was also well attended, mainly because many people were increasingly receptive to Western medicines.[43]

In 1941, Abraham Ng'elech requested an assistant from Kapsowar, and Noah Chesus, who had converted earlier in Kibuswa under Elijah Kilimo, was sent to help. Noah took over the school, and Abraham concentrated on the dispensary. At weekends, they both visited the communities for evangelism and Sunday School and continued with the work till early 1942 when Mr. Ngelech was moved back to Kapsowar Station for another assignment to Ng'echer. During that time, tension arose between the mission and the community of Sengwer around traditional beliefs and values. The tension resulted in the departure of some of the Sengwer to West Pokot. As a result of that move, the colonial government stepped in and curtailed mission activities around Cherangany.

In 1949, the mission decided to send Abraham Ngelech (again) and George Kendagor to Kapcherop outstation. As he made plans to move his family, Abraham Ngelech sent his son Benjamin Kipkorir to proceed

---

42. Personal correspondence with Dr. Stanley Lindsay, October 1991.

43. The Kapcherop out-station suffered no setbacks, possibly because it was close to Tranzoia and many settlers. There was more interaction between the Marakwet, and the settlers' farms and Western values were, therefore, more acceptable.

ahead with Mr. Kendagor the new schoolteacher. Abraham Ng'elech had planned to follow but his plans were delayed when his wife left him, and he had to look after small children on his own. He was also worried that with his wife gone, he might lose his employment with the mission and his assignment to Kapcherop might be revoked. Instead, the mission was sympathetic and kept him in their employ. He could have married another wife according to Marakwet culture, but his Christian teaching prevented him. Meanwhile, Benjamin Kipkorir recalls how difficult it was for him to be away from the rest of his family, but at the same time, he credits George Kendagor for his formal education.

> My formal education career was effectively launched in the course of 1949 by the tall, lanky, self-assured, severe, and highly religious man, Mwalimu George Kendagor.[44]

In 1950 Abraham Ng'elech finally moved to Kapcherop to run the clinic while George Kendagor continued to manage the school. Kapcherop School grew and expanded under George Kendagor. He ran the school effectively and with considerable discipline. Abraham Ng'elech came from Arror location in Kerio valley. He converted in 1934 and was one of the first to do so at the station. After conversion, he enrolled at the school and was instructed by Joel Chemibei. Following completion of the three-year program, he married a woman from his village called Sarah. The young couple decided to settle at Kapsowar, where Abraham was employed as a cook to the Reynolds household. When the Reynolds returned to Kapsabet in 1935, Abraham Ng'elech trained as a dresser at the hospital before going to Ng'echer in 1936. His experience prior to arriving at Kapcherop stood him in good standing and he remained there until his retirement in 1965. His wife, Sarah Kabon was never interested nor involved with the church, and she left him and the children at least three times. However, Abraham found his identity in the church and his business. In the week, he ran his variety shop and on Sundays he participated at AIC Kapcherop where he was a prominent elder.

During his years of work at Kapcherop, Abraham had managed to acquire a shop and a piece of land where he settled his family. Following his retirement, he expanded his variety shop in the growing market centre to provide for his children's education. His third son Dr. Benjamin Kipkorir went to Tambach in the 1950s and proceeded to Alliance High school and Makerere University. After working for Sirikwa County Council for a brief period he went on to Cambridge University in England for advanced studies in history and graduated with a PhD in 1969. Dr. Kipkorir returned to

---

44. Kipkorir, *Descent from Cherang'any Hills*, 74.

Kenya and taught at the University of Nairobi until 1985, when President Daniel Moi appointed him as the executive chairman of the Kenya Commercial Bank, the largest financial institution in Kenya. After leaving the Banking sector, he was deployed by Moi as Kenya's ambassador to Washington, DC. Dr. Kipkorir has published several academic works, but he is famously known for his first book *The Marakwet of Kenya*. His memoirs were published in 2009 and he died in 2015.

In 1950s, AIM had been forced by several factors to accept government funding and educational demands for Africans. Eventually, in the 1960s the government took over all primary schools. With new government regulations, Noah Chesus lost his job due to his limited education. However, his son Elias Cherop, who had trained at the Teachers' College in Mosoriot, became the headmaster at Kapcherop. In 1970, Elias resigned from his teaching career and became the chief of Cherangany location.

Abraham's replacement at Kapcherop was Clementi Rotich, originally from Katilit in Kaben location. Apart from short transfers to Liter and Kapsowar, Clementi remained at Kapcherop dispensary. When Clementi was absent on an assignment elsewhere, several nurses in succession were sent from Kapsowar to Kapcherop on short-term assignments to gain an out-station experience. In 1972, Clementi returned to Kapcherop from another assignment and stayed until 1978, when he was sent to open a new dispensary at Kaptalamwa. Unfortunately, this dispensary was not a success, and Clementi returned to Kapcherop where he retired in 1980. Clement Rotich's son Daniel Yano completed Bible College and later served as a pastor and High School Chaplain. He decided to return to Kapcherop.

The active ministry of the Mission through the dispensaries and schools resulted in the considerable growth of the Christian community at Kapcherop. There is now a large church with over two hundred regular members, and six small church plants in Chebororwa, Kaptalamwa, Kamoi, Kapyego, Tenden, and Kibikos.

Boroko and Liter

When Dr. W. B. Young and his wife Margaret arrived at Kapsowar in 1942, they released Elijah Kilimo to open a new out-station in Endo location. Elijah searched for an appropriate spot and finally chose to settle at Boroko, at the extreme edge of Marakwet region. Apart from being a suitable area, the place was also the village of his maternal uncles, and he used his affinity to his advantage and was welcomed there. His business partner Elolia Kwananyang (author's grandfather) was also a resident of Boroko. It is not known how they met but they developed a friendship and partnership in business. Although Elolia Kwananyang did not go to church, his first wife did, and their second born son Jeremiah Kipkeu was one of Elijah Kilimo first students at Boroko school. Jeremiah proceeded to Tambach to train as a brick layer and worked for the Kenya ministry of works in Eldoret, Nakuru, Lokitaung and Narok. He was at Lokitaung when Jomo Kenyatta was in detention there.

Elijah Kilimo was born in Sibow location around 1900. When he was about twenty years old, he joined some of his peers from the village and traveled to work on settler farms. During this period, most of the able-bodied young men were being recruited by the colonial administration to go and work on the European farms in Uasin-Gishu and Tranzoia. A hut tax of two rupees had been introduced early in 1904. While, this tax was to increase government revenue, it was later used by European settlers to induce Africans to work on the European-owned farms.[45] The Marakwet men traveled to the far away settler farms just to earn the tax money and return home.

> At present nothing will induce a man to accept employment once he has collected his tax money and few who go out to work will not remain for more than 2 months.[46]

Those without the cash money to pay were forced to part with a few heads of their precious cattle or goats. The majority, however, managed, somehow, to obtain the two rupees tax by selling livestock a head of time before the tax men arrived. In 1919, the government hut tax was increased to five rupees. This made it difficult for many Marakwet people to pay and, fearing to losing their livestock, a greater number of people signed on to work on settlers' farms. The Assistant District Commissioner, Mr. N. R. R. Vidal, reported the Marakwet response:

> This is the first year that Marakwet have been out to work on farms in any numbers and they have been most fortunate in their employers whose fair and kind treatment of them in this their initial effort will. I am sure it has a favorable effect on the future output of labour from the Reserve. This current year is also the first in which the Marakwet have been called on to pay a Rs.5 tax. This tax was very promptly paid, in fact the greater majority paid up. Rs.27000 being brought in 15 days.[47]

Apart from obtaining the tax money, the people also acquired the newly arriving merchandise of cotton cloth (shuka) which was brought in by the

---

45. Mungeam, *British Rule in Kenya*, 110–11.
46. Vidal, "Annual Report 1918."
47. Vidal, "Annual Report 1919–1920."

Europeans. The shuka became so fashionable that every person wanted one. Those with more money could purchase the famous blanket that came to be called "maalsenji" means no simpleton or poor person can afford it.

In 1922, the District Commissioner offered jobs to able bodied men from the district to work as laborers on the construction of the railway in Uasin-Gishu. The response was poor, especially in Kerio Valley.[48] However, Elijah and a few young men accepted the offer and were taken to work at Kaptagat near Eldoret. Their pay for work on the railway was Sh.12 per month.

While working at Kaptagat, Elijah Kilimo heard the Christian message through some evangelists from Africa Inland Mission at Eldama Ravine. Towards the end of 1922, cholera struck the camp, and many died.

Fearful of the dreadful disease, Elijah Kilimo left work and went back to Kerio Valley where he remained until he underwent the rites of circumcision in 1923. When the government school at Tambach was opened in 1930, Elijah applied for admission, but he was somehow refused entry. He was considered to be too old. He approached the Mission school at Kapsabet and was enrolled in January 1932. Daudi Kisang, from Kamogo was already at Kapsabet Mission School and Elijah was happy to meet another student from Marakwet.

When Kapsowar Mission opened in 1933, Elijah and Daudi were recruited to assist the missionaries. As previously stated, Daudi taught at the school, while Elijah worked as a dresser at the hospital. In 1934, the two were baptized along with Abraham Ng'elech of Kapsogom, Arror, Andrea Kirotich of Kaben and Job Birech of Nandi. Elijah loved to preach, and immediately after his baptism took leave of absence from the hospital for a preaching tour of the Tugen territory. He went with a Tugen Christian to the Baringo area. Whenever they met a crowd, Elijah took the opportunity to preach; he often preached in Kiswahili and his friend, Landa Kiti, translated it into Tugen.

In 1935, Elijah and Daudi traveled to Kabartonjo for a double wedding ceremony was conducted by the Rev. B. Dalziel, the AIM missionary in charge of the station. After the marriage, the two couples returned to Kapsowar.

As previously stated, Elijah Kilino was sent out to start a new outstation at Katkok/Kibuswa. When War broke out in 1939, Elijah was recalled to Kapsowar hospital. The school at Kibuswo was closed, and the pupils transferred to Kapsowar. In 1942, Elijah offered to open a new station in Kerio Valley. After a considerable search for an appropriate site, he chose

---

48. The *Marakwet* initially resisted working for the settlers; however, when the hut tax was introduced, they were forced to do so or lose some of their livestock.

Boroko in Marich sub-location. It happened that Boroko was the community of his maternal uncles. Furthermore, his one-time business partner Elolia Kwananyang (author's grandfather) and Lokotiyan Mwatabei hailed from there. The latter two were engaged in the business of trading maize flour (posho) and tobacco for goats and cattle in Turkana. One of the trading posts was Kobono Kuruch/Karena which was located about six kilometers below Boroko.

In February, Elijah started classes with a handful of pupils. He worked hard in persuading parents to send their children to school. At first, he faced resistance from parents but before long he succeeded with a few students. He also opened a dispensary. He attended to the sick in the morning and taught the school in the afternoon. In the evenings and at weekends he visited homesteads. By 1950, the school attendance had grown to over fifty pupils. The Mission employed William arap Muna to assist Elijah Kilimo, thus freeing the latter to spend more time at the dispensary. Once a week he took his small mobile clinic to the small shopping center at Chesegon which is located at the border between Marakwet and East Pokot. The medical supplies had to be transported on foot from Kapsowar. The regular carriers were Mwaitum and Lokitam, both from the Talai clan in Boroko. They walked the forty miles to Kapsowar and back in two days for a small stipend. Lokitam was recognized for his sportsmanship, especially in the long-distance running.

William arap Muna came from Kaben, the next sub-location to Boroko. He had gone to Kapsowar and had been converted to Christianity employed by the Mission and sent to assist Elijah at the school at Boroko. Former students reported that Arap Muna was quite stern with the pupils and not liked. As a result, some of the children dropped out of school to the distress of Elijah Kilimo who oversaw the out-station. Eventually, arap Muna was removed and returned to Kapsowar. His replacement was Daniel Kitum from Kakisagur. William arap Muna remained at Kapsowar until 1960 when he was appointed assistant chief of Kaben sub-location.

Elijah Kilimo's work at Boroko met with success and surpassed his earlier work at Kibuswo. He attracted many children to his school. Elijah Kilimo Kleu was well liked by the people and his efforts at the dispensary were highly appreciated. However, his evangelistic endeavors did not win many converts except a few women. The mission's negative attitude towards traditional honey beer, and Marakwet traditions did not impress the men. This was also the reason his two close friends, Elolia Kwananyang and Lokotiyan would not join him socially, although some of their children attended the school. Elolia Kwananyang sent his second son, Kipkeu Elolia to school at Boroko and later to the government school at Tambach to train in masonry. The most famous student was Vincent Arap Too who became the first member of parliament when Kenya attained independence in 1963. One of Kwananyang's daughters, Lillian Tabarno Elolia, became a Christian and accompanied Elijah's daughter, Susan, to the girl's home at Kapsowar. She later resided near her brother Jeremiah at Chebiemit before acquiring a piece of her own land at a former settler's land at Uswo. She has since donated a small piece for the construction of a Church. Many people appreciate her ability in evangelism and public prayer. Enock Suter was also a student at Boroko and later an effective teacher and headmaster at Liter and Cheptulon primary schools. He made his home at Cheptulon, and he and his wife Nancy Suter are known for their generosity in opening their home to many young people including John Ng'imor who rose to become the Headmaster of Chewoyet High school and later Assistant Secretary and Philemon Kilimo who was once the provincial engineer of roads in Rift Valley.

The first women attendants at Elijah's little church were Koyano Luguget and Kimoi Elolia Kwananyang (the author's grandmother). They were soon joined by others, including Kochebe Lokotiyan. These women were very faithful attendants, but none were baptized because they did not reject their traditional practices. The same apply to the men who came to church later on. Kisang Kariwotum and Karaninyang showed a keen interest and started to attend literacy classes but discontinued contact when the mission relocated the school to Liter.[49] Elijah Kilimo was the most sympathetic to traditional culture; he never forced the Mission's views onto his audience. He was gentle and moderate in presenting the gospel and rarely attacked the Marakwet tradition.

> Some of the dances, such as Kimosop and Kirap were not necessarily sinful as far as I was concerned, but the missionaries rejected all of them. No Christian was permitted to involve in traditional dances nor partake of any ritual meal.[50]

When the road from Kapsowar to Chesegon was completed in 1949, the mission saw it necessary to move the school and dispensary from Boroko down to Liter which was on the new road. Tom Collins, who had been working among the Pokot at Nginyang also moved to Liter. For Collins, Liter was chosen for two reasons. Firstly, it had a good source of water which was essential for a mission station; secondly, it was situated on the Marakwet and Pokot border, an ideal place from which to reach both groups of people. The construction of the dispensary was carried out by Dr. Philip Morris who replaced Dr. Young for a short period at Kapsowar. He was assisted by

---

49. Personal interview with Kisang Kariwotum, February 1989.
50. Personal interview with Elijah Kilimo, December 1988.

Mr. Checkley, an Australian missionary at Kapsabet. By the end of 1952, construction was completed, and Elijah resumed work in the new building. At the start, the relocated school met under a tree until a classroom was completed with the help of the community.[51]

In 1957, Elijah was asked by the District Commissioner to be an elder in the African Native Court based at Kapsowar.[52] The Mission was reluctant to release him, but Elijah was excited by his new assignment. He left his dispensary work in the hands of one assistant, Johana Lobeiluk, whom he had trained. While at Kapsowar, Elijah worked diligently in the African Court, alongside Job Kisang and others and on weekends he assisted in church work. He was respected by both the missionaries and colonial administration for his prudence in customary law and with people. In 1965, he retired from the African Native Court and moved to Suwerwa in Tran-zoia where he and his wife, Maria, settled. They got involved in Suwerwa's church work until 1975, when Elijah became blind. He died in 1989.

With the arrival of Collins, Liter station expanded slightly. Ruth Collins, who was a trained nurse, took charge of the dispensary and managed it well. She was assisted by Johana Kanda Lobeiluk who had been trained by Elijah Kilimo. Ruth Collins was the daughter of Mrs. Elma Elizabeth and Rev, Arthur Barnett, who were pioneer missionaries in Masai and Eldama Ravine. Her four brothers had also become missionaries with the Africa Inland Mission in various parts of Africa. Ruth was influenced by her Swiss mother, Elma Elizabeth Barnett, was a massage therapist. This training was most useful in rehabilitating the sick in Africa, and she guided her children into the field of medicine. Two of her sons were doctors with the Africa Inland Mission.

Ruth became a Christian early on and was baptized by Charles Hurlburt in 1926. She attended Rift Valley Academy at Kijabe and later trained as a nurse in the United States. She returned to Kenya and worked as a nurse at the Kijabe mission hospital. In 1942, she met Tom Collins a fellow missionary who was a British Army chaplain during WWII. They were married

---

51. Personal interview with Elijah Kilimo, December 1988.

52. The African native courts were established by the British to administer law and order among the Africans. They were presided over by European District Officers working with African elders and assessors. They were guided by local laws and customs as they existed. In 1930, these courts were given jurisdiction over whole divisions, instead of committees as previously. Their appeals also went to the District Commissioners and Governors rather than to the High Court. These changes enhanced the powers of the native tribunals manned by elders and chiefs for deliberations. See Mungeam, *British Rule in Kenya*, 54.

at Kijabe in 1944. When the war ended in 1945, they moved to Nginyang where Tom Collins had previously established a mission station.[53]

Tom Collins was born in South Africa in 1915 and attended Cambridge University. On one of his visits to South Africa he met Reginald Reynolds who was returning to South Africa on furlough after a term in Kenya with the Africa Inland Mission. Their conversations resulted, eventually, in the conversion of Tom Collins, who later recalled this experience:

> I was interested in Mr. Reynolds' work. I wanted to speak to him but decided to wait and let him approach me. It was the first time anyone had asked me about my relationship to Christ. It was the first time I confessed Jesus as my Saviour.[54]

Reynolds shared with him the challenge of the Mission in the Eldoret area and the need for British missionaries to pioneer work in Northern Kenya among the Pokot and Turkana. After Tom Collin's return to Cambridge, he corresponded with Reynolds and made further enquiries about the Pokot people. His interest regarding the Pokot began to grow and he recognized this to be God's call to missionary service. He made preliminary application to the Africa Inland Mission in London and was told to take a course on Bible and missionary training at the London Missionary College. After two years he completed the program which included, apart from studying the Bible, how to build a house without using nails. He again applied to the Africa Inland Mission, but was rejected because of a seriously damaged heart, the result of rheumatic fever earlier in his life.[55]

Although he was physically weak, he was a strong-willed man, and persistent in what he believed to be right. His conviction regarding missionary work was so strong that he decided to make his own way to the Mission in Africa.[56] With a minimum of baggage, a motorcycle and a ticket bought with his own money, he boarded a ship for Kenya. When he arrived at Mombasa, he rode his motorcycle to Nairobi, then by train to Eldoret, and the final thirty-two miles by road to Kapsowar. He was welcomed there by the Reynolds and the Ashtons.

Tom Collins remained at Kapsowar for the entire year of 1934, awaiting news from the Pokot chief. Finally, he received word from chief Naro, inviting him to open a station in his area. He immediately got down to

---

53. Personal interview with Mrs. Ruth Collins of Eldoret, April 1989.
54. Phillips, *Tom Collins of Kenya*, 37.
55. Personal interview with Mrs. Ruth Collins of Eldoret, April 1989.
56. Richardson, *Garden of Miracles*, 85.

the task and pioneered the East Pokot territory. Although he did try other methods, Tom's trips within the Pokot area were mainly done on foot:

> He tried his motorbike, but it proved a hindrance. He tried a bicycle, but it was difficult riding on desert sand. He even tried a mule. A missionary had to smile as he recalled "I saw that the mule throws Tom three times over its head until it finally submitted to Tom's leadership."[57]

Between trips in the hot Pokot country, which lasted about a month, Tom resorted to a few weeks in the cooler climate of Kapsowar or Kabartonjo.

> There were no holidays, for Tom was spending many hours a day on language study, not only of Suk (Pokot) but also Swahili. In both of which he became fluent.[58]

After about three years, having exceeded accomplishments of the average medically fit missionary, Tom re-applied to the Africa Inland Mission, and was accepted immediately. No further questions were raised, for Tom had proved himself more than equal to the challenging task he had taken among the Pokot.

When war broke out in 1939, Tom joined the British Army as a Chaplain. In 1944 he married Ruth Barnett, and in 1945, after the end of the war, he took his wife to Nginyang station where they settled and worked among the Pokot people. The task of communicating the Christian message to the Pokot people was extremely difficult and often frustrating. The Pokot, deeply rooted in their traditions, were slow in responding to the Christian message.

In 1950, trouble surfaced in the territory stirred by Lukas, a Pokot charismatic leader who had embraced the Msambwa religion.[59] Lukas Pkech made great promises to those who would follow him in his venture to repel the white people (*wazungu*). Tom overheard a conversation concerning the plot in a little shop in Nginyang and reported it immediately to the police. Reinforcements were sent, but not before many lives were lost, including those of some government officials. Lukas was killed in the affray, and many of his followers were dealt with by the law. Tom was called to give evidence at the official enquiry and spent many hours in the witness

---

57. Phillips, *Tom Collins of Kenya*, 37.
58. Phillips, *Tom Collins of Kenya*, 48.
59. Msambwa Religion was started by Elijah Masinde from Western Kenya. He combined traditional African beliefs and Christianity and attempted to resist the colonial domination. In 1952 the Kolowa branch of Msambwa was crushed by colonial administration.

box. After one of these sessions, when Tom had spoken of his work among the Pokot, a member of the enquiry team remarked:

> Tom Collins is one of the finest men I have ever met. To work in that difficult country for so many years with so little to be seen in the way of results demands the highest of a man.[60]

In 1952, Tom Collins moved to Liter with the approval of Reynolds to establish a new station to serve the Pokot and Turkana regions. Liter also offered a better climate compared to the Kinyang station. While his wife worked at the dispensary, Tom Collins embarked on the translation of the Pokot New Testament; his collaboration with a Church Missionary Society missionary, Mrs. Totty, who was based at Kapenguria. They worked tirelessly for several years to give the Pokot the Scriptures in their own language. Finally, in 1964, revisions were done, and Tom Collins agreed to type the fair copy to be sent to London for printing. Just before completing the typing, Tom Collins succumbed to a long-time illness and died. Despite many obstacles, the Pokot New Testament was eventually published.[61]

After Collins' funeral at Kijabe, Ruth Collins returned to Liter with her adopted son, Malcolm. She was soon joined by her brother Paul Barnett and his wife, Dorothy. The Barnetts had been sent to take over the station. Paul Barnett was one of the twins born to Elizabeth Barnett and Albert Barnett at Rumuruti. He went to the Rift Valley Academy for his elementary education, and then to Columbia College in the United States. After completing his engineering studies, he applied to the Africa Inland Mission, but was turned down on the grounds of his inadequate theological understanding. He was encouraged to study for a year at Moody Bible Institute in Chicago and was then accepted by the Mission. His first assignment was in Eldama Ravine, where his parents were missionaries for many years.

Paul Barnett was incredibly good with his hands, an asset in pioneering work. The first thing he did when he came to Liter in 1965 was to construct the church building planned by Tom Collins. This was followed by building the dispensary and a large semi-permanent home for his family; this included a swimming pool in a nearby stream which became a point of controversy later. Paul Barnett was also responsible for the construction of the churches at Tot and Koitilial. He also assisted at some of Kerio Valley schools which came under the Africa Inland Mission sponsorship.[62]

---

60. Phillips, *Tom Collins of Kenya*, 48.
61. Phillips, *Tom Collins of Kenya*, 48.
62. Personal interview with Johana Kanda Lobeiluk, March 1989.

In the early 1960s, the Roman Catholic Mission at Nerkwo (near Kapsowar) started out-reach work in the Kerio valley. Dr. Stanley Lindsay agreed to hand over the dispensary at Chesongoch to them because it was almost impossible to supply it from Kapsowar. The Catholic Missionaries expanded the clinic into a health center, constructed a church and visited villages. New missionaries arrived from Europe to assist in the expansion of the Catholic Church in Kerio Valley. Arror Catholic mission was opened in the early seventies followed by Endo Mission. When Paul Barnett came to Liter in 1965, he saw them as the main threat to the Africa Inland Mission's work in Kerio Valley. On some occasions, the two Missions confronted each other over sponsorship of schools and preaching spaces.[63]

An example was a contest over Chepkum Primary School. The community first invited the Africa Inland Mission to help build a classroom block. When the Africa Inland Mission delayed, the chief approached the Roman Catholic Mission and, being eager to get a foothold in the Kerio valley, they put up the classroom block within two months. When the Africa Inland Mission evangelist went to the school to preach as he had previously done, he was refused entry and told the sponsorship of the school had been given to the Roman Catholic Mission. Paul Barnett appealed to the government District Education Officer, but he was told that the community had the prerogative to choose whichever mission they wanted.

Another incident took place at Sangach, three miles from Liter. The Catholic evangelist came to hold services on Sundays which were most attended by children. When Paul Barnett heard about this, he dispatched two of his employees from Liter to go and disrupt the meeting, but their efforts yielded no success. The assistant chief Kiberenge Karupe intervened. He called a public meeting (baraza) and asked the Kowow community to decide which mission it favored. A majority chose the Africa Inland Mission on condition that they provide a school. After two years, nothing had been done about the school. The assistant chief Kiberenge Karupe, asked the Africa Inland Mission for reasons why the building of the school had been delayed. The Mission advised that, as the school at Liter was close to the area in question, he felt that the children should attend the school already established in Liter.[64] In 1980, the Kowow community invited the Roman Catholic Mission to build a school for them. The Mission did not only build a school, but also a mission station capable of serving the whole of Endo location. The Endo health center was established. Already, the dispensary at Chesongoch has

---

63. Personal interview with Chief James Cheserek of Endo, March 1989.
64. Personal interview with Paulo Kibore of Liter, March 1989.

been transformed into an impressive health center to serve Mogoro location. There is also another one at Arror location.

Chebara

Two factors were responsible for the starting of Chebara out-station. First, the growing population at Kapsowar had reached its breaking point. Secondly, there was an agricultural incentive by the colonial government to encourage native populations on the cooler highland areas along the forest line to practice modern agriculture of contour terracing, padlock fencing, and new crops such as maize, beans, potatoes, and pyrethrum and the promotion of European dairy cows. These agricultural activities were to spread from Kapsowar and Chebara to other parts of Marakwet. In 1950, they were further enhanced by the Swynnerton Plan which was aimed to raise agricultural output in small farms commonly found in cooler climates. This smallholder agriculture program was the brainchild of a colonial agricultural officer Roger Swynnerton. He had been involved in the development of cash crops in Tanzania for seventeen years and had been brought to Kenya to promote research for food and cash crops in small farm holdings.

The combinations of the two incentives motivated several Christians from Kapsowar station to relocate to Chebara. Additionally, the Christians sought and found comfort with other likeminded families in a setting where they could practice the two mission benefits of Christianity and commerce. In his memoirs, *Descent From Cherang'any Hills*, Dr. Kipkorir captures the dramatic move that commenced in 1946–47 led by Dr. Young. The first project was the construction of a school and a teacher's house which was done by a team from Kapsowar led by Dr. Young, Joshua Chebobei, Samson Chelang'a, Daudi Kisang (*koikoi*), Ezekiel Chebet (*Sungula*), Isaiah Arap Chemwal and his brother Solomon Chemwal, Samuel Koilege, Kimuron Arap Tolkos, Josiah Kipsarno, Arap Yego, and Marko Mengich relocated to the new outstation. Dr. Young noted.

> It was . . . school holidays and the schoolboys were all set to joining in when they heard about it. The mission would supply maize meal and a side of beef from a killing up at the shops for rations and with the [LNC] government grant for nails and equipment, their free work would do the rest. Every able-bodied man who could possibly make it was going. . . . In the end 25 men and 12 schoolboys formed the party.[65]

---

65. Young, "Eldoret Area Report," 9. Kipkorir, *Descent From Cherang'any Hills*, 63.

Isaiah Chemwal was employed at the Kapsowar hospital, and his brother Solomon and Joshua Chebobei conducted evangelistic visits around Chebara. On the weekends they were joined by Isaiah Chemwal and other evangelists from Kapsowar. Before long, a church and school were established. In his yearly report, the regional mission director Rev. Reg. Reynolds wrote:

> We opened a new out-station late in the year and the buildings were put up by the Kapsowar Christians without pay. They camped on the site in wet weather for a fortnight and the school and teachers house were up in double quick time.[66]

Joshua Chebobei was the first teacher at Chebara Out Station School until he moved to Chebiemit, where he constructed his own shop and ran a small business. He was replaced at the school by Ezekiel Chebet and Solomon Chemwal. Mr. Chebet ran the school efficiently and conducted church services on Sundays, well into his retirement. He also ran a successful shop and a gas station. He died in 1986.

In subsequent years, additional Christians who had been converted at Kapsowar moved to Chebara and formed a strong Christian community. Among them were Barnabas Kalacha, Marko Kotut, and Josiah Marrir. Most of these men started small shops at Chebara and established the shopping center by the main road. Joshua Chebobei opened a shop at Chebiemit and was later joined by Marko Mengich. Joshua helped in starting a church at Chebiemit with the support of Chebara Christians.

By 1952, the Christian community at Chebara was almost equal to that of Kapsowar. The school under Ezekiel Chebet had attracted over a hundred pupils and taught standards one through four. As the number of students increased, more teachers were needed, and some of the evangelists were brought in to teach in the morning and conduct their evangelistic work in the afternoons and weekends. The dispensary, which was earlier started by Dr. W. B. Young and Joshua Chebobei, was also active in serving the community that already had a building of its own.

The Christian community of Chebara lived around the school, and like the Christians at Kapsowar they organized Bible studies in Christian homes on Mondays. Mid-week prayer meetings were on Wednesdays and women's meetings on Fridays. On Sundays, some of the elders took the Christian message to neighboring communities and Sunday schools and

---

66. Young, "Eldoret Area Report," 9.

churches were soon established in some of these communities, such as Chebiemit and Cheptongei.[67]

In 1955, a small church had been started under the care of Joshua Chebobei. Although Joshua was tending his shop at Chebiemit center, he continued to offer guidance in the church for several years. He was later joined by other Christians, including Kibanwa Kesium who had been converted at Mathare Mental Hospital in Nairobi. The son of Kibanwa, Francis, went to Kapsabet Bible Institute in 1978 and served for a while as the pastor of AIC Chebiemit.[68]

The evangelists from Chebara covered large tracts of land in their evangelical trips. Some travelled up the Mosop route through Yemit and Kapcherop, spreading the Christian message along the way. Occasionally, they joined some of the evangelists from Kapsowar. By 1958, there were Christian gatherings at Cheptongei, Yemit, and Kimnai. Some evangelists returned to Kibuswo and revived the station originally opened by Elijah Kilimo; they established a church and a school. However, the church was later moved to a better location with more land in Kaptabuk. One of the first converts from Kaptabuk was Paulo Chepkiyeng. He became a Christian in 1960 and in 1961, was baptized by Dr. W. B. Young. He became interested in the work of the mission and was recruited by Dr. Stanley Lindsay to be an evangelist alongside Amos Kipkech from Samar, Marko Kandie from Sambirir, and Silvano Kipkatam and Barnaba Kalacha—both from Kapkamak. Once a month, they went to a selected community for an evangelistic mission using the book *Sobondab Betut age Tugul* published by Scripture Gift Mission. In an interview with Rev. Paulo Chepkiyeng, he recounted.

> The format was the same in every house we visited. One introduced the team, another prayed and one preached. We persuaded and asked the people to think about the message and respond by going to a Church near them.[69]

Paulo Chepkiyeng went on to Kapsabet Bible Institute and graduated in 1965 as the first Marakwet trained pastor. His ordination was delayed until 1978 when he completed the fourth year of Bible training at Narok.[70]

Most of the evangelists were men, but there were a few women among them. The Christian gatherings at Kimnai area were established by a woman named Eunice Tula. She was the first convert in the area and

---

67. Personal correspondence with Dr. W. P. Young, December 1991.
68. Personal correspondence with Dr. Stanley Lindsay, November 1991.
69. Personal interview with Rev. Paulo Chepkiyeng, December 1988.
70. Personal interview with Rev. Paulo Chepkiyeng, December 1988.

was instrumental in starting a Sunday school and, later, church services in her community. Also, a dispensary was opened due to her endeavors. Although she could hardly read, Tula was able to sing numerous hymns by heart. As time passed, she learned to read the Bible and was able to lead Bible studies in her home and in church. Dr. Stanley Lindsay, who met Tula from time to time, said:

> Without wanting to overlook others ... mention must be made of Eunice Tula of Kimnai, one of the first converts there. She emerged as a leader and through her visitation and evangelism some ten other church centres were opened in that area. As with many others, she was illiterate and must have learned every hymn in the book by heart, but though of mature years she learnt to read to feed her own soul and to be able to share the Scriptures with others.[71]

Eunice Tula emerged as a leader, not only among the women, but also among the male evangelists. She travelled frequently in her vicinity, telling people about her faith and challenging many to consider the Christian message. She became a noted speaker in women's meetings in the Mosop churches. She was also active in the annual women's meetings at Kapsowar. Through her influence and example, many Marakwet women became active in their churches. Some of them acted as preachers when no male evangelists were available.[72]

In 1965, Chebara Secondary school was established. The classes began at the boarding School at Kapsowar while construction was underway on the land next to the church. In 1966, the buildings were ready for use and the students moved from Kapsowar to their new location. My uncle Jeremiah Kirop Elolia who had relocated from Kerio Valley and settled with his family at Chebiemit was one of the builders of the school. He trained in masonry at Tambach and Kabete.

Sambirir

Sambirir location was the most difficult of all the Marakwet areas to accept Christianity. The people generally considered the missionaries as colonial invaders. Sambirir was also noted for non-payment of the hut tax and that may have been one of the reasons why they did not trust white people in their territory. Another fundamental fear was the missionaries' known attitude

---

71. Personal correspondence with Dr. Stanley Lindsay, November 1991.
72. Personal interview with Elijah Kilimo, January 1989.

towards the Marakwet culture and beliefs which they had observed since the Mission became active at Kapsowar.[73] In later years, Sambirir men acquired another reputation of abducting girls. For a long time, no female passed through Sambirir unaccompanied by few men because of that fear.

The missionary doctors from Kapsowar, and the evangelists, visited Sambirir on medical trips, with little success. People stayed away as much as possible. Anyone found collaborating with the missionaries was ridiculed and shunned. The government dispensary, which had been established by the District Commissioner earlier, was used as a legitimate excuse that a duplicate dispensary run by the Mission was unnecessary. Whatever the reason, Sambirir closed its doors to the missionaries for two decades, while the rest of Marakwet, with some reservations, welcomed the mission to open schools and dispensaries.

Dr. Stanley Lindsay made several trips to Sambirir with the purpose of starting a dispensary. He was also interested in studying the Marakwet traditional herbal medicine. By the end of 1953, the District Commissioner asked him to take over the government dispensary at Chesoi in Sambirir. This was most welcomed news for the Mission as it would allow them a foothold in Sambirir. Without wasting any time, Dr. Lindsay accepted the offer and transferred Paulo Katisei from Ng'echer to run the dispensary.

By this time, the road had been constructed to Chesoi which enabled Dr. Lindsay to transport medical supplies by car. By 1959, a church had been established and weekly services were conducted by Paulo Katisei. Margaret Armstrong and Maria Kilimo paid weekly visits from Kapsowar to attend the women's meetings they had earlier started.[74]

> On Wednesday morning, we visited a place called Chesoi, thirteen miles from here (Kapsowar). It was a great joy to us last month when thirteen women and one old man were baptized. None of these folk can read, so we feel we should make our visits weekly to teach them the word of God that they in their turn may become evangelists to their own people.[75]

In 1962, another congregation was started, by women, at Choruo Kimnyikeu where Eunice Tula lived. With encouragement from Kapsowar, the women conducted Friday Bible studies and literacy classes.

> One place rejoices in the wonderful name of Choruo Kimnyikeu. It is about 15 miles from Kapsowar, in a location

---

73. Personal interview with Joseph arap Kipkore of Kapsowar, April 1989.
74. Personal interview with Mrs. Maria Kilimo, January 1989.
75. Margaret Armstrong, Kapsowar Mission Station Records.

which for years has been hard and barren spiritually. I have been there a few times with Margaret Young and an African Christian woman (Maria Kilimo). We usually meet some fifty women and children . . . it is such a joy to teach the word to these women many of whom listen attentively. . . . We long to see them established, really rejoicing in the Lord, and weaned away from all the old customs of heathenism.[76]

The Mission did not start a school in Sambirir as there was already a government school at Chesoi run by the District Education Board. However, the Mission started a dispensary and used it as a stepping-stone for village evangelism and successfully gathered converts.[77] In the mid-1960s, the church attendants in Sambirir were few, but their numbers were increasing steadily. One of their major challenges was the men and clan members who were openly hostile particularly when the Christian women refused to brew beer or partake of it during ceremonies. As a result, many women who would have wished to join the Christian women had second thoughts about Christianity.

In 1972, Musa Chelang'a, the grandson of one of the early converts, became a Christian and later was sent by the church to Kapsabet Bible Institute for two years. He is a gifted preacher and through his sermons many young people converted. Later Musa Chelang'a relocated to the highlands of Kapsigoria/Cheptongei. Another talented young man, Joseph Cheserek, converted and attended Kapsabet Bible Institute. At the end of his studies in 1975, he returned to Sambirir and became the pastor at Choruo Kimnyigeu. His efforts brought many youths to the church. He also established a church at Iboi.[78] He married Pastor Mary Chelang'a, also from Sambirir and a graduate of Kapsabet Bible college. Mary Chelanga's mother is considered a pioneer Christian in Sambirir as she was one of the early mission converts. Rev. Cheserek was sidelined from leadership by political forces within and outside the church but through it all he maintained his equilibrium. He turned his energies to local initiatives and even started a church school at Chorwo that has posted remarkable results in national examinations. He has now been recognized for his leadership abilities and has been elected as the Regional Chairman of the AIC churches in Marakwet East.

76. Margaret Armstrong, Kapsowar Mission Station Records.
77. Personal interview with Joseph arap Kipkore of Kapsowar, April 1989.
78. Personal interview with Joseph Cheserek, April 1989.

Tot

Tot centre was established by the colonial government in the 1920s as a Colonial administrative post to collect taxes and recruit workers for settler farms. In 1950, Tot supplied a few soldiers to suppress the followers of Luka's P'Kech which was seen as a threat to the colonial government. Apart from that, Tot served as an ordinary small government post.

When Tom Collins moved to Liter in 1952, he made frequent visits to Tot intending to start a church; however, that dream was not realized due to lack of workers. It was not until 1959 that Christian activities were realized under the guidance of Hezekiah Kaino a man from the Sibow village who was, at that time, a dresser for the Mission at Ngecher.[79]

Hezekiah Kaino was born in Sibow village near Tot. After his conversion at Kapsowar hospital in 1948, he returned to his village and opened a small business at Tot. He had to close it when the Mission employed and posted him to Ng'echer. There he met Pilipu Chepkong'a, a dedicated Christian teacher. On Sundays Pilipu preached at Ng'echar while Hezekiah went to Tot to run a Sunday school class that attracted children from several villages. The beat of his big drum, which he carried over his shoulder signaled to the children that it was time for Sunday School. His lessons lasted for two hours and today many adult Christians credit those classes for their faith. Children came from as far as Kotut in Mogoro location, and Chebilil in Endo location. Hezekiah did not only teach them the Bible but instructed them to read and write.[80]

Hezekiah was transferred to Chesongoch in 1960 when Ng'echar closed. From Chesongoch he continued to walk the seven miles each Sunday to teach his Sunday school at Tot. To buy reading material for the children, Hezekiah asked every child to bring one shilling. The number of children grew steadily and were eager to read. Some did not distinguish Sunday school from regular school. Because both involved literacies.[81] When the District Officer heard about this, the Sunday school was investigated and Hezekiah was accused of running a parallel school illegally, especially as there was an established government school already at Tot under the District Education Board. Hezekiah was forced to discontinue the literacy part of his Sunday school. He took the matter to Tom Collins at the Liter mission station, but nothing was resolved. The missionaries often tried to cooperate with the colonial authorities in fear of subordination.

---

79. Personal interview with Nelson Kibiwot, March 1989.
80. Personal interview with Hezekiah Kaino, March 1989.
81. Equivalent to five cents Canadian.

When Paul Barnett succeeded Tom Collins at Liter in 1965, the work at Tot expanded. Barnett was a builder, and aggressive in his approach to evangelism. He visited Tot at least one Sunday a month, and, occasionally, showed Christian films in the evenings. Hezekiah was delighted to observe the fruits of his hard work. The first Christians to go through the two-year catechumen classes were baptized in 1968.[82] In 1969, Paul Barnett began the construction of the church and completed it within a year. In 1970, the church was officially opened and Rev. Samuel Yego from Kotut and his wife Helen Yego were sent to lead the Church. He was the first Marakwet to be ordained.

Samuel Yego was converted through Hezekiah's Sunday school classes. He proved keen and soon became Hezekiah's assistant. As he had a good education in the government school, he was encouraged to attend Kapsabet Bible Institute. He completed his training at Kapsabet Bible Institute in 1968 after which he went to Moffat Bible Institute in Kijabe in preparation for ordination. In 1970, he was ordained at Kapsowar as the first Marakwet to receive such an honor. He was sent to Tot.[83] In 1972, the Mission bought him a motorcycle so that he could travel all over Marakwet to conduct weddings and baptisms. He was also elected chairman of the District Church Council in Kerio valley. At the same time, his former Sunday school teacher and an elder at Tot Church Hezekiah Kaino, was accused of adultery. The church confirmed the allegations and stopped him from all his official church activities including his work at the dispensary at Chesongoch. Eventually, Ezekiah married the young woman as his second wife. He continued to attend church faithfully, but the mission could not accept him back into the church leadership unless he divorced his second wife.

In 1985, the Rev. Samuel Yego was accused of infidelity and was forced to resign. Following the fall of these two Marakwet key leaders in the church and the transfer of Paul Barnett to Kijabe in 1986, the church at Tot experienced a severe setback. The membership, once in the four hundred, declined to only twenty in 1987. In 1990, I was assigned to Tot after graduating from Scott Theological College. In addition to the church work, I also taught at Kerio Valley Secondary School. After a few months of consulting with the elders, I decided to take the risk and went against the mission church polity and reinstated Hezekiah Yego as an elder. I was nervous of the potential repercussions. Fortunately, my small board of elders was totally in support of my decision. They comprised of Johnston Chelanga, and his wife Rose Kilimo, Thomas Labero, and his wife Albinah, Perisi Chelanga, and Emily Kipkech. The church attendance started to go up slowly, due to the following

---

82. Personal interview with Hezekiah Kaino, March 1989.
83. Personal interview with Hezekiah Kaino, March 1989.

factors. The government administration had elevated Tot to the status of divisional headquarters with several government offices. Also, the nearby GSU camp had a few Christians who were regulars on Sunday. The subsequent influx was beneficial to the growth of AIC Tot. Moreover, a few students from Kerio Valley Secondary School where I taught attended the Sunday services. Also, Emily Kipkech was active with the youth and held Sunday school meetings at Kokwo Tolimo. In about the same time, the World Vision International was making inquiries to start their child program in Kerio Valley. They were given space at the church plot to construct their offices. Their work in the Valley went beyond local expectations through child sponsorship, relief, and development. I had already left for further studies in Canada during the operations of World Vision. However, in 1989, I returned to Kenya to conduct research for my dissertation but got sidetracked and was offered a job as one of the project managers by Mrs. Rebecca Cherono, the then Director of World Vision, Kenya. My responsibilities were to oversee several projects that included Tot where Vincent Krellkutt was the manager. I enjoyed the one year I worked for the World Vision organization, but I had to go back to Canada to complete my studies.

Koitilial

In 1951, a few evangelists were sent from Kapsowar mission to Chepkum and Koitilial. Among them were Job Kibor Kabiron, and Dr. Morris. Later, Amos Kipkech and Barnaba Kalacha traveled the whole Kerio Valley as evangelists. In 1960, Silvano Katam Sogo, Daniel Kakisakur, and his wife, Miriam Kakisakur gathered the few converts and started a church at Koitilial. Daniel Kakisakur taught at the school. Another prominent leader was Job Kapnyonge, a builder by profession who later helped Paul Barnett in the building of the Koitilial Church. Silvano Katam was born in a small village in Koitilial in the Kerio valley. When he was about twenty years old, just after initiation, he joined some of his friends in search of work in settler farms in Uasin-Gishu near Chebororwa. One day, Silvano developed a quarrel with someone that ended with Silvano shooting the man with an arrow. Silvano was taken into police custody and later tried in Eldoret for murder. Dr. Stanley Lindsay, the medical doctor from Kapsowar mission, was asked to examine him and give a medical report. Dr. Lindsay confirmed to the court that Silvano was mentally ill.[84]

---

84. Personal correspondence with Dr. Stanley Lindsay, November 1991.

Being able to speak at his trial in Eldoret, the judges accepted my evidence of mental instability and Silvano was committed to Mathare mental hospital.[85]

While in Mathare mental hospital in Nairobi, Silvano met another Marakwet named Kibanwa Kesium, who was at the hospital for a similar reason. Kibanwa had become a Christian, possibly at Mathare. After several months, Silvano also converted. His mental health improved greatly, and he was released after six months and transferred to Muthaiga prison to serve a year's sentence before returning to his home at Koitilial. Encouraged by Dr. Lindsay and other Christians at Kapsowar, Silvano became an evangelist in his home area, establishing several small churches, including one at Kipyebo in the late 1960s.[86]

When Paul Barnett succeeded Tom Collins at Liter, he travelled extensively in the Kerio valley building and repairing schools. He became interested in the work at Koitilial where he conducted monthly evangelistic meetings and, occasionally, showed Christian films. One of the Marakwet interpreters would explain the content and meaning of the film, followed by invitations for conversion. These efforts brought several young people into the church, especially school children. When church attendance increased, Rev. Paul Barnett and Job Kapnyonge constructed a permanent church building.[87] Job Kapnyonge's family was significant in the church and his daughter Leah who is a hotelier in Eldoret continues to support the church at Koitilial financially.

Silvano Katam served Koitilial church as an evangelist for over twenty years. He preached in open markets, villages, and schools. He died in 1985, but not before he saw one of his proteges, Elijah Yego, attend Kapsabet Bible Institute for pastoral training. Yego graduated in 1986 and became the pastor of AIC Koitilial for several years before he relocated to Cherangany where he has continued to be the Pastor of the Marakwet community who bought and subdivided a settler farm of Kamendi. There are about four churches that emerged under Koitilial. The adult attendance has been poor for a long time, but the young people and children are active. Very few men come to church, probably because they prefer the less rigid Catholic Church which started in Arror in the mid-1970s.[88]

The Protestant churches and homes in general became refuge centers for Christian youth escaping the traditional circumcision rites of passage. They had been taught that their conversion involved rejecting such rites as

---

85. Personal correspondence with Dr. Stanley Lindsay, November 1991.
86. Personal correspondence with Dr. Stanley Lindsay, November 1991.
87. Personal interview with Joseph Kilimo, March 1989.
88. Personal interview with Elijah Yego, Koitilial, March 1989.

antithesis to Christianity. On the other hand, the Marakwet felt that their traditions were being undermined by the missionaries. Before the advent of the Christian missionaries, the youth accepted the norms of the tradition. As it were, many Christian youth who were advised by the missionaries to ran away to escape the traditional rites were given shelters and protection at Christian homes at the highlands until the circumcision season was over. The rejection of this rite by the youth was praised as a measure of their Christian commitment. While in Christian homes, the boys were sent to Kapsowar hospital for circumcision while the girls were to reject the rite altogether. After the circumcision season, some of the youth returned to their homes while others remained in their host homes until they completed their primary or secondary education. After completing primary education of grade seven, some were considered for the nursing training program and employment at Kapsowar hospital. Others who performed well in their Kenya Certificate of Primary Education and had the money or sponsors proceeded on to secondary school for higher education. Benjamin Chelimo was one of those young people to escape to the highlands and was hosted at the home of Peter Rotich, a Christian teacher and prominent Christian in Yemit area, Benjamin Chelimo eventually went to Kapsabet Bible College and after graduation was a Pastor in his community of Kipyebo He later joined the Bible translation team for a few years. Disagreements with church leaders forced him to seek employment with the power and electricity company in the city. Some of the Christians who have left that area and residing in the urban areas continue to support their village church at Koitilial. One of those supporters, worth mentioning is Leah Job a businesswoman, in Eldoret. Her generosity for her community is remarkable.

— CHAPTER 6 —

Theological Reflections

Salvation/Conversion and New Names

WHAT WERE THE MOTIVATING factors for conversion to Christianity? Was it for religious change or was it a way to take advantage of the modern benefits that came with European civilization? Was it motivated by the fear of damnation and eternal fire in hell or the love and embrace of God? Why did some convert and later revert? Why was mission Christianity unpopular with the adult men? The best way to explain it in my view lies in the conversion process and its expectations.

The term "conversion" comes from the Latin *convertere*, which means "to change" or "to turn around." It suggests a change from one form of life experience to another or a shift from one religion to another. From the biblical perspective, the concept is developed with primary reference to those who were once close to God but needed to return and renew their loyalty to the God who had entered a covenant relationship with them. For Israelites, such a return to God often involved sackcloth and ashes since this was culturally appropriate for showing humility and repentance.[1] Although this implies repentance, it is also associated with conversion.

In the New Testament, the word conversion is represented by synonyms such as repentance, regeneration, restoration, or turning around. The central focus is to change directions. The direction is given in the Bible, but the response it should elicit is not specifically determined in the Bible. Rather, it is to be based on the cultural appropriateness of those to whom the appeal is made.[2] Leslie Newbegin confirms this point of view by describing the historical characteristic of conversion as follows:

---

1. Kraft and Ramm, *Christianity in Culture*, 333.
2. Kraft and Ramm, *Christianity in Culture*, 333.

It is a call to concrete obedience here and now in the context of the actual issues of the day. . . . Conversion is not some sort of purely inward and spiritual experience which is later followed by a distinct and different decision to act in certain ways. The idea that one is first converted, and then looks round to see what one should do consequently, finds no basis in scripture. And yet this idea is very common. A careful study of the biblical use of the language of conversion, of returning to the Lord, will show that, on the contrary, it is always in the context of concrete decisions at the given historical moment.[3]

Conversion here implies that the convert accepts this new pattern of conduct as that which is relevant for the doing of God's will and the fulfillment of his reign at a particular place and time.

The missionaries appreciated this factor and demanded a radical change. The question that follows is to what must one convert? That is where the blurring and confusion emerge. When missionaries made their appeal, they demanded a total conformity to moral and cultural shift to the ideals of Western culture, with the assumption that this was synonymous with Christianity. The opposite or contrast is the African culture that was castigated as dark and backwardness from which one must convert. It is no wonder missionary endeavors were viewed as part of the colonial civilizing mission.

In the Marakwet context, becoming a Christian involved moralistic do's and don'ts. It also meant forgoing and rejecting many of the Marakwet's religious and social practices, such as rites of passage, marriage rituals and replacing them with Western Christian ones. Dualistic vocabulary was employed to draw the stark distinction between darkness and light. The converts were baptized and given Western or Jewish biblical names and encouraged to adopt Western styles of dress. At Kapsowar and Liter, Christians were expected to settle around the mission station to fulfil the mission's goal for "a model new society."[4]

As conservative evangelicals, the missionaries stressed, above everything else, the following points: (1) the Reformation doctrine of the final authority of the Scripture, (2) the doctrine of the original sin and eternal salvation through personal confession of Christ, (3) the importance of evangelism and missions, (4) rejection of the worldly practices, and (5) the importance of spiritually transformed life.[5] These principles were interpreted in

---

3. Newbegin, *Finality of Christ*, 93–94.
4. Schreuder and Oddie, "What Is Conversion?" 498.
5. Ford, *Modern Theologians*, 132.

Marakwet as rigorous regiments including abstaining from alcoholic drinks and smoking and the rejection of Marakwet traditional rites such as child naming, circumcision, and polygamy. Most of these rules touched the core of the Marakwet social life. To many non-Christian adults then, becoming a Christian was almost synonymous with ceasing to be a Marakwet.

A good example of this sentiment was when young Marakwet converts were refused to take part in the most important rite of circumcision. This is the rite of passage from childhood to adulthood. Failure to participate in this rite excluded one from participating in the Marakwet social life. The early missionaries and the Christian pioneers discouraged girls rite but did not interfere with the boys' rite. However, the missionaries who came after 1950s discouraged Christian boys from undergoing the traditional rite. Alternatively, Christian boys went to Kapsowar hospital to be circumcised but were ridiculed and ostracized from their families when they returned home.

John Kiptoo, (not his real name) who converted to Christianity in the mission through the influence of the early missionaries, was circumcised at Kapsowar mission hospital. Upon his return to the village, he was ridiculed by his relatives and peers until he succumbed to pressure. Since he had gone to the hospital, he didn't need excision, but he had to go to the camp for the training. Many years later, he submitted his application to be an assistant chief. His education positioned him on top of the other candidates, and he was easily selected. It is doubtful that he would have been considered for the job had he not undergone the traditional circumcision ritual.

The principal target for the missionary in rejecting the traditions of Marakwet was to cast away the looming darkness in the culture associated with the devil. According to Aylward Shorter, the early missionaries saw the devil everywhere in African culture and religious practices. It was principally for that reason that the central message for the Mission was salvation from traditional practice.[6] In other words, the African cosmology was to be ignored or rejected altogether. All they saw in Marakwet culture were superstitions and trappings of religion that had nothing to do with the true God of Christianity. The revision of that view is being undertaken by a growing number of Marakwet Christians who recognize the God of the Bible to be the same deity of their tradition called *Iriin*—the Creator.

The common methods exploited in accelerating conversions were the school and the hospital. Both institutions were spaces of vulnerability, and both provided many opportunities for evangelism and conversion. The school was used to convert the young before they were grounded in the traditions of their own culture and religious beliefs. This process was gradual but

---

6. Shorter, *African Christian Theology*, 21.

consistently successful. Those who responded to the Christian message were instructed in the basic Bible lessons on how to live as good Christians, including rejecting African traditions such as consulting herbalists, medicine men, witches, and diviners. The ancestors were to be completely ignored. Catastrophes usually attributed to supernatural powers were acts of God. Similarly, infant mortality, sickness, childlessness, and premature deaths were purely medical matters. They were told that witches did not exist.

When the young people returned to their communities after such orientation, they confronted traditional beliefs in which supernatural powers were not just superstitions or speculations but real. These traditions had been suppressed from the view of the missionaries who did not see them kindly; however, they came alive in the absence of missionaries. As a result, many Marakwet are Christians on Sundays, but resort to their old traditions in times of weekly hardships. There were no rules or discrimination with regard to attendance at the mission schools which allowed all children regardless of their beliefs. However, the teachers were expected to be Christians and to conform to the Mission's regulations.[7] Through the influence of Christian teachers, the Mission expected the students to convert, and those who did were always treated favorably.

Johana Kanda, an elder of one of the AIC churches, sent his son Edward to Kapsowar boarding school. While there, Edward converted and was baptized by Dr. Lindsay. He was admitted with the first batch of students to Chebara secondary school in 1965. When Edward returned home during holidays, he taught Sunday school and was an occasional interpreter to visiting missionary preachers at Liter mission station. After high school, Edward was employed by the Standard Chartered Bank in Eldoret and attended the mission-founded church famously known as the Fellowship Church. Jacob Kitum (not his real name) also, was at Kapsowar boarding school and was baptized at the mission station. He became a teacher, and when he got married, he chose the traditional wedding, thus earning the fury of the missionaries.[8] Since then, his relationship with the church deteriorated, and eventually he stopped going to church altogether. He had his daughters circumcised and married according to tradition. Many Christians found themselves in similar circumstances. They converted while at the mission schools but stopped going to church altogether because of the unreconciled tension between their culture and

---

7. The Mission's regulations for teachers were to abstain from drinking beer and smoking, as well as regular attendance at church services.

8. No ceremony or ritual was complete without the use of the traditional beer and the pouring of libations, something that is absent from church weddings.

Christianity. The Roman Catholics who came to Marakwet later were slightly better in bridging this cultural gap.

The hospital and its dispensaries provided more converts. The patients were exposed to the Christian message from both the nurses and doctors. Those who were healed and relieved of their sufferings felt indebted to the hospital and its workers and above all God's healingand were receptive to conversion. The dispensaries and frequent doctors' visits to the villages served to reach new people, as well as follow up with previously converted patients. At every dispensary, the day began with an evangelistic service, followed by treatment of the sick. Those who converted were sent to their respective churches for further instruction and baptism.

In the Marakwet society, women are not directly active participants in the decision making in public matters. When Christianity came, it provided women with minimal alternative leadership roles. They found space to meet, learn to read, organize, and express themselves freely in their gatherings where literacy classes were given. The church provided leadership opportunities that were denied in the traditional structure. These factors attracted many women to Christianity. Also, by virtue of their general role as mothers, the women had a close relationship with their children who attended the mission schools, thus providing another reason for their conversion. Many Christian communities were established on these lines. When Elijah Kilimo closed his station at Boroko in favor of Liter in 1952, some of his converts, including Kisang Kariwotum, Karaninyang, Koyano Lukuket, Kimoi Elolia (*kochemeitoi*), and Josiah Cheptenderwo, followed him and continued to attend his services despite the distance, but discontinued when Elijah returned to Kapsowar.[9] There is a possibility that they would have continued to attend church if there was one in their community. Today, there is a church across river Karengor at Cherutich, but unfortunately the early contacts are dead except for Josiah Cheptenderwo who no longer attends.

During conversion, the prospective convert must first accept the message and ask forgiveness from Jesus Christ, followed by catechism classes for a period of two to three years before baptism. During the catechism period, converts were closely monitored by other Christians. On the day of baptism, the sponsor or any member of the congregation is to reveal any cause that might prevent the baptism. If there is no reason to withhold baptism, the candidate is baptized, preferably in the river by immersion before all the Christians and given a new Western or Bible name to signify his/her new identity.

---

9. Personal interview with Elijah Kilimo in Suwerwa, January 1989.

It was not uncommon for church elders at Kapsowar to spy on young converts, mostly to make sure they weren't dating. A fair number were denied baptism for failing to conform to Christian expectations of abstaining from dating or smoking. Those who broke the rules, especially after they had been baptized, were disciplined, and asked to repent publicly and be fully re-instated into the church. The unbaptized were held back from baptism until further notice. To prevent temptations, Christians were encouraged to join one of the prayer meetings in a mission station. These prayer meetings at the station, were, to a great degree, worlds apart from the village where such Bible study meetings were non-existent. As a result, converts came to the mission stations for refuge, and to escape from what was deemed to be ungodly village life.[10]

Apart from being a refuge for Christians, the mission stations also offered opportunities for cash employment or small business ventures. Others found jobs with the government as teachers and clerks. Very soon, Christians controlled the economy of the growing town in comparison to their peers in the village. Some of the Christians who engaged in trade saw their fortunes grow rapidly, and their time in weekly meetings and Bible studies declined. This did not escape the notice of the other Christians and the missionaries. A case in point is Samson Chelang'a, a skilled builder from K'Marich who was trained at the Tambach government school. He opened a shop and became a successful businessman at Kapsowar. While at Tambach government school, he was introduced to Christianity, along with a fellow Marakwet student Joshua Chebobei, by a Nandi teacher called Job Birech. The two students were baptized at Kapsowar by Rev. Reg. Reynolds. Samson Chelang'a met Ana, who had come to Kapsowar with an ulcerated leg, and upon recovery she converted and entered the girl's home. They married a year later. Samson was intrigued by the business opportunities at Kapsowar. When he had saved enough money, he opened a small kiosk next to the one owned by Abdi Garbash, a Muslim originally from Somalia. Samson attracted all the Christians to his shop and, after a short period, resigned his job at the mission station and enlarged his business. He sold well sought commodities such as salt, sugar, cooking oil, Paraffin, and maize flour. As the shop expanded, he added blankets, cotton cloth material (*Shuka*), and other newly arrived outfits for both men and women. As his business grew, he started missing prayer meetings as he spent more time running his shop.

Samson Chelang'a worked in his shop on weekdays and closed on Sundays to go to church. He was too busy to attend, Wednesday prayer and from then on, a tension developed between Samson and the other Christians in

10. Personal interview with Johnstone Chelang'a, February 1989.

the station. The Christians who had initially encouraged him in his business turned against him for engaging in worldly affairs instead of seeking God's kingdom. The missionaries were ambivalent towards Samson's entrepreneurship. However, the relationship turned sour only when Samson turned down the missionaries' request to be an evangelist in the valley. None of it bothered Samson Chelang'a, who was becoming the richest man in Kapsowar. As the center expanded, so did Samson's business. He enlarged his shop by adding an extension, and by 1958 his was the largest shop in Marakwet. In 1963, Samson purchased a Land Rover, becoming one of the first Marakwet to own a vehicle. Since he had a vehicle, the missionaries initially relied on him to bring their mail from Eldoret. Samson could not understand the fuss from the station as the missionaries also owned vehicles. Samson could only conclude that he, a "native," was getting close to becoming equal to a white man.[11]

Although the mission station offered financial opportunities to the converts, it also gave the missionaries permission to monitor and, frequently, force their views and perceived standards of conduct on the converts. Failure to conform to the Mission's ethical norms could lead to the loss of jobs, disciplinary actions, and even ostracism. The rules were a bit hard to enforce on the converts who lived further away in the villages. Sometimes sympathy was extended to them because they were understood to suffer a great deal of temptations from the village life and its pagan activities. A majority of the adult converts succumbed and returned to such pressure, and when they could no longer balance it well, they returned to the traditional life. Only some of those employed by the mission schools and clinics did better. Similarly, some of the students in the boarding school at Kapsowar received Christian instructions and encouragement as part of their new program and progress.

The question, often asked by social scientists, is why some Africans converted and later abandoned the faith. The most stimulating attempt at an explanation, and one which has provoked strong reactions during the last four decades, is what Robin Horton proposed in his theory. His thesis proposes that African conversion to Christianity or Islam is due to the development of traditional African cosmology responding to aspects of modern Western values.[12] He characterizes African cosmology on two levels. The first relates to what he called the lesser spirits concerned with the local community and its environment (microcosm), and the second level is he associated with the Supreme Being concerned with the whole world (macrocosm). In his view, the modern changes affecting Africa could not be

---

11. Personal interview with Samson Chelang'a in Kapsowar, May 1989.
12. Horton, "African Conversion."

resisted because the process of change had already begun. He proposes that beliefs and practices are only accepted where they happen to coincide with changes in traditional cosmology.[13]

Horton's theory was criticized by H. Fisher and Caroline Ifeka-Moller. Ifeka-Moller is ambivalent. She agrees with Horton's notion that people turned to Christianity because it promised a new kind of power identified with the white man's power, which was sought out due to the new technological discoveries. However, she disagrees with Horton on his intellectual theory that suggested, among other things, that conversion would have occurred with or without Christianity. As an alternative, Ifeka-Moller proposes a social structural explanation as a more valid interpretation for conversion in Africa.[14]

Although these scholars seem to disagree in some areas, their arguments are limited to the social aspect of conversion. They neglected to deal with the spiritual or religious factor which is one of the fundamental principles in religious conversion. It is possible that their enlightenment worldview did not consider spirituality to account in explaining social changes. In fact, Horton accuses Christian scholars of not looking at the issues from his own intellectualistic point of view.

The socio-cultural factor was fundamental in conversion. Many people joined the church through the schools and hospitals. Indeed, some converted or affiliated with the church in order to gain some of these advantages. The question to ask is whether one can convert for both social and spiritual reasons and cannot be separated by the many people I interviewed. They agreed that many converts have benefited materially from their faith and Church. In fact, majority of the elites in Marakwet benefited from mission schools or christian families. After the Second World War, a few people in Marakwet gradually being exposed to the outside world, and some had seen the benefit of Western education. In fact, education was considered the only means to gain admittance to the emerging world of Western technology. Parents were eager to send their children to schools, run mainly by missions such as the Africa Inland Mission and the Roman Catholic Mission. Many young people became members of these churches to ensure continued access to schools. Teachers, too, had to conform to the church regulations which meant that they had to teach religious lessons, and possibly assist in the promotion of mission work. At times, Church attendance was mandatory. Failure to attend might result in serious punishment or even expulsion from the mission school. One man

---

13. Horton, "On Rationality of Conversion."
14. Ifeka-Moller, "White Power."

told how he was punished when he decided to help his parents and failed to attend Sunday school. Because permission had not been sought, he and others in the same situation were ordered to fence the school garden for two evenings after school.[15]

The need for education and the job security offered by mission resulted in the church's growth after the second world war. However, after independence in December 1963, the government took over most of the mission schools and staffed them with government teachers. All the mission schools in Marakwet were taken over by the government during this period. As a result, church attendance gradually declined. Religious obligations were no longer a prerequisite for schooling. Kapsowar Boarding School also received some government teachers. Conversion or going to church was recommended but no longer mandatory to keep a job in the mission schools.

The above supports the socio-cultural theory discussed in part by both Horton and Ifeka-Moller—that conversion was necessary to gain the privileges of Western civilization. However, it must be argued that there were also those who converted solely for spiritual needs. The latter continue to remain faithful in the church, even in times of difficult challenges such as health or loss of material gains. Although they, too, benefited from the material gains offered by the missions, they consider the latter as a utility to advance the faith. If the material benefits were unavailable, they still have something of religious significance in their lives. The basis of this view is biblically grounded, and for evangelicals it is influenced by their view of eschatology. Unfortunately, this view gets convoluted with Western cultural interpretation of salvation and its end goal.

Conversion to Christianity is believed to be ultimately an act of God's grace, and it must affect all aspects of life. It is believed to be a supernatural change touching the total life of the convert because it is driven by the Spirit of God. This view concurs with Louis J. Luzbetak's explanation that conversion is a whole-hearted acceptance of a new set of values affecting the totality of one's life day in and day out.[16]

The evangelicals explain salvation in the Johannine language of new birth. However, the missionaries to Africa interpreted this to include the rejection of worldly vices of alcohol, tobacco, fornication, dances, and traditional rites of passage. Such a view of salvation has received surmountable criticism from the theologians of the global south.

---

15. Personal conversation with Ruto Kibiwot, who attended Liter Primary School from 1964–68.

16. Luzbetak, *Church and Cultures*, 6.

The Latin American theologian Gustavo Gutierrez underlines two levels of salvation. The first is the quantitative and extensive aspect of salvation. The focus in this case is otherworldly. The thrust is moralistic, and the spirituality is one of flight from this world.[17] Gutierrez along with other theologians including Karl Rahner and Clark Pinnock have challenged this view and advocated for the widening the scope beyond the visible frontiers of the church. Their thesis is that people are saved if they open themselves to God and the world.[18]

What exactly are we saved from? In the Christian context, salvation implies freedom from bondage or enslavement of sin. What is sin? An African would define sin as a refusal to be open to God and to others. The opposite is withdrawing into oneself. This boils down to refusing to love God and others—a breach of friendship with God and with other human beings. Sin is negation of love or withholding love. In this case, salvation is to reverse those characteristics by loving God through our neighbors.

In the liberationist approach, sin is not just an individualistic and private affair to be addressed only privately, but sin is also evident in oppressive structures that exploit and enslave people. The work of justice is the fruit of salvation. The liberation of Israel from Egypt is a model of God's salvific plan. Similar vision is seen in the exile of the same people as recorded in the exilic writings of Second Isaiah:

> Wake, awake, put on strength,
> O arm of the Lord!
> Awake, as in days of old,
> the generations of long ago!
> Was it not you who cut Rahab in pieces,
> who pierced the dragon?
> Was it not you who dried up the sea,
> the waters of the great deep? (Isa 51:9–10)

The words and images in this passage refer to creation in the beginning and liberation from Egypt. Rahab symbolizes both Egypt and the chaos that Yahweh had to overcome to create the world. But the chaos is also the waters of the red sea which Israel crossed to begin the exodus. God's historical actions in both events for creation and liberation from Egypt are considered creative and salvific. It comes as God's response to their cry. Their salvation included a long journey to the promised land where they would create a new society based on justice. The incarnation of God in Jesus continues the same liberative theme in the Hebrew Bible but with more clarity and solidarity. As

---

17. Gutierrez, *Theology of Liberation*, 84.
18. Gutierrez, *Theology of Liberation*, 84; Pinnock, *Wideness of God's Mercy*, 17–47.

Gustavo Gutierrez puts it; Jesus' work encompasses all comprehensiveness of liberating process in its full meaning.[19]

In response to a question by a Pharisee lawyer, on the greatest commandment in the law, Jesus pointed him to the ten commandments and summarized them thus "'You shall love the Lord your God with all your heart, and with all your soul, and with all your mind.' This is the greatest and first commandment. And a second is like it: 'You shall love your neighbor as yourself'" (Matt 22:37–39). The grounding salvation to the love for one's neighbor resonates with African ethos of community than the missionaries' Western individualism.

Similarly, for most Protestant evangelical missionaries, salvation was mostly about going to heaven and tied to eschatology especially the premillennialism doctrine. It is true that the Bible is the book of promise per excellence and the promise is to be unlocked by faith. Abraham was given a promise that his posterity would be the heirs of the world. The promise is fulfilled in Jesus Christ, the Lord of history for in him we are the heirs by promise (Gal 3:29). The resurrection as a fulfillment of a promise is also the participation of a future event. On the other hand, a part Jesus' prayer to his disciples says, "thy Kingdom come on earth as it is in heaven." Don't you think that the earth portion is important for our consideration?

In reflecting from his Peruvian context, Gustavo Gutierrez understands liberation on three levels namely liberation from: (1) oppressive socio-economic structures, (2) oppressed consciousness /psychological, and (3) sinful centeredness. By stating the social, psychological, and spiritual, Gutierrez was at the same time warning against restricting the idea of salvation to just one of its dimensions. If we understand salvation spiritually as most missionaries did, then it fails in addressing the concrete human life as per Jesus' manifesto in Luke 4:16–20—which include freedom of captives and slaves. The sign of the kingdom is when we struggle for a just world in which there is no colonizing or enslaving colonizing other people. It calls for a is better living conditions for all human beings, not some. The taste of the Kingdom of God starts here on earth and its fullness is yet to come. [20]

The problem with the missionaries and, by extension, the evangelical church seems to orient itself to the future and ignoring the present. Some of the missionaries were complacent with an oppressive colonial system that oppressed and stole African resources. On the other hand, Jesus taught and lived the kingdom promise here on earth while recognizing its future fulfillment. He taught his disciples to consider Gods' reign

19. Gutierrez, *Theology of Liberation*, 92.
20. Gutierrez, *Theology of Liberation*, 184.

here on earth now as if it is in heaven. "Your kingdom come, your will be done, on earth as it is in heaven" (Matt 6:10). While the kingdom of God is at the heart of the message of Jesus, it calls for a certain behavior from those who receive it, and that does not only mean moralistic behavior but loving God through the neighbor. This translates to standing alongside them in their fight to survive while at the same time resisting the forces of evil that oppress them socially, psychologically, and spiritually. For some reasons, this interpretation of Scripture was not promoted by the missionaries. What concerned the missionaries was the theology of eschatology and life beyond the physical life and the fewness of those who will attain it.

The fewness doctrine and the optimism of salvation are both based on interpretations or the misinterpretation of the Scripture. The fewness view restricts salvation to those who have made a confession of faith with their own lips. "If you confess with your lips that Jesus is Lord and believe in your heart that God raised him from the dead, you will be saved" (Rom 10:9). Both Augustinian tradition and the evangelicals have understood this to mean that God chooses a few who will be saved, leaving out most of humanity to eventually perish in hell. This pessimistic interpretation has shaped the view of many missionaries to Africa.

Some progressive evangelical theologians have challenged such pessimistic reading of the Scripture. The Canadian evangelical theologian Clark Pinnock has called for a revision and correction. He writes:

> I want to make the case for salvation optimism, and for a hermeneutic of hopefulness that may assist us in negotiating a necessary paradigm shift away from our current pessimism. To put it out in the open, I want evangelicals to move away from the attitude of hopefulness based upon Good News, from restrictive to openness, from exclusivism to generosity. If we could but recover the scope of God's love, our lives and not just our theology of religions could be transformed.[21]

Pinnock locates his optimism of salvation with the Noahic covenant in Genesis 9:8–17. After the flood, God establishes a covenant for all people in Noah, represented by the rainbow in the sky. By this pledge, God announces God's saving purposes, not just among a single chosen few, but among all peoples. The point is that God does not belong to a tribe or race, nor to the Jews or even Christians only, but is the Lord and judge of all peoples of the earth. From the beginning, God raised up priests to take care of God's people: Abel, Seth, Enoch, Noah, Melchizedek, and Job. They all responded to the grace of God given to them, thus confirming what Paul

---

21. Pinnock, *Wideness of God's Mercy*, 20.

later stated, that God has never left himself without witness in the world. (Acts 14:17). In this sense, the unevangelized are judged based on the light they have received and how they have responded to that light as per (Romans 2:14-16). What matters is faith in God. In the Gospel of John we read, "For God so loved the world that he gave his only Son, so that everyone who believes in him may not perish but may have eternal life" (John 3:16). Questions have been asked about the millions who died before the gospel reached them? Does one need to be conscious of the work of Christ done on one's behalf to benefit from that work?

In the context of God's concern for the world Abraham is called, not for his own sake or his family's sake, but for the sake of the entire world so that all the families of the earth might be blessed in and through him (Gen 12:3). The notion of choosing a single representative to represent the whole group appears singularly in Jesus being presented by Paul as the last Adam who represents human race as its Savior (1 Cor 15:22). These examples go to show that God's plan is to bless the whole human race and not just a few. Otherwise, we might join Clark Pinnock in asking:

> What kind of God would create men and women in love, only to irrationally punish most of them? A God who would play favorites with his children, condemning some to eternal separation . . . based on the accidents of history or geography, over which they had no control?[22]

As we anticipate an answer, another question arises as to how we understand the evangelical interpretation of Matthew 7:14 that supports the fewness doctrine. Could it be that Jesus is encouraging the few disciples to choose the hard and unpopular path? Whatever the meaning, it is doubtful that the fewness view should eliminate the optimism of salvation that many other portions of Scripture explain. Otherwise, how will God's house be filled as in the parable in Matthew 22?

The overall picture one finds in the Scriptures is God's boundless generosity especially regarding the salvation of all including those that have been considered to be out of the covenant deal. The story of Jonah among others should shed some light here. Based on this, there is a reason to conclude that a tremendously large number of people are going to be saved. Jesus said, "Then people will come from east and west, from north and south, and will eat in the kingdom of God" (Luke 13:29). In Revelation, John writes "After this I looked, and there was a great multitude that no one could count, from every nation, from all tribes, and peoples and languages,

---

22. Pinnock, *Wideness of God's Mercy*, 150.

standing before the throne and before the Lamb, robed in white, with palm branches in their hands" (Rev 7:9).

The second-century Greek fathers like Justin Martyr, Clement of Alexandria, Origen, Theophilus of Antioch, and Athenagoras believed that God was concerned and at work with all people. They had developed a new understanding that they were not to become Jews first but to live actively within Hellenistic pagan society but converting its institutions and its thought patterns to Christ. Conversion also called for high standards of moral and social conduct as approved in the Hellenistic traditions. The Greeks understood conversion from the Greek technical term *metabile* commonly used by the philosophical schools for the decision to embrace a certain philosophy. When Justin Martyr gives an account of his own conversion, that conversion comes directly from his pursuit of philosophy as a means of achieving *metabile*. Here philosophy is not understood as an academic achievement but a religious quest that guides him toward the Hebrew prophets.

> A flame was kindled in my soul, and a love of the prophets and of those men who are friends of Christ possessed me. And while resolving his words in my mind, I found this philosophy to be safe and profitable? Thus, and for this reason I am a philosopher. Moreover, I wish that all making a resolution similar to my own do not keep themselves away from the words of the savior. They possess a terrible power in themselves and are sufficient to inspire those who turn aside from the path of rectitude with awe, while the sweetest rest is afforded to those who make diligent practice of them. If then you have any concern for yourself and are eagerly looking for salvation and if you believe in God, you may become acquainted with the Christ of God and after being initiated live a happy life.[23]

Justin's quest begins entirely within his own pre-Christian tradition. They read the prophets and adopted them into the preexisting framework of Greek thought. The use of Scripture enabled him to make the connection between the Greek logos and Jesus the divine Word and show that Greek thinkers like Plato had participated indirectly in the Logos of God. Justin's conversion therefore is also the conversion of the culture.[24]

---

23. Andrew Walls, "Considerations on the Cultural History of Christian Mission and Conversion," transcriptions of four 1996 lectures reproduced for a symposium sponsored by the Center for Mission Study & Research at Maryknoll, October 1997, p. 18.

24. Bediako, *Theology and Identity*, 153.

On the other hand, St. Augustine, the famous Latin father of the fifth century, embraced a pessimistic view of salvation represented by Cyprian's slogan "outside the Church there is no salvation." Since then, the exclusivism of salvation has grown steadily. From this perspective, African religion and spirituality were demonized. Our people were baptized into Christianity with Western names and values. Was the mission about Christianization or a civilizing mission? Hard to tell. However, while there are many ways of looking at this, I tend to agree with one wisdom tradition that God can use a crooked stick to accomplish God's purposes.

Clark Pinnock makes a good point that the debate on the universality of salvation should not sacrifice fundamental Christian convictions like the trinity and Christology. In this sense, Scripture can provide a way forward for a life-giving spirituality for Marakwet and African Christians. Already, they have discovered the discrepancies in mission theology and are on the way to affirming their place in God's salvific plan that does not reject their valued traditions.

The African Religious traditions which the missionaries attacked is nature oriented. In other words, cosmology plays a key role in communicating with the Divine. Unfortunately, the missionaries negatively called it "animism." The dictionary description of animism is positive. It means "the belief in a supernatural power that organizes and animates the material universe." Reasoning from this point of view, a keen observer can easily tell that African spirituality of animism tends to be closer to the Bible than the modern secular view of the west. At this juncture, it is safe to say that African spirituality is cognizant of God's inclusive and universality of salvation that is not just exclusive to Africa. That can serve as a foundational context for which the bible can be read and interpreted.

In addition, there is a renewed awareness of salvation in relation to the ecosystem. Increasingly, scholars are writing extensively about the universal nature of salvation that is inclusive of humans and all creation. This new emphasis challenges the historic Christianity that has focused on the human (anthropocentric) and lost sight of the strong scriptural evidence for God's expansive creation. God is at one and the same time creator and redeemer (Isa 42:5–6; 44:24). Romans 8:22-23 acknowledges an existential reality that the whole creation (humans included) is groaning with pain potentially, climate change could be as bad as pandemic. These days, global warming has resulted in unprecedented life-threatening conditions. In addition to natural events, the groans come from socially constructed oppression of human civilizations. What happens if the groans are not taken seriously? The great hymn in Colossians draws on the Wisdom tradition and the history of Jesus in equal measure,

> He is the image of the invisible God, the firstborn of all creation; for in him all things in heaven and on earth were created, things visible and invisible, whether thrones, dominations or rulers or powers—all things have been created through him and for him. He himself is before all things, and in him all things hold together.... For in him all the fullness of God was pleased to dwell, and through him God was pleased to reconcile to himself all things, whether on earth or in heaven, making peace by the blood of his cross. (Col 1:15–17, 19–20)

In the book of Revelation, we hear the same hope with divine promise for all creation "every creature in heaven and on earth and under the earth and in the sea, and all that is in them" singing praises to the Lamb (Rev 5:13), and the one who sits on the throne says, "See, I am making all things new" (Rev 21:5).[25]

Contested Themes

In the early years, the Protestant missionaries attacked key elements of Marakwet culture and beliefs. Initially, the Marakwet met such attacks with indifference. The missionary was determined to undermine the Marakwet culture through the school where the African youth came under their tutelage. In that setting the students were taught to despise, denigrate, and undermine their traditional practices in favor of Western culture that was promoted as Christian, civilized, and therefore superior. However, not all the missionaries shared this radical view. There were a few who were sympathetic to African culture and sought to apply a less damning approach by seeking some good elements in African culture. One of those missionaries was the Belgian missionary Placide Tempels whose sympathetic study of the Luba religion resulted in the famous book *Bantu Philosophy* published in 1948. Tempels argued that the Bantu peoples of Sub-Saharan Africa have an implicit philosophy. Similarly, at the Protestant Missionary conference held at Le Zoute in 1926, attended by the representatives of Africa Inland Mission, the following resolution was passed:

> Everything that is good in the Africa's heritage should be conserved, enriched, and ennobled by contact with the spirit of Christ. While the Church cannot sanction any custom which is evil, it should not condemn customs which are incompatible with the Christian life.[26]

25. Johnson, *Ask the Beasts*, 223–24.
26. Smith, *Christian Mission*, 108.

This proposition, suggest a change of heart on the part of African Inland Mission, albeit it's paternalism. The missionaries claimed to determine which aspects of African culture are worth their respect and acceptance. As far as they were concerned, most African cultures were condemned—if not in total, at least large segments of it. Aspects of cosmology/religion and rites of passage were totally ignored except when it clashed directly with the mission's work. The most significant practices, such as circumcision and polygamy, became chief areas of contention. Other important practices, such as child naming and funerary rites, produced minimal discussions. It is important to underline such topics for further research and a better understanding of a Marakwet Christian. Undoubtedly, the identity of a person begins at birth and the time of their naming is followed by their initiation.

Child Naming

As previously discussed, the birth of a child is one of the most important occasions for every family. It is well celebrated by the family and kin. Usually, , after the child's birth, the mother is confined to the house for a week or more to allow her to regain her strength and to attend to her baby. She is then released from seclusion by a ritual. The naming rite is an important event as it identifies and welcomes the new baby into society. At this stage, the elders gather to pray and invoke God and the ancestors for the happiness and prosperity of the baby. The ancestor's names are given to the baby to maintain continuity. When missionaries came to Marakwet, they did not understand what the naming rite represented and rejected it outright without bothering to find out its value and significance. To them, communication with the ancestors was considered evil. Therefore, child naming rituals were forbidden for Christians.

In the first four decades of Christianity in Marakwet, the missionaries were more tolerant and did not challenge the traditional rituals for fear of driving possible converts away too soon. As time passed and more of the Marakwet had converted, missionaries began to teach against some of the traditions, especially those linked to ancestors for whom the missionaries, considered to be synonymous with evil spirits.[27] After 1970, the Marakwet pastors who were graduating from Kapsabet Bible Institute spoke against the practice and several Christians discontinued the child naming rite. Some of the evangelists and Christians at Kapsowar mission hospital and station practiced the rite in secret, despite the constant opposition from

27. Personal interview with W. B. Young, February 1992.

Church officials. The Christians who were discovered to have transgressed were advised to desist and occasionally were refused communion.[28]

Women who deliver their babies at the hospital would not observe the seclusion period of rest ritual purification and recuperation until they got home. At some point the elders are invited to perform the ancestral naming rite. Similarly, those living in the cities take their children to the village for the naming ceremony. Failure to do so is believed to result in bad health for the child. Those who had moved away and could not return to the village for their child ritual, have often requested for the ritual to be performed in their absence. The general rule is that the ancestral naming rites must be done in the village where the ancestors are believed to reside. It remains unclear to most Marakwet as to why this practice conflicts with Christianity.

John Kipkeu (not his real name), a successful man with a good government job, was married in a Nairobi church where he later became an usher. He was respected as a good Christian, not only in his Church in Nairobi, but also in the Marakwet Christian circles. When their first child was born, John was against ancestral names for his child since he was a Christian. His wife did not share her husband's views and begged that the child be taken to the village for the naming ceremony. A month later, John's mother visited and tried to persuade him not to neglect traditions and the ancestors, but John stood by his newfound convictions. Eventually, John's wife took the child to John's village where the elders were waiting to perform the ritual. When it became known to the Christians that John's wife insisted on the traditional naming ceremony, both John and his wife were barred from church leadership until they had duly repented. Although John was not involved directly, he was held responsible for having allowed his wife to return to the community with their baby. John and his wife left the church and joined a non-denominational church in the city, where he is currently an usher.[29]

Another example is Joseph Kaino and his wife Magdalena. The two had converted to Christianity at a church in Tran-Zoia. They had four children before conversion and followed all the traditional requirements, including the child naming ceremony. When they had their fifth child, they were advised by some of the Christians that they were no longer subject to the traditional rite of child naming because God was going to protect their baby from the seemingly evil intentions of the ancestors. For a while they debated the issue. On the one hand, there were some who did not want them to follow the naming ritual. On the other hand, there were the clan's folk who insisted that they obey the culture and respect

---

28. Personal interview with Elijah Kilimo, January 1989.
29. Personal interview with Samuel Chepkong'a, April 1989.

the traditions of the ancestors. When the baby got sick a second time, Magdalena's parents, who were also Christians, visited and persuaded them to consider having the naming ritual to guarantee the baby's health and finally they obliged. However, to maintain their fellowship with their church, Joseph and Magdalena kept their plan secretive and visited one of the clan elders at night for the naming ritual. When their sixth child was born, they also had a secret naming ceremony.[30]

Today, ancestral naming has become very contentious among Marakwet Christians, partly because some are convinced that the practice is unchristian, as taught by the missionaries. Christians who support the ancestral naming ceremony see no harm in remembering their ancestors. Some have argued that the biblical names they have taken at baptism such as Abraham, Isaac, Jacob, Hezekiah, Jeremiah, Job, David, and John are Jewish ancestors who were not Christians. On the other hand, they never objected adding another Christian name in keeping with their own tradition where one took a new name at various stages of life. For Marakwet Christians, baptismal names or Christian names were parallel to the Marakwet traditional nicknames such as Chemuttut, Chesorom, Chebeiywa, Lomukeng'ura, Lobokong'ar, Lobetanguria, Loywalan, Lokinyang'a, Loikwongobong, Losili, Lormotum, Kemerio, Loribongura, Lotuma, Ribosia. Some of the Marakwet in the highlands of Cherang'any have adopted names from their Nandi and Keiyo neighbors such as Arap Moek, Arap Arusei, Arap Kandie, Arap Kurgat, Arap Kendagor etc.

It might be safe to think that there is no theological reason whatsoever for Marakwet Christians to reject their traditional names and naming ceremonies that give them a sense of identity. In the same way, there is no reason not to use Marakwet names for baptism if the candidate so chooses. Moreover, Marakwet names have a greater significance and meaning than European names such as Johnstone, Richard, Kevin, Irene, Lucy. On the other hand, biblical names might have been chosen due to their character, admiration, and motivation of faith. In fact, many Christians choose a baptismal name based on the character or faith of a Biblical person.

The Circumcision Rite

What is it that offends God in African circumcision rites? How do circumcision rites affect one's pursuit for salvation? I have been asked those questions, and I am afraid my answers have not been convincingly satisfactory. The debate over circumcision in Marakwet came into the limelight in the mission

30. Personal interview with Kisang Kirop, n.d.

station after the "Kikuyu Controversy" of 1913. The Protestant missionaries were united in attempting to deal with this matter and managed to succeed in soliciting the support of the government to stop the practise. The general missionary position on the subject was formulated and adopted during those debates. Therefore, by looking at the wider debate, a better understanding of the Marakwet situation can be attained. At least some of the measures that the missionaries applied in *Marakwet* were those adopted during the Kikuyu Controversy. I will underline some of the key points briefly.

As early as 1906, the Church of Scotland Mission started systematic instructions to its followers against circumcision of women. Other missions, including the Africa Inland Mission, followed a similar pattern. The Church Missionary Society was not emphatic in its teachings on this issue until 1928, when all the missions operating in East Africa convened a conference in Nairobi to discuss, among other topics, the issue of circumcision of girls. At this conference, the following resolution was passed:

> The allied societies should unite in absolutely forbidding the circumcision of girls in their missions, and that Government should be approached to legislate for its abolition among the heathen.[31]

Having passed this resolution, the Africa Inland Mission, like the other mission organizations, campaigned against the practice of circumcision among its followers. This was done largely at Kijabe through their leading missionaries, Dr. and Mrs. Elwood Davis, and in the hospital through Virginia Blakeslee, the director of the boarding school, and Hulda Stumpf. The latter was murdered during the height of the conflict.[32]

The Mission asked its followers, especially the elders/evangelists and the schoolteachers to sign a statement repudiating the practice. This request resulted in a rift within the African Christians A majority saw nothing wrong with the practice. The conflict erupted in Githumu mission station and caused a rift between some Kikuyu and the mission resulting in a break away in 1927. Reginald Reynolds confirmed this as follows:

> Mission adherents divided themselves into two bodies. One body was loyal, the other otherwise. The second body, which constituted the larger portion of the church members, boycotted Githumu and all its activities. . . . The teachers were likewise divided. Those who belonged to the second body were dismissed.[33]

---

31. Gration, "Africa Inland Mission," 163.
32. Gration, "Africa Inland Mission," 138.
33. Gration, "Africa Inland Mission," 139.

Worse still, the Christian children who were at the Mission Station were smuggled out at night by relatives and taken away to be circumcised. In other cases, Christians who saw nothing wrong with circumcision but did not want to jeopardize their reputation with the missionaries often sent their children secretly to relatives to be circumcised. The latter was done to make it look as if they were not involved in the decision. However, when their plan was discovered, was discovered, the individual was disciplined. The discipline varied from excommunication of the parents from partaking of the Holy Communion to losing employment to Discipline was not effective in Kikuyu land because there were alternative schools run by the Africa Independent Churches. In areas where there was no alternative, the families conformed to the discipline for the sake of their children.

In 1928, the battle over circumcision in Central Kenya was intensified by the involvement of the Kikuyu Central Association. This body was initially started to provide a well-rounded education when the missions' schools refused to provide it. The Kikuyu Central Association members refused to have teachers within their schools who had sided with the missionaries. Consequently, in many places it became a matter of choosing between the church and the Kikuyu Central Association. Mostly, the choice meant a loss to the Mission. At Kijabe and its surroundings, church attendance dwindled to a handful of followers. A missionary described the general situation as follows:

> The whole Kikuyu church is practically gone. The persecution is great and constant. Schools where the teacher or evangelist has signed are left, not a soul attend. Worse still is that all these who are refusing are singing vile filthy songs cursing those in favour of the church's firm stand.[34]

The stations that were hardest hit were Kijabe and Githumu. Lee Downing observed that the Kikuyu churches which had become involved in the circumcision controversy were reduced to about 10 percent of their former membership.

The crisis worsened when Miss. Huldah Stumpf was murdered by an unknown person at her house in Kijabe. She was murdered because the girls in her school had refused to be circumcised. Naturally, her death created a stir in both European and African communities. The colonial government became involved and apprehended many who had forced their daughters to be circumcised.

---

34. Gration, "Africa Inland Mission," 143.

To demonstrate its support for the mission, the colonial government passed a law to have the practice stopped, but soon realized this would create renewed tension among the native population. It opted to modify this by allowing a "mild" operation that might appease the mission. Chiefs and councilors were asked to pass these instructions to the public. Parents had to be convinced that this kind of superficial circumcision was as good as the previous one. It was hoped that this policy would eventually end the practice. Unfortunately, the government's alternative did not convince the missionaries nor the Africans. The mission societies rejected the government's option outright. They understood it as an infringement of St. Paul's teaching in 1 Corinthians 7:18–19. Here, Paul states that a person who is uncircumcised at the time of his call to faith should remain in that state. Moreover, on medical grounds, the operation was considered hygienically harmful. The only solution was to ban the practice completely. The government found itself in a dilemma, and consequently, the practice continued among the people who disagreed with the Mission.

The problem surrounding circumcision was not only confined to Central Kenya. The Marakwet region had its share of tension, not necessarily in similar magnitude to cause a considerable conflict. In the early years, the missionaries had learned from their previous experiences in Kijabe and were quite careful in their approach. Before long, however, it became a known fact among the Marakwet converts that to be a Christian was to abandon traditional practices, including the rite of female circumcision. This was not always received well by most of the early converts, even among those who worked in the mission stations.

Up until the early 1950s, most of the Marakwet Christians observed the circumcision rite with no radical opposition from the mission. The young Christians who might have been advised against the practice could not refuse to participate in the rite for fear of their extended families and peers. The only people who did not circumcise their children in the traditional way during those early years were the evangelists and the dispensers (nurse-aids) who were employed by the Mission and resided near the mission station. They also harbored young female converts who refused the rite and escaped to Kapsowar Mission station for safety and education. Some of the mission agents, like Elijah Kilimo, Daudi Kisang, and Paulo Katisei, married uncircumcised Christian women from the mission girls' school (*Kaptipin*). These men and women, though few, became dedicated role models for the rest of the Christians, although sometimes at a cost of social intimidation. Through their perseverance and successful marriages with children, they challenged the traditional rumor that children could not be born to uncircumcised women.

Paulo Katisei, who married Grace Cherop Cheboi. Grace was born in Kasang sub-location. She became a Christian at a young age and was taken to the mission home at Kapsowar where she obtained an education and protection. When her parents asked her to return home and undergo circumcision with her peers, she refused, and her furious parents stormed the mission station intending to abduct her. They were unsuccessful as the mission had hidden her. Her disappointed parents vowed to disown her. After completing her basic training at the mission school, Grace was wedded by Paulo Katisei, another Christian from Kapsogom in Endo, who was training as a dresser at the hospital. The marriage took place at Kapsowar church in 1943. In 1947, they were sent to Ng'echar to re-open the dispensary previously closed due to lack of workers.

The marriage to an uncircumcised woman sparked a lot of debate all over Marakwet. Parents warned their children against such a disgrace. Songs of ridicule were composed and sung during public gatherings, expressing the disgrace Grace had brought on her parents and clan. Some of the people mistook Grace's refusal to undergo the rite as cowardice. Apart from those individual cases, there were no serious controversies on the issue of circumcision until the 1970s. The mission had learned a lesson from the Kikuyu controversy of 1928 and had chosen slow down, lest they re-open wounds that might split or retard the progress of the young church. Also, there were not many adults converts in the church to raise a concern. The majority of the Christians at the time were younger converts in mission sponsored schools.

In the early '70s, the first patch of Marakwet pastors had graduated from Kapsabet Bible School. Through their zealous preaching in Marakwet schools, villages, and churches, many youths became Christians. To encourage the converts, the church began to hold a yearly, week-long youth conference at Kapsowar. Its popularity grew every year and drew youth from all corners of Marakwet and neighboring districts. The preaching was strictly evangelical, emphasizing St. Paul's notion "to come out from among them." The idea was to come out and denounce the traditional practices. Polygamy, circumcision, alcohol, and smoking were some of the target areas. Christian girls were encouraged to abstain from circumcision, while the boys were asked to be circumcised in hospitals. In addition, they were to avoid other traditional ceremonies that were considered incompatible with mission teachings. Many boys and girls who had escaped the traditional rites were given space to give their detailed testimonies. Youth gave incredible stories of heroic escapes that could make for an interesting novel or movie.

I do not say this to diminish the potency of those stories, for they were real, and a number of youths did suffer a great deal. For example, one evening at Liter, some of us had gathered to discuss what to do because earlier on in the day one of the members of our Christian youth group, Anna Cherop (not her real name), had been abducted by men who happened to be her relatives. They took her up the hill to be circumcised. The missionary in charge of the station, Paul Barnett, was away. We were few and young, and there were no adult Christians to help. We prayed for Anna and went to sleep at Nelson's house, where we often met to hang out. At about 2:00 a.m. we heard a soft knock at the door. We inquired as to who it was, and a faint whisper said, "it is me Anna." We opened the door, but she could not come in. Instead, she stood in the dark and said she didn't have any clothing. Nelson's wife, Paulina, handed her some clothes, to cover herself, and came in. We were all happy to see her intact, though she had been ruffled quite a bit. She narrated how she was taken by force by her male clansmen. When she reached the village, she joined the other girls who were already in the process getting ready for the ordeal. Anna cooperated and went along for a while. They had their hair shaved and had dinner together. After dinner they were taken to the place where she had to surrender her regular clothing in exchange for the ritual. Because she had cooperated up to that point, nobody was worried that she would escape. When the girls were busy, she took advantage of that moment to escape. She went outside into the dark, as if going for a short goal and escaped. She left the ritual garment in the bush and ran unnoticed. She hid for a while and along the way and continued to run in the dark for five miles until she reached the mission station. We were happy to see her but were faced with what to do if those people followed suit. Nelson, who worked as a cook for the Barnett's went and woke him up and told the story. Paul Barnett had been tipped off about what happened earlier and was equally delighted that Anna had escaped. He dressed quickly and drove Anna across to Maron Mission Station, where the Staufficher's were stationed. At about 6:00 a.m., Paul Barnett returned to the station. Similar stories were common in the 1970s and 1980s. The young people's courageous testimonies of escape were intended to encourage others to denounce the practices.

When the Marakwet elders felt that the fabric of their culture was being threatened, they sought ways to re-enforce the rite. Firstly, they reported the matter to the local government authorities; secondly, they put undue pressure on the boys who were initiated at hospitals by shaming them. When the church leaders and missionaries realized what was happening, they doubled down and assisted any youth who wanted to escape, sometimes taking them secretly at night to safe grounds. Such acts added undue tension between Christianity and Marakwet traditional culture. Those who defied the tradition openly were beaten and, occasionally, forced into the rite. The following are two instances of youths who suffered persecution because they refused the traditional rite.

Christine Kibiwott had lost her mother at an early age. At fifteen, she became a Christian while attending Liter Primary School near the mission station. Because her father objected to her newfound faith, Christine decided to live with other Christian girls at the mission station. Besides, it was close to her school. When the girls of her village of Kamariny were getting ready for the circumcision rite, Christine did not join them. Her father wondered why his daughter was not joining the other girls in preparations. Finally, Christine explained to her father that she was not going to be circumcised because she was a Christian. The father was quite disappointed that his firstborn daughter had chosen to let him down at this crucial time. He tried to threaten her that the ancestors would be upset, and, furthermore, she might not find a husband or have children if she disobeyed. When initiation time finally came, Christine's brothers and cousins stormed the station and abducted Christine. She was taken to join the rest of the clan girls to undergo the rite. Christine convinced her brothers that she would comply, but when people were tired and sleepy from the night's dancing, she escaped. She ran to the mission station and to one of the Christian houses where people had gathered to pray for her. They were relieved to see her, and the missionary in charge of the station, the Rev. Paul Barnett, drove her immediately across the border to another mission station in Baringo district. She was to remain there until the circumcision months were over.

After a week of searching, Christine's clansmen discovered that the missionary had helped her to escape. They demanded she be brought back, and when this was not heeded, they laid ambush and attacked the missionary on the main road at Krel near their village. Paul Barnett was badly injured and was airlifted to Kijabe mission hospital where he underwent eye surgery. When the government learned of the incident, police were sent out to arrest the culprits. Christine's two clansmen were arrested and served a jail term. Paul Barnett never returned to Liter. He was blinded in one eye and was reassigned to Eldama Ravine near Kijabe. I remained close to the Barnetts and occasionally exchanged letters. I visited them at Eldma Ravine where they had retired. By that time, he was completely blind—probably from those early injuries. Thankfully, his two daughters, Kathy and Ellen, and son in law Roy Stover lived with them. They had developed an impressive home on a piece of land given to them by Kenyan former President Daniel Arap Moi. Apparently, Paul Barnett had officiated the president's wedding.

In 1981, Christine attended Bible College with the support of Ms. Mary Lucking. After graduation in 1985, she was married to Daniel Lopuriang, a Christian school teacher. Her father, who had denounced her earlier for rejecting circumcision and thought she would never get married, has since changed his mind and is proud of his daughter. In fact, Christine is in a good financial situation to assist her father in his old age. She is an influential Christian woman leader in her community and a role model to many girls.

Another example was Benjamin Ruto. He converted to Christianity and was baptized in 1978. When the boys of his clan took part in the traditional ritual in 1979, Benjamin refused to join them. He and two other Christian boys were sent by the Rev. Paul Barnett to be circumcised at the Mission hospital. His non-Christian relatives did not understand why Benjamin abandoned his clan's age mates during the most crucial cultural rite. Some thought that he was afraid, but most of them knew it had to do with the church and the missionary. After two weeks at the hospital, they had recovered and returned home. Benjamin was not received well. In fact, he was constantly shamed. He felt like a stranger in his own village. One evening, at the instigation of the elders, the men of his clan invaded Benjamin's hut and took him by force to the circumcision camp where all his age-mates were recuperating. They saw no reason to perform the operation again since it had already been done at the hospital. However, he had to go through the remaining time of instructions and bonding. He was also fined for what he did. The penalty involved two goats and a large quantity of beer prepared on his behalf by his larger family.[35]

It seems inevitable that the Marakwet traditions have been undermined by both Christianity and Western culture. For example, its leadership preparation, based on the rites of passage and age-set system, has been replaced by Western education. These changes have contributed to enormous cultural erosion and confusion, in the modern Kenya, where government leaders come from anywhere, including the tribes that do not practice the rite of circumcision such as the Luo and Turkana. When such leaders are deployed to Marakwet, the locals often judge them from Marakwet standards. If they are not circumcised for whatever reason, they are often not taken seriously. They were often judged from the Marakwet standards, and their opinions were not heeded regardless of their education. There was an incident in the late 60s where I learned that a District Commissioner from the Luo people went to address a baraza (gathering) in Endo. When the audience learned that he was not circumcised, they walked out protesting that the District Commissioner was a boy, as far as they were concerned, and could not, therefore, offer them anything sensible. That is no longer the case.

---

35. Personal interview with James Cheserek, January 1989.

The Marakwet put a lot of premia on their rites. The most important aspect of which is the pain which must be endured. Pain is a teacher; for through it, the youth become adults. Failure to submit to the pain is interpreted as cowardice. These are valuable principles that hold in balance the traditional education that is passed from one generation to the next. The disruption could affect the equilibrium of social harmony.

While reminiscing on the past glory of their traditions, the Marakwet are aware of the imminent change that comes because of an encounter with outsiders, especially Westerners. Those changes have altered traditions and forced the Marakwet to adjust accordingly. For example, in 1964 the three-month duration of being at the circumcision camp was slightly adjusted for the few initiates who attended school. However, the latter would join their fellow initiates at the circumcision camp in the evenings. From the age-set of Kipnyigeu in the mid-1970s, most of the youths were attending school. This meant that they were released after a month. By the 1990s, almost every initiate was attending either primary or secondary school, and it became the norm for the circumcision to last for only one month. The changes have altered the rite considerably. Today, most of the youths going through the initiation rite are in their early teens, and the initial training in marriage and family responsibilities can, therefore, no longer be imparted in full. The only sure thing is the lasting impression of the pain during the operation. What is lost is the space necessary to teach the young men to be responsible adults in their family and community matters.

The girls' circumcision, on the other hand, has faced a lot of opposition from both Christianity and the government. The opposition intensified when the civil society was involved, especially when the health of the novice was in danger.[36] President Daniel Arap Moi his time, took a strong stance and condemned the practice. In most cases, families who forced their girls into circumcision were punished by law. This opposition has induced many families to circumcise young girls before they are able to rebel. In the most Christian-influenced quarters, such as Kapsowar, Chebara, and Kapcherop, circumcision has ceased as a communal practice. A few families who still revere the old traditions circumcise their girls secretly in the highlands. However, down in the valley, the practice continues unabated. Neither the church nor the government, with all their efforts, have managed to discourage the practice in those places.

While it is easy to see the reason for circumcision of boys, Christians do not see any benefit in the circumcision of girls. In fact, a lot of

---

36. The operation is often done by untrained people under unhygienic conditions. For that matter, infections are virtually inevitable.

men whom I interviewed have confessed that they had no problem marrying uncircumcised women. If this is true, then, why has the practice continued? To answer this question, it is important to underline that the entire subject of women's circumcision is shrouded in secrecy of taboos and tradition. In many cases, those who defend the rite do so because they say it has always existed and must not be questioned. Consequently, the supporters of the rite have clashed with both Christians and government authorities. Most of the people fear the consequences of not conforming to the ancient tradition that has been instilled since childhood to be responsible for ill-health, barrenness, and other misfortunes. Similarly, many are convinced that there are social and moral privileges granted by going through the experience. These factors have promoted the continuation of the practice of circumcision from generation to generation.

During the 1980s, there was a consistent outcry from both the church and the global society for eradication of female circumcision, not only in Marakwet, but in the rest of Africa. From the medical point of view, the rite disadvantages millions of African women who still have to endure circumcision every year. Medically, the practice deprives women of their most sensitive part of their bodies and, hence, their natural rights to sexuality. In 1984, the World Health Organization (WHO) and UNICEF organized a seminar in Dakar in collaboration with the Senegalese government to discuss harmful traditional practices in the continent of Africa. They adopted steps to stop some of the rites, especially the circumcision of women. National committees and other special bodies able to handle the problem in a manner acceptable to Africans were established. These bodies were to define strategies and programs aimed at educating women and men regarding the dangerous consequences of the practice. In his speech to the delegates, Abdul Diouf, the then President of Senegal, remarked:

> Let us not rush into the error of condemning (circumcision) as uncivilized and sanguinary practices. In traditional Africa, it evolved out of coherent system with its own values, beliefs, cultural values, and ritual conduct. They were necessary ordeals in life because they completed the process of incorporating the child in society.... These practices raise a problem today because our societies are in a process of major transformation and are coming up against new socio-cultural dynamic forces in which such practices have no place or appear to be relics of the past. What is therefore needed are measures to quicken their demise. The main part of this struggle will be waged by education rather than by anathema and from the inside rather than from the outside. I

hope that this struggle will make women free and "disalienated" personifying respect for the eminent dignity of life.[37]

In the same manner, President Moi had repeatedly opposed the circumcision of women. The only problem with such presidential declarations is that they do not give specific means to implement them. The Kenyan government, with the support from the international agencies, continues to discourage the practice by adopting specific ways and means which would appeal to the grass-roots level.

As far as the traditional circumcision of boys is concerned, many in Marakwet are lost as to why it is considered unchristian when the Jews, including Jesus, practiced it according to the Jewish tradition. In fact, the early listeners to Christian teachings often asked how a positive education given to their youths at the circumcision camp could possibly be considered as sinful? This question still has not been answered. Some feel that the Christian boys should not be encouraged to go to the hospital, instead, the entire rite should be Christianized and openly performed and observed in the community. In this case, the tutors (*motiren*) are to be superseded by Christian elders who would be responsible for teaching the young both Christian and Marakwet values. This is understood to be the best way for the church to be relevant and active in Marakwet society. At the beginning of this millennia, many Christians abandoned the hospital and circumcised their boys in groups at Christian centers. The current rituals with Christian influence are intended to parallel the ancient tradition in form only without the traditional substance. I think a discourse between Marakwet Christians, and traditionalists might strike a middle ground where the best traditions and mentorship can be practiced without the actual cut for the girls.

Marriage

The Marakwet requirements for the preparation for marriage are observed by both Christians and non-Christians. The only major distinctions are in the sequence and manner in which the wedding ceremony is conducted. In the traditional way, the wedding is performed when the wife is pregnant, whereas the Christians begin marriage with a Western Christian wedding. Once the Christian man has picked a Christian partner, he informs his church elders to proceed with the wedding negotiations, a method similar to the traditional one, but instead of taking honey beer, the Christian

---

37. Koso-Thomas, *Circumcision of Women*, 106.

elders take soft drinks.[38] The purpose of the negotiations is to ensure that there is no blood relationship or any other impediments that might hinder the marriage, and once this is satisfactorily resolved, the couple can plan the wedding. The Christian wedding is usually quite expensive because of the required clothes—suits, bridal gown—as well as festive food. Fortunately, the Christian community and friends assist with the cost.

Daudi Chemeitoi, a member of the Christian community at Liter, had found a lovely Christian woman from Luguget to whom he wished to marry. The only problem was that Daudi had no job and no money for the wedding. He took the matter to his pastor Rev. Samuel Chepkong'a who promised assistance from the church. The pastor summoned his elders and put Daudi's predicament before them. They all agreed to help and made a list of the required items which included ten cases of soda, several kilograms of sugar and rice, salt, and four goats for meat. Daudi only had to buy his own suit, and one of the women agreed to lend her own wedding gown to the bride.[39]

On the wedding day, the church was decorated with plastic flowers, balloons, and ribbons. The missionaries had rejected the evergreen creeper plant (*seretyon*) and the hard wood (*yemit*), which are usually used in traditional weddings. Instead, Western symbols were appropriated.[40] At about 11:00 a.m., the groom and best man entered the church while a girls choir began to sing outside as they waited to welcome the bride. The bride had arrived earlier and had been taken to the pastor's house to get dressed and to await the car, which would take her the two hundred meters to the church. The girls serenaded her with songs praising her beauty and good character. The singing continued for at least an hour before she entered the church for the ceremony. The officiating pastor, the Rev. Samuel Cheserek, led the service with a few songs before performing the actual ceremony. Although the church was too small to accommodate everyone, some looked from the big wire mesh windows to witness the solemn event. After the exchange of vows, the couple walked out and the remainder of the ceremony such as the cutting of the cake and reception was done outside under the mango trees. Several choirs performed and speeches were given by relatives and friends. The wedding cake, prepared by Mary Lucking, the station nurse, was cut and distributed.[41]

---

38. Because the church does not permit the drinking of beer within its membership, soft drinks, and sometimes meat, are used as substitutes.
39. Personal interview with Joseph Cheserek, May 1989.
40. Personal interview with Joseph Cheserek, May 1989.
41. Personal interview with Joseph Cheserek, May 1989.

At about 2:00 p.m., presentations of gifts were made. Some brought goats and sheep, while others brought money. The parents of the groom presented a heifer, not only as a practical gift, but as a symbol of fertility. The church women from the bride's community gave a big carton box full of utensils.[42] The wedding concluded with a prayer led by a church elder. Since this was a strictly Christian wedding, the Marakwet traditional blessings (*kise'eno*) was not allowed nor the ceremonial traditional elders' colobus monkey headgear of colobus monkey nor the marriage ritual spear (*swoger*).

A renewal of wedding vows has also become mandatory for people who wish to have their marriages recognized by the Kenyan government. Apparently, the Kenyan law, which is based on the English common law, does not provide registration of customary marriages.[43] Recognized marriages according to the Kenyan law are those performed in the church or in an attorney's office. In Marakwet, the former is only available.

The Church and Polygamy

Technically, the term polygamy might have a different meaning, but for the purpose of our discussion, the word will refer to the union of a husband with several wives at the same time.[44] From the moment the missionaries from the west landed in Africa, polygamy was condemned outrightly as uncivilized and unchristian. It received similar treatment as adultery if not worse. The only sympathetic churchman on record was the Anglican Bishop John Colenso of Natal, South Africa. When he first arrived, he held the prevailing missionary views that polygamy was unchristian and must be discouraged at all costs. After his first year in the parish, Colenso met polygamous people and had known them to be honest good people. After giving it some consideration, he come to a different position which he made clear in 1888.

> I must confess that I feel strongly on this point, that the usual practice of enforcing the separation of wives from their husbands upon their conversion to Christianity is quite unwarrantable and opposed to the plain teaching of our Lord. It is putting new wine in old bottles and placing a stumbling block, which he has not set directly in the way of receiving the Gospel.[45]

42. Personal interview with Joseph Cheserek, May 1989.
43. Kisembo et al., *African Christian Marriage*, 20.
44. Mbiti, *African Religions*, 142.
45. Hillman, *Polygamy Reconsidered*, 32. See also Harris, "Christian Marriage in African Society," 32.

This precipitated the fullest ecclesiastical debate ever undertaken on the question by missionaries. Colenso reaffirmed his position and criticized the mission societies for mistreating African polygamous converts. The debate was later to the taken to the Anglican Lambeth Conference in London in 1888. Unfortunately, John Colenso was not there to defend his position; he died before the debate reached a conclusion. However, the Lambeth Conference discussed the matter and voted against any changes. Polygamy was condemned as adultery. However, the wives of polygamists, who denounced polygamy, could be admitted to the church. Bishop Crowther made a plea for the wives under polygamy to be pardoned as they were involuntary victims of the social institution. A baptized convert, who later took a second wife, was to be excommunicated.[46]

Another group that sympathized with the polygamists was the Bremen Mission. They maintained a positive policy and stressed the historical significance that:

> Polygamy existed at the time of Christ and the apostles, but we do not find that monogamy was made a condition for acceptance into the Church. Therefore, a man who has several wives must be admitted to baptism and communion. However, all are always to be reminded that monogamy is the true marriage according to God, and that only in this way can the purpose of marriage be reached.[47]

Most of the Protestant mission societies, including the Africa Inland Mission, opposed polygamy on the grounds of maintaining a united front against it with other missionaries operating in Africa. Surprisingly, theological argument played a minor role in determining the missionaries' attitude. Their basic reasons were motivated by Eurocentric values, as expressed by B. Webster:

> They proposed to make Africa conform to the Victorian bourgeois society of England which appeared to them as the highest morality yet attained. . . . They never failed to point out that monogamous people were conquerors, the civilized, the inventors—in short, the master races. Polygamist people were the conquered, the savage, the imitators, in short, the lesser breeds without the law.[48]

---

46. Nkwoka, "Church and Polygamy," 144.
47. Grau, "Missionary Policies," 68.
48. Webster, "Attitude and Policies," 228.

When the Africa Inland Mission arrived in Marakwet, their view on polygamy was negative. All they saw was a people blinded by darkness that needed the light of Christianity and education. Moreover, most of the converts were young and posed no threat during the early years. The polygamists who joined the church were denied baptism, while their wives were baptized. Like most of the Protestant missions, the Africa Inland Mission took an active role on the issue of polygamy. Eugene Hillman has conveniently summarized those propositions as follows:

(1) All the women and children may be baptized, but not the husbands.

(2) Only men who are not married polygamously could be baptized.

(3) The husband may be baptized if he retains his first wife while divorcing the others.

(4) The husband may be baptized with the understanding that any subsequent plural marriages are forbidden.[49]

These propositions became the general guidelines for the missions whenever they encountered polygamous marriages, not only in Marakwet, but in the rest of Africa. Arthur Phillips made a personal observation that:

> On this crucial issue, the mission authorities of all denominations have consistently refused to surrender their ground. They have always maintained, and still maintain, that acceptance of polygamy would be fundamentally inconsistent with the teachings of Christianity.[50]

The question of polygamy has been a major issue of debate in the church in Africa since the arrival of the first missionaries and has continued to be a conundrum to the present. African Christians are also divided over the issue of polygamy. Some accepted uncritically everything the missionaries proposed. In fact, they assisted the missionaries in implementing discipline and order in the churches. On the other hand, others could not tolerate the missionaries' attacks on their cultural values. They refused to accept the missions' position on polygamy and found support in the Old Testament polygamous practices of the patriarchs like Abraham, David, and Solomon. In the Mosaic law, polygamy is clearly mentioned and regarded as a normal and licit practice (Exod 21:10; Lev 18:18; Deut 21:15–17). Nowhere in the Old Testament is this form of marriage questioned, apart from when it was abused. While it is true that many people of the Old Testament were monogamists, it is evident that some

---

49. Hillman, *Polygamy Reconsidered*, 165–67.
50. Phillips and Morris, *Marriage Laws in Africa*, 16.

were polygamists. Elkanah and his wife Hannah are singled out in the Bible as an example of affectionate expression of conjugal love, although Elkanah had another wife at the same time. The patriarchs were polygamous, yet they are held up highly as godly people. Jacob had two wives and Christians continue to use the example of Rachel (the second wife) as a role model for newly married women (Gen 29:15-30).

Many African Christians ask why the missionaries condemned polygamy as evil if such a practice was congenial to the Old Testament custom. On the other hand, those who support monogamy as the ideal Christian marriage, take the story of Adam and Eve in the garden (Gen 2:18-25) as God's universal law of monogamous marriage. Along this line, some have cited the words of Jesus (Matt 5:31-32; 19:3-9; Mark 10:2-22) and interpreted them as an attack on polygamy. The subject under consideration in the Gospels of Matthew and Mark has nothing to do with a particular form of marriage but discourages easy divorce. In this context, divorce and polygamy are diametrically opposed. Divorce means breaking up, while polygamy is building up. It would, therefore, be unfair to read into the text what it does not say. In their 1988 Lambeth working paper on polygamy, the African Bishops put it rightly:

> Where Jesus has not spoken, as in the case of polygamy, the Church has done so on his behalf; where it has spoken, as in the case of divorce, the Church has ignored him and gone on to institutionalize that which He explicitly forbids.[51]

The Pauline use of the term "one flesh" and Christ's love for the church is often interpreted to imply monogamous marriage. This may not necessarily be confined to the conjugal union of one husband and one wife, but rather a metaphor describing intimacy, especially that engendered by sex relationships between a man and a woman. This is not impossible in polygamous situations. Elsewhere, Paul argues that a man who joins himself to a prostitute becomes one flesh with her (1 Cor 6:16-17). On the same thought wave, Eugene Hillman suggests that a man can become one flesh with more than one wife in Africa where this form of marriage is accepted.[52] In dealing with Old Testament polygamous citations, the monogamists see it as practices which were never approved by God, and therefore, could not be taken as ideal marriages. For example, Lamech, the first polygamist, had come from a deviant lineage of Cain (Gen 4:17-19). Also, despite Abraham, Jacob, David, and Solomon being godly men, their polygamous

---

51. Muge, Private Papers, Anglican Diocese of Eldoret, Kenya.
52. Hillman, *Polygamy Reconsidered*, 167.

marriages were probably not approved by God as noted in Solomon's case. These biblical interpretations demonstrate, that when people are bent on having their own ways, God will not stop them.

The "one wife" rule in the Pastoral Epistles (1 Tim 3:2, 12; Titus 1–6) was most likely given because some of the men in the church had more than one wife and would, therefore, not qualify for leadership. It is very likely that when Christianity penetrated the world of the Greco-Roman Empire, polygamists who genuinely responded to the gospel were allowed to keep their believing wives and children. They might have considered it unchristian to put away their extra wives and children. However, for leadership purposes, it was important to get a man who was married to only one wife. That means monogamy was confined only to those in leadership positions.

According to Eugene Hillman, the text might have come from nothing more than the church's need to align itself to the Greco-Roman world where monogamy was the practice. During his time, St. Augustine acknowledged the influence of Greco-Roman culture on monogamous marriages. With his fellow early church fathers, he was convinced that this kind of marriage was rooted in the teachings of the New Testament. He admitted that polygamy was not sinful in the Old Testament when the social conditions permitted it. But in the New Testament times, the practice was no longer permitted because the cultural situation had changed. Paul's understanding of marriage was developed out of this context.[53]

Following this tradition, the Western Church, with very few exceptions, has consistently affirmed the absolute incompatibility of polygamy with the Christian life. This view, as we have noted, is based on the interpretations or misinterpretations of some scriptural texts. Some have argued further that, although polygamy is allowed in the Old Testament, there is a gradual evolution towards monogamy. Because of this argument, monogamy is viewed as the divinely willed form of marriage. In addition to that, the modern cultural setting in Africa with the Western influence has made it easier to adopt monogamy, among other things. Almost all Christian churches in Africa, except for some of the African Independent Churches, have adopted monogamy as the ideal Christian marriage. For Christians, it is the equality of love and the intensity of the relationship between husband and wife that matters. This qualitative value of relationship is taken from the New Testament. These ideas are in harmony with the inspirations of African women as they seek to benefit from modern education and economic emancipation.

Now, the most critical issue of concern in the Marakwet Church is whether polygamists should be baptized and accepted into the church

---

53. Joyce, *Christian Marriage*, 564; see also Hillman, *Polygamy Reconsidered*, 22.

membership. We interviewed a cross section of Marakwet Christians of all ages and sexes, particularly those related to the Africa Inland Mission on this topic. Fifty people were questioned in each category and fifteen pastors, and the responses varied as indicated on the following table:

Age Group	Sex	Should Baptize (%)	Should not Baptize (%)
20–30	male	20	80
	female	30	70
31–45	male	25	75
	female	25	75
46+	male	25	75
	female	20	80
Pastors	male	10	90
	female	—	—

Table 7.1 Group Survey on Polygamy for Baptism

Due to the influence of the missionary teachings, a few of the Christians felt that a polygamist who converted should be baptized based on his faith in Jesus Christ and be accepted into full membership of the church. The women who participated did not particularly favor polygamy. Most of them felt that polygamy was only chosen as a last resort when monogamy is not foreseen. Most of the pastors who were trained and influenced by Western missionaries were strongly opposed to the practice and the baptism of polygamists. They believed that a polygamist was living in a state of sin because he was continuously committing adultery, thus breaking the marriage vows and covenant. One pastor went to the extent of suggesting that a polygamist should not be allowed to participate in any of the church's activities until he shows signs of true and genuine repentance by sending away all his wives except the first one. The reason behind this position, as far as he was concerned, is to protect the constitution of the church.

However, there were a few pastors who were obviously sympathetic to polygamists, some of whom came from polygamous families. They felt that further discussions on the subject should be encouraged through the local Church Councils. As far as they were concerned, the subject of polygamy had never been discussed in full by the Marakwet Christians. One of the reasons for this is the hierarchical structure of the Africa Inland Church, whereby most of the final theological decisions are made by the Central Church Council and passed down through several Church Councils to the local church level. One evangelist expressed his disappointment on the whole matter and suggested that if he were an ordained pastor, he would baptize a polygamist who was a true believer.[54] Another older pastor expressed his deep concern over the large number of people who were turned away from the church because of their polygamous marriages. He cited the case of several polygamous chiefs who were turned away during the early years of the Mission.

Kisang Kirop Chemuttut was appointed chief of Endo by the Colonial government in 1955. He interacted frequently with the missionaries who operated in his location. Before long, the chief expressed interest in becoming a Christian. He received the Christian instructions and before baptism, he was told that he would have to abstain from drinking alcohol and send all but his first wife away. This idea did not sit well with the chief. He could not reconcile such action in good conscience, especially with his status in society. He stopped attending church. Later when the Roman Catholic Mission came to the area in the early 1960s, he appreciated their generous attitude towards alcohol and the Marakwet cultural practices. Before long, however, he learned that the Catholic Church was also strict regarding polygamy. After those attempts, the Chief became disinterested with the Catholic Church. In the early 1980s, when he had settled all his wives in their respective properties and he was now living alone at Tot, he returned to the Catholic Church and sought baptism. His request was granted, and the chief was finally baptized with the name Paul.

A similar example is Paulo Kibore. He was a polygamist when he was employed at the Liter mission station. After two years he was ready for baptism; the only obstacle was his polygamous marriage. To receive baptism and retain his job with the Mission, Paulo agreed to keep one wife. In this case it was his second wife with whom he lived near the mission station, and that satisfied the missionaries. His first wife lived at his other home on the escarpment. In the eyes of the Mission, such a separation was considered legitimate divorce. According to mission policy, Paulo should have kept his first wife and sent the second away. After baptism, Paulo was chosen as an elder in the church and enjoyed a close friendship with Paul Barnett for many years. He was removed from church leadership in the mid-1970s when the young

---

54. Only men are ordained in the Africa Inland Church, and they are the only ones authorized to baptize or conduct marriages.

Marakwet Christians, who had graduated from Bible College, took over the leadership of the church. A majority felt that Paulo had lived a double life and should not continue as an elder in the church. Some questioned Paul Barnett's integrity in involving Paulo in the church leadership.

These instances might seem hypocritical, but one must consider the pressure imposed on the African family unit. Because of the failure of the church in dealing with polygamy, many polygamists who became Christians have adopted the role of "indirect separation" in order to find acceptance in the church. Although missionary teachings and influence still prevail in guiding the Marakwet churches, many Christians foresee the need for new directions in which honest contextual theological discussions are undertaken. Meanwhile, pastoral counselling should be offered to polygamists and their families to guide and help them to lead meaningful Christian lives in their own setting. Instead of sweeping condemnation each case should be considered carefully with compassion and love.

Already, some of the churches in Africa have attempted to deal with the matter of polygamy. Most of the Africa Independent Churches in particular have shown considerable tolerance towards polygamy, hence their tremendous growth. Others, especially those with foreign links like the Africa Inland Church, have chosen to ignore the subject. The Anglicans have recognized the problem, and after many discussions, they have adopted a constructive policy for those who were refused entry into the church on grounds of polygamy. This followed great pressure from the African Bishops, who raised this subject at several synods. At the Lambeth Conference of 1988, the Anglican commission dealt seriously with this matter. As a result, they altered their century-old policy that barred many polygamists from the church sacraments. In resolution no. 26, they passed the following statements:

> The Conference upholds monogamy as God's plan, and as the ideal relationships of love between husband and wife; nevertheless, recommends that a polygamist who responds to the Gospel and wishes to join the Anglican Christians may be baptised and confirmed with his believing wives and children on the following conditions:
>
> (i) A polygamist shall promise not to marry again if any of his wives at the time of his conversion are alive.
>
> (ii) The receiving of such a polygamist has the consent of the local Anglican Community.
>
> (iii) A polygamist shall not be compelled to put away any of his wives, on account of the social deprivation they would suffer.

(iv) The provinces where the Churches face problems of polygamy are encouraged to share information of their pastoral approach with Christians who become polygamists so that the most appropriate way of disciplining and pastoring them can be found, and that the Anglican Consultative Council be requested to facilitate the sharing of that information.[55]

The problem of polygamy in Marakwet as well as in the rest of Africa is widespread, and therefore cannot be tackled in isolation. The ACK's obligation is to guide the family as a creative force for the improvement of the quality of life and promotion of the church's mission. To accomplish such a goal, the church tries to work together regarding issues of common concern such as polygamy. The Africa Inland Church in Marakwet might follow suit in accepting the directives adopted by the Anglicans for those polygamists who have either been driven away or shied away from the church. As it stands now, most Marakwet Christians recognize the problems pertaining to Christianity and culture, but they have not, so far, brought up the subject for serious deliberation. The missionary views still prevail in many quarters. Many polygamists are aware that they could never be accepted as potential church members unless they disposed of their wives.

One example is the previous story of Hezekiah Yego Kaino, a respected leader of his clan. Hezekiah was born in 1914, the year his village of Sibow was set on fire by the British. In 1926, Ezekiah followed some of his friends in search of cash employment so that he could buy the newly arrived cotton calico. Fortunately, he found work at Kapsowar as a 'shamba boy' for a Nubian soldier attached to the District Commissioner. After a month, Ezekiah had earned enough to buy the *Shuka* and returned home. Following his initiation in 1932, he travelled with another group to Tranzoia district to work for a European settler in Naikam near Kapcherop. Within six months he had earned enough to return home, pay the hut tax, and start a small business of selling the home-made brew (*buzaa*) made from maize flour. In 1947, he became ill and was taken to the mission hospital at Kapsowar. While in hospital, he heard the Christian message and was converted to Christianity.

On his return home from the hospital, he received further religious instructions by Pilipu Chepkonga, a Christian teacher at Ngecher. During Christmas of 1949, Hezekiah and his family were invited to join Elijah Kilimo, the mission Evangelist, stationed at Boroko. During this visit, Hezekiah

---

55. Muge, Private Papers, "The Lambeth Conference 1988," 220–21. Also, see the Lambeth Conference Resolutions Archive from 1988, "Resolution 26: Church and Polygamy."

was instructed against alcohol and tobacco since his trade entailed the sale of both. He had to think of another business if he was to live as a Christian. Elijah advised him to sell tea and other foodstuffs instead. To do that well, he acquired a proper business plot at Tot trading centre. He continued his business at Tot until 1952, when Dr. Morris invited him to train as a dresser at Kapsowar hospital. He qualified in 1953 and was posted to Ng'echer. There he worked tirelessly as a preacher and dispenser. He attracted many youths wherever he went. Ng'echer had to be closed in 1960 as people in the area relocated, and Hezekiah moved to Chesongoch, where a new dispensary had been started. He worked there until 1970, when his services were terminated. He had become involved with a young woman and married her as his second wife. The dispensary had to close, and on the recommendation of Dr. Lindsay, and it was transferred to the Roman Catholic Mission which had started work in the area.

Hezekiah moved back to Tot and reopened his small shop. Although he was dropped from the church leadership, he was a faithful attendant and generous contributor to church. As far as the church is concerned, Ezekiah failed; but in the eyes of the Marakwet society, he is an honest and respectable man. According to the church constitution, only divorce from his second wife would bring about his full reinstitution in the church. Ezekiah admitted his mistake but refuses out of conscience and family commitment to divorce any of his wives. Although he does not encourage anybody to follow his example, he does not feel that his second marriage situation affects his relationship with God.[56] The church continues to encounter similar problems, but it has not developed the capacity to dealt with them constructively. Instead, it ignores them in fear of conflict with the teachings of the mission, and with such an approach, nothing is solved. This prevarication is also one of the reasons why for many years, the Africa Inland Church did not attract many adult men.

Funeral Rites

The general position of the Africa Inland Mission was to steer away completely from any traditional rite they viewed as non-Christian, especially those that required the invocation of ancestors. Although funerary rites belong to this category, it has created the least controversy, simply because the Marakwet Christians have not adopted a particular funeral rite. Even if the missionaries and the church introduced a Christian funeral pattern, the traditional funerary rites continued to be followed by the clan elders.

56. Personal interview with Hezekiah Kaino, May 1989.

In any case, most of the rites are performed after the body has been buried. The missionaries are mostly unaware of them and have, not directly challenged them.[57]

Apart from a Christian service being held at the funeral site, the traditional and Christian funerals are conducted in a similar fashion. Due to the warm climate and lack of mortuaries, the dead are buried within twenty-four hours.[58] As mentioned in chapter 2, the senior elders in the community who will perform the traditional funeral rites, are asked to perform the actual internment. The ritual goat is brought forth and the ensuing ritual is done at the homestead followed by two days of mourning for the whole village. No work of any kind is undertaken during this time.

When a Christian dies, the whole Christian community go to the deceased person's home to console the family at the wake vigil. On the following day, the Church conducts a funeral service with singing, during which time a Christian message is delivered. After the service, the clan elders and the dead person's spouse are left to complete the burial according to tradition. This is done in the absence of any youths and pregnant women.[59] After the burial, the people move to the home of the deceased, where the ritual goat is killed and prepared for eating. Part of the goat's entrails are appropriated as cleansing elements; these are scattered throughout the compound by an elder primarily to appease the ancestors. In the same manner, the dead person's property is ritually cleansed before being distributed to family members. At this time, the women and children belonging to the dead person's family have their heads shaved, while the initiated men remove a bit of hair on their forehead as a symbol of their loss. Two days of mourning are observed in the whole territory, and anyone found working is cursed by the elders. Some Christians have refused to participate in the traditional rites, especially the shaving of hair and sacrifices given to the ancestors. However, the whole community observes the mourning period.

James Kipkiror Loshamba was killed at his home near Liter in 1970. His funeral was the first Christian burial as I recall. Christians went to his home and stayed the whole night singing to comfort the family. On the following day, the clan elders came to oversee the burial. Some Christians volunteered to dig the grave. Because most of the Christians were youths, they were prohibited by custom to stay for the actual internment. After the internment, Selina, James's widow, buried her husband with the help of the elders. After

57. Personal interview with Musa Chelanga, March 1989.
58. Personal interview with Musa Chelanga, March 1989.
59. Anybody who encounters a dead person is considered unclean in Marakwet. Youths and pregnant women are, therefore, kept away in case they are corrupted. If by chance a pregnant woman comes close to a corpse, she must undergo a cleaning ritual.

that, Selina and the elders returned to her home where they shared a meal. Other rituals were also observed, but the Christians did not actively participate except those belonging to the family. Selina was also a Christian, but she adhered to tradition and stayed inside her home for a whole month until the cleansing ritual was performed to set her free. During this period of seclusion, she was visited by the Christian women almost every night.[60]

Teriki Kisang (my mother) had become a Christian a few days before she died suddenly at Tot Health center. Due to the lack of transport to take the body home, she was buried near the hospital. The funeral was conducted on the day she died, and Christians from Tot area and a few from Liter and Kerio Valley secondary school where I taught attended the burial. A Christian elder from Tot offered the timber for a casket and another one volunteered to make it. By 3 o'clock in the afternoon, everything was ready for the funeral service for which I conducted. The Catholic priest Fr. Benedikt Ruegg a.k.a Kaberur was present to offer support which we appreciated. After I managed to give a brief message based on John 11:25-26, the youths were asked to leave and my father, with the help of my uncles, buried my mother according to tradition. Because he buried my mother, he was considered ritually polluted and could potentially contaminate the land on his way home. For this reason, the elders had to ritually clean him temporarily by applying sheep's oil to his feet so that he would not contaminate other people's land.[61] On the following day, our family met in our own home and observed all of the traditional ritual protocols including the killing of the ritual goat and the shaving of hair. That rite was followed by two days of rest and mourning throughout K'Marich location. Although she was not buried there, the same rules still applied in the community.

From the two cases quoted above, it is evident that whether the deceased and their family are Christian or not, traditional funerary rites are still observed with a few differences. Failure to observe the rites creates fear and uneasiness amongst the living. The major distinctions between the Christian and traditional funerals are the moral support and the hope of heaven from the Christians. Everything else is almost the same. A couple of years before Covid19 Pandemic, funerals became elaborate and

60. Personal interview with Johana Kanda, March 1989. The sheep's oil was readily available from some of the elderly women who usually carry it in their ornamental necklace "laal."

61. Personal interview with Hezekiah Kaino, April 1989. I am still left with many unanswered questions as to why we did not take her body home when she died in 1982. As I recall, my father was having a difficult time and wanted the burial done there. I was about 22 years old and in shock and unable to process what had just happened. My younger sister Nelly, who was there, was just a teenager and equally in shock. My mother died when her twin babies had turned two years old. May her memory be blessed.

expensive. Increasingly, funerals are posted on social media particularly WhatsApp. Following the announcement, an M-Pesa account is created with a designated name to receive contributions and every contributor is listed with their corresponding donation. While this has been helpful to defray hospital expenses or assist the deceased children, it has the opposite potential to cause undue social pressure on some.

God and God's Emissaries

Like many other African people, the Marakwet believe in one Supreme God who is the original source of all things. God has absolute power and authority over everything. Bolaji Idowu is correct in asserting that there is no place, age, or generation which did not, at some point in its history, receive some form of revelation.[62] The names attributed to God, as discussed in chapter 3, are indicative of the Marakwet view of God. When the missionaries came to Kapsowar and travelled throughout Marakwet, they did not bother to study the Marakwet concept of God. Instead, they presented God using their own terms and concepts. That attitude came from the general mission outlook on African cultures, considering them as heathen with no true perception of the true God—any ideas that existed were dismissed as superstitious and animistic.[63]

Unfortunately, the missionaries did not employ the Marakwet terms for God, such as *Chebeto chemataw*, *Asis*, or *Cheptalel*. Instead, they introduced a new concept to Marakwet- in the Jewish term "Jehovah." Some of the missionaries suspected the many names in Marakwet cosmology to imply polytheism or idolatry. Many African societies use diverse names for God. The names are descriptions of the same God whose self-revelation occurs to many people throughout the world. This notion is supported by Malcolm J. McVeigh, who said:

> The God of African traditional religion and Christianity is in fact the same God who revealed himself fully in Jesus Christ is none other than the one who continually made himself known to African religious experience.[64]

Many of the educated Christians have managed to reconcile the missionary notion of God and their own notion of God. However, they see the mission understanding of God to be more refined and better because it has

62. Idowu, *African Traditional Religion*, 140.
63. Idowu, *African Traditional Religion*, 142.
64. McVeigh, *God in Africa*, 81.

been committed to writing. At the same time, they understand, *Chebeto Chemataw*, or *Asis*, and Jehovah be synonymous. For those who could not read, the term "Jehovah" conveyed a different message and suggested a different deity from the Supreme Being they already knew as Iriin (the creator). Unfortunately, the missionaries did not embrace the Marakwet terms for the divine and chose instead to portray their own views. Meanwhile, Marakwet Christians internalized that tension. Paulo Kibore, a church elder at Liter, was once asked to pray at a church meeting, and in his prayer, he addressed Jehovah as a separate deity from the Marakwet Supreme Being.

> Jehovah, you are great and equal to Chebeto Chemataw, the creator. Your powers and authority are equal to those of thunder. Give us life and prosperity.[65]

In this prayer, Paulo conceptualized two deities that are in parallel terms, yet equal. Apart from such undeveloped notions, the majority of the Marakwet who became Christians accepted the Western concept of God. Although they do not use the Marakwet terms for God, the majority do not necessarily differentiate it from their own traditional notions of the Supreme Being. The human and the superhuman forces that act as intermediaries in the Marakwet cosmology, namely the sun, thunder, ancestors, witchcraft, divination, incantations, and healers are internalized by some of the Marakwet Christians because they were outrightly rejected by the missionaries as pure idolatry and function in the society is deemed as works of the devil that must be rejected and avoided by the Christians. Jesus Christ and the Bible are sufficient to reveal God. While the latter is true, the process of contextualization cannot be ignored.

As discussed in chapter 3, the Marakwet believe that God uses the superhuman powers such as the sun, thunder, oaths, and ancestors to maintain balance and justice on earth. If anybody steals another's property and denies it, the ultimate appeal is made to the Supreme Being through the administration of the oath. The outcome is, therefore, severe, unless the person repents and obtains mercy through the necessary intermediaries such as the diviners and medicine experts. The missionaries have rejected these forces and dismissed their powers as nothing more than superstitions. They taught their followers to do the same but, knowing a bit more than the missionaries, they reject them but acknowledge their potency. Most of the Christians might not be actively involved with these powers, but in times of crisis they resort to them. Other Christians recognize those powers and draw a safe

---

65. Personal interview with Samuel Chepkong'a, April 1989.

boundary as possible. The latter respond in relation to the principalities or cosmic powers that St. Paul warns the believers in Ephesians 6:12.

David Kirui, a church elder, who owns a shop at Kapsowar, had his money stolen from his home. He suspected three of his guests, but none of them would admit to the theft. The only way to resolve the matter was to administer the oath to the three men, and they agreed. After three months, the wife of one of the men had a miscarriage and her neighbors attributed this to the oath. While the woman was recovering, the clan elders appealed to the husband to repent if he were the one who had taken David's money, otherwise his wife would die. He confessed to having stolen the money and agreed to repay it. He asked for the elders who administer the oath to reverse it. The elders performed the required ritual to correct the situation. He was also penalized to pay a fine to the elders.[66] Whether the miscarriage was caused by the oath or not, the Marakwet were quite convinced that it was so. The power of the oath is not to be taken lightly. This illustrates that Christians may appeal to the traditions in times of anxiety. It may not be acceptable to the missionaries, but it continues to be practiced secretly.

The ancestors, or the living dead, were another subject of contention. The reason for this biased attitude was based on the missionaries' alternative agenda and program to promote Christianity. In the African experience, the ancestors are viewed as human beings with personal identities and not as gods to be worshipped as the missionaries contended. The words used in describing the ancestors are father, grandmother, or great-grandfather, and they are indeed viewed as persons and never as deities.[67] However, ancestors, though human, are believed to possess supernatural powers. Their key role is to hold the community together, and they are invoked when life in the community is threatened. Like other African societies, the Marakwet believe that the ancestors, if pleased, can make things well for their living families. If the ancestors are displeased, a disaster is bound to follow.[68] Whether one is converted to Christianity or not, the Marakwet consider the ancestors as a part of the community. The Christians may not openly admit this, but they consider the ancestors, especially in child naming and at funerals. The ancestors are also consulted when there is a crisis, such as illness, in the family. The ancestors are, therefore, believed to mediate for the family before God because of their position in time and space.

The mediatorial notion is widespread practice among the Marakwet, and because of this concept, they easily understand the mediatorship of

---

66. Personal interview with Joseph Kore, March 1989.
67. Sawyer, *Creative Evangelism*, 26.
68. Muzorewa, *Origins and Development*, 13.

Jesus on the Cross and formulate an African eschatology based on life beyond mere physical existence. The significance of the belief in the ancestral spirits for Christianity are that it places emphasis on the reality of the spirit world. In doing so, it provides an African eschatology based on both the present life and the hereafter.

Witchcraft is viewed negatively, not only by the missionaries but also by the Marakwet. The missionaries hold the general Western view that witchcraft is an illusion or superstition which could be eliminated through conversion to Christianity. Others thought that the practice would disappear in time due to the influence of Western education, Christianity, and technology. Surprisingly enough, this has not happened. It is rare to find a Marakwet Christian who thinks that witchcraft is an illusion, although they consider the practice and consultation of witchcraft as sinful to be avoided.

Divination belongs to the category of healers or experts with the ability to reveal the secrets of witchcraft. Through their accessibility to the spirit world, diviners are credited to know what the ancestors and divinities desire from the people and vice versa. For that reason, they are constantly consulted, especially in times of misfortunes such as illness, unusual death, or rain failure.[69]

After four years of marriage, a Christian couple from Liter still did not have a child. They became quite desperate and visited several health centers including Kapsowar mission hospital, without success. Throughout the period, their clansmen had advised that they visit Lotibar, the famous diviner at Boroko, but they refused because of their Christian faith. The church elders encouraged them to have faith in God and pray. After a long time of waiting, they finally agreed to see the diviner. The diviner they consulted promised to help them. They were taken through the divination rite. Two years later they had their first child, and many people in the community attributed this to the work of the diviner, while the Christians maintained that it was due to the prevailing prayers of the church. I couldn't find out what the couple thought.[70]

Regarding illnesses and misfortunes, the Marakwet perceive them to be caused by either supernatural or natural phenomena. On the supernatural level, the forces at play are manipulated by witchcraft or oaths. Because of this sentiment, the missionaries discouraged consultations with herbalists or traditional doctors, as well as their medicines. Christians were encouraged to use the mission hospitals and dispensaries for their ailments instead of traditional remedies. A few Christians, particularly those living close to or

---

69. Personal interview with Elijah Kilimo, January 1989.
70. Personal interview with Joseph Kibor and Maria Kobilo, May 1989.

working at the mission stations, abandoned the use of traditional medicines. One pastor vowed never to touch anything connected with traditional medicine. Another Christian elder at Kapsowar taught people that it was a sin to depend on traditional remedies.[71] However, not all Christians followed these injunctions and most of them continue to consult herbalists and other specialists. It is still widespread practice to use traditional medicines on the sick; only if this fails can they be taken to the hospital.[72]

Dr. Stanley Lindsay, who came to Kapsowar in 1953, studied the traditional medicines under a famous herbalist called Chebo Kamichan and encouraged Christians to use the herbs. However, he could not do so openly and thus challenge the prevailing negative position of AIM on the subject.[73]

Incantation, which is a form of prayer in Marakwet, is completely absent in the liturgies of the church. The missionaries did not trust anything in the Marakwet culture to be worth borrowing or adopting. However, like any prayer in a church service, the incantation is performed on any special occasion, such as a marriage ceremony, child naming, circumcision rite, or in preparation for a journey or hunting expedition. Incantations are also needed to settle disputes within a family or neighbors. It is really a form of prayer and has not been a subject of contention like other practices such as circumcision. However, it is still a suspect in some Christian quarters.

In August 1989, there was a wedding at Sambalat between a Roman Catholic catechist and his Protestant bride. After the priest had completed the church ceremony, he invited two elders to offer traditional Marakwet incantation to bless the couple and bind together not only the two individuals, but also the two families. The first elder recited the incantation and called on their clan ancestors to bless the couple with a joyful and successful marriage, with abundance of children and prosperity. The second elder, from the bride's side, also called upon the ancestors to bless the young couple but refrained from using the Marakwet term for God *(Iriin)* instead he used the Hebrew term of Jehovah.[74]

After the wedding, there was a heated debate among some of the Christians about the elders' use of the Marakwet term of *Iriin*, was syncretistic. The discussion extended to whether a Christians should adopt the traditional incantation in a church function. One of the pastors who had trained under the missionaries argued that traditional incantations were

---

71. Personal interview with Joseph Kore, February 1989.
72. Personal interview with Ezekiah Kaino, March 1989.
73. Personal interview with Dr. Stanley Lindsay, March 1992.
74. Personal interview with Joseph Cheserek, August 1989.

tainted with idolatry and therefore unacceptable in a church setting.[75] It is clear from such a discourse that the Marakwet Christians are at a crossroads. While most Marakwet Christians constantly negotiate what they need in the two contesting religious traditions, there is need for a serious discussion on contextualization or inculturation.

Inculturation/Contextualization

One of the major areas to suffer a set back with the coming of the missionaries is the cultural front which comprises everything from religion to social practices. The process of learning a culture begins at birth. Moreover, it is commonly held by all cultures that children might be born culture-less, but not without a distinctly human competence to learn a culture through the process of enculturation. This is a lifelong process of learning to adapt to a system of culture. Before we proceed, it is important to define culture. in 1871, the father of modern anthropology Edward B. Tylor defined culture as a complex whole[76] They include knowledge, belief, art, morals, law, custom, and any other abilities and habits acquired by people as members of society. Children might be born cultureless but not without a distinctly human competence to learn a culture through the process of inculturation. This is a lifelong process of learning. Louis J. Luzbetak defines culture as (1) the set of ideas a society has for coping with its physical, social, ideational environment, (2) patterns that allow for individual variations, and (3) traditions or a social heritage that constantly changes, deteriorates, develops, and adapts.[77] What unites these definitions is the fact that culture is the behavior acquired through social learning. It is composed of the set of ideas that a society has at its disposal to help its members cope with their physical, social environment and moral environment. Some patterns may be expected for all the members of a society, some only for certain groups or individuals. While culture can take hold in society, human beings are not automatons or slaves to their culture. Individuals can exercise their free will and rebel against the culture on the ground of fear, frustrations, socio-political threats, or other life threats. Some of the early Marakwet Christians found themselves in such a predicament. They did not want to abandon their culture but due to the demands placed on them, left little choice especially if they were to enter the employment of the mission. Some found a way of having one foot on the missionary Christianity and another foot in their tradition.

75. Personal interview with Joseph Cheserek, August 1989.
76. Tylor, *Primitive Cultures*, 1.
77. Luzbetak, *Church and Cultures*, 172.

Louis J. Luzbetak further underlined three levels of inculturation to which Christianity must consider. The three levels are (1) the form, (2) function, and (3) underlying psychology. Inculturation takes place only in the second and the third levels of culture. The first basic or outward level is Form which means the shape of cultural patterns that relate to the questions who, what, when where and how? The *why* is concerned with the meaning of the form which is represented in the deeper second and third levels of culture. However, all the levels are significant to inculturation or contextualization process. For example, as Luzbetak puts it, it is of little concern to God as a rule whether a particular society prefers bowing to genuflecting, standing to kneeling, wearing shoes or being barefooted with head covered to show one's reference and submission to God. At the Last Supper, it wasn't the form (washing of feet) that Jesus wanted to be perpetuated as much as the meaning of this dramatic act of service to others.[78]

The second level of culture is the Function, which answers the question why? Such a question will enable us to appreciate the meaning that is attached to a particular cultural event. For example, why do people wear clothing? The answers range from protection from weather, religious, ceremonial, professional, status, fashion etc. In preaching the gospel, we must be aware of meanings in a culture; in other words, we must be aware of the prize tags attached to cultural item, such as cultural grammar meanings and purposes and the appropriate usages.

The third level of culture is what anthropologists call underlying psychology or mentality. It deals with the linkages between the various constituents of culture. Philosophy seeks answers to such questions as who and what am I? Why am I here? It is concerned with the mentality of personality of a culture—its configuration and orientation, thought process, assumptions, underlying values, and interests. It relates to birth, parental and sibling relations, filial respect, kinship, courtship, marriage, death, and relation to the ancestors. The gospel succeeds when it has been integrated into all the above areas and the community has the capacity to express faith values meaningfully.[79]

Inculturation and contextualization are interchangeable terms whose goal is to integrate Christianity with culture. This approach deviates from the accommodation approach of the past that put emphasis on the missionary's culture and on individual converts who have decidedly rejected their culture. Accommodation respected other's culture only as containing some good elements that might serve as contact points and stepping-stones for the

---

78. Luzbetak, *Church and Cultures*, 76.
79. Luzbetak, *Church and Cultures*, 78.

gospel. Unlike accommodation or indigenization, contextualization goes much further into the very roots of culture. It views other cultures as already containing the germ of Jesus' message reminding us of the early church Fathers' *appropriation of logoi spermatikos* as the seed that was brought into existence through the mercy of the Father, planted by Christ through his death and resurrection, and watered though the refreshing rain and warm rays of the Holy spirit. Evidently, the active presence of God in the world began on the day of creation and continues to the present time. Going from this logic, the missionary does not go to introduce Jesus Christ to the world of cultures but to recognize him in non-Christian cultures. God who desires the salvation of every person is already active in the world through the Holy spirit laying down the foundation of the gospel. Those people might not have heard of Jesus, but Jesus already knows them. The seeds of the word or a ray of that truth which enlightens all are already present.

> Eventually Christ must be fully born (incarnated) into a given culture not as a Jew of two thousand years ago, or as a westerner of the twentieth century, but as someone born here and now for the first time. The Gospel is not so much transplanted as it is sown for faith to rise out the native soil. . . . Mission must make it possible for Christ to be reborn again and again in every time and place.[80]

Unlike the Western missionary who encouraged individualism, the contextual approach does not get lost in the individual at the expense of the community. African cultures focus on the community over the individual. Culture is expressed in the community. Individuals may behave actualize values that have been formulated in community and managed by the same. While the local is important, genuine contextualization never loses sight of the fact that however important the local Christian community is an integral part of the universal church which is more important than the sum of its parts.

> The ultimate purpose of inculturation is not only the benefit to be derived by the local church qua local but the enrichment of the whole body of Christ. The good of the local church is the good of the whole body of Christ, and the good of the whole body of Christ is the good of the local church.[81]

The process of appropriating the gospel in every culture has been determined in various terms such as assimilation, adaptation, indigenization,

---

80. Luzbetak, *Church and Cultures*, 74.
81. Luzbetak, *Church and Cultures*, 72.

contextualization, inculturation, and translation. All these terms are the interpretation of the New Testament term Incarnation, which was the epic event of God taking on human flesh in Jesus of Nazareth. The notion of the divine taking on a human form is indeed a mystery. In this union neither reality is destroyed or downgraded or absorbed, yet each is enriched and mysteriously transformed by the other. In other words, the mystery of incarnation is not only humans that tend towards God and become one with God (kenosis), but it is God who tends towards humanity and becomes one with us (Eph 5:32).

In the Gospel according to John Chapter 1, we read that Jesus took human flesh and adopted a human culture as a necessary concomitant of his human nature (incarnation). He was willing to accept both the minority Samaritan sub-culture and the dominant Greco-Roman culture as a process of his own inculturation. By adopting a cultural identity, Jesus accepted the ways in which that culture influenced and was influenced by other cultures. As an adult, Jesus challenged certain aspects of the culture he had inherited. He defied the legalistic Jewish traditions and challenged the regulations of the Sabbath and ritual rules that were hindering his mission of the kingdom of God. He opposed the severe punishment that was legally due to a woman found in adultery. Further, he interacted with the tax collectors and publicans. The opposition of Jesus to these aspects of Jewish religious culture earned him the hatred and hostility of the religious authorities which led to his death.

The central hermeneutical concern for the early church was whether Jesus of Nazareth, the Messiah promised by God in the Old Testament, extended beyond Israel, the covenant people of God, to the gentiles. As the chosen people, the Jews had been brought up to regard themselves as God's unique and holy people set apart from the gentiles, who were altogether regarded as sinners. Salvation was dependent upon the observance of the law, and gentiles were expected to go to Jerusalem and be taught the law. In addition, the Jews had been taught to observe strict ritual cleanliness which included disassociation with those deemed to be polluted by sin. With the coming of Jesus, a new era had dawned, and such attitudes had to change. That did not mean that their Jewish identity was lost, but it meant that the Jewish Christians had to change from their Jewish religious fundamentalism and embrace Jesus' teaching of love and compassion. That involved welcoming those who respond to the gospel, including gentiles, into their fellowship as a response to the *Good News*.

The church believes that after the resurrection, Christ transcended the physical limitations of an earthly life bound by time, space, and culture. Therefore, he identifies with every culture, everywhere. The resurrection and the coming of the Holy Spirit were symbolized at Pentecost when people of diverse languages heard and understood the gospel in their own tongues. This is viewed as an ideal act of inculturation. Following the ideals of Jesus, Paul extended his mission beyond the Hellenized Jews. He reached out to the gentiles in their own world; where he travelled both geographically and culturally as he encountered non-Jewish ideas and world views. Instead of pushing his own Jewish culture along with the gospel, he was committed to Christ who, to him, transcended the cultural categories and expectations of both Jews and gentiles. He rejected the Judeo-Christian form of the gospel imposed on the gentiles and opposed the imposition of circumcision and other rules from the Mosaic law upon his gentile converts. The controversy on this matter came to a head at the Council of Jerusalem when the church leaders decided to accept the gentile Christians without forcing Jewish ideals onto them (Acts 15:4–35).

The radical change did not come easily to the Jews. Sometimes, it took painful experiences in the battle ground of ideas to understand the meaning of the incarnation. It meant that Jewish Christians had to reject their inherited prejudices and their exclusionary or separatist theology. Peter was instructed through a vision to accept invitation of a God-fearing Cornelius, a gentile who was a high-ranking Roman official (Acts 10). This was revisited later in the surprise of the Jerusalem Council when Peter was found eating with the gentiles in Acts 11:1–3. The debate came to its climax in Jerusalem when the early followers of Jesus blocked the entry of the uncircumcised gentiles into the fellowship. Eventually, the messianic question in relation to the gentiles was resolved by the same Council (Acts 15). It is, therefore, in their struggle to answer this question that we understand the full extent of incarnation as an agent of salvation for all humanity and other forms of creation. The breakthrough lay in the official acceptance and declaration that circumcision and the observance of the law were not necessary for salvation, that both Jews and gentiles are equal before God, and that both could receive salvation only by the grace of God through faith in Jesus Christ. The emphasis is the utter absolute gratuitousness of God's gift of salvation in Christ for all. Acts 15 is regarded as the Magna Carta of freedom given to the gentiles to live their Christian faith according to their own cultures.[82]

Saint Paul stands out on the gentile question due to his missionary work to the gentiles. He was positioned to fight it out pastorally and theologically in his letters to the Galatians and Romans. This struggle led to the recognition that since salvation lay solely on the incarnation of Jesus Christ, the gentiles were to be accepted by God on equal terms without keeping

---

82. Okure et al., *Inculturation of Christianity*, 67.

the Jewish law (Rom 3:21–31). Moreover, Paul freely regarded his previous Jewish heritage as nothing compared to the surpassing worth of knowing Christ and the righteousness, based on faith (Phil 3:7–11).

As he stated in one of his Epistles, Paul identified with any culture or social category in order to preach the gospel:

> To the Jews I became as a Jew, in order to gain Jews. To those under the law I became as one under the law (though I myself am not under the law) so that I might gain those under the law. To those outside the law I became as one outside the law (though I am not outside God's law but am within Christ's law) so that I might gain those outside the law. To the weak I became weak, so that I might gain the weak. I have become all things to all people, that I might by all means save some. (1 Cor 9:20–22)

He took other people's views seriously and attempted to initiate a dialogue between them. In his approach he used the terms and the vocabulary of popular Hellenistic philosophy. When he was in the Greek world, he employed the Greek language and wisdom. In his speech before the council of the Areopagus, Paul used secular wisdom to challenge idolatry. He referred to the practice of dedicating altars to unknown gods and used the occasion to call the people to faith in Christ (Acts 17:15–34). This was an attempt on Paul's part to acknowledge other people's views though he might not necessarily have approved of them.

The same was true of the post-apostolic church. The gospel was inculturated through translations of the faith into varieties of liturgies, such as Syriac, Greek, Roman, Coptic, Armenian, Maronite, and Ethiopian. Prof. Lamin Sanneh is, therefore, correct in asserting that the church was born in a cross-cultural milieu with translation as its birthmark.[83] When Christianity came under the political influence of Constantine, the church assumed that its theology was universally valid and had to be exported together with its culture to the rest of the world. It saw itself as a body from the civilized and superior culture versus the inferior culture of the savages—a process in which the latter had to be conquered and subdued. Despite this, a small element of religious groups within the church continued to respect other people's cultures. Some of the founders of such groups, such as the Jesuits and White Fathers, impressed upon their missionaries to defer to the cultures of the people they would encounter. In their Policy of 1659, the Jesuits, for example, advised their missionaries not to force people to change their customs if these were not opposed to the faith. They were to present the faith and forget their European culture and become Asians to the Asians

---

83. Stackhouse, *Apologia*, 58.

and Africans to the Africans. Charles Lavigerie, the founder of the White Fathers, instructed his group of Missionaries to East Africa to assimilate into societies they were to evangelize and adopt local manners and be sympathetic to such customs as polygamy.

Two other examples of inculturation from the sixteenth century were Matteo Ricci and Roberto de Nobili. These two Jesuits went to Asia as missionaries and integrated well with the local people. Matteo Ricci was an Italian Jesuit priest born in 1552. He was sent to China as a missionary in 1578 and his first attempt at inculturation was to adopt the dress and lifestyle of a Buddhist monk. When he discovered that Confucianism was the dominant religion, he took on the identity of a Confucian scholar to win over the intellectual experts in a society controlled by Confucian ideas. By 1595, Ricci, who had changed his name Matteo to the Chinese "Ma Dou," had succeeded in penetrating the higher ranks of diplomats and bureaucrats through his contribution to Chinese scholarship. His proficiency in astronomy, mathematics and the physical sciences was greatly appreciated by the Chinese. He was the author of more than twenty works in Chinese, including books on social and religious life. Ricci and his fellow Jesuits aimed to achieve the presentation and interpretation of Christianity in a manner comfortable to the Chinese. By the time of Ricci's death in 1610 about three thousand people had been baptized.[84]

Roberto de Nobili, another Jesuit missionary, went to India in 1604. Like Matteo Ricci in China, he intended to convert the elite of India. He penetrated the world of scholarship and learning after he adopted the costume and lifestyle of a Hindu holy man. His aim was to enter into the highest caste of the Brahmins. The success of his mission was realized when an eminent Brahmin scholar was converted to Christianity and kept his former lifestyle. When de Nobili left India, there were more than a thousand converts. His approach and efforts were, however, challenged by the Catholic Church authorities and finally censured in 1623.

At the beginning of the eighteenth century, the Inquisition and those who advocated a narrow view of the church objected to the inculturation methods of Ricci in China and de Nobili in India. The controversy that arose concerned the Chinese and Indian rites which were accepted by the two missionaries as compatible with the Christian faith. The church condemned these rites as superstitious and recalled the two missionaries, In fact, all the Jesuit missionaries were accused for their openness to non-Western cultures and were similarly recalled from their mission assignments. Two hundred years later, in the Vatican II Council, these adverse decisions were rescinded,

---

84. Dunne, *Generations of Giants*, 23–50.

and the wisdom of Matteo Ricci and Roberto de Nobili was recognized.[85] Following this, Christian ashrams began to emerge all over India.

The main purpose of the Vatican II Council, which convened in Rome in 1962–65, was to make Christ's message relevant to modern times. It was to open a window of fresh air into the church. The Council affirmed, among other things, that Christianity was for every age and culture and, as such, it cannot be monopolized by Western culture.

> Whatever good is in the minds and hearts of men, whatever good lies latent in the religious practices and cultures of diverse peoples is not saved from destruction but is also healed, and perfected into the Colony of God, the confusion of the devil, and the happiness of man.[86]

In these and other similar affirmations, the Council was recognizing the positive aspects that existed in other cultures. The new approach was to promote the endeavours that consider the cultural aspirations of every people and use whatever is good in them in the presentation of the Christian faith.

> Thus, in imitation of the plan of the incarnation, the young churches rooted in Christ and built up on the foundation of the apostles, take to themselves in a wonderful exchange all the riches of the nations which were given to Christ as an inheritance. From the customs and traditions of the people, from their wisdom and their learning, from their arts and sciences, these churches borrow all those things which can contribute to the glory of their creator, the revelation of the Saviour's Grace. . . . Finally, the individual young churches adorned with their own traditions, will have their own place in the ecclesiastical communion.[87]

In July 1969, Pope Paul VI, in his efforts to promote inculturation, addressed African Bishops in Kampala and challenged them to promote an African Christianity:

> From this point of view, a certain pluralism is not only legitimate but desirable. An adaptation of the Christian life in the field of pastoral, ritual, didactic and spiritual activities is not only possible, it is even favoured by the church. The liturgical

---

85. Rajamanickam, *First Oriental Scholar*.
86. Waliggo, *Inculturation*, 25.
87. Waliggo, *Inculturation*, 23–24.

renewal is a living example of this. And in this sense, you may, and you must have an African Christianity.[88]

Pope John II followed faithfully in his predecessor's footsteps. In his speech to the African Bishops in Nairobi in 1981, he reiterated that Christianity was not only relevant in Africa, but Christ was himself an African. A move in this direction would lead to Christianity as a way of life and not a bookish Christianity.[89]

The Pontiff made these remarks as a response to Vatican 2, otherwise the history of Catholic church in African, Asia, and Latin America is closely linked to the European colonialism that was pioneered by the Catholic nations of Portugal and Spain. In Africa, it began with the enslavement and the exploitation of millions of Africans. In the nineteenth century the renewed exploitation began when other European nations met in Berlin in 1884/5 to divide Africa among themselves as if it were a cake. That event led to the rise of modern missionaries who followed the footsteps of their own nations into the colonized spaces of Africa. Both Protestants were fully engaged in it. Vatican 2 might have been a realization of that error though it was not explicitly acknowledged as such. They should have but such an expectation is remote given the participants at the conference. I wonder how many African bishops were in attendance.

The Protestant involvement in inculturation was very slow. Although they were the pioneers of the nineteenth century missionary expansion. Their approach was influenced by Puritan spirituality and colonial imperialism, as well as general European cultural arrogance. Instead of taking Jesus and St. Paul's mission approach, modern Western missionaries framed and transmitted the Christian message in European cultural forms, where Jesus and God looked European. At one point, it was impossible for an African to think of Christianity as separate from the Western cultural forms which had culturally conditioned and shaped it to reflect their culture while suppressing African cultures. The overarching aim for Western missionaries, whether be Protestant or the Roman Catholics, was to create ecclesiastical institutions like those in Europe and North America. In the 1960s, when most African nations were gaining political independence, many African Christians also demanded a change of leadership in their churches. Unfortunately, they were met with a strong resistance that resulted in the rise of the independent churches. The Western-linked churches lost many of their members to the new spiritual movement.

---

88. Paul VI, "Homily."
89. Waliggo, *Inculturation*, 76.

Occasionally Western missionaries would unintentionally advance African culture. An example were the Protestant missionaries who pioneered in the translation of the Bible into vernacular. Providentially, they laid the groundwork by establishing alphabets and developing literacy. In 1974, the Protestant missions at the Lausanne Congress on World Evangelization invited African participants and as a result reviewed some of its mission strategies. They commissioned a consultation team to study, among other things, the interrelation of the gospel and culture. The team affirmed that:

> No Christian witness can hope to communicate the Gospel if he or she ignores the cultural factor. . . . Sometimes people resist the Gospel not because they think it false but because they perceive it as a threat to their culture. There are features of every culture which are not incompatible with the Lordship of Christ, and which therefore need not be threatened or discarded, but rather preserved and transformed. Messengers of the Gospel need to develop deep understanding of the local culture and a genuine appreciation of it. . . . The missionaries are resented, and their message rejected because their work is seen not as an attempt to evangelize but as an attempt to impose their own customs and way of life.[90]

Although some attempts have been made in cross-cultural missions, most of the evangelical churches in the West are still rigid and continue to exercise exclusive guardianship over the shape of the theology and material resources in Africa. The Africa Inland Church finds itself in this position.[91] Its relationship with its parent mission, the Africa Inland Mission, is not that of partnership. The Africa Inland Mission continued to function as a separate body despite several attempts to make it one with the national church.

The Africa Inland Church has not suggested the idea of moratorium (though that might be sometimes necessary), but what is needed is a balanced theology free from theological imperialism. Such a theology can be developed through the integration of faith and culture. It is through such honest attempts with the guiding insights of the Holy Spirit and the Scriptures that the church will make itself at home in Marakwet as well as in every society.

The African church should strive for ecclesiastical existence in which it ceases to be an extension of the Western churches and take full account

---

90. Stott and Coote, "Willow Bank Report," 441.

91. The AIC Theological Institutions, which are eight in number, continue to teach Western conservative theologies in its curriculum using mostly Western literature.

of its existence in the African soil. It must break free of all the foreign appendages that have alienated it from the needs of the people. In addition, the church must address its worshippers in their respective socio-economic and political situation. The Willow Bank Report supports these objectives in its statement:

> (The church) must challenge what is evil and affirm what is good to welcome and seek to promote all that is wholesome and enriching in art, science, technology, agriculture, industry, education, community development . . . to denounce injustice and support the powerless and the oppressed; to spread the good news of Jesus Christ which is the most liberating and humanizing force in the world, and actively engage in good works of love.[92]

One of the essential methods for inculturation especially in relation to world religions is engagement through dialogue. The term comes from the Greek *dia-logos*, which means mutual communication. The purpose of the communication is to acknowledge the diversity and universality of each culture. No dialogue is possible unless two concerned groups are ready to engage in it. It can be impeded if one side sees the other as a threat; in other words, if any group or party comes with "a priori" assumption that its story is the only true story, the dialogue is doomed before it begins. To maintain the flow of a dialogue, barriers of prejudice and defensiveness must be overcome. True dialogue, therefore, requires courage to take risks and humility to accept the possibility of change. These ingredients are only gained if there is love and trust. Failure to do so would make room for hypocrisy and nothing lasting can be built on such a false foundation.[93] African traditional religion does not have written dogma; therefore, dialogue is both verbal and non-verbal. The latter can be reached through active observation and experience. It is also important to observe and listen to an African traditionalist's reaction to Christian beliefs.

Aylward Shorter's proposes that the ideal people to conduct a meaningful dialogue between Christianity and African culture are the African Christians. At conversion, the African Christians repudiate very little of their African ways. They may be obliged to turn their backs on certain traditional practices which the church has condemned. Consequently, they easily return to the forbidden practices as occasion arises. Most African Christians operate between these two thought-systems which are, after all, close to each other. It is here, in the consciousness of the Christian, that the dialogue can take place. African scholars, like J. S. Mbiti, Bolaji Idowu, H. Sawyer, Lamin

---

92. Stott and Coote, "Willow Bank Report," 457.
93. Shorter, *African Christian Theology*, 7.

Sanneh, Gwynyai Muzorewa, Mercy Oduyoye, Musa Dube have had such experiences, and their dialogues are verbally explicit.[94]

The method of inculturation is illustrated in Vincent J. Donovan's book *Christianity rediscovered* based on his missionary work among the Masai which like the Marakwet are members of the Nilo-Hamitic family. Donovan's book has been widely read and embraced by missiologists who claim to have been challenged and transformed by it. There is no question that the book has broad, missiological and theological breadth which obviously reflects the depth and breadth of Donovan's reflections based on his years of missionary work among the Masai in Tanzania. Donovan critiques missionary strategies as imperialistic and out of step with the gospel principles of St. Paul. His approach through the process of inculturation takes seriously the gospel and cultures. Donovan was convinced that missionary work is better undertaken by a gospel-oriented community with a vision to carry the gospel to the nations of the world. That discovery began with the critical evaluation of the previous mission work that stretched one hundred years back during the era of colonial rule in Africa. There is consensus among historians that the missionaries operated in tandem with the colonial agenda of their respective countries. Overall, the colonial agenda was brutal, exploitative, and oppressive. While most missionaries did not operate in that fashion, they were gradually complicit.

Part of the book critiques the prevailing missionary methods of the Western church that proposes to transport the Western church to the rest of the world with minor changes simply because the West could not imagine a church different in form from their own. The missionaries were sent out to perpetuate it indefinitely. From their mission station, the missionaries evangelize the natives, build churches that look like Western churches, write the catechism, set up dioceses, establish seminaries, and ensure their finances. In his case, Donovan observed the prevailing strategies of the mission station of Liliondo, with its four successful schools, a hospital, and a small chapel. He noted that there was little to show in the way of conversions of the Masai. At this point, he asked for permission to break away and to go directly to the Masai in their villages to talk to them about God and the Christian message.[95]

He knew that his novel approach was a radical departure from the traditional Catholic procedure and beliefs that it is impossible to preach the gospel directly to the Masai. He chose to take that risk with no theory,

---

94. Shorter, *African Christian Theology*, 7, 10; see also Schreiter, *Constructing Local Theologies*, 40.

95. Donovan, *Christianity Rediscovered*, 15.

nor strategy, but confidence in God and his own instincts. He was introduced to the classic writings of Roland Allen, a fellow missionary who had worked in China. In his book *Missionary Methods: St. Paul's or Ours?*, Allen had become convinced that modern missionary methods had strayed far from the methods of the early church. Echoing Allen, Donovan insisted that any action taken in mission should be measured by the Bible—whether it is biblical or evangelical.[96] On that basis, the task of evangelization or the missionary's sole work is a temporary work in any given place, for once a Christian community is established, the missionary moves on, as per the example of Apostle Paul.

Donovan commenced his new mission strategy of direct evangelization in the village of Chief Ndangoya—one of twenty-six villages of the district of Loliondo. He had given himself a five-year target to evangelize the entire area and move on. The process was simple. He would introduce a religious theme or topic and ask to hear their opinion on it and then he would tell them what he believed or thought on the same subject. In the first week of instructions, he asked the Masai to tell him what they thought about God. For the Masai, there is only one God, Engai, who goes by many names. Unlike the West's obsession with the masculine God, the Masai use diverse names. When God is kind and propitious, they call him the Black God, and the Red God when angry. Sometimes they call him rain or the God of the Blue Stomach. Regardless of the descriptive colorful names, God is always the one God, the Creator. Donovan was to discover that the Masai understanding of God is quite similar to God's many names in the bible—fire, breeze, rock. God is neither male nor female but certainly embodies the qualities which exist in both.

Donovan took the next step to introduce them to another tribe in the bible—the Hebrew tribe or the Israelites and their knowledge of the One True God. At the same time, he introduced Abraham and his relationship with God, in doing so he was careful not to limit God to one tribe.

> Perhaps the story of Abraham speaks also to you. Perhaps you Masai also must leave your nation and your tribe and your land, at least in your thoughts, and go in search of the high God, the God of all tribes, the God of the World.[97]

Finally, someone asked Donovan: if he or his tribe has found the high God. Donovan admits having been startled by the question but after a moment of reflection, he responded with humility:

---

96. Cited in Donovan, *Christianity Rediscovered*, 33.
97. Donovan, *Christianity Rediscovered*, 45.

No, we have not found the high God. My tribe has not known him. I have come a long distance to invite you to search for him with us. Let us search for him together. Maybe, together we will find him.[98]

Donovan seems to show his vulnerability and humility as a fellow traveler searching for the divine.

It seems clear that Donovan had come to believe that the gospel claims have been compromised by the errors of exporting Western cultural baggage with the gospel. This understanding has been advanced by those scholars who propose an alternate approach through dialogue and recognition that:

> Goodness and holiness are the beginning of salvation and they do not reside exclusively in Europe and America. I have seen too many good and holy Pagans in Africa to believe that.[99]

The next main theme he tackles were sin and salvation. First, he had no difficulty explaining salvation to be the result of God's love. However, his next attempt to explain sin from the bible flopped miserably. He had misgivings on the Christian assumption to convince the world of sin or the world would never feel the need for redemption and the redeemer. With no other tradition to rely on, he did just that with the Masai—the story of Adam and Eve, the garden and the fruit tree and the serpent and finally, the fall.[100]

The Masai complained that the story sounded agriculturally biased with the garden and the command to till the soil. For them, tilling the soil is repugnant. Only a farmer—a barbarian (*olmeg*) would cut open the thin layer of topsoil of the Masai slopes exposing it to the equatorial sun and turning it into desert within a short time. The Masai had their own stories about their origins and their cattle, but no part of that story is about a consciousness of guilt or a need for personal redemption.

Donovan followed the story of the garden with a worse one, the story of Cain, the first farmer, murdering Abel, the first cattle herder. With some justification, they began to wonder if the bible that I held with great reverence was not some kind of an agricultural or government plot against them. He never told the story again. After such difficulties of relating biblical notions of sin and salvation, he was not sure how to explain forgiveness.[101]

---

98. Donovan, *Christianity Rediscovered*, 46.

99. Donovan, *Christianity Rediscovered*, 54. Other noted proponents of this view include Paul Knitter, Jacques Dupuis, Mark Heim, Leslie Newbigin, Marjorie Suchoki, and Clark Pinnock.

100. Donovan, *Christianity Rediscovered*, 56.

101. Donovan, *Christianity Rediscovered*, 58.

While evangelizing the first villages, Donovan noticed a man on the outskirts who belonged to another Masai village. He seemed poorer than the average Masai. Apparently, he had committed a great sin and broke the taboos of the Masai tribe. The man had broken a cultural norm or a taboo which is close to the biblical view of sin. It was considered sin for a son to offend his father for the act brings disruption in the relationship. In extreme cases, the son is banished from the community and shunned by his age-mates. It was believed that a curse or misfortune followed a sinful person. The recourse or remedy would be to ask the father or his "spittle of forgiveness" so that he could forgive his son and restore the broken relationship.

> Spittle, is a very sacred element of a living, breathing human, was considered the sign of forgiveness.[102]

Sometimes, sin occurs between groups within the same community or between two communities. In such cases, reconciliation is attained when the two parties share the holy food (*endaa sinyati*). The transition from sin and reconciliation to Jesus was easily understood.

Donovan found it exciting, challenging, and rewarding to read discussions of Jesus with the Masai. Jesus' connections to his clan of Judah in the tribe of Israel resonated well with the Masai who valued clan and tribal relations. Similarly, the stories of Kings were told to explain the mission of Jesus using Maasai cultural framework. Other stories of David as a warrior and a brave man, battling lions, resonated well with the Maasai.

> David was the greatest *Legwanian* the Jewish tribe ever had. They called him the lion of the clan of Judah.[103]

Donovan tried to build an historical portrait of Jesus by appropriating the Masai age-set system and steered away from Euro-American cultural misappropriations. To explain the gospel, Donovan drew on Jesus' parables. For the illiterate Masai, no other method could better serve the purpose. He would convey the stories and ask them to recount afterwards what they remembered of them.[104]

For some reasons, Donovan focused on the adult stories of Jesus. He told them that from the first day he became an elder, Jesus spoke about the land of green pastures that God is preparing for God's people of the earth—a land and a state of peace. God is the shepherd of that land, and it is for those God loves with a special love—the poor, the meek, the humble, the little

---

102. Donovan, *Christianity Rediscovered*, 59.
103. Donovan, *Christianity Rediscovered*, 69.
104. Donovan, *Christianity Rediscovered*, 76.

ones—for those who mourn and those who are crying. God will dry their eyes. God loves those who hunger and thirst after justice and those who suffer unjustly. God will satisfy them. God loves the merciful who do not seek revenge. God will be merciful to them, and they will be blessed. To bring it home, Donovan contextualized that the pastures of God are like a wedding feast or a circumcision feast where there will be dancing and singing and sugarcane for the children and beads for the women and tobacco for the elders to chew on and milk and meat and honey beer. Many will come from as far as the mountain of Kilimanjaro to Serengeti Plains.[105]

Some of the Bible stories captured the Masai imagination like no other. One was the story of Isaac and Ishmael as a story of an old man with two sons and one a good brave warrior and the other a lazy herder who ran away in disgrace. It is the story of the father going up on the hill each night to ask for the spittle of forgiveness for his wayward son and of the son finally returning to the village and the father returning to meet him. The most favorite and most popular story of all is the story of the good Olmeg (barbarian) whom Jesus identified as the neighbor we must love. After he explained the story as best as he could, Donovan was convinced that his job had been accomplished and what was left now was for the Masai to respond by either accepting or rejecting the gospel.

> First, they must believe in all that God had done, and in Christ, then they must be sorry . . . be forgiven . . . and begin again. They must not keep all this to themselves, they must go forth in the Spirit and witness to the good news . . . letting others see the meaning of it all, by their words and by their lives until the time that Jesus comes again.[106]

From his initial contacts with this Masai group, and their Chief Legwanan, Donovan had discovered that they operated as a community and therefore, he expected them to respond to the gospel as a community. He gave them time to think and discuss things among themselves. Donovan's method deviated from the traditional method geared to individual conversions. The mission and catechetical practice are based on that premise. After a week, they responded affirmatively "We believe." Donavon had never heard of such a response, but he was thrilled. The baptisms in the six communities were devoid of many symbols except live-giving water which was sacred to them long before missionaries got there. The Masai usually change their names at any important life-changing event; therefore, they were prepared to do so like the Old Testament people—Abram to Abraham, Jacob to Israel.

105. Donovan, *Christianity Rediscovered*, 79.
106. Donovan, *Christianity Rediscovered*, 82.

However, there was no harm if they wanted to keep their old beloved names. The church needs some saints with names like Ole Timbau, Ole Kiyiapi, or Kurmanjo in the litany of Saints. The next step was to find the name of the community of believers like an initiation age-set. After considering several names, they settled on Orpororo L'Engai which means brotherhood of God: the age group of the last age, the final age of the world reaching to the Kingdom. As the people of Ndangoya Community gathered on the banks of the stream for baptism, Donovan spoke to them thus:

> I have finished my last instruction in your village. I will never come back to teach anyone else here. From this day on, it is you people who must teach the Word of Christianity. You must anoint the people with sheep fat. You must baptize them. The brotherhood is yours . . . guard this, Gospel. Do not change it for anyone. . . . I will return to you another time to break bread together as Jesus told us to do.[107]

All the men and women of Ndangoya's community chose new Masai names except *Ndangoya* who took the name of Abraham because Abraham had left everything and led his people from the worship of a tribal god in search of the Unknown High God. Now, with the whole neighborhood and visitors watching, Donovan poured water from the stream over his head. Donovan baptized Ndangoya, son of Parmwat, with his new name, Abraham.

After such a success in Ndangoya's community, Donovan felt confident to move to the next community and repeat the same formula with a gained experience. After a year, he had completed the instructions in that community after which he left them for a week to decide. When he returned, he found them waiting in the place where they had met every week. He asked for their decision on the gospel. The Chief spoke for his people:

> We have heard what you mean by the Christian message. For a year we have talked about it. . . . We thank you for coming to us. We think we understand what you have said about Jesus Christ. But we cannot accept it. . . . We do not want baptism. Forgive us—our answer is no![108]

Donovan was devastated by the rejection. He wondered how they could follow instructions for a whole year and then reject it. He saw himself as a total failure. He composed himself and tried to make them feel guilty but that didn't work. Donovan was able to learn the most important

---

107. Donovan, *Christianity Rediscovered*, 96.
108. Donovan, *Christianity Rediscovered* 107.

lesson that day that Christianity by its very essence is a message that can be accepted or rejected.

> No Christianity has any meaning or value if there is not freedom to accept it or reject it. It must be presented in such a way that rejection of it remains a distinct possibility.[109]

In his next evangelization, Donovan developed a completely different approach. He would work with someone in a given community—someone who seemed to understand the message better than the others. That person would summarize the previous lesson before Donovan starts a new instruction. That strategy seemed to work well until he met a brave Masai—Ole Sikii, to whom he had been introduced as a religious man in the Masai sense of the word. Donovan instructed Ole Sikii and baptized only him and in turn, Ole Sikii instructed and baptized his own people. The celebration of the Eucharist in Ole Sikii's community signified a major step in Donovan's inculturation efforts.

Donovan was cautious in passing on to the people the liturgy of the Eucharist in fear of cultural infringement, but he realized that ritual is part of the culture. Besides, the Eucharist is a response to the good news they had heard, a celebration of the belief in the good news. So, the first Masses in the Masai communities were quite simple. Donovan would take the bread saying.

> This is the way it was passed on to me, and I pass it on to you that on the night before he died, Jesus took bread and wine . . . [and] blessed them.[110]

It is considered a taboo for Masai men to eat in the presence of women. But here in the Eucharist, they were accepting the gospel that in Christ there is neither slave nor free, Jew nor Greek, male nor female.

> The first time when I blessed the . . . gourd . . . and passed it on to the woman sitting closest to me and told her to drink from it and then pass it on to the man sitting next to her. I don't remember any other pastoral experience in which the sign of Unity was so real.[111]

Donovan attempted to teach the Masai that the Eucharist was not an act of magic accomplished with the saying of a few words in the right order—but that the Eucharist is their whole life—the raising of family, herding, milking,

109. Donovan, *Christianity Rediscovered*, 108.
110. Donovan, *Christianity Rediscovered*, 120.
111. Donovan, *Christianity Rediscovered*, 121.

and working. If the life in the village had been less than human, then there would be no Mass. Similarly, if there had been selfishness and hatefulness and lack of forgiveness, then the body of Christ had not been achieved or if someone, or some group, in the village had refused to accept the grass as the sign of the peace of Christ, there would be no Eucharist.[112]

In summary, the most compelling aspect of Donovan's book is its noble attempt to present the bare gospel unencumbered by Western culture that he calls "the mission station captivity." Donovan understands the missionary as one called to divest himself of his culture so that he/she can be a naked instrument of the gospel to the culture for which he/she is called. He highlights apostle Paul's example to be "all things to all people" (1 Cor 4:19–23). He was unimpressed by the Western imperialistic development agenda of the twentieth century that was promoted by both government agents and missionaries. The same agenda masqueraded as nation building by the newer national governments. Donovan is not against all development. His primary concern is when development consumes much of the missionary's time, leaving the work of evangelization undone. What he calls for, is a fresh assessment of the church's mission to bear fruit in a joyful sharing of the gospel. When that is done, the people will respond to the gospel on their own terms and produce their own theology and social action that is authentically theirs.

As he prepared to leave Africa, Donovan wrote: "it is missionary evening in Africa."[113] This is interpreted to signal that missionaries are no longer needed in Africa. This idea is not new. In fact, other African Christian leaders had proposed the same idea at the time of national independence. The noted proponent was John Gatu who called for Moratorium of missions at an ecumenical conference at Lusaka, Zambia. The moratorium call was meant for the child to cut the dependency from the mother church so the child can grow and be independent. It is possible that Donovan might have been aware of those discussions. Moratorium is good for some time. However, due to the universal nature of the church, the best option is partnership on equal terms.

From Donovan's example, inculturation or contextualization does not change the essence of the message of the gospel but rather it makes it culturally relevant. For example, baptism is always the same in Christian traditions everywhere. Similarly, the Holy Communion remains the ritual meal for Christians across the ages. However, what is contextualized are the containers or vessels and the officiants. Some traditions permit women to officiate

---

112. Donovan, *Christianity Rediscovered*, 127.
113. Donovan, *Christianity Rediscovered*, 161.

while other traditions unfortunately do not. What is important is for Jesus Christ to be born in every culture. That means Christ and his gospel must become the very heart and soul of the way of life or the very *raison d'etre* of human existence. Listening to the local Christian communities is paramount, for they surely know where it itches. The African people have often criticized foreign missionaries for scratching where it didn't itch.

Conclusion

THIS BOOK ATTEMPTS TO provide the ethnography of the Marakwet as well as its encounter with foreigners who came as colonizers and missionaries. The broad objective is to understand how the missionaries and the gospel they preached interacted with the Marakwet culture. This helps us understand the extent to which the Marakwet world has been influenced by Christianity and little on the reverse. It is not my aim to question the missionaries' commitment but rather their overall view of Marakwet culture. Also, I am not trying to retrieve what has been lost in the passage of time as far as the culture is concerned. This is not the place to satisfy our nostalgia. Neither do I advocate for a wholesale acceptance of tradition without critique. Some aspects of it need to be examined carefully, not by an outsider but by the Marakwet. However, I call attention to what has been preserved and passed on to us. Obviously, the Marakwet culture like many African cultures have undergone an evolution in the last century some of which have been detrimental while others are good. It is no wonder that the elders complain that the European educational model has had positive and negative impacts on society. The negative impact is evident in the moral latitude among the youth, which include delinquency, moral lapse, and the deterioration of values especially the institution of marriage. On the other hand, traditional education is disappearing fast because the children are no longer instructed by the extended family. Secondly, the circumcision rite no longer follows the communal calendar where all the youth go through the ritual as a group to maintain group solidarity. Similarly, the girl's circumcision rite has faced attacks due to health hazards. However, there is no reason for the community not to reform the rite and embrace all the formative lessons without the cut. For that to happen, the church must dialogue honestly with the tradition.

While acknowledging the impact that Christianity has made in Marakwet, I have presented several cases to indicate that however well-educated or Christianized the Marakwet have become, the majority still find it difficult to bid farewell to their tradition. There are exceptions especially in those who have moved away into mission stations or cities and raise their children outside. My argument pertains to the majority of the Marakwet people. In saying this I am not advocating for any negative practices in society but rather life affirming practices that do not contradict God's word. On the opposite are death dealing practices that are anti God. Many of those who embraced Christianity are faithful church attendees, but at a time of crisis, some of them revert to the traditional beliefs and practices. Does this indicate that Christianity cannot supersede traditional beliefs? The Marakwet's beliefs and traditions are deeply rooted in their lives and cannot easily be extirpated. It is difficult, if not impossible, for Marakwet converts to disassociate themselves from the traditional practices in the way the missionary Christianity expects. Therefore, they maintain divided loyalties to both traditional practices and Christianity. It is common to find a Christian with one foot in the church and the other in the rituals. The dichotomy comes because of Western imposed dualism. It is about time for Marakwet Christians to interrogate this kind of dichotomy and hopefully find a way to harmonize life. Isn't it possible to move from the choice of either/or and entertain the possibility of both/and? Can't one be a total Marakwet and a total Christian? In other words, can't one be unapologetically Marakwet and Christian? When life is threatened, a Marakwet attempts to act in a practical manner. A Christian woman for example goes to the hospital for the birth of her child, to the traditional elder for the naming ceremony and to church to dedicate the baby to God. She will have her baby vaccinated in the mission dispensary and go to their herbalist or a diviner when the child is sick, and she may not see any contradiction whatsoever. Her basic concern is the preservation of life, which is the general aim of all humans. The Marakwet concept of sin as *ng'oki* does not negate the biblical view. In fact, the Marakwet has no problem with the Bible but unsure of some of the interpretations rendered by the missionaries. For example, the missionaries never raised a finger to condemn the colonial mistreatment of African people, but they were quick in condemning as sin key of Marakwet tradition. The missionary warned the Christians against such a practice calling it syncretism instead of contextualizing. It was for that reason that some Marakwet Protestant Christian who sought help from the traditional healer does so in secret lest he loses his standing in the church. In the eyes of the church, such an act is considered syncretistic, or a lack of faith. For the desperate Marakwet Christian such an act is an attempt to reconcile both his culture and Christianity.

It is due to these factors of cultural alienation from the church that the majority of adult Marakwet men and women have not accepted Christianity in large numbers. This book has shown that the few adults who have embraced Christianity benefited first from the missions materially, mainly through employment. For the majority in the older generation, to accept Christianity would be to lose their heritage, therefore there is a degree of hesitancy. Although most of my arguments in this study show how missionaries rejected most of Marakwet beliefs and culture, it must also be pointed out that not all the Marakwet culture was rejected. Some have therefore been integrated to the Marakwet Christianity. For example, the concepts of sin and sacrifices as well as the belief of life after death or immortality of the soul are commonly held. Also, the use of traditional musical tunes has been adopted in the church. A case in point is the Endo Choir of AIC Cherutich under the leadership of Laban Cheserek and Martha Kilimo. In this synthesis, authentic elements of both Marakwet culture and Christianity have established a meaningful dialogue however minimal. It awaits more theological reflection and engagement towards contextualization.

However, today, African Christians face the challenge of how to take charge of their own house as far as the Christian faith and theology is concerned. For Africans, incarnation has to do with bringing the gospel into the heart of African life and recognizing the African culture as the fertile soil in which the gospel is planted, fertilized, and watered. Without that happening, Jesus Christ remains a foreigner. Incarnation therefore means Jesus taking the Marakwet flesh, so that they can truly experience him as a living person. Similarly, the Marakwet people need to hear him speak in Marakwet idioms and relate to the best of the Marakwet values. In return, the Marakwet need to express their gratitude by praising him in the best Marakwet fashion. This may involve planned communion celebrations in homes as well as churches using not foreign but honored indigenous materials such as honey, mango drink and millet cake instead of bread and grape wine or juice. Isn't it true that the Eucharist should reflect the local produce (fruit of the land) and the sweat of the people? Such may also change, for we also recognize that cultures are dynamic and open to cross-cultural impact. We owe it to God to render our cooperation in God's ongoing work of restoring all things in Jesus the incarnate. Indeed, the complexity of cultures manifests the richness of Christ and therefore a beautiful thing not an obstacle.

Additionally, the church must engage the traditional religion of Africa, which the missionaries previously called "animism." Marakwet Traditional Religion and culture is still alive and dynamic, and it is the context from which most Christians come, and to which many of them still practice to some degree. At critical moments in their lives, some Christians may consult a traditional religious practitioner for help. For this reason, it is important for the church not to repeat the mistakes that the missionaries did by disparaging African religions. Instead, the church needs to have a positive engagement with African Religion and culture. The better African culture is understood, the more suitable the presentation of the gospel. Moreover, the underlying needs of the Marakwet will be identified. In this way the church can be more at home in the culture and the Marakwet people can be more at home in the church.

The dialogue with traditional religion is two-pronged. First, dialogue with the active adherents of traditional religion who are not yet interested in Christianity. Such a dialogue can promote good will, mutual understanding, and respect. The second dialogue is with Christians who have recently converted. Obviously, there are common objects of beliefs that can be shared by both participating parties, such as God the creator (*Iriin*), fundamental religious rituals, and values. Such values include respect for life, a sense of family and community, authority, gender, and religious practice. The dialogue can also spell out the negative aspects that can be found in both traditions. Undoubtedly tribalism, like its counterpart racism in the west, constitutes the single most adverse factor crippling the health of Christianity anywhere.

Christianity in Marakwet awaits a full inculturation or contextualization whereby the most valuable assets of the culture will be appreciated by the Church. There is another urgent matter of concern. The church needs to address what affects people socio-economically in their daily existence. In other words, how can people experience a glimpse of the kingdom of God in their situation while they are still alive here on earth and in anticipation of the fullness of the Kingdom.? Africa has been identified with disease, poverty, and violence and these three are experienced in Marakwet. It is incumbent for the church to stand in solidarity with the people to resist such dangers.

In the past, Africa was pillaged and raped by the colonial empire. Today, Africa stands in danger of further pillaging by home grown exploiters some of whom are affiliated with the churches. It is therefore incumbent upon the church to initiate some reforms that are aimed at addressing grave social and economic concerns.

Religion can be a two edged sword and has been used to oppress as well as liberate, Karl Marx understood only the oppressive side of religion, when he made the statement in 1843 that "religion is the opium of the people, It is the sigh of the oppressed creatures, the heart of heartless world, and the soul of our soulless condition."[1] The missionaries seemed to have justified Marx for instead of critiquing the injustices of the colonial government,

---

1. Cited in Ela, *African Cry*, 41. Philip J. Kain, 'The Young Marx and Kantian Ethics', *Studies in Soviet Thought*, 31 (1989), 277-299.

the missionaries used the Bible to advance colonialism. The missionaries taught their adherents to obey those in authority as per their interpretation of Romans 13. They justified oppression by pointing to a divine will that calls for obedience and not question the corrupt political establishments. Compensation for such obedience is a heavenly reward where they will make up for their earthly unhappiness. This supports Feuerbach expression that, "you have to be a slave on earth for heaven not to be in vain."[2] All of these conspire to incline human beings to accept misery and socio-economic injustice passively with no resistance.

The other side of religion that Karl Marx didn't see is the liberative side. Over the centuries Black people have been relatively sustained by their religious beliefs in their struggles against calamities and oppression. Slaves revolted against their enslavers and early African Messianic prophets resisted the colonial rule. It is without question that Karl Marx was mistaken in his blanket assertion that religion is the opium of the people, unless he confined it to nineteenth century England. Contextualization or inculturation are excellent methods for the gospel otherwise what good is worship service with knee bells, dancing, and ululation if the poor are being trampled on and have not enough food to eat? How can the church in Marakwet be silent while its people face starvation and relentless insecurity for decades? Who will hear the cry of mothers and fathers who have buried their young people? Who speaks for the farmer who has no road to take their mangoes, bananas, and vegetables to the market? Our theology lacks courage and boldness when it is only spiritualized and not embodied.

In the same manner, salvation is not only limited to humans. The whole creation cries out for redemption as St. Paul puts it 'We know that the whole creation has been groaning in labor pains until now; and not only the creation, but we ourselves, who have the first fruits of the Spirit, groan inwardly while we wait for adoption, the redemption of our bodies'. (Romans 8:22-23) This means all life-forms will be restored.

Evangelical Christianity has concerned itself largely on humans (anthropocentric) and ignored, the rest of God's creation. That is a mission drift that needs to be corrected by a fresh look at the scriptures. In Genesis, Adam was given the privilege to name all the animals. To name things in Marakwet and the rest of Africa means knowing them in their special characteristics, color, size, food and their habitat. In the Biblical narrative, God is telling Adam to go out and explore the land and get to know his neighbors in order to name them accordingly as Chemarmar, Meril, Kong'ol, Cheplanget, Belio etc. As Adam becomes acquainted with

---

2. Ela, *African Cry*, 41.

them, they in turn get to know him and a relationship is developed. Job understands this as he puts it poetically.

> But ask the animals, and they will teach you;
> the birds of the air, and they will tell you;
> ask the plants of the earth, and they will teach you;
> and the fish of the sea will declare to you.
> Who among all these does not know
> that the hand of the Lord has done this?
> In his hand is the life of every living thing
> and the breath of every human being".
> Job 12:7–10

Another important area that requires the church's immediate attention is the marginalization of women in church leadership after all, they are the majority in the Churches. Understandably, the Marakwet society is patriarchal, but the Holy Spirit breaks such barriers as exemplified on the day of Pentecost in Acts 2. The question to ask is why did the missionaries protect patriarchal leadership in the Church? History might be helpful in this case. St. Thomas Aquinas who was influenced by Aristotle represents the European medieval views of women. He stated categorically that women are "defective and misbegotten,"[3] which means that women should not have been part of the original creation. Conclusively for Aquinas, good order would not be possible if some were not governed by others wiser than themselves.

Aquinas believed that it was the male, by virtue of his fuller intellectual capacity, who was able to reveal the image of God most fully, for only creatures with intellect are made in God's image.[4]

In the Marakwet patrilineal society, women have been brought up to believe that their place in life is to be under her father brothers or husband. Her husband can beat her at will with no consequences on his part. On the other hand a free single woman who manages her affairs successfully without a man is frowned upon or castigated as immoral. The church has not challenged this thinking even though some women have been doing it subtly for centuries. The theological question is who defines the humanity of women? Is it the culture or God? The missionaries in Marakwet represent churches that have a long history of patriarchy. In that case women have been locked out of ordained leadership and therefore excluded from participating in the most important rituals of the church. The secular world has done better. In 1985, the Women's movement met in Nairobi. While the session was on, African men mocked it saying that liberation of women was a foreign import and did

3. Pipic, "Philosophy of Women."
4. DeCrane, *Aquinas, Feminism, and the Common Good*, 48.

not apply to African women. In the last thirty-five years since the Nairobi conference, women in Kenya have made giant steps. Many have competed with men in politics and have won. Some have taken leadership roles as managers, doctors, professors, and politicians. Marakwet has had a woman cabinet minister in Linah Jebii Kilimo, and more women are competing at all levels of government. The church however still lacks behind due to its long missionary view of women reinforced by the biblical patriarchal culture where God has taken a male gender especially as it appears in the English language translation. But the same Bible introduces a God who introduces Godself to Moses not a male but as "I AM WHO I AM" and comes to us through Jesus of Nazareth—a champion of liberation and equality of people therefore a champion of all God's children regardless of their gender. If the church is in the business of performing Christ-like functions in the world, then why isn't it leading in the liberation of women?[5]

The poor and the marginalized (*Wanyonge*) in Marakwet and the whole of Africa for that matter yearn for someone like Jesus who listens to their cries with compassion and stand in solidarity with them and resist the social sin that marginalizes and oppresses them. In reading the Scriptures diligently and contextually, Marakwet Christians will discover a God who liberates people from personal and social dimensions of sin which was absent in missionary consciousness. While denouncing sin, the Christians safe both the guilty and the victim. John wrote 'A man who does not love the brother or sister that he can see, cannot love God who he does not see (1 John 4:20). The one who claims to love, one born in Bethlehem over two thousand years ago but closes his heart to the one across river Kerio has failed the discipleship test. In God's eyes, every person is a bearer of God's image (*imago Dey*). Each is a special creation, loved, and in need of God's love and forgiveness. Correspondingly, I agree with Brian McLaren that in the gospels, Jesus doesn't dominate the other, avoid the other, colonize the other, intimidate the other, demonize the other, or marginalize the other. Instead, he incarnates into the other, joins the other in solidarity, protects the other, listens to the other, serves the other, and even lays down his life for the other.[6] God is love and anyone who loves God loves that which God loves.

---

5. Oduyoye, *Daughters of Anowa*, 26.

6. Brian McLaren, *Why Don't They Get It? Overcoming Bias in Others (and Yourself)* (self-pub., 2019), [45, 90]. http://brianmclaren.net/store/.

Bibliography

Anderson, David M. "Massacre at Ribo Post: Expansion and Expediency on the Colonial Frontier in East Africa." *International Journal of African Historical Studies* 37 (2004) 33–54.
Ashby, Godfrey. *Sacrifice: Its Nature and Purpose.* London: SCM, 1988.
Ashton, L. P. "Annual Report." *Inland Africa* (1935) 19.
———. "Annual Report." *Inland Africa* (1936) 1.
———. "Annual Report." *Inland Africa* (1937) 39.
———. "Field Report." *Inland Africa* (1936) 16.
Ashton, Leigh P. "Annual Report." *Inland Africa* (1937) 2.
Awolalu, J. Ọmọṣade. *Yorùbá Beliefs and Sacrificial Rites.* Brooklyn: Henrietta, 1996.
Baur, John. *2000 Years of Christianity in Africa: An African Church History.* Nairobi: Paulines, 1994.
Beane, Wendell C., and William G. Doty. *Myths, Rites, Symbols: A Mircea Eliade Reader.* New York: Harper & Row, 1976.
Bediako, Kwami. *Theology and Identity: The Impact of Culture upon Christian Thought in the Second Century and Modern Africa.* Oxford: Regnum, 1992.
Beidelman, Thomas O. *Colonial Evangelism.* Bloomington: Indiana University Press, 1982.
———. *The Cool Knife: Imagery of Gender, Sexuality, and Moral Education in Kaguru Initiation Ritual.* Washington, DC: Smithsonian Institution Press, 1997.
Billy Graham Archives (BGA). Wheaton, Illinois, Collection 81, Boxes 40–62.
Bosch, David J. *Transforming Mission.* Maryknoll, NY: Orbis, 1982.
Kisembo, Benezeri, et al. *African Christian Marriage.* London: Chapman, 1977.
Carson, Brian. "Hospital Annual Report." *Inland Africa* (1988) 2.
Collier, Frances. "Kapsowar Report." *Inland Africa* (1934) 3.
Collins, Tom. "Kapsowar News." *Inland Africa* (1935) 79.
Critchley, W. B. S. "Agricultural Development in Marakwet: Some Controversial Issues." In *Kerio Valley: Past, Present, and Future,* edited by B. E. Kipkorir et al., 19–26. Nairobi: Institute of African Studies, 1983.
Davidson, Basil. *Africa in History: Themes and Outline.* New York: MacMillan, 1991.
DeCrane, Susanne M. *Aquinas, Feminism, and the Common Good.* Washington, DC: Georgetown University Press, 2004.
Donovan, Vincent J. *Christianity Rediscovered.* Notre Dame: Claretian, 1978.
Driskel, Pauline. "Kapsowar Report." *Inland Africa* (1952) 15.

Driver, Tom F. *Liberating Rites: Understanding the Transformative Power of Ritual*. Boulder, CO: Westview, 1991.
Dunne, George Harold. *Generation of Giants*. Notre Dame: University of Notre Dame Press, 1962.
Ela, Jean-Marc. *African Cry*. Maryknoll, NY: Orbis, 1986.
Firth, Raymond. *Symbols: Public and Private*. London, 1974.
Ford, David F. *The Modern Theologians*. New York: Blackwell, 1989.
Gennep, Arnold van. *The Rites of Passage*. Translated by Monika B. Vizedom and Gabrielle L. Caffe. London: Routledge & Paul, 1960.
Gration, John Alexander. "The Relationship of the Africa Inland Mission and Its National Church in Kenya Between 1895 and 1975." PhD diss., New York University, 1974.
Grau, E. "Missionary Policies as Seen in the Work of Missions with the Evangelical Presbyterian Church, Ghana." In *Christianity in Tropical Africa*, edited by C. G. Baeta, 60–78. London: Oxford University Press, 1968.
Gutierrez, Gustavo. *A Theology of Liberation*. Rev. ed. Maryknoll, NY: Orbis, 2002.
Halliday, Margaret. "Annual Report." *Africa Inland* (1950) 39.
Harrison, Alexina Mackay, and A. M. Mackay. *A.M. MacKay, Pioneer Missionary of the Church Missionary Society in Uganda, by His Sister*. London: Cass, 1970.
Hennings, R. O. *African Morning*. Toronto: Clarke, Irwin, & Co., 1951.
Hillman, Eugene. *Polygamy Reconsidered: African Plural Marriage and the Christian Churches*. Maryknoll, NY: Orbis, 1975.
Horton, Robin. "African Conversion." *Africa, Journal of the International African Institute* 41 (1971) 85–108.
———. "On Rationality of Conversion: Part I." *Africa, Journal of the International African Institute* 45 (1975) 219–35.
Huxley, Elspeth. *A New Earth: An Experiment in Colonialism*. London: Chato and Windus, 1960.
Idowu, Emanuel Boḷaji. *African Traditional Religion: A Definition*. London: SCM, 1974.
Ifeka-Moller, Caroline. "White Power: Social-Structural Factors in Conversion to Christianity, Eastern Nigeria, 1921–1966." *Canadian Journal of African Studies* 8 (1974) 55–72.
Jackson, Julian. "A Battle for a School." *Inland Africa* (1958) 9.
Johnson, Elizabeth A. *Ask the Beasts: Darwin and the God of Love*. London: Bloomsbury, 2014.
Jones, Thomas Jesse. *Education in East Africa: A Study of East, Central, and South Africa*. New York: Phelps-Stokes, 1925.
Joyce, George Hayward. *Christian Marriage: An Historical and Doctrinal Study*. London: Sheed and Ward, 2009.
Kain, Philip J. 'The Young Marx and Kantian Ethics', *Studies in Soviet Thought*, 31 (1989), 277-301.
Kayongo-Male, Diane, and Philistia Onyango. *The Sociology of the African Family*. New York: Longman, 1948.
Kilimo, Jacob Kisang. *The Beauty and Pitfalls of Cultural Transformation: An Autobiography*. Nakuru: Oracle, 2020.
Kipkorir, B. E. *Descent from Cherang'any Hills: Memoirs of a Reluctant Academic*. Nairobi: Moran, 2009.

———. "The Sun in Marakwet Religious Thought: A Note." *Journal of Eastern African Research and Development* 6 (1976) 175–78.

Kipkorir, B. E., with F. B. Welbourn. *The Marakwet of Kenya: A Preliminary Study*. Nairobi: East Africa Education, 1973.

Kipkorir, B. E., et al., eds. *Kerio Valley: Past, Present, and Future*. Nairobi: Institute of African Studies, 1983.

Kisembo, Benezeri, et al. *African Christian Marriage*. Nairobi: Paulines, 2015.

KNBS. "2019 Kenya Population and Housing Census Results." https://www.knbs.or.ke/2019-kenya-population-and-housing-census-results/.

Koso-Thomas, Olayinka. *Circumcision of Women: A Strategy for Eradication*. London: Zed, 1992.

Kraft, H. Charles, and Bernard Ramm. *Christianity in Culture*. Maryknoll, NY: Orbis, 1979,

Langley, Myrtle S. *The Nandi of Kenya: Life Crisis Rituals in a Period of Change*. London: Hurst, 1979.

Lindsay, Stanley. Kapsowar Mission Station Records, Kapsowar Hospital, 1963.

Lonsdale, John. "The Conquest State of Kenya." In *Unhappy Valley—Conflict in Kenya and Africa: Book 1, State and Class*, edited by Bruce Berman and John Lonsdale, 13–44. Athens: University of Ohio, 1992.

Luzbetak, Louis J. *The Church and Cultures*. Techny, IL: Divine Word, 1970.

Maillu, David G. *Our Kind of Polygamy*. Nairobi: Heinemann Kenya, 1988.

Mbiti, John S. *African Religions & Philosophy*. Nairobi: Heinemann, 1969.

———. *Concepts of God in Africa*. Nairobi: Acton, 2012.

McLaren, Brian. *Why Don't They Get It? Overcoming Bias in Others (and Yourself)* (self-pub., 2019), [45, 90]. Available from https://brianmclaren.net/store/

McMinn, P. W. "Progress in Marakwet." *Inland Africa* (1934) 12.

———. "Report from Kapsowar." *Inland Africa* (1946) 3.

———. "Report from Kapsowar." *Inland Africa* (1952) 2.

McVeigh, Malcolm J. *God in Africa: Conceptions of God in African Traditional Religion and Christianity*. Cape Cod, MA: Stark, 1974.

Middleton, John, and Edward Henry Winter. *Witchcraft and Sorcery in East Africa*. London: Routledge, 1963.

Miller, Catherine S. *Peter Cameron Scott, the Unlocked Door*. London: Jackman, 1955.

Miller, D. M. "Annual Report" *Inland Africa* (1931) 20.

———. *Central Africa Revisited*. London: Africa Inland Mission, 1938.

Moore, Henrietta. *Space, Text, and Gender: An Anthropological Study of Marakwet of Kenya*. New York: Guilford, 1999.

Muge, Alexander. Private Papers, Anglican Diocese of Eldoret, Kenya, 1989.

Mungeam, Gordon Hudson. *British Rule in Kenya, 1895–1912: The Establishment of Administration in the East Africa Protectorate*. Oxford: Clarendon, 1966.

Muzorewa, Gwinyai H. *The Origins and Development of African Theology*. Eugene, OR: Wipf & Stock, 2000.

Newbigin, Lesslie. *The Finality of Christ*. Richmond, VA: John Knox, 2009.

Nkwoka, A. O. "The Church and Polygamy: Lambeth Conference Resolution." *African Theological Journal* 19 (1990) 139–54

Nyamiti, C. *Christ as Our Ancestor: Christology from an African Perspective*. Gweru: Mambo, 1984.

Oduyoye, Mercy Amba. *Daughters of Anowa: African Women and Patriarchy.* Maryknoll, NY: Orbis, 1995.

Ogot, B. A. "Kenya under the British, 1895–1963." In *Zamani: A Survey of East African History*, edited by B. A. Ogot and J. A. Kieran, 255–89. Nairobi: East African, 1968.

Okure, Teresa, et al. *Inculturation of Christianity in Africa.* Eldoret: AMECEA Gaba, 1990.

Orobator, A. E. "'After All, Africa Is Largely a Non-literate Continent': The Reception of Vatican II in Africa." *Theological Studies* 74 (2013) 277–94.

Ostberg, wilhelm "Life among the Marakwet," Kenya Past and Present, Issue 42 (2015)59.

Paul VI, Pope. "Homily, July 31, 1969." https://www.vatican.va/content/paul-vi/en/homilies/1969/documents/hf_p-vi_hom_19690731.html.

Phillips, Arthur, and Henry Francis Morris. *Marriage Laws in Africa.* Nairobi: Law Africa, 2011.

Phillips, Kenneth, N. *Tom Collins of Kenya: Son of Valour.* Nairobi: Evangelical, 2003.

Pinnock, Clark. *A Wideness of God's Mercy: The Finality of Jesus Christ in a World of Religions.* Grand Rapids: Zondervan, 1992.

Pipic, Kristin M. "The Philosophy of Women of St. Thomas Aquinas." https://www.catholicculture.org/culture/library/view.cfm?recnum=2793.

Pius XII, Pope. *Evangelii Praecones.* https://www.vatican.va/content/pius-xii/en/encyclicals/documents/hf_p-xii_enc_02061951_evangelii-praecones.html.

Rajamanickam, Savarimuthu. *The First Oriental Scholar.* Tirunelveli: De Nobili Research Institute, 1972.

Reynolds, Reg. "Annual Report." *Inland Africa* (1935) 36.

———. "Kapsowar News." *Inland Africa* (1937) 6–7.

Richardson, Kenneth. *Garden of Miracles: The Story of the Africa Inland Mission.* London: Africa Inland Mission, 1976.

Rosberg, Carl G., and John Nottingham. *The Myth of "Mau Mau": Nationalism in Kenya.* Stanford: Praeger, 1966.

Sanneh, Lamin O. *Translating the Message: The Missionary Impact on Culture.* Maryknoll, NY: Orbis, 2008.

Sawyer, Harry. *Creative Evangelism: Towards a New Christian Encounter with Africa.* London: Lutterworth, 1968.

Schreiter, Robert J. *Constructing Local Theologies.* Maryknoll, NY: Orbis, 2015.

Schreuder, Deryck, and Geoffrey Oddie. "What Is Conversion? History, Christianity, and Religious Change in Colonial Africa and South Asia." *The Journal of Religious History* 15 (1989) 496–518.

Shorter, Aylward. *African Christian Theology: Adaptation or Incarnation.* Maryknoll, NY: Orbis, 1975.

———. *Prayer in the Religious Traditions of Africa.* Nairobi: Oxford University Press, 1975.

Smith, Edwin W. *The Christian Mission in Africa: A Study Based on the Work of the International Conference at Le Zoute, Belguim, Sept. 14th to 21st, 1926.* New York: International Mission Council, 1926.

Smith, Roland. "British Council Business Report." *Inland Africa* (1937) 9.

Soper, R. C. "A Survey of the Irrigation System of the Marakwet." In *Kerio Valley: Past, Present, and Future*, edited by B. E. Kipkorir et al., 75–95. Nairobi: Institute of African Studies, 1983.

Ssennyonga, J. W. "The Marakwet Irrigation System as a Model of a Systems-Approach to Water Management." In *Kerio Valley: Past, Present, and Future*, edited by B. E. Kipkorir et al., 96–111. Nairobi: Institute of African Studies, 1983.

Stackhouse, Max L. *Apologia: Contextualization, Globalization, and Mission in Theological Education*. Minneapolis: Eerdmans, 1988.

Stauffacher, Gladys. *Faster Beats the Drum*. Pearl River, NY: Africa Inland Mission, 1978.

Stott, John R. W., and Robert T. Coote. "Willowbank Report." In *Gospel & Culture*, edited by John R. W. Scott and Robert T. Coote. Pasadena: Carey, 1979.

Sundermeier, Theo. *The Individual and Community in African Traditional Religions*. Hamburg: Lit, 1998.

Sutton, J. E. G. "Towards a History of Cultivating the Fields." *Azania* 24 (1989) 98–112.

Sylvester, J. M. *Annual Report*. DC/ELGM/1/3 Kenya National Archives, Nairobi, 1934.

Thomson, Joseph. *Through Masai Land: A Journey of Exploration among the Snowclad Volcanic Mountains and Strange Tribes of Eastern Equatorial Africa*. London: Low, Marston, Searle, & Rivington, 1885.

Tillich, Paul. *Systematic Theology: Three Volumes in One*. Chicago: University of Chicago Press, 1967.

Turner, Victor. "Sacrifice as Quintessential Process Prophylaxis or Abandonment?" *History of Religions* 16 (1977) 189–215.

Tylor, Edward B. *Primitive Cultures*. New York: Holt and Company, 1889.

Vidal, N. R. R. "Annual Report 1918." Kenya National Archives, Nairobi, Kenya. DC/Elgm/1/1.1.

———. "Annual Report 1919–1920." Kenya National Archives, Nairobi, Kenya. DC/Elgm/1/1.1.

Waliggo, John Mary. *Inculturation: Its Meaning and Urgency*. Kampala: St. Paul, 1986.

Watson, Elizabeth E., et al. "Indigenous Irrigation, Agriculture and Development, Marakwet, Kenya." *The Geographical Journal* 164 (1998) 67–84.

Webster, J. B. "Attitude and Policies of the Yoruba African Churches towards Polygamy." In *Christianity in Tropical Africa*, edited by C. G. Baeta, 224–48. London: Oxford University Press, 1989.

Welbourn, F. B. "Keyo Initiation." *Journal of Religion in Africa* 1 (1968) 212–32.

Wittgenstein, Ludwig. *On Certainty*. Edited by G. E. M. Anscombe and G. H. von Wright. Translated by Denis Paul and G. E. M. Anscombe. New York: Harper, 1969.

Young, W. B. "Eldoret Area Report." *Inland Africa* (1947) 9.

———. "Field Report." *Inland Africa* (1944) 39.

———. "Marakwet Report." *Inland Africa* (1945) 32–33.

Zibor, Jacob Z. "The Growth and Development of African Inland Mission and Africa Inland Church in Marakwet, Kenya." *Africa Journal of Evangelical Theology* 24 (2005) 107–28.

Index

America Academy of Religion/ Society of Biblical Literature (AAR/SBL)
Adams, J. Davis, 120
African Native Court, 177
Age-set system, 49–53, 58
Agriculture, 17–20
Allen, Roland, 252
Almo, 1
Africa Inland Church (AIC), 138, 139, 230, 231, 249
Africa Inland Mission (AIM), 111–40, in Marakwet, 127–40, 178, 212
African Traditional Religion, 142, 263
Aluta continua, viii
Agriculture, 17–20
Ancestors, 43, 69–70, 71, 77, 80–83, 100, 237
Anglican commission resolution of polygamy, 230, 231
Animism, 207
A Priori, 250
Aquinas, Thomas, 265
Arab traders, 103, Arap Swahili caravans, 107
Ara kapterik, 100
Ara beel, 103
Aristotle, 265
Arror, 1, 77–79
Arukwomoi, 146
Ashton, Leigh, Marion, 131,132, 167
Asis, 80, 102, 101
Athenagoras, 206
Augustine, St., 207, 227

Awalolu, J. Omosade, 86, 100
Ayebisio, 92–93
Austria, 109

Baibai, 92
Baker, Samuel, 112, 135
Bagamoyo, 110
Bagnall, Archibald, 106
Bangert, William C., 118
Banks, J.M.W., 134, 158
Baptism, 228, 229
Baraka, AIC, 170
Barbarisio, 61
Barnett, Albert, 120, 126, Elma, 177
Barnett, Ruth, 121
Barnett, Paul, 132, 180, 189, 216, 217
Baringo, 1, 6
Bartholomew, Elmer, 119
Barsiron, Jonathan, 152
Baxter, Jane, 167
Beiledman, T. O., 149
Benedictine, 144, 143
Berekimoi, Samuel, 147
Bee keeping, xi
Beech, M.W. H., 10
Berlin, 111
Berur, 42
Birech, Ezekiel, 140
Birech, Job, 174
Birthmark, 37
Bito Karin, 69
Biwott, Mary Jeruto, 144, Joseph, 160
Biwott, Sabina, 144

INDEX

Black God, 152
Blakeslee, Virginia, 212
Boit, Milkah, 153
Bolaji, Idowu, 250
Bomet, Mica, 123
Bonesetters, 95x
Bore, 54
Boroko, 134, 154n9, 172–77, 238
Borokot, 1
Botner, Fr. Reinhard, 145
Breech, 37
Bremen Mission, 224
Brennan, Fr. Michael, 142
British Colony, 3
British East Africa Protectorate, 113
British Missionaries, 121–27
Brown, Nancy, 134
Bryson, Stuart M., 124, 127

Canada, vii, 138
Canadian International Development Aid (CIDA) 140
Cambridge University, 171, 178
Carson, 138
Chawis, 169
Chebara, 161, 183,185
Chebet, Ezekiel, 152, 167, 183
Chebeto Chematau, 72, 235, 236
Chebiemit, 184
Chebisas, 122
Chebo Kamichan, 137, 239, 239
Chebobei, Joshua, 170, 183
Cheboi, Colleta, 144
Cheboi, Grace Cherop, 169
Cheboi, Rev. Edward, 160
Cheboi, James, 144
Cheboi, Peter, catechist, 144
Cheboi, Rev. Zechariah, 162
Chebororwa, 3
Chelalam, Maria Komen, 151
Chelang'a, Johnstone, wife Rose, 189
Chelang'a, Pastor Mary, 187
Chelang'a, Rev. Musa, 187, 233n57
Chelang'a, Samson and Ana, 198, 199
Cheles, 149
Chelimo, Antonio Murkomen, 144
Chelimo, Edward, 144
Chelimo, David, 152n6, 160

Chepite, 48
Chemeitoi, Daudi (jokinda), 222
Chemeri, 48, 59
Chemibei, Joel and Jeni, 127, 128, 168
Chemosop, 88, 89
Chemurey, Linah, 154
Chemuttut, Justice Charles, 143
Chemuttut, Paramount Chief Kisang, 229
Chemwal, Isaiah, Leah, 152, 153, 183
Chemwal, Solomon, 153
Chepkiyeng, Rev. Paulo, 154
Chepkorowo, 10
Chepkurui, Josephat, 143
Chepkwony, Elija, 123
Chepseng'ei, 20
Cheptalel, 235
Cheptenderwo, Josiah, 197
Cheptendur, 59
Chepyegon, 42
Chepsagitian, 95
Chepseng'eny, 20
Chepkiyeng, Rev. Paulo, 167, 184n69, 70
Chepkong'a, Anthony, 144
Chepkon'ga, Pilipu, 168, 231
Chepkong'a, Rev. Samuel, 222, 235n65
Chepkosir, Truphena Johnstone, 160
Chepkwony, Johnston, 160
Chepsagitian/Chepsagitin, 96
Cheptoo, Dominic, 143
Cheptorus, Leah,123
Cheptulel, 92
Cherang'any, 3
Cheratum, Jeremiah, Salome, 153
Cherang'any Hills, xi
Cherang'any/Chebororwa, 2
Cherelmo, 73
Cherono, Rebecca, 190
Cherop, Raphael, 144
Checkley, Rev. A.R., 163
Chelang'a, Samson, 170
Cherop, Elias, 172
Cherop, Susana, 144
Chesang, Simon, 153
Chesegon, 12, 88
Cheserek, Amos, 153
Cheserek, James (sr. Chief), 160, 181n63
Cheserek, Rev. Joseph, 187, 222n39

INDEX 275

Cheserek, Laban, 262
Cheserek, Pius, 145
Cheserek, Rev. Samuel, 222
Cheserem, Joseph (simba), viii
Chesir, Anyesi, 144
Chesir, Elias
Chesoi, intermediate, 142
Chesus, Noah, 153, 170, 171
Cherwon, John, 145
Chesegon, 176
Chesongoch, 23, 143, 232
Chewosot, 95
Choruo kipnyikeu, 186
Church Missionary Society, 116, 119
Chyme, 100
Chereko, Michael, 143
Chilanyang, 146
Child naming, 209–211
Chiibo yim, 70
Christianity Rediscovered, 251
Circumcision, 211–21, 239
Clans, 13–14,
Cleansing rite, 68–69
Clement of Alexandria, 206
Colenso, Bishop John, 223
Collins, Malcolm, 180
Collins, Tom, 121, 164, 178–79, 176,
    Ruth, 177, 180, 189
Cone, Prof. James, vii
Constitution, 2
Contextualization, 240–59, 258
Cormie, Prof. Lee, vii
Covid 19 Pandemic, 234
Circumcision, 40
Creation, 76
Crow, pied, 10.
Cyclical calendar, 54

Dalziel, Rev. B., 151, 174
Daniel, Milcah, 153
Davis, Elwood, 212
De Nobili, Roberto, 246
Dia-logos/dialogue, xv, 250, 263
Diouf, Abdul, president, 220
Divination, 77, 86–89
Divorce, 226
Donavan, Vincent, 252
Dube, Musa, viii, 251

Divination, 238
Dominico of Kaplenge, 143
Donavan, Vincent J., 251,253, 256
Downing, Lee H., 119, 213
dualistic, 194

Economic structure, 16–27
Eldama Ravine, 104, 121, 126
Eldoret area, 125
Eliade, Mircea, 71
Elolia, Kisang Ng'elecha (the author's
    father), vii, 36n37, 88, 92n39
Elolia, Kwananyang' (author's
    grandfather), 173, 175, 176,
    kimoi, 197
    Lobokong'ar and Ribosia, 92n38
Embobut/Embolot 2,
Endo, 1, 2, 86, 100
Emmanuel Christian Seminary at
    Milligan University, viii
Ethnography, 260
Eucharist, 257
Eva Maria, Sister, 145
Evil eye, 95

First Baptist Church, Toronto, viii
funeral rites, 66–68, 232–35

Garbush, Abdi, 149
Gatu, Rev. John, 258
Gichuhi, Andrew, 139
Gladstone, William E.110
Gorges, Capt. E.H., 107, 108
Grillo, Laura, viii
Gutierrez, Gustavo, vii, 202

Haight, Roger, vii
Halliday, Margaret, 161
Hamilton, Zan, 127
Hansen, Marie, 122
Hardinge, A.H. 113
Hartman, Fr., 127
Healers, 92–96
Hearing and doing, 116.
Henderson, Dr. J. 119
Hennings, R. O, 20, 103
Herbalists, 96, 239
Herman, Prisca, 153

INDEX

Hillman, Eugene, 225, 226, 227
Hinga, Teresia, viii
Hoehler-Fatton, Cynthia, viii
Holy Ghost Fathers, 112
Holy Spirit, 265
Hopkins, Dwight, viii
Horton, Robin, 199, 200, 201
Hotchkiss, Willis, 115, 117
Hurlburt, Charles, 118, 177
Huxley, Elizabeth, 21
Hyde-Baker, Harold, 105, 106
Hurlburt, Charles, E., 116, 120
Hut tax, 231

Ibin, 62
Idi Amin, 12
Idowu, Bolaji, 83
Ifeka-Moller, Caroline, 200, 201
Ilat, 77, 79, ilot, 80
Il Chamus, 104, 106, Il Chamus Maasai, or Njemps, 107, 109
Imago-Dey, 266
Incantation, 91–92, 242
Inculturation, 240–59, 242, 243, 247
Indigenization, 241
Iriin (the creator), 73, 195, 239, 263
Irrigation furrows, 20
Ivory trade, 103

Jerotich, Gladys, viii
Jesinen, Joan, viii
Jemtai, Metrine, viii
Jesuits, 245
Johnson, C. F., 119
Johnson, Sir Harry, 104, 108

Kabarsiran, 22
Kabarsumba, 87
Kabartonjo, 151, 154, 165
Kaben, 3
Kabeldemet. 88
Kaberur, 51
Kabetwa, 137
Kabisioi, 83
Kabor, 12
Kachebisas, 160
Kaino, Hezekiah Yego, 83, 188, 189n82, 231, 232, 232n56

Kakisakur, Daniel and Miriam, 190
Kalacha, Barnaba, 152, 153, 154, 183, 184
Kalenjin, 1, 8, 9, 40
Kalesi, Jane, and David, viii
Kamama, 12,22, 85
Kamorir, 68
Kapchebai, 23
Kapchebau, 169
Kapchelos, 159
Kapchesewes, 149, 159
Kapcherop, 170–72, 184
Kapchesom, 23
Kapkamak, 12
Kapkechir of Katemko, 143
Kapkore, 48
Kapkikoi/Kapikoi, 12
Kaplelach, 12, 53
Kapsiliot, 3
Kapsiren, 23
Kapsowar Mission Station, xiii, hospital, xiii, 195, 238
Kapyego, 2, 23
Kaptabuk, 167, 184
Kaptalamwa, 172
Kaptipin, 160, 214
Kapnyonge, Job, 191, daughter Leah, 192
Karaninyang, 197
Karena, 175
Kariwotum, Kisang, 197
Karube, Kiberenge, 146, 181
Kasagat, 89
Katkok, 164, 175
Katam, Sylvano (kipkatam), 167, 184, 190
Katisei, Grace, 153, Paulo, 168, 186, 215
Kasenyang, Maria Kochemeitoi, 147
Kasororot, Josiah, 153
Katkok (the first AIM outstation),164, 17
Katisei, Grace, 153, Paulo, 168,
Katongole, Fr. Emmanuel, viii
Kayongo-Male and Onyango, 11
kelyekab chebiosok, 162, 153, 154
Kimengich, Mariko, 153
Kendagor, George, 166n34, 170, 171
Kenosis, 243

INDEX

Kenneson, Philip, viii
Kenyatta, Jomo, 149
Kenya-Uganda railway, 113
Kenyision, 74
Kerio river, 6
Kerio Valley, 3
Keiyo, 1
Kew, 5, 6
Khenti, Akwatu, viii
Klein, Prof. Martin A. vii
Kibaki, Mwai (President), 2
Kiban, 84
Kibarber, 93
Kibiwot, Christine, 217, 218
Kibor, Dr. Jacob, 160
Kibor Talai, 20
Kibor, Ziborah, 153
Kibore, Paulo, 229, 236
Kiboret, 43
Kibuno, 47
Kibuswo, 164 -167, 175
Kikuyu controversy, 212
Kilimo, Elijah (Kleu), 128, 131, 134, 150, 151, 164, 174, 175, 176n50, 197, 214, 231
Kilimo, John (kapkorin), 143
Kilimo, Martha, 262
Kilimo, Eng. Philemon, 176
Kilimo, Rebecca, Hezekiah, 160
Kiltegan missionaries, 142
Kipkech, Cheserek, 152
Kipkech, Zachariah, 152
Kipkemoi, Jeffrey, viii
Kipkeres, Musa, and Clara, 153
Kipkeu, Jeremiah, 173
Kipkoimet, 51, 53,59
Kipkorir, Benjamin E., 20, 75, 87, 166, 171
Kipkorir, Robert, MP, 157, 160
Kiptaber, 9, 11
Kiptani, 1
Kiptoo, Obadiah, 169
Kiptoo, Wilfred, 144
Kipketin, 35
Kipnyigeu, 51
Kipses, 10, 95
Kimaget, 46
Kimaiyo, David, 170

Kimisoi, James, 143
Kipsigis, 9
Kimu (author's son), ix
Kinship, 11
Kapanda, 159
Kipchumba, Catherine, 144
Kipkwomei, Philip, 145
Kipkech, Emily, 189, 190
Kiplabat, Ruth, 151
Kipnyigei, Rev. Samuel, 123, 167
Kirala Ma, 60
Kirong'o, 26
Kirop, Joseph Biwott Elolia, 160
Kirop, Jeremiah (author's uncle), 185
Kirop Elolia, Lillian (author's aunt), 153, 176
Kirop, Magdalena, 144
Kiror, 65
Kingdom of God, 243
Kisang, Kariwotum, 176
Kisang, Daudi (koikoi), 128, 131, 150, 152, 214
Kisang, Job, 170
Kisang, Teriki (author's mother), viii, 234
Kisiten, 35
Kitony, 90
Kitum, Florence, 144
Kitung'a, 41
Kobeno Kitum (Kitum's cave), 9
Koilege, 9
Koitilial, 181, 190–92
Kokwo, 7, 15, 84, 87, Kokwo Tolimo, 190
Kolomber, 35
Komen, Jennifer, 145
Kombo moren, 63, 80
kong'asis, 41
Kore, Joseph, 152
Korongoro, 53
Korosion, 40n26
Kotut, Marko, 152, 183
Kowow, 84, 100
Koyelel, Gabriel, 143
Koyer, 58, 59
Kuhn, Fr. Joseph, 141
Kukotum, 43
Kutwo, 65, 83

K'Marich, 234
Knife, cool, 43
Kraft, J. Ludwig, 114
Krellkutt, Vincent, 190
Krieger, F. W, 116, 118
Kristensen, Signe, C., 122

Labero, Thomas, wife Albina, 189
Landa Kiti, 174
Lakam, 7
Lake Baringo, 104, 109
Lake Turkana, 103
Lake Victoria, 105
Lambeth Conference, 224, 230
Laussane congress, 249
Lavigerie, Chrales, 246
Lelan, 2, 20
Levasseur, Pere, 112
Lezo, 61
Libation, 43, 69
Liliondo, 251
Liminal, 40, 44, liminal stage, 44–46
Lindberg, Minnie, 116
Lindsay, Dr. Stanley, 136, 169, 185n71, 186, 190, 231, 239, 191n84, 191n85
Litamoi, Joseph Kibiwot, 144
Liter, 121, 132,136, 177–82, 229
Livingston, Davis, 114
Lobeiluk, Johana Kanda, 177
Lokotiyan, Kochebe, 176
Logere, Benjamin, 168
Logo, 160
Logoi spermatikos, 242
Lokiles, Jacob Kibor, 160
Lokitel, 103
Lord Delemare, 104
London Missionary Society, 178
Long'aile, Jonathan, 160
Lopuriang, Daniel, 217
Loshamba, James Kipkiror, 233
Lotipar, 238
Loyei, Sogomo, 145
Lucking, Mary, 217, 222
Lukuget, Koyano, 197
Lukwob, 99
Lunn, Harry, 127
Luzbetak, Louis, J., 240, 241
Lyakat, 43

Mackay, Alexander, 115
Magna carta of freedom, 244
Mahood, 155, 161
Makere University, 171
Marakwet culture/tradition, beliefs 195, 261–63
Marir, Josiah, 152, 183
Markweta, 1
Martyr, Justin, 206
Marriage, 56–61, 221–23
Masai inculturation, 251–59
Martin, James, 102
Marx, Karl, 263, 264
Mathare Mental Hospital, 191
Mbiti, John, 11, 73, 132, 250
McCreary, George, 122
McMinn, Philip, 1, 163, 167
McNicholas, Fr., 143
McIntire, Thomas C., vii
McVeigh, J. Malcolm, 235
Mead, Eustace, viii
Mengich, Marko, 183
Mensah, David, viii
Meiberg, Fr. Peter, 144
Metabile, 206
Mildenhall, Bessie, 129, 167
Middleton, John, 84
Miis, 91
Mill Hill Fathers, 140–43
Misri legend, 8, 9
Mogoro, 1, 24, 25,86
Moi, Daniel President, 2, 152, 219
Moiben/Kureswo, 2
Mombasa, 111
Monogamy, 226, 227
Moody Bible Institute, 127, 180
Moore, Henrietta, 59, 50n44, 57, 76n86
Moratorium, 258
Morgut, 38, 67, 70, 98
Mosaic law, 225
Mosop, 7
Morris, Dr. Philip, 134, 177, 232
Mosowo, 26
Motiren, 48
Moody Bible Institute, 120
Mooy, 98
Motiren, 221
Msambwa, 179

INDEX

Mt. Elgon, 8
Mucherera, Tapiwa, vii
Mulwa, Wellington, 139
Muna, William Arap, 175
Mundy, William, 123
Muma, 78, 90
Musoke, Alix, viii
Muzorewa, Gwinyai, viii, 251, 237n68
Mwatabei, Lokitiyan, 175
Myth, xiii, 71

Naam ak iaam, 161
Nandi, 110, 113, 121, Nandi Bible, 123
Nerkwo, 141, 162
Nganaset, 160
Ng'echer (cheptororio), 143, 167–70, 188, 232
Ng'elech, Abraham, 152, 166, 170, 171, 174
Ng'eny, 63
Ng'imor, 27, 92, 176
Nginyang, 177, 179
Ng'oki, 94, 95, 261 sin, 253.
Ng'oroko, 88,
Ng'osho, 63
Nicher, Elma, E.,120
Nile, 8
Njiru, Emilio, Njiru., 144
Nubian Askaris, 107

Oaths, 89–90, 237
O'Brien, Fr. Morgan, 143
Odagame, Afe, viii
Olmeg (barbarians), 253
Olupona, Jacob, viii
Okiek, 10
Opoku, Kofi, viii
Origen, 206
Orpororo L'Engai, 256
Ossis (miis), 83
Ostberg, Wilhelm, 21n23

Panentheist, 75
Parapiy, Tabrandich, 153
Para Tipin, 16
Peters, Karl, 105, 109, 110
Pentecost, 243
Peramiho Abbey, 144, 146

Philadelphia Missionary Council, 115, 116, 118, 120
Philips, Arthur, 225
P'Kech, Lukas, 179
Pippa (author's daughter), ix
Pinner, Jack, 137
Pinnock, Clark, 202, 207
Pokot, 1
Postcolonialism, viii
Polygamy, 66–68, 215, 223–32
Pritchard, John Evans, 84
Probst, Lawson S., 121

Rahner, Karl, 202
Raynolds, Rev. Reginald, 127, 149
Reckling, Bertha, 116
Red God, 252
repes, 36
Ricci, Matteo, 246
Rionoki, 146
Ribo Post, 104, 107
rites, 29, 30, 33,
rites of passage, 40
ritual goat, 233, 234
rituals, 29, 34
Robin (author's wife), ix
Roger Swynnerton, 19
Roman Catholic Mission, xiv, xiii, 229, 232
Rorok, 149
Rotich, Clementi, 172
Rotich, Peter, 192
Ruegg, Fr. Benedikt (kaberur),144, 234
Rudolf, Prince of Austria, 109

Sabondab betut age tugul, 161, 184
Sacred, 71
Sacrifices, 97–101
Sadi Ben Abedi, 103, 104
Sabbath, 243
Sambalat, 239
Sambirir, 185–90
Sambu, Kipkoeech Araap, 9n7
Sambirir, 1,2, 86, 153
Samoei, Koitalel Arap, 110
Sandeman, Pat, vii
Sangach, 181
Sanneh, Lamin, 245, 250
Sawyer, 250

INDEX

Seretyon, 222
Seroney, Jean Marie, 149
Seroney, Reuben, 123, 149
Scott, Maragaret, 116, 117
Scott, Peter Cameron, 116, 117
Stover, Roy, 217
Shaban, 24
Shaeffer, Dr. Ethel, 137
Shorter, Aylward, 75, 195, 250
Sengwer, 91, 170
Seretyon, 63, 92
Severn, Lester, 116
Sexual taboos, 47
Sibow, 24, 173, 188
Siew, 53
Sikiip, 145
Sikoom, 18
Sile, 58
Siman, 49
Sindiit, 60
Sinon, 141, 149
Slater, Peter, vii
Smith, Roland, 124
Somokwony, Nelly
Sonok, 38
Soyon 18
Spittle of blessings, 68n89, 92
Spittle of forgiveness, 254, 255
Ssenyonga, 21n23
Sundermeier, Theo, 29
Supreme Creator, 76, Deity, 91, 93, 99, 100, Being, 236
Suter, Pastor Edwin, 160
Swoger. 59
Swynnerton plan, 19
Stauffacher, John, 120
Stam, Fr. Nicolas, 141
Steinmann, Fr. Paul. 144
Stumpf, Ms. Hulda, 213
Supreme Deity, 76, 236
Suter, Enock (author's primary teacher), 176
Suter, John Long'ura, 143
Suwerwa, 162
Swoger, 223

Taboo, 58, 257, taboos, 62, 254
taboot, 18
Talaa, 33
Talai, 9, 10, 159
Talai Kibor, 19
Talam, Edward, 160
Tambach, 20, government school, 142, 171
Tartar, 141
Tehindrazanarivelo, Emmanuel, viii
Teleki, count, 109
Teriki, 33
Thompson, Joseph, 21, 105, 109
Tiati Hills, xi
Tiren, Susana, 153
Tillich, Paul, 47n38
Tilya, 26, 27
Time concepts, 53–56
Tirioko, 27
tiswo, 36, 37
Tot, 137, 188–90, 232
totem, 79
toyoi, 79
Tran-Zoia, 113
trepanning, 96
Trinity College, vii
Tula, Eunice of kimnai, 184, 185, 186
tumbo sorun, 53
tugen, 4
tum, 64
Turkana,
Tylor, Edward B. 240

Uasin-Gishu, 4, 107, 113
ugali, 27

Van Gennep, Arnold, 39
Vatican Council II, 247
Vidal, N. R. R. (District Commissioner), 173

Wakwafi, 109
Wanyonge, 266
Wawa mwatian, 98
Webster, B, 224
Wedding, 61–64
Weech, Fr. Lester, 142
Weijden, Fr. Koos Van der, 141
Willow Bank Report, 250
Winfred, Fr. (kipchurmet), 144

White Fathers, 245
White highlands, 114
Wicker, Kathryn
Wilcart, Sr. (koko) 145
Wilberforce, William, 112
Wilson, Waler McLellan, 116, 117
Witchcraft, 83–86, 238
Wittgenstein, Ludwig, 45
World Health Organization (WHO), 220
white highlands, 89

Yano, Anna, 144
Yano, Daniel, 172
Yano, Emmanuel, 143
yashan, 22
Yego, Rev. Elija, 191
Yego, Rev. Samuel (Cheburwa), 137, 189, Helen, 189
yombo, 39
Young, Dr. W. B., 134, 153, 158, 183, 209n27

zamani, 74
Zanzibar, 110
Zechariah, Rebecca, 153
Zelaya of Kakisegei, 143